Digital Forensics in the Age of AI

Marwan Omar
Illinois Institute of Technology, USA

Hewa Majeed Zangana
Duhok Polytechnic University, Iraq

IGI Global
Scientific Publishing
Publishing Tomorrow's Research Today

Vice President of Editorial Melissa Wagner
Managing Editor of Acquisitions Mikaela Felty
Managing Editor of Book Development Jocelynn Hessler
Production Manager Mike Brehm
Cover Design Phillip Shickler

Published in the United States of America by
IGI Global Scientific Publishing
701 East Chocolate Avenue
Hershey, PA, 17033, USA
Tel: 717-533-8845
Fax: 717-533-8661
Website: https://www.igi-global.com E-mail: cust@igi-global.com

Library of Congress Cataloging-in-Publication Data

Names: Omar, Marwan, 1982- editor. | Zangana, Hewa Majeed, 1987- editor.
Title: Digital forensics in the age of AI / edited by Marwan Omar, Hewa Zangana.
Description: Hershey, PA : IGI Global Scientific Publishing, 2025. | Includes bibliographical references and index. | Summary: "The primary objective of the book is to explore the intersection of digital forensics and artificial intelligence, addressing the challenges and opportunities that arise in this rapidly evolving field"-- Provided by publisher.
Identifiers: LCCN 2024056694 (print) | LCCN 2024056695 (ebook) | ISBN 9798337308579 (hardcover) | ISBN 9798337308586 (paperback) | ISBN 9798337308593 (ebook)
Subjects: LCSH: Digital forensic science. | Artificial intelligence. | Criminal investigation--Technological innovations.
Classification: LCC HV8078.7 .D54 2025 (print) | LCC HV8078.7 (ebook) | DDC 363.250285/63--dc23/eng/20250218
LC record available at https://lccn.loc.gov/2024056694
LC ebook record available at https://lccn.loc.gov/2024056695

British Cataloguing in Publication Data
A Cataloguing in Publication record for this book is available from the British Library.

Table of Contents

Detailed Table of Contents

This chapter explores the intersection of digital forensics and artificial intelligence (AI), emphasizing the transformative impact AI is having on digital investigative techniques. Digital forensics, traditionally focused on the collection, preservation, and analysis of electronic evidence, is facing new challenges and opportunities in the era of AI. The rapid proliferation of digital devices and the sophistication of cyber threats demand enhanced methods for accurate and timely evidence gathering. AI technologies, including machine learning, natural language processing, and deep learning, are empowering forensic professionals to detect, analyze, and interpret vast volumes of data with unprecedented efficiency. This chapter discusses the fundamentals of digital forensics, examines the integration of AI tools within forensic processes, and addresses the ethical and privacy concerns that arise. The insights provided will help readers understand how AI can bolster digital forensics, enabling more proactive and precise responses to cybercrime.

The increasing reliance on Artificial Intelligence (AI) in digital forensic investigations has brought forward significant advancements in the identification, analysis, and interpretation of digital evidence. However, one of the major challenges remains the "black-box" nature of many AI models, which often hinder trust, accountability, and transparency. Explainable AI (XAI) emerges as a critical solution, providing clarity into the decision-making processes of AI systems. In the context of digital forensics, XAI facilitates investigators' understanding of AI-driven tools, ensuring that conclusions drawn from automated analyses are interpretable, verifiable, and legally admissible. This chapter explores the role of XAI in digital forensics, highlighting its potential to enhance the reliability and transparency of AI-based forensic systems, while addressing key challenges and ethical considerations. We examine the integration of XAI in forensic workflows, discuss various techniques for explainability, and evaluate real-world case studies where XAI has contributed to improved forensic outcomes.

Today's world has seen rapid advancements in technology. With that comes even more rapid advancements in cybersecurity. And to combat that, criminals and adversaries have also developed even more advanced techniques to combat cybersecurity. Many of these techniques fall under the field of anti-forensics. Digital forensics is the branch of cybersecurity that deals with investigating incidents in cyberspace. So, to hide themselves even more, cybercriminals have come up with very created anti-forensic techniques to evade these investigators and make it harder to prove that they actually committed a crime. This paper highlights published and proven anti-forensic techniques across different devices. It covers the technical details of these techniques, as well as the forensic techniques that they evade. Although many of the techniques in this paper can be used for malicious purposes, forensic investigators should nevertheless know these so that they can continue to perform their jobs effectively despite the rapid growth of techniques that are used against them.

The rapid evolution of artificial intelligence (AI) has introduced transformative possibilities for cybercrime investigation and fraud detection, enabling enhanced accuracy, efficiency, and adaptability. AI-powered tools such as machine learning algorithms, natural language processing, and computer vision offer robust solutions for detecting fraudulent activities, tracing digital evidence, and identifying anomalous behaviors across diverse platforms. This chapter explores the fundamental technologies that underlie AI applications in digital forensics, discussing key methodologies, challenges, and case studies that illustrate AI's role in combating cybercrime. Emphasis is placed on how AI techniques support law enforcement in recognizing sophisticated fraud schemes, performing predictive analysis, and adapting to ever-changing cyber threats. Additionally, we address ethical and privacy concerns related to AI-driven surveillance and investigation processes, underscoring the need for a balanced approach in leveraging AI for crime prevention. This chapter provides valuable insights for cybersecurity professionals, digital forensics experts, and law enforcement agencies on the effective deployment of AI to counteract fraud and secure digital ecosystems.

In the following paper, we look at file system forensics intricacies for four dominant ones: EXT, FAT, NTFS and HFS. In this book, each of the system is discussed with its structure, operational characteristics and forensic challenge to collect evidence against it. The EXT family (EXT2, EXT3, EXT4) gets its turn on being evolutionary and providing tons of improvements around journaling and data integrity. It describes the FAT file system for its simplicity and great acceptance, then it presents common forensic techniques such as metadata examination and cluster chain analysis. Although NTFS has some advanced features of its own, such as the Master File Table (MFT) and strong journaling system that it uses to recover both resident and non-resident files, it's really not too much different from other file systems. Now comes to its proprietary nature with the analysis of HFS file system including Catalog file corruption, encryption handling, and more details about the entire structure of its Cloud.

This survey explores the landscape of Intrusion Detection Systems (IDS) in 5G wireless networks, with a specific emphasis on those leveraging Machine Learning (ML) techniques. The deployment of 5G is poised to revolutionize telecommunications with unprecedented data rates, reduced latency, and enhanced capacity. However, the advanced infrastructure also brings heightened security challenges, necessitating robust and adaptive security measures. IDS have emerged as a key strategy to counteract these vulnerabilities, particularly those that exploit machine learning for anomaly detection and rapid response. This paper reviews several 5G IDS implementations across different domains, including the 5G Core Network, Internet of Things (IoT), and Smart Grids. Each domain's technical and cybersecurity environment is explored for better context in understanding the different implementations available, which are scrutinised based on ML models used, datasets for training and testing, and architecture.

Machine learning (ML) is transforming digital forensic analysis by enhancing the speed, accuracy, and depth of evidence examination and interpretation. This chapter explores the integration of ML algorithms into digital forensic workflows, including anomaly detection, pattern recognition, and predictive modeling. It discusses how various machine learning techniques, such as supervised and unsupervised learning, deep learning, and reinforcement learning, are applied to tasks like data classification, incident response, and evidence triage. Challenges such as model interpretability, data privacy, and adversarial attacks are addressed alongside emerging solutions to improve robustness and reliability. Through case studies and practical applications, this chapter underscores the impact of machine learning on evolving forensic capabilities, contributing to more efficient investigations and enhanced decision-making processes.

In the rapidly evolving field of digital forensics, the integration of behavioral analysis and user profiling has emerged as a critical component for enhancing investigation accuracy and efficiency. This chapter explores the role of behavioral analysis in forensic investigations, focusing on how user profiling techniques can be utilized to identify behavior patterns, track digital footprints, and detect anomalous activities. We examine various methods for collecting, analyzing, and interpreting user data from diverse digital sources, including social media, browsing history, and mobile devices. Furthermore, we discuss the challenges forensic experts face in handling large volumes of data, maintaining privacy, and ensuring the integrity of evidence. This chapter aims to provide insights into the growing importance of behavioral analysis and user profiling for modern forensic investigations in the digital age through a combination of AI-driven tools and traditional forensic methodologies.

In the internet era, images and videos face significant danger from criminals seeking to manipulate and conceal evidence of their crimes. The authenticity of image and video evidence cannot be guaranteed, making it challenging to consider them strong proof in a law court. The ongoing competition between researchers developing forgery detection tools and forgers creating more sophisticated manipulation techniques adds complexity to creating a universal tool for efficiently detecting various types of forgeries. Numerous approaches have been proposed to assess the authenticity of images; this chapter conducts a comprehensive literature review and comparative analysis of recent effective techniques designed to discover image forgeries. The emphasis is on addressing copy-move and splicing attacks frequently encountered in such scenarios. The chapter also identifies commonly used datasets and evaluation metrics in this field. The chapter also highlights existing challenges and provides valuable insights into potential future directions for research in image forgery detection.

Artificial Intelligence (AI) has transformed digital forensics and cybersecurity, enhancing efficiency and accuracy in combating cybercrime and analyzing evidence. This chapter will explore AI's capabilities in handling vast data, identifying patterns, reconstructing crime scenes, and detecting anomalies that have revolutionized investigations.. However, these technologies also pose challenges, including ethical concerns, algorithmic bias, privacy issues, and potential misuse. In cybersecurity, AI facilitates real-time threat detection, fraud prevention, and cross-border cooperation against cyberattacks. Despite these advancements, addressing challenges like international legal inconsistencies, transparency, and ethical implications is critical. As AI evolves, its integration into forensic science and cybersecurity holds immense potential to uphold justice and security, demanding balanced governance to ensure ethical and lawful applications.

As artificial intelligence (AI) continues to evolve, it is reshaping the landscape of digital forensics, introducing new tools, methodologies, and challenges. This chapter explores the anticipated future trends in AI that are poised to transform digital forensic practices. Key areas of focus include the integration of machine learning for enhanced evidence analysis, AI-driven automation for streamlining investigative processes, and advances in natural language processing to improve data interpretation. The chapter also addresses emerging challenges such as adversarial

Preface

The digital era has ushered in unprecedented changes in the field of forensics, particularly as artificial intelligence (AI) emerges as a transformative force. Digital forensics, a cornerstone in the fight against cybercrime and the quest for digital truth, is undergoing a paradigm shift driven by AI's capabilities in automation, accuracy, and scalability. **"Digital Forensics in the Age of AI"** is a timely exploration of this evolving landscape, offering a comprehensive overview of AI's integration into forensic practices.

This volume brings together leading voices from academia and industry to examine the intersections of AI and digital forensics. By addressing both foundational principles and cutting-edge advancements, the book serves as a valuable resource for practitioners, researchers, and students alike. The chapters provide insights into the practical application of AI technologies in solving forensic challenges, while also delving into the ethical, legal, and technical complexities that arise from this integration.

Our objectives with this book are to:

1. **Enhance Understanding**: Present foundational and advanced topics in AI-driven digital forensics to broaden readers' perspectives.
2. **Promote Practical Applications**: Highlight real-world applications of AI in forensic investigations to bridge theory and practice.
3. **Foster Critical Thinking**: Address the ethical and legal challenges inherent in the field to encourage responsible AI adoption.
4. **Inspire Future Research**: Outline emerging trends and opportunities for innovation in AI and digital forensics.

ORGANIZATION OF THE BOOK

The book is structured to provide a cohesive journey through the interplay of AI and digital forensics. The chapters are as follows:

- **Chapter 1**: *Introduction to Digital Forensics and Artificial Intelligence*

Sets the stage with an overview of digital forensics and AI's transformative potential in this domain.

- **Chapter 2**: *The Role of Explainable AI (XAI) in Forensic Investigations*

Explores the critical role of interpretability in AI models to ensure transparency and accountability in investigations.

- **Chapter 3**: *Anti-Forensics: The Art of Deceiving and Evading Cybersecurity Analysts*

Discusses the emerging threats of anti-forensic techniques and how AI can counteract these methods.

- **Chapter 4**: *Cybercrime Investigation and Fraud Detection with AI*

Highlights AI-driven approaches to identifying and addressing cybercrimes and fraud.

- **Chapter 5**: *Machine Learning in IoT and Mobile Device Forensics*

Examines the challenges and solutions AI offers in analyzing data from IoT devices and mobile platforms.

- **Chapter 6**: *Legal and Ethical Challenges in Digital Forensics Investigations*

Discusses the legal and ethical dilemmas that arise with AI's integration into digital forensics.

- **Chapter 7**: *Understanding File System Forensics – FAT, NTFS, HFS & EXT*

Provides a detailed examination of file system structures and their forensic implications.

- **Chapter 8**: *A Survey on 5G Wireless Network Intrusion Detection Systems using Machine Learning Techniques*

Investigates the role of machine learning in securing next-generation wireless networks.

- **Chapter 9**: *Machine Learning in Digital Forensic Analysis*

Explores machine learning's transformative impact on forensic data analysis.

- **Chapter 10**: *Behavioral Analysis and User Profiling in Forensic Investigations*

Details AI methodologies for profiling user behavior in digital investigations.

- **Chapter 11**: *Advancements in Image Integrity Verification Techniques and Challenges in AI-Driven Forensics*

Examines innovative techniques for ensuring image authenticity in forensic contexts.

- **Chapter 12**: *Navigating Emerging AI Technologies and Future Trends in Cybersecurity and Forensics*

Surveys the landscape of new AI technologies and their potential applications in forensic science.

- **Chapter 13**: *Future Trends in AI and Digital Forensics*

Concludes the book with a forward-looking perspective on the role of AI in the future of digital forensics.

IN CONCLUSION

As the digital forensics field continues to evolve, the role of AI will only grow in significance. This book is not only a reflection of current advancements but also a guidepost for future exploration. We hope it serves as a source of inspiration and a foundation for further innovation, encouraging collaboration and responsible AI adoption in the pursuit of digital justice.

Marwan Omar
Illinois Institute of Technology, United States

Hewa Majeed Zangana
Duhok Polytechnic University, Iraq

Chapter 1
Introduction to Digital Forensics and Artificial Intelligence

Hewa Majeed Zangana
https://orcid.org/0000-0001-7909-254X
Duhok Polytechnic University, Iraq

Marwan Omar
Illinois Institute of Technology, USA

ABSTRACT

This chapter explores the intersection of digital forensics and artificial intelligence (AI), emphasizing the transformative impact AI is having on digital investigative techniques. Digital forensics, traditionally focused on the collection, preservation, and analysis of electronic evidence, is facing new challenges and opportunities in the era of AI. The rapid proliferation of digital devices and the sophistication of cyber threats demand enhanced methods for accurate and timely evidence gathering. AI technologies, including machine learning, natural language processing, and deep learning, are empowering forensic professionals to detect, analyze, and interpret vast volumes of data with unprecedented efficiency. This chapter discusses the fundamentals of digital forensics, examines the integration of AI tools within forensic processes, and addresses the ethical and privacy concerns that arise. The insights provided will help readers understand how AI can bolster digital forensics, enabling more proactive and precise responses to cybercrime.

DOI: 10.4018/979-8-3373-0857-9.ch001

1. OVERVIEW OF DIGITAL FORENSICS

Digital forensics involves the identification, acquisition, analysis, and reporting of electronic evidence from digital devices to investigate cyber incidents, criminal activities, and security breaches. With the widespread adoption of digital devices and networks, digital forensics has evolved into a critical discipline that plays an essential role in supporting law enforcement, cybersecurity, and regulatory compliance. This overview provides insights into the foundational aspects of digital forensics, including key processes, challenges, and the discipline's growing interconnection with artificial intelligence (AI).

Digital forensics traditionally covers various domains, including computer forensics, network forensics, mobile device forensics, and cloud forensics (Adam & Varol, 2020). Each of these domains focuses on extracting, preserving, and analyzing digital evidence from different environments. For example, computer forensics involves recovering data from computers and storage devices, while network forensics emphasizes monitoring and analysis of network traffic to detect and reconstruct cyber events (Jeong, 2020; Wright, Dawson Jr, & Omar, 2012).

Forensic analysis spans various evidence types, each necessitating specialized handling techniques. This bar chart illustrates common digital evidence types and their relative prevalence in investigations.

Figure 1. Forensic Evidence Types

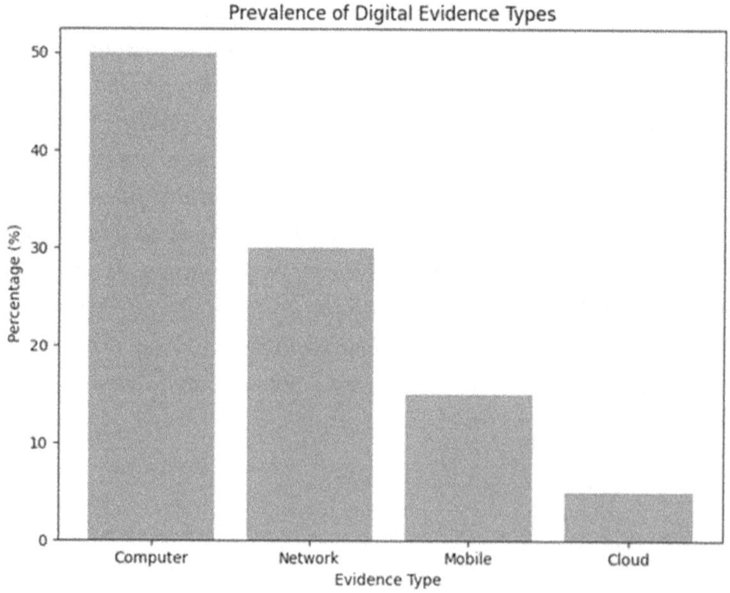

1.1 Key Processes in Digital Forensics

The digital forensic process generally follows a structured approach, often referred to as the digital forensic process model. The main stages are:

1. **Identification and Preservation**: This phase involves identifying digital sources that may contain relevant evidence and securing them to prevent tampering. Devices are collected, documented, and protected to ensure data integrity, which is critical for maintaining a legally defensible chain of custody (Irons & Lallie, 2014).
2. **Acquisition**: In this step, forensic practitioners create exact copies of the data for analysis. Bit-by-bit imaging techniques ensure that the original data remains unaltered, allowing investigators to work on duplicates without risk of modifying the original evidence (Moustafa, 2022).
3. **Analysis**: Forensic analysts search through acquired data to uncover meaningful information. Techniques include examining file metadata, recovering deleted files, and tracing user activity. Advanced analysis methods, including timeline creation and anomaly detection, support investigators in reconstructing events and identifying suspects (Hall, Sakzad, & Choo, 2022).
4. **Interpretation and Reporting**: The final phase involves interpreting the findings and preparing a detailed report, which must be clear, thorough, and legally sound. This report is often used in court, making precision and adherence to legal standards essential (Kelly et al., 2020).

The digital forensics process is systematic, ensuring evidence is identified, acquired, analyzed, and interpreted methodically. The following flowchart outlines the key steps in the digital forensics process, from data preservation to reporting.

Figure 2. Digital Forensics Process

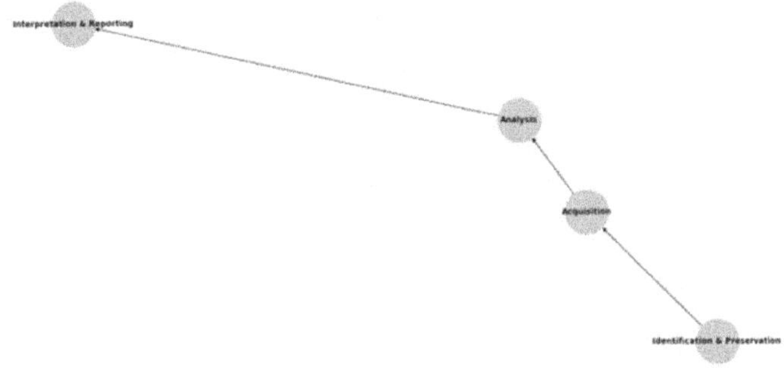

1.2 Challenges in Digital Forensics

As the scope of digital forensics expands, so do the challenges it faces. One primary challenge is the rapid advancement of digital technology, which continuously introduces new devices, software, and encryption methods. This makes it difficult for forensic tools and methodologies to keep pace. Other challenges include:

- **Data Volume and Complexity**: Modern devices generate vast amounts of data, making it challenging for forensic analysts to process and analyze within limited time frames (Iqbal et al., 2020).
- **Encryption and Privacy**: Encryption safeguards user privacy but complicates forensic investigations, as encrypted data can be nearly impossible to access without the correct decryption keys (Hamza & Omar, 2013).
- **Cloud and Distributed Environments**: With the rise of cloud storage and computing, digital evidence may reside on remote servers rather than on local devices, making the acquisition of evidence challenging and raising jurisdictional concerns (Bhawna & Mahajan, 2024; Zangana, 2024).
- **Legal and Ethical Considerations**: Digital forensic investigations often involve sensitive information, necessitating strict adherence to privacy laws and ethical standards to prevent violations of individuals' rights (Ganesh, 2017; Costantini, De Gasperis, & Olivieri, 2019).

The complexity of digital forensics grows with data volume and diversity, posing challenges in analysis and investigation. The heatmap below highlights primary areas of complexity.

Figure 3. Data Complexity and Forensic Challenges

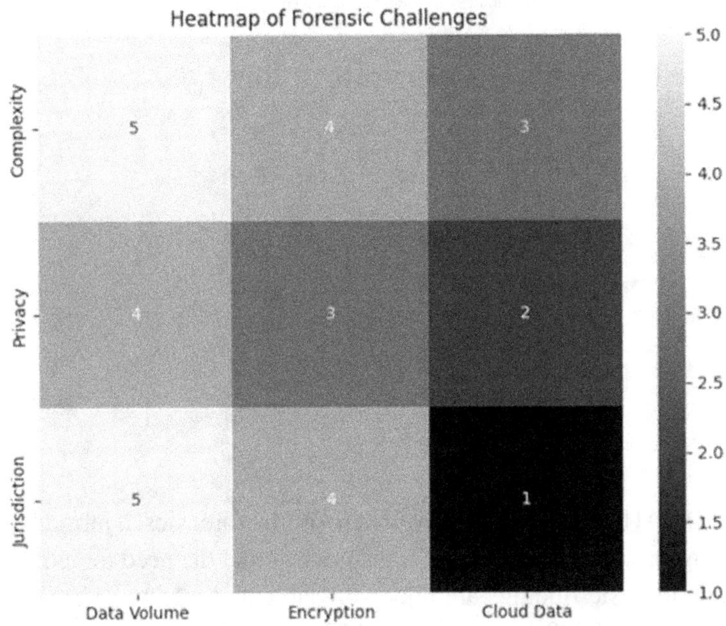

1.3 Digital Forensics and Artificial Intelligence

The introduction of AI in digital forensics is transforming the field by enhancing the efficiency and accuracy of forensic investigations. AI-driven tools assist in analyzing large datasets, detecting patterns, and automating repetitive tasks, such as scanning log files or identifying anomalous behaviors (Sikos, 2021). Machine learning, in particular, is instrumental in digital forensics for tasks like file classification, anomaly detection, and predicting user behaviors based on digital traces (Dunsin, Ghanem, & Quazzane, 2022).

AI's integration in digital forensics enables analysts to conduct investigations more quickly and with greater precision. For instance, AI-based image recognition can help locate specific objects within digital media, while natural language processing (NLP) assists in parsing large volumes of text and identifying keywords relevant to a case (Gholami & Omar, 2023; Jarrett & Choo, 2021). These advancements are especially valuable as forensic teams face growing data complexity and time constraints in modern digital investigations.

AI tools have revolutionized forensic processes. The following pie chart illustrates the distribution of various AI technologies applied within digital forensics.

Figure 4. AI Tools in Forensics

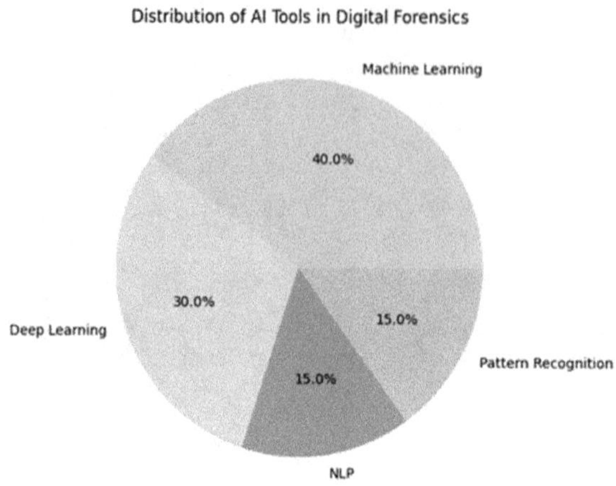

However, as AI becomes more prevalent in digital forensics, it introduces its own set of challenges, such as algorithmic transparency and the need for explainable AI to ensure that forensic findings are understandable and legally defensible (Hall et al., 2022; Kelly et al., 2020). Additionally, AI-based methods require robust datasets to train models effectively, and ensuring the reliability and authenticity of these datasets remains a critical concern (Tyagi, Kumari, & Richa, 2024).

1.4 Summary

Digital forensics is a rapidly evolving field, facing both traditional and emerging challenges as technology advances. AI's integration offers transformative benefits for digital forensic investigations, but it also introduces new considerations, including transparency, legal compliance, and data integrity. As digital forensics continues to develop, AI will play an increasingly significant role in enhancing investigative capabilities, setting the stage for a future where forensic processes are more efficient, scalable, and adaptable to new digital landscapes (Zangana & Omar, 2025; Huff et al., 2023; Manasa & Kumar, 2022).

2. INTRODUCTION TO ARTIFICIAL INTELLIGENCE (AI)

Artificial Intelligence (AI) has evolved significantly since its inception, driven by advancements in computational power, data processing capabilities, and algorithmic sophistication. AI encompasses a broad range of technologies aimed at enabling machines to perform tasks traditionally requiring human intelligence, such as learning, reasoning, problem-solving, perception, and language understanding (Ganesh, 2017). The integration of AI into diverse fields has created a paradigm shift in sectors like healthcare, finance, manufacturing, and cybersecurity (Karthikeyan, Pande, & Sarveshwaran, 2023). AI's interdisciplinary nature also facilitates its convergence with other fields, including digital forensics, where AI algorithms improve efficiency and accuracy in forensic investigations (Dunsin, Ghanem, & Quazzane, 2022).

The application of AI in digital forensics has revolutionized how data is analyzed and interpreted. Forensic tasks that previously required extensive manual effort can now be automated through machine learning algorithms, which can sift through vast amounts of data to identify patterns, anomalies, and critical evidence faster than human investigators (Costantini, De Gasperis, & Olivieri, 2019; Jeong, 2020). Advanced AI techniques, such as deep learning and neural networks, have further enhanced forensic capabilities, enabling more precise detection of complex cyber threats and incident responses (Dunsin, Ghanem, Ouazzane, & Vassilev, 2024). The synergy between AI and digital forensics opens new avenues for forensic science, transforming traditional practices into more agile and proactive approaches (Irons & Lallie, 2014; Manasa & Kumar, 2022).

AI's role in cybersecurity also extends to addressing sophisticated cyber threats. By applying AI-driven techniques, organizations can bolster their security postures through predictive analytics, anomaly detection, and real-time threat intelligence (Bhawna & Mahajan, 2024). In digital forensics, these AI capabilities allow for effective handling of incidents such as email phishing and network intrusion, which require rapid response and robust analysis to mitigate damages (Zangana et al., 2024; Rizvi et al., 2022). According to Jones and Omar (2024), AI-based approaches enhance both the speed and precision of cybersecurity measures, a necessity given the increasing sophistication of modern cyber threats.

Explainable AI (XAI) is emerging as a critical area within AI research to provide transparency in decision-making processes, especially in forensic applications where trust and accountability are paramount. For instance, XAI techniques make it possible for forensic investigators to understand and validate AI-driven conclusions, ensuring that evidence used in legal contexts remains comprehensible and justifiable (Hall, Sakzad, & Choo, 2022; Kelly et al., 2020). This approach addresses the "black box" challenge of AI, where complex models often provide results without clear explanations, posing challenges in environments where verification is essential (Iqbal et al., 2020).

AI's application in digital forensics has introduced novel analytical methods, yet it also raises concerns around ethical issues, data privacy, and potential biases in AI algorithms (Jarrett & Choo, 2021; Tyagi, Kumari, & Richa, 2024). As AI continues to be integrated into digital forensic practices, researchers emphasize the importance of developing standards and regulatory frameworks to ensure ethical use of AI technologies (Huff et al., 2023; Zangana & Omar, 2025). Furthermore, the rise of cloud-based digital forensics and AI-powered tools has introduced additional complexities related to data integrity, access control, and cross-border data sharing, all of which require careful consideration to ensure the security and reliability of forensic processes (Hamza & Omar, 2013; Mitchell, 2014).

In conclusion, AI has become an indispensable component in digital forensics and cybersecurity, enhancing analytical capabilities, accelerating incident response, and enabling more resilient security frameworks (Sikos, 2021; Moustafa, 2022). The integration of AI into forensic science represents an evolution in the field, pushing it toward a future where data-driven insights and predictive analytics play central roles in safeguarding digital systems against evolving cyber threats (Wright, Dawson, & Omar, 2012; Zangana, 2024). As AI and machine learning continue to evolve, digital forensic practices are poised to become even more precise, efficient, and indispensable in an increasingly digitized world.

3. INTERSECTION OF DIGITAL FORENSICS AND AI

The integration of artificial intelligence (AI) within digital forensics represents a transformative approach to managing the vast complexities and volumes of data involved in cyber investigations. Traditional digital forensics has primarily relied on expert analysis, manual processes, and rule-based methods for identifying and analyzing digital evidence. However, the exponential growth of data generated by individuals, organizations, and systems has made it increasingly challenging for forensic analysts to process, investigate, and interpret digital evidence manually. As such, AI methodologies, particularly those involving machine learning and deep learning, have emerged as pivotal tools for enhancing efficiency, accuracy, and scalability in digital forensic investigations (Bhawna & Mahajan, 2024; Zangana, Omar, Al-Karaki, & Mohammed, 2024).

3.1. Enhancing Data Analysis and Pattern Recognition

AI has greatly augmented forensic analysis by automating data categorization, pattern recognition, and anomaly detection, thereby reducing the manual effort required for initial evidence sorting and triage (Costantini, De Gasperis, & Olivieri, 2019). AI algorithms, such as deep learning models, can detect intricate patterns in unstructured data, allowing forensic investigators to rapidly identify potential threats or suspicious behaviors. This capability is especially useful in investigations involving vast data sources like emails, network logs, or social media activity (Ganesh, 2017; Wright, Dawson Jr, & Omar, 2012). By automating these processes, AI minimizes human error and accelerates the response to cyber incidents, enabling investigators to focus on higher-level analysis.

The decision-making process in forensic analysis involves selecting appropriate techniques based on the evidence type and investigation needs. This decision tree illustrates the main choices in forensic analysis.

Figure 5. Decision Tree of Forensic Analysis

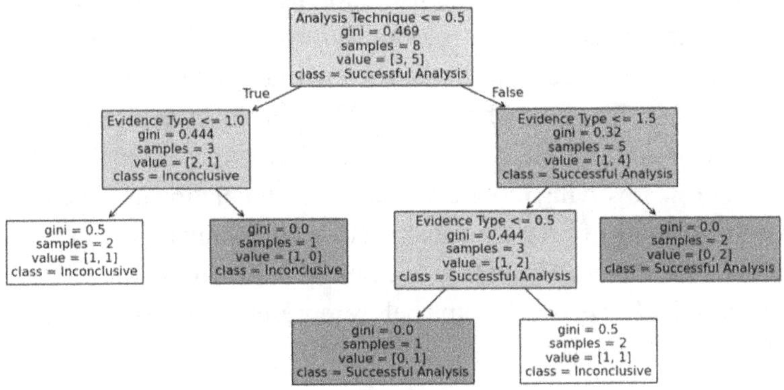

3.2. Application in Incident Response and Predictive Analysis

AI-powered predictive models have become instrumental in forecasting and preventing cyber incidents, thus adding a proactive layer to digital forensics. Machine learning algorithms, for example, analyze historical data to predict patterns of criminal behavior, identify vulnerable system configurations, and detect anomalies indicative of unauthorized activities (Dunsin, Ghanem, & Quazzane, 2022; Manasa & Kumar, 2022). In incident response, these predictive capabilities support the swift identification of potential entry points and attack vectors, streamlining the investigative process (Jeong, 2020).

3.3. Explainable AI and Interpretability in Digital Forensics

One of the most critical aspects of integrating AI into digital forensics is ensuring the interpretability of AI decisions, particularly in legal contexts where transparent evidence is paramount. Explainable AI (XAI) frameworks have been developed to address this challenge, enabling forensic tools to provide clear, interpretable rationales for their findings. This capability is crucial for establishing the reliability of AI-derived evidence and ensuring that it can be presented confidently in court (Hall, Sakzad, & Choo, 2022; Kelly et al., 2020). AI-driven tools can now articulate how a model arrived at a particular conclusion, making them more credible and legally admissible in digital forensics.

3.4. Automation of Evidence Collection and Processing

AI technologies have proven valuable in the automation of routine forensic tasks, such as evidence extraction, classification, and preservation, which significantly enhances operational efficiency. Automated forensic tools equipped with machine learning can autonomously extract relevant information from digital devices and identify critical evidence, freeing up human investigators to focus on complex analysis (Rizvi, Scanlon, Mcgibney, & Sheppard, 2022; Karthikeyan, Pande, & Sarveshwaran, 2023). This automation is especially beneficial in handling high volumes of cases, such as those involving mobile devices or cloud platforms, where traditional manual methods are insufficiently scalable (Hamza & Omar, 2013; Omar, 2022).

AI components interact within forensic investigations to optimize evidence collection and analysis. The network graph below represents the AI-driven components in digital forensics.

Figure 6. AI-Driven Forensic Components

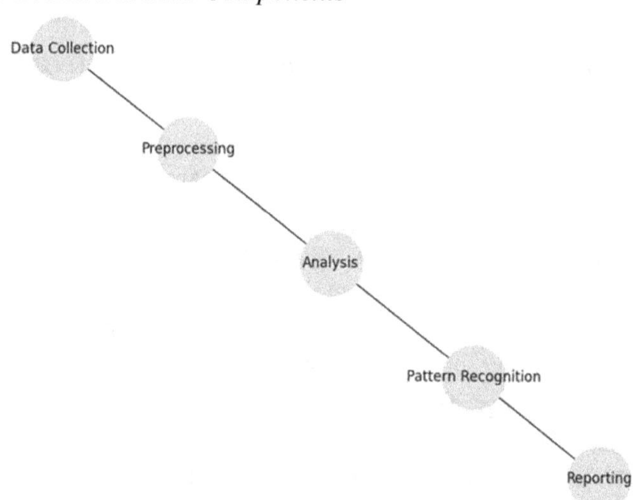

3.5. Challenges and Ethical Considerations

Despite the advantages AI brings to digital forensics, it introduces several ethical, legal, and operational challenges. AI algorithms must be carefully managed to avoid bias in investigations and ensure the accuracy and fairness of forensic outcomes (Irons & Lallie, 2014). Moreover, the complexity of some AI models, particularly deep learning-based models, can introduce interpretability issues, complicating the legal use of AI-derived evidence in judicial proceedings (Jarrett & Choo, 2021). Privacy concerns also arise, especially when processing personal or sensitive data. Therefore, balancing the benefits of AI with rigorous ethical and legal standards is essential to maintain trust in AI-driven forensic practices (Tyagi, Kumari, & Richa, 2024; Huff et al., 2023).

AI model accuracy in forensics can be affected by the size and complexity of evidence datasets. This scatter plot compares accuracy rates with evidence sizes across AI models used in forensics.

Figure 7. AI Accuracy vs. Evidence Size

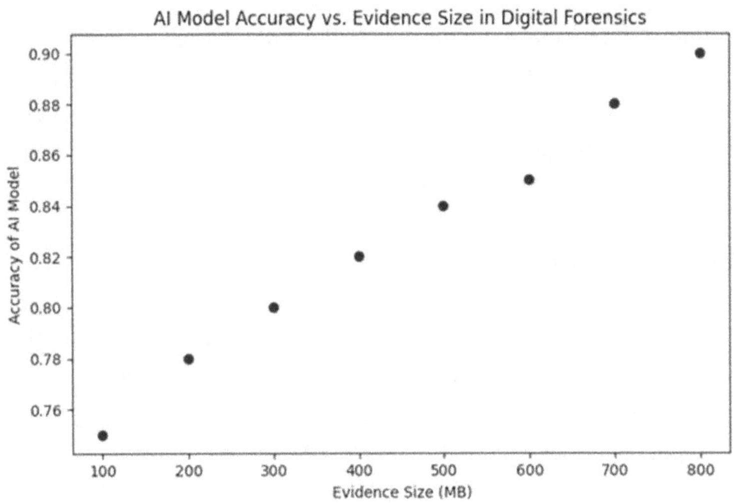

3.6. Future Directions in AI-Driven Digital Forensics

The future of AI in digital forensics includes the development of more sophisticated models capable of handling encrypted data and identifying deeper contextual insights from limited or incomplete datasets. Innovations such as natural language processing (NLP) and large language models (LLMs) hold promise for understanding linguistic patterns in social engineering attacks, thereby aiding in the detection of fraudulent or malicious communications (Zangana & Omar, 2025; Gholami & Omar, 2024). Additionally, advancements in AI-enabled blockchain forensics are anticipated, which could improve the tracking and investigation of cryptocurrency transactions used in illicit activities (Zangana, 2024; Omar & Zangana, 2024).

In summary, AI's integration into digital forensics marks a significant shift towards a more automated, efficient, and predictive investigative paradigm. By leveraging AI, forensic investigators can respond to cyber incidents more swiftly and thoroughly, although careful consideration must be given to the ethical and legal implications that accompany these advancements (Adam & Varol, 2020; Iqbal et al., 2020). The continued evolution of AI will likely drive transformative changes in forensic practices, ultimately enhancing the ability to protect digital assets and bring cybercriminals to justice.

4. CHALLENGES IN INTEGRATING AI WITH DIGITAL FORENSICS

Integrating artificial intelligence (AI) with digital forensics presents promising advancements but also significant challenges. The convergence of these two fields can enhance forensic capabilities in analyzing complex data and uncovering hidden insights. However, multiple obstacles must be addressed to ensure the seamless and effective deployment of AI in digital forensics.

4.1. Data Complexity and Volume

The vast amount of digital evidence generated today is one of the primary challenges in digital forensics. AI, particularly through machine learning and deep learning, can assist in managing and processing this data efficiently. However, the complexity of digital evidence—such as encrypted data, multimedia, and data from IoT devices—makes it difficult for AI to interpret without sophisticated models and substantial computational power (Adam & Varol, 2020; Dunsin et al., 2022). Processing these complex data types often requires advanced algorithms, such as neural networks trained for specific forensic applications, which can be computationally expensive and resource-intensive (Ganesh, 2017).

4.2. Trustworthiness and Explainability

Another critical challenge is the need for AI models in digital forensics to be explainable and trustworthy. Explainable AI (XAI) enables forensic experts to understand and justify AI-driven insights, especially in legal settings where evidence must be transparent and defensible. The opacity of some AI models, particularly deep learning networks, complicates their adoption in forensics (Hall et al., 2022). Developing XAI tools specific to forensic applications is essential to build confidence among practitioners and legal professionals (Kelly et al., 2020).

4.3. Ethical and Privacy Concerns

The application of AI in digital forensics raises ethical questions, especially regarding data privacy and the potential misuse of sensitive information. AI models often require large datasets for training, which can involve personal data from individuals unrelated to the cases under investigation. Protecting the privacy of these individuals while ensuring the integrity of forensic data is a delicate balance (Jarrett & Choo, 2021; Moustafa, 2022). Moreover, the misuse of AI technologies could lead to ethical violations, such as infringing on privacy rights or improperly handling sensitive evidence (Zangana & Omar, 2025).

4.4. Adversarial Vulnerabilities

AI systems are susceptible to adversarial attacks, where slight perturbations in input data can lead to incorrect or misleading results. In digital forensics, this vulnerability could be exploited to manipulate forensic findings, potentially affecting case outcomes. Techniques such as adversarial training and robust model design are essential to mitigate these risks, but they add complexity to the deployment and maintenance of AI models in forensics (Omar, 2024; Wright et al., 2012).

4.5. Skills Gap and Resource Limitations

The integration of AI into digital forensics requires a workforce skilled in both domains. Many digital forensic professionals may lack expertise in AI methodologies, and the demand for specialized training poses challenges. Additionally, implementing AI tools in constrained environments, such as remote incident response, can be problematic due to resource limitations, including limited bandwidth and processing capabilities (Dunsin et al., 2024; Rizvi et al., 2022).

4.6. Legal and Compliance Issues

The use of AI in digital forensics raises legal and compliance challenges, as forensic findings often serve as critical evidence in legal proceedings. The legal community may view AI-based results skeptically, given the potential for algorithmic bias or errors. As forensic evidence must adhere to strict standards, developing AI models that align with these standards is essential. Legal frameworks and forensic standards must evolve to accommodate AI-driven analyses without compromising on legal integrity (Irons & Lallie, 2014; Bhawna & Mahajan, 2024).

4.7. Algorithm Bias and Fairness

Algorithmic bias in AI systems is a significant concern, especially in forensic applications where bias can lead to unjust conclusions. Bias in AI models can arise from biased training data, which may inadvertently influence forensic findings. Addressing this issue requires diverse, representative datasets and continuous monitoring to minimize potential biases (Jeong, 2020; Tyagi et al., 2024). Ensuring fairness in AI algorithms is critical to uphold the objectivity and impartiality of forensic investigations.

4.8. Integration with Existing Forensic Tools

Integrating AI with existing forensic tools and frameworks poses additional challenges. Legacy systems often lack the compatibility needed to work seamlessly with AI solutions, requiring extensive modifications and updates. Additionally, as forensic practices evolve with AI, there is a need for standardized protocols to ensure consistent integration across different tools and platforms (Costantini et al., 2019; Sikos, 2021).

4.9. Real-Time Forensic Analysis

Real-time analysis is increasingly crucial in digital forensics, especially for incident response in dynamic environments. While AI can expedite data processing, achieving real-time analysis is challenging due to the computational demands of AI models and the rapid evolution of cyber threats. Developing efficient, lightweight AI algorithms capable of delivering timely insights is essential for forensic teams handling urgent cases (Hamza & Omar, 2013; Jones et al., 2023).

In summary, while AI has the potential to transform digital forensics, overcoming these challenges is essential for its effective adoption. Addressing these issues requires advancements in AI technology, updated legal frameworks, and a skilled workforce capable of leveraging AI to enhance forensic investigations. With ongoing research and development, AI can become an invaluable asset to digital forensics, providing faster, more accurate, and more reliable insights into cyber incidents.

5. CURRENT AND EMERGING APPLICATIONS

In recent years, the convergence of Artificial Intelligence (AI) with digital forensics has led to transformative changes, addressing limitations and introducing efficiencies in forensic investigations. AI-based digital forensic applications focus on augmenting data analysis, automating detection, and enhancing threat intelligence capabilities. These advancements are essential given the rising complexity and volume of digital evidence and the proliferation of sophisticated cybercrimes.

5.1 AI-Enhanced Data Collection and Evidence Gathering

AI techniques have revolutionized how digital forensic experts collect and analyze data. Traditional methods often rely heavily on manual processes, which can be time-consuming and error-prone, especially when dealing with large datasets. Modern AI approaches, such as machine learning and natural language processing, streamline the collection and categorization of evidence, aiding in quicker and more accurate investigations (Adam & Varol, 2020). AI algorithms can scan vast amounts of data, identify relevant artifacts, and even detect hidden or obscured evidence. These advancements are particularly effective in filtering through noisy data, making digital forensics more manageable and less resource-intensive (Irons & Lallie, 2014; Jarrett & Choo, 2021).

Forensic investigations categorize data across multiple types, each with specific characteristics. The histogram below presents the distribution of data types collected in digital forensics.

Figure 8. Forensic Data Categories

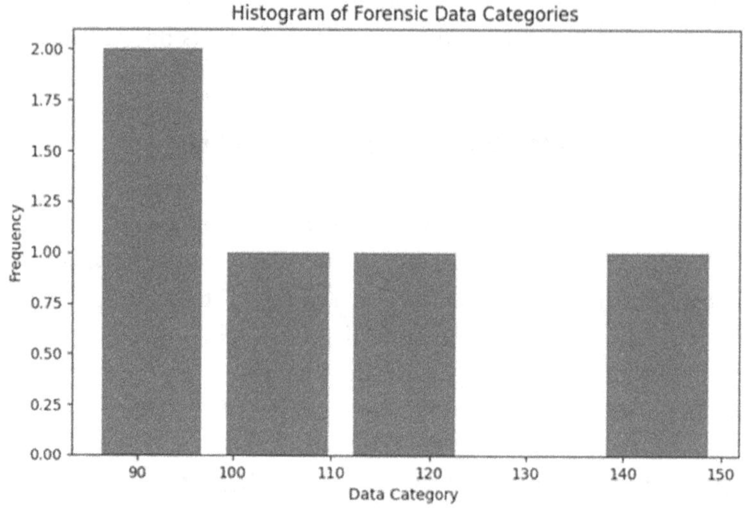

5.2 Automated Malware Detection and Analysis

AI-driven malware detection has become a core component of cybersecurity. Advanced neural networks and deep learning models can identify patterns associated with malware, even those obfuscated by encryption or other techniques. Convolutional neural networks (CNNs) and recurrent neural networks (RNNs) have proven highly effective in detecting and analyzing malware characteristics, offering a significant improvement over traditional signature-based method (Omar, 2024). The shift to AI-driven detection enables a more proactive stance in threat response, facilitating real-time threat intelligence and automated incident response (Jeong, 2020; Mohammed, Omar, & Nguyen, 2018).

5.3 AI for Network and Cloud Forensics

The integration of AI in network and cloud forensics is another emerging application with considerable promise. Network forensics often requires the analysis of large volumes of traffic data to detect anomalous behaviors that could indicate a breach or attack. AI-based anomaly detection systems, using both supervised and unsupervised learning methods, can identify these subtle deviations in network patterns with high accuracy (Zangana & Omar, 2025). In cloud environments, AI tools assist forensic investigators in overcoming the challenges of data dispersion across multiple locations and virtualized environments, making it possible to conduct effective forensic analysis without compromising data integrity (Hamza & Omar, 2013; Moustafa, 2022).

5.4 Explainable AI for Forensic Decision-Making

Explainable AI (XAI) models are increasingly used in digital forensics to ensure transparency and accountability in decision-making processes. XAI methods allow forensic analysts to understand and interpret AI-generated outputs, thus building trust in AI-driven findings. This is crucial in forensic investigations, where evidence often needs to be presented in a court of law. XAI applications in digital forensics can help elucidate complex decision-making processes, making it easier to validate findings and address potential biases (Hall, Sakzad, & Choo, 2022; Kelly et al., 2020). By incorporating explainable models, forensic professionals can better justify AI-derived conclusions, enhancing credibility in legal contexts.

AI models provide distinct capabilities in forensic analysis. The radar chart below compares key capabilities of AI-based forensic models in data interpretation, anomaly detection, and decision-making.

Figure 9. AI-Based Forensic Model Capabilities

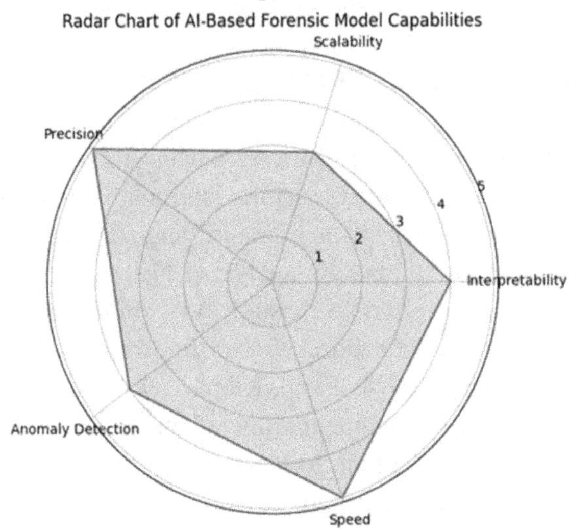

5.5 Large Language Models for Threat Analysis

Large Language Models (LLMs), such as GPT-3, have demonstrated significant potential in forensic applications, especially in analyzing textual data. These models can be employed to sift through logs, emails, and communications, identifying patterns that might indicate insider threats or phishing attempts (Zangana & Omar, 2025). LLMs can generate comprehensive threat reports and offer summaries that help analysts identify pertinent details quickly, thus improving response times (Gholami & Omar, 2023; Wright, Dawson Jr., & Omar, 2012).

5.6 Blockchain-Based Forensics for Data Integrity

Blockchain technology is emerging as a robust solution for ensuring data integrity in digital forensics. By using blockchain's immutable ledger, forensic investigators can timestamp evidence, ensuring that it remains tamper-proof throughout the investigation. This technology not only helps verify the authenticity of digital evidence but also provides a transparent audit trail, which is critical in legal proceedings (Zangana, 2024). AI models are also being integrated with blockchain systems to automate the process of data validation, further enhancing the reliability and efficiency of forensic workflows (Costantini, De Gasperis, & Olivieri, 2019).

5.7 Advanced AI for Cyber Threat Detection

Cyber threat detection has seen significant advancements with AI, particularly through the application of advanced machine learning techniques and intelligent algorithms. AI models are now capable of identifying zero-day vulnerabilities and even predicting future cyber threats by analyzing historical attack patterns. This proactive approach is made possible through AI's ability to recognize patterns across diverse datasets, often uncovering new forms of attacks that might otherwise go unnoticed (Jones & Omar, 2024; Tyagi, Kumari, & Richa, 2024). For instance, supervised and unsupervised machine learning algorithms are employed to detect anomalies in network traffic, helping to identify and mitigate threats before they escalate (Dunsin, Ghanem, & Quazzane, 2022).

5.8 AI-Driven Deception Technologies in Digital Forensics

Another innovative application in digital forensics is the use of AI-driven cyber deception techniques, designed to lure attackers into controlled environments where they can be monitored and analyzed. These technologies create decoy systems or digital "honeypots" that trap malicious actors, allowing investigators to gather valuable intelligence on attack methods and strategies (Zangana et al., 2024). Deception technologies not only provide critical insights but also serve as a proactive defense strategy, potentially deterring attackers by creating uncertainty about the legitimacy of their targets (Ganesh, 2017).

5.9 Future Directions

Looking forward, the integration of AI in digital forensics is expected to become even more sophisticated. Research into AI's role in enhancing forensic capabilities across decentralized systems, such as blockchain and cloud-based networks, shows great potential for improving both security and response times. Additionally, the rise of ethical considerations in AI application for forensics calls for a responsible approach to AI deployment, balancing innovation with transparency and accountability (Huff et al., 2023; Jarrett & Choo, 2021).

In summary, AI applications in digital forensics are rapidly advancing, addressing both current needs and anticipating future challenges. The synergy between AI and digital forensics not only enhances the efficiency and accuracy of investigations but also paves the way for more robust security infrastructures across sectors. These technologies promise to transform forensic practices, ensuring that they remain agile, adaptive, and equipped to handle the complexities of the digital age.

6. LEGAL AND REGULATORY CONSIDERATIONS

In the evolving landscape of digital forensics, artificial intelligence (AI) has significantly enhanced investigative capabilities, yet it raises complex legal and regulatory considerations. The increasing reliance on AI-driven tools necessitates frameworks that ensure compliance with data privacy laws, ethical standards, and evidentiary admissibility in judicial systems.

6.1 Data Privacy and Compliance

One of the foremost legal concerns in AI-powered digital forensics is data privacy. Data privacy regulations such as the General Data Protection Regulation (GDPR) in Europe mandate strict guidelines for handling personal information. This is particularly relevant for digital forensics, where sensitive data is often processed. The regulation emphasizes data minimization and purpose limitation, both of which must be incorporated into forensic practices to prevent legal repercussions (Iqbal et al., 2020). Ensuring AI systems comply with these standards involves embedding privacy-centric methods into the forensic analysis process (Ganesh, 2017; Kelly et al., 2020).

6.2 Admissibility of AI-Generated Evidence

The admissibility of AI-generated evidence in courts is another significant regulatory challenge. Courts require that evidence be reliable, which is complicated when dealing with machine learning (ML) algorithms that may not be easily explainable (Hall et al., 2022). The opacity of certain AI models, often called "black-box" systems, could lead to legal challenges as forensic experts may struggle to provide clear and understandable evidence in court. Explainable AI (XAI) solutions are being developed to mitigate this issue by making ML processes more transparent, thereby aligning AI-generated forensic evidence with legal standards (Costantini et al., 2019; Jarrett & Choo, 2021).

6.3 Ethical and Bias-Related Concerns

AI models can inadvertently introduce biases, affecting the fairness of forensic analyses and raising ethical concerns (Manasa & Kumar, 2022). For instance, biases in training data can result in skewed or unfair outcomes, particularly in systems trained on data that lacks demographic diversity. This could lead to potentially biased forensic conclusions, which could influence the outcome of cases unfairly. Addressing these biases is vital, and implementing fairness algorithms and bias audits in forensic AI models is necessary to uphold ethical standards (Dunsin et al., 2024).

6.4 Cross-Jurisdictional Challenges

Digital forensics investigations often span multiple jurisdictions, as digital evidence may traverse different countries with distinct laws regarding data collection, processing, and sharing. This complexity is exacerbated when AI is employed across borders, as regulations on AI and data usage vary widely (Sikos, 2021). Harmonizing cross-jurisdictional legal frameworks is essential to enable AI-driven forensic investigations that are legally sound internationally (Irons & Lallie, 2014). This requires collaborative legal standards that allow the smooth sharing of digital evidence across borders without breaching local privacy or regulatory standards (Hamza & Omar, 2013).

6.5 Accountability and Liability Issues

In cases where AI-based forensic systems make critical decisions, questions of accountability and liability arise. Determining who is responsible when AI systems produce erroneous or misleading evidence remains a grey area in current regulations. Policymakers are examining ways to assign accountability for AI-based decisions in forensic applications, especially when errors could have severe legal implications (Bhawna & Mahajan, 2024; Jeong, 2020). It may be necessary to develop laws that hold AI tool creators, users, and forensic investigators jointly accountable for the accuracy and reliability of AI-driven forensic evidence.

6.6 Emerging Regulatory Frameworks and Standards

Globally, regulatory bodies and standard-setting organizations are working to establish guidelines for using AI in digital forensics. Emerging standards, such as those developed by the IEEE and the ISO, are creating frameworks to ensure that AI tools used in digital forensics are transparent, reliable, and ethically aligned (Rizvi et al., 2022). These frameworks aim to guide organizations in implementing AI in ways that comply with existing legal structures while fostering innovation. For instance, developing guidelines on model interpretability and privacy protection measures can enhance AI's role in forensics while maintaining regulatory compliance (Moustafa, 2022).

6.7 Future Directions

To address the complex regulatory landscape in AI-based digital forensics, continuous dialogue between technologists, legal professionals, and policymakers is essential. This collaboration can help create adaptive policies that keep pace with technological advancements, addressing both current and anticipated challenges (Omar & Zangana, 2024; Zangana et al., 2024).

7. FUTURE DIRECTIONS AND RESEARCH AREAS

The rapid advancement of digital forensics and cybersecurity highlights emerging opportunities for integrating artificial intelligence (AI) into investigative processes. Future research directions in this field focus on enhancing digital forensics through machine learning (ML) models, exploring innovative approaches for threat detection, and addressing the unique challenges posed by new technologies and cyber threats.

1. **Enhanced AI-Driven Forensic Analysis**

Research into AI and ML applications in digital forensics continues to gain traction, offering substantial improvements in data analysis efficiency and accuracy. Digital forensics requires handling vast amounts of data, where traditional analysis methods fall short. AI-driven solutions, such as pattern matching and anomaly detection, streamline the investigation process by identifying critical evidence faster. As Costantini et al. (2019) and Dunsin et al. (2024) suggest, implementing AI in forensics can improve evidence extraction from complex datasets, enabling investigators to detect cyber incidents with greater accuracy.

The adoption of AI in digital forensics has accelerated over recent years. This line graph shows the increase in AI applications in forensics over the past decade.

Figure 10. AI in Forensics Over Time

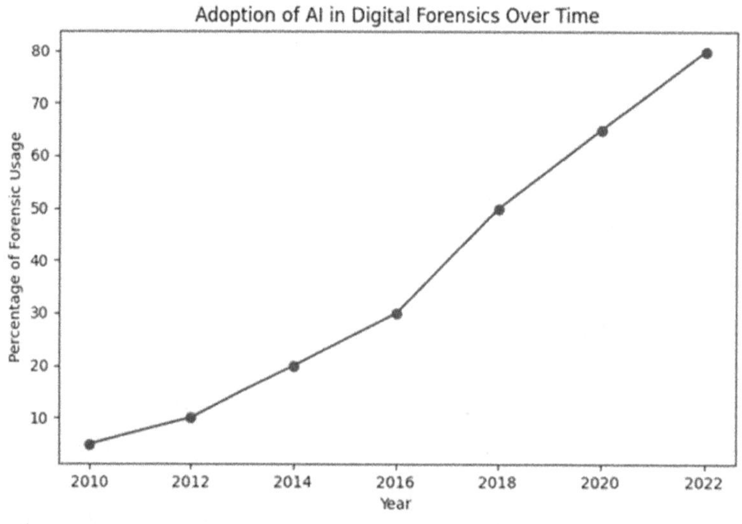

2. **Explainable AI (XAI) in Forensics**

With the growing reliance on AI, there is a pressing need for explainable AI (XAI) solutions to ensure transparency and accountability in digital forensics. Hall et al. (2022) underscore the role of XAI in making AI decisions interpretable, which is vital for maintaining legal standards and ensuring that digital evidence is admissible in court. Moreover, studies by Kelly et al. (2020) highlight how XAI can assist investigators in understanding AI-generated results, helping reduce bias and improve reliability in forensic analysis.

3. **Blockchain-Enhanced Evidence Management**

Blockchain technology offers potential solutions for enhancing evidence security and integrity in digital forensics. As Zangana (2024) explores, blockchain can be employed to create immutable records of forensic evidence, ensuring data integrity from collection through analysis. Such advancements are critical for establishing trust in forensic processes and supporting chain-of-custody protocols, particularly in high-stakes investigations where evidence tampering poses a significant risk.

4. **Integrating Large Language Models (LLMs) for Automated Analysis**

The advent of LLMs opens up new possibilities for automating text-based forensic analysis, including evidence documentation and interpretation of digital communications. Gholami and Omar (2023, 2024) examine the potential of synthetic data to enhance the efficiency of LLMs, which could be leveraged for automated report generation and multilingual forensic analysis. Future work may investigate how LLMs can streamline investigative processes, particularly in cyber forensics where language barriers and data volume pose challenges.

5. **Cyber-Physical System (CPS) Forensics**

With the rise of IoT and cyber-physical systems, new forensic approaches are required to investigate attacks on interconnected devices. Bhawna and Mahajan (2024) discuss the impact of AI on digital forensics within CPS, emphasizing the need for adaptive forensic tools that can respond to threats targeting critical infrastructure. As these systems are susceptible to unique vulnerabilities, future research should address forensic methodologies tailored to CPS to mitigate risks and preserve evidence from interconnected devices.

6. **Forensic Automation and Response Optimization**

Automation plays a critical role in expediting forensic investigations, particularly in environments with limited resources. According to Jarrett and Choo (2021), leveraging AI and automation in digital forensics minimizes manual intervention, reduces human error, and accelerates the incident response process. Research efforts in this area should focus on developing automated tools that can analyze and classify forensic artifacts in real time, enabling more agile responses to emerging threats.

7. **Cybernetic Deception Techniques in Forensics**

Future research could also explore the application of cybernetic deception techniques to mitigate phishing and other social engineering threats. Zangana et al. (2024) highlight the importance of understanding the dynamics of deception in cyber-attacks to enhance forensic analysis. Investigating AI-based detection systems that can identify and counteract deception techniques used by attackers could advance the field of digital forensics, enabling more comprehensive threat assessment and mitigation.

8. **Forensic Investigations in Cloud and Virtual Environments**

As organizations increasingly shift to cloud-based environments, digital forensics faces challenges in investigating incidents across distributed infrastructures. Research by Hamza and Omar (2013) on cloud security underscores the need for forensic frameworks capable of capturing and analyzing evidence in virtualized environments. Future research should address methodologies for conducting forensic investigations in multi-cloud and hybrid cloud environments, considering data privacy, jurisdictional concerns, and cloud provider limitations.

9. **Developing Ontologies for AI-Driven Forensic Knowledge Bases**

Ontology engineering is crucial for structuring and standardizing knowledge in digital forensics, enabling AI algorithms to interpret forensic data accurately. Sikos (2021) presents the potential of AI-based ontologies for organizing forensic information, thus facilitating more efficient data retrieval and decision-making. Future work may involve constructing comprehensive ontologies that support cross-domain forensic investigations, aiding in the seamless integration of diverse forensic data sources.

10. **Security and Ethical Challenges in AI Forensics**

While AI offers significant advancements for digital forensics, its application raises ethical and security challenges. Irons and Lallie (2014) emphasize the need for ethical guidelines to prevent AI misuse in forensics, particularly in areas like surveillance and privacy. Jeong (2020) explores the potential risks AI-based systems might introduce, such as data manipulation or model biases. Continued research is essential to develop ethical frameworks and security protocols for AI forensics, balancing the benefits of automation with the need for responsible and transparent AI use.

In summary, the integration of AI and advanced technologies into digital forensics holds substantial promise for transforming the field. However, ongoing research is crucial to address challenges such as explainability, data integrity, security, and ethical implications. By exploring these future directions, the field of digital forensics can evolve to meet the demands of an increasingly complex digital landscape, ensuring robust, efficient, and reliable investigative processes.

8. CONCLUSION

The rapid advancements in digital forensics have unveiled a new era in cybersecurity, marked by the increasing integration of artificial intelligence (AI) to enhance investigative capabilities and efficiency. This fusion of AI and digital forensics promises to reshape how digital evidence is analyzed, interpreted, and applied, allowing for faster, more accurate, and increasingly proactive responses to cybersecurity threats. By leveraging machine learning algorithms, data-driven insights, and predictive modeling, digital forensic tools can now detect anomalies, recognize complex patterns, and even predict potential threats with an accuracy that was previously unattainable.

However, with these innovations come new challenges. The complexity of integrating AI into digital forensics requires a deep understanding of both technological and ethical considerations. Ensuring the reliability and interpretability of AI models remains essential to maintain trust in forensic processes, especially in legal contexts. The challenge is compounded by issues related to data privacy, ethical use of AI, and the need for robust regulatory frameworks that address the rapid evolution of digital technologies. As AI systems become more autonomous, the risk of bias, security vulnerabilities, and misuse also grows, underscoring the importance of stringent standards and ethical guidelines in their development and deployment.

Looking ahead, the role of AI in digital forensics is expected to expand further as technology evolves. Emerging fields, such as large language models and deep learning, show promise for improving digital forensics' reach and accuracy, particularly in areas like natural language processing for analyzing communications, pattern recognition in malware detection, and enhancing cybersecurity protocols. However, achieving these advancements requires collaborative research, cross-disciplinary expertise, and investments in developing secure, transparent, and interpretable AI systems tailored to forensic needs.

In conclusion, the integration of AI in digital forensics marks a transformative shift, bringing new levels of sophistication and speed to threat detection and response. While the journey is not without obstacles, the potential benefits to cybersecurity and public safety make it an endeavor worth pursuing. As researchers, practitioners, and policymakers work together, the future of digital forensics will likely be characterized by powerful, ethical, and highly adaptive technologies that redefine how we safeguard digital environments.

REFERENCES

Adam, I. Y., & Varol, C. (2020, June). Intelligence in digital forensics process. In *2020 8th International Symposium on Digital Forensics and Security (ISDFS)* (pp. 1-6). IEEE. DOI: 10.1109/ISDFS49300.2020.9116442

Bhawna, & Mahajan, S. (2024). Artificial Intelligence Perspective on Digital Forensics. *Applying Artificial Intelligence in Cybersecurity Analytics and Cyber Threat Detection*, 33-44.

Costantini, S., De Gasperis, G., & Olivieri, R. (2019). Digital forensics and investigations meet artificial intelligence. *Annals of Mathematics and Artificial Intelligence*, 86(1), 193–229. DOI: 10.1007/s10472-019-09632-y

Dunsin, D., Ghanem, M. C., Ouazzane, K., & Vassilev, V. (2024). A comprehensive analysis of the role of artificial intelligence and machine learning in modern digital forensics and incident response. *Forensic Science International Digital Investigation*, 48, 301675. DOI: 10.1016/j.fsidi.2023.301675

Dunsin, D., Ghanem, M. C., & Quazzane, K. (2022). The use of artificial intelligence in digital forensics and incident response in a constrained environment. *International Journal of Information and Communication Engineering*, 16(8), 280–285.

Ganesh, V. (2017). Artificial intelligence applied to computer forensics. *International Journal (Toronto, Ont.)*, 5(5).

Gholami, S., & Omar, M. (2023). Does Synthetic Data Make Large Language Models More Efficient? *arXiv preprint arXiv:2310.07830*.

Gholami, S., & Omar, M. (2024). Can a student large language model perform as well as its teacher? In *Innovations, Securities, and Case Studies Across Healthcare, Business, and Technology* (pp. 122-139). IGI Global. DOI: 10.4018/979-8-3693-1906-2.ch007

Hall, S. W., Sakzad, A., & Choo, K. K. R. (2022). Explainable artificial intelligence for digital forensics. *Wiley Interdisciplinary Reviews: Forensic Science*, 4(2), e1434.

Hamza, Y. A., & Omar, M. D. (2013). Cloud computing security: Abuse and nefarious use of cloud computing. *International Journal of Computer Engineering Research*, 3(6), 22–27.

Huff, A. J., Burrell, D. N., Nobles, C., Richardson, K., Wright, J. B., Burton, S. L., Jones, A. J., Springs, D., Omar, M., & Brown-Jackson, K. L. (2023). Management Practices for Mitigating Cybersecurity Threats to Biotechnology Companies, Laboratories, and Healthcare Research Organizations. In *Applied Research Approaches to Technology, Healthcare, and Business* (pp. 1-12). IGI Global.

Iqbal, F., Debbabi, M., Fung, B. C., Iqbal, F., Debbabi, M., & Fung, B. C. (2020). Artificial intelligence and digital forensics. *Machine Learning for Authorship Attribution and Cyber Forensics*, 139-150.

Irons, A., & Lallie, H. S. (2014). Digital forensics to intelligent forensics. *Future Internet*, 6(3), 584–596. DOI: 10.3390/fi6030584

Jarrett, A., & Choo, K. K. R. (2021). The impact of automation and artificial intelligence on digital forensics. *WIREs Forensic Science*, 3(6), e1418. DOI: 10.1002/wfs2.1418

Jeong, D. (2020). Artificial intelligence security threat, crime, and forensics: Taxonomy and open issues. *IEEE Access : Practical Innovations, Open Solutions*, 8, 184560–184574. DOI: 10.1109/ACCESS.2020.3029280

Jones, R., & Omar, M. (2024). Revolutionizing Cybersecurity: The GPT-2 Enhanced Attack Detection and Defense (GEADD) Method for Zero-Day Threats. *International Journal of Informatics* [INJIISCOM]. *Information System and Computer Engineering*, 5(2), 178–191.

Jones, R., Omar, M., Mohammed, D., Nobles, C., & Dawson, M. (2023). Harnessing the Speed and Accuracy of Machine Learning to Advance Cybersecurity. In *2023 Congress in Computer Science, Computer Engineering, & Applied Computing (CSCE)* (pp. 418-421). IEEE. DOI: 10.1109/CSCE60160.2023.00074

Karthikeyan, P., Pande, H. M., & Sarveshwaran, V. (Eds.). (2023). *Artificial intelligence and blockchain in digital forensics*. CRC Press.

Kelly, L., Sachan, S., Ni, L., Almaghrabi, F., Allmendinger, R., & Chen, Y. (2020). *Explainable artificial intelligence for digital forensics: opportunities, challenges and a drug testing case study*. Digital Forensic Science.

Manasa, S., & Kumar, K. P. (2022). Digital forensics investigation for attacks on artificial intelligence. *ECS Transactions*, 107(1), 19639–19645. DOI: 10.1149/10701.19639ecst

Mitchell, F. R. (2014). An overview of artificial intelligence based pattern matching in a security and digital forensic context. *Cyberpatterns: Unifying Design Patterns with Security and Attack Patterns*, 215-222.

Mohammed, D., Omar, M., & Nguyen, V. (2018). Wireless sensor network security: Approaches to detecting and avoiding wormhole attacks. *Journal of Research in Business. Economics and Management*, 10(2), 1860–1864.

Moustafa, N. (2022). *Digital Forensics in the Era of Artificial Intelligence*. CRC Press. DOI: 10.1201/9781003278962

Nguyen, V., Mohammed, D., Omar, M., & Banisakher, M. (2018). The Effects of the FCC Net Neutrality Repeal on Security and Privacy. [IJHIoT]. *International Journal of Hyperconnectivity and the Internet of Things*, 2(2), 21–29. DOI: 10.4018/IJHIoT.2018070102

Omar, M. (2021). New insights into database security: An effective and integrated approach for applying access control mechanisms and cryptographic concepts in Microsoft Access environments.

Omar, M. (2022). *Machine Learning for Cybersecurity: Innovative Deep Learning Solutions*. Springer Brief. https://link.springer.com/book/978303115

Omar, M. (2024). From Attack to Defense: Strengthening DNN Text Classification Against Adversarial Examples. In *Innovations, Securities, and Case Studies Across Healthcare, Business, and Technology* (pp. 174-195). IGI Global.

Omar, M. (2024). Revolutionizing Malware Detection: A Paradigm Shift Through Optimized Convolutional Neural Networks. In *Innovations, Securities, and Case Studies Across Healthcare, Business, and Technology* (pp. 196-220). IGI Global. DOI: 10.4018/979-8-3693-1906-2.ch011

Omar, M., & Zangana, H. M. (Eds.). (2024). *Redefining Security With Cyber AI*. IGI Global., DOI: 10.4018/979-8-3693-6517-5

Omar, M., & Zangana, H. M. (Eds.). (2025). *Application of Large Language Models (LLMs) for Software Vulnerability Detection*. IGI Global., DOI: 10.4018/979-8-3693-9311-6

Rizvi, S., Scanlon, M., Mcgibney, J., & Sheppard, J. (2022). Application of artificial intelligence to network forensics: Survey, challenges and future directions. *IEEE Access : Practical Innovations, Open Solutions*, 10, 110362–110384. DOI: 10.1109/ACCESS.2022.3214506

Rughani, P. H. (2017). Artificial Intelligence Based Digital Forensics Framework. *International Journal of Advanced Research in Computer Science*, 8(8), 10–14. DOI: 10.26483/ijarcs.v8i8.4571

Sikos, L. F. (2021). AI in digital forensics: Ontology engineering for cybercrime investigations. *WIREs Forensic Science*, 3(3), e1394. DOI: 10.1002/wfs2.1394

Tyagi, A. K., Kumari, S., & Richa. (2024). Artificial Intelligence-Based Cyber Security and Digital Forensics: A Review. *Artificial Intelligence-Enabled Digital Twin for Smart Manufacturing*, 391-419.

Wright, J., Dawson, M. E.Jr, & Omar, M. (2012). Cyber security and mobile threats: The need for antivirus applications for smartphones. *Journal of Information Systems Technology and Planning*, 5(14), 40–60.

Zangana, H. M., Mohammed, A. K., Sallow, A. B., & Sallow, Z. B. (2024). Cybernetic Deception: Unraveling the Layers of Email Phishing Threats. [INJURATECH]. *International Journal of Research and Applied Technology*, 4(1), 35–47.

Zangana, H. M., & Mohammed, D. (2025). Foundations of Large Language Models in Software Vulnerability Detection. In Omar, M., & Zangana, H. (Eds.), *Application of Large Language Models (LLMs) for Software Vulnerability Detection* (pp. 41–74). IGI Global., DOI: 10.4018/979-8-3693-9311-6.ch002

Zangana, H. M., & Omar, M. (2020). Threats, Attacks, and Mitigations of Smartphone Security. *Academic Journal of Nawroz University*, 9(4), 324–332. DOI: 10.25007/ajnu.v9n4a989

Zangana, H. M., & Omar, M. (2025). Harnessing the Power of Large Language Models for Cybersecurity: Applications, Challenges, and Future Directions. In Omar, M., & Zangana, H. (Eds.), *Application of Large Language Models (LLMs) for Software Vulnerability Detection* (pp. 1–40). IGI Global., DOI: 10.4018/979-8-3693-9311-6.ch001

Chapter 2
The Role of Explainable AI (XAI) in Forensic Investigations

Yara Shamoo
https://orcid.org/0009-0004-2459-0807
Saint Leo University, USA

ABSTRACT

The increasing reliance on Artificial Intelligence (AI) in digital forensic investigations has brought forward significant advancements in the identification, analysis, and interpretation of digital evidence. However, one of the major challenges remains the "black-box" nature of many AI models, which often hinder trust, accountability, and transparency. Explainable AI (XAI) emerges as a critical solution, providing clarity into the decision-making processes of AI systems. In the context of digital forensics, XAI facilitates investigators' understanding of AI-driven tools, ensuring that conclusions drawn from automated analyses are interpretable, verifiable, and legally admissible. This chapter explores the role of XAI in digital forensics, highlighting its potential to enhance the reliability and transparency of AI-based forensic systems, while addressing key challenges and ethical considerations. We examine the integration of XAI in forensic workflows, discuss various techniques for explainability, and evaluate real-world case studies where XAI has contributed to improved forensic outcomes.

DOI: 10.4018/979-8-3373-0857-9.ch002

1. INTRODUCTION

Explainable Artificial Intelligence (XAI) refers to a set of processes, techniques, and methods that make the decision-making process of AI models understandable to humans. In contrast to traditional "black-box" AI models, which often operate in ways that are not easily interpretable, XAI aims to provide transparency, accountability, and interpretability for complex AI systems. By making AI's reasoning transparent, stakeholders—including investigators, policymakers, and end-users—can gain trust in the system's decisions and ensure they are making fair, responsible, and ethical choices. In the realm of digital forensics, where the need for transparency and reliability is paramount, the application of XAI can significantly enhance the effectiveness and accountability of forensic investigations.

AI has increasingly become a core component in modern digital forensic investigations, aiding in the collection, analysis, and interpretation of digital evidence. However, the inherent complexity and opacity of many AI techniques, especially deep learning models, pose challenges in forensics, where decisions need to be explained and validated. The inability to explain why or how an AI system made a particular decision can lead to trust issues, especially in high-stakes legal and security contexts (Hall, Sakzad, & Choo, 2022). Thus, XAI has become crucial in ensuring that AI's role in digital forensics is both effective and justifiable.

The core advantage of XAI lies in its ability to offer decision-making transparency. It enables forensic analysts to understand the rationale behind an AI model's predictions, which is vital in legal contexts where the findings of forensic investigations can be challenged in court. In digital forensics, where evidence can be easily contested, it is critical that AI systems offer explanations for their actions in a manner that is accessible and understandable to non-experts.

Moreover, XAI can help uncover biases that may influence AI predictions. This is of particular concern in forensics, as any unintended bias in the data or the AI model could lead to incorrect conclusions, such as misidentifying a suspect or overlooking a critical piece of evidence. By allowing forensic investigators to trace and understand AI's decision-making process, XAI can prevent these types of errors (Costantini, De Gasperis, & Olivieri, 2019).

As the field of AI and digital forensics continues to evolve, the integration of XAI techniques into forensic workflows will be critical. Investigators will be able to leverage AI for tasks such as anomaly detection, pattern recognition, and evidence authentication while ensuring that the results remain explainable and verifiable. The combination of AI's powerful analytical capabilities and XAI's transparency could lead to more effective, equitable, and defensible forensic processes.

Recent studies highlight the potential of XAI in specific forensic applications, including network forensics, incident response, and the analysis of digital evidence from smartphones and cloud systems (Dunsin, Ghanem, & Ouazzane, 2024; Zangana & Omar, 2020). As researchers continue to explore and develop more sophisticated methods for explainability, XAI's role in digital forensics will undoubtedly expand, making AI-driven investigations more robust and trustworthy.

For example, in network forensics, AI-powered tools are used to detect suspicious patterns, identify vulnerabilities, and track down cybercriminal activities (Rizvi, Scanlon, McGibney, & Sheppard, 2022). With XAI, investigators can better understand how the AI arrived at specific conclusions, helping them refine their strategies for evidence collection and attack mitigation. Similarly, in incident response, AI can be used to predict and counteract cyber threats, but the lack of transparency could hinder its full potential. By adopting XAI techniques, investigators gain insights into the AI's decision-making, allowing them to act decisively and with confidence in complex situations.

As the capabilities of AI continue to grow, the need for explainability in digital forensics becomes more pronounced. Without the integration of XAI, the use of AI in digital forensics may lead to outcomes that are difficult to challenge or defend. It is essential, therefore, that XAI becomes an integral part of forensic AI systems, ensuring not only accuracy and efficiency but also fairness, accountability, and transparency.

In this chapter, we will explore the role of XAI in digital forensics, examining its benefits, challenges, and the future of AI-driven forensic investigations. Additionally, we will discuss how XAI enhances the forensic process by providing insight into AI decision-making and how it helps mitigate the risks associated with black-box AI models in forensic contexts.

2. CHALLENGES OF BLACK-BOX AI MODELS IN FORENSIC INVESTIGATIONS

The integration of Artificial Intelligence (AI) into digital forensics has proven transformative, offering advanced capabilities for data analysis, pattern recognition, and incident detection. However, the use of black-box AI models—those whose decision-making processes are not fully interpretable by humans—presents several significant challenges in forensic investigations.

To better understand the limitations of black-box AI models in forensic contexts, the chart below categorizes the primary challenges, including lack of interpretability, risk of bias, dependency on large datasets, and real-time processing limitations. This visualization highlights areas where XAI methods offer potential solutions.

Figure 1. Challenges of Black-Box Models in Forensic Investigations

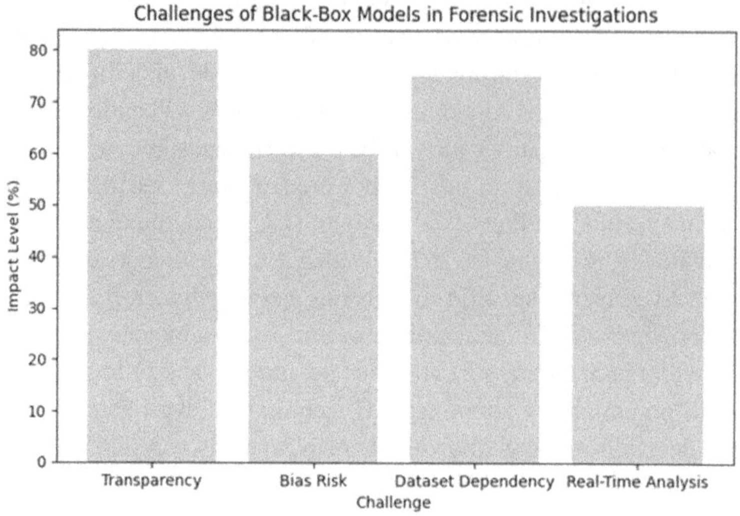

2.1. Lack of Transparency and Interpretability

One of the core issues with black-box AI models in digital forensics is their lack of transparency. These models, which include many deep learning and neural network-based systems, can provide accurate results but at the cost of understandability (Bhawna & Mahajan, 2024; Hall, Sakzad, & Choo, 2022). In forensic investigations, it is crucial to not only know the outcome but also understand how that outcome was reached. Without this interpretability, forensic experts may struggle to validate the results or present them in a legal context, where transparency is key for admissibility (Jarrett & Choo, 2021).

The inability to trace decision-making processes can result in challenges when defending AI-driven results in court. If forensic investigators cannot explain why a particular action was flagged or a pattern identified, it may diminish the credibility of the findings (Costantini, De Gasperis, & Olivieri, 2019). This issue is particularly concerning in high-stakes criminal or civil investigations where the authenticity of evidence is under scrutiny.

2.2. Risk of Bias and Inaccuracy

Black-box AI models are susceptible to bias, particularly if the data used to train them is unbalanced or flawed. In digital forensics, this could lead to misclassification of evidence or incorrect conclusions regarding an investigation (Dunsin, Ghanem, & Quazzane, 2022). For example, if an AI model is trained predominantly on data from specific geographic locations or demographic groups, it may not accurately detect or interpret evidence from different contexts or populations (Zangana, H. M., & Omar, M., 2020). This poses a serious risk in global cybercrime investigations, where diverse data sources need to be considered.

Moreover, the complexity of black-box models can lead to a lack of robustness, resulting in misinterpretations or false positives. In forensic contexts, where even a small error can compromise an investigation, the accuracy of AI models is paramount (Ganesh, 2017; Zangana, H. M., Omar, M., Al-Karaki, J. N., & Mohammed, D., 2024).

2.3. Dependency on Large and High-Quality Datasets

For AI models to function optimally, they require vast amounts of data. This presents a challenge in digital forensics, where relevant, high-quality datasets may not always be available. Models trained on insufficient or poor-quality data may generate inaccurate or irrelevant results (Sikos, 2021). In many forensic investigations, especially those involving niche or emerging cybercrimes, the data necessary for training AI models may be scarce, making the deployment of these technologies less effective or prone to error (Jeong, 2020).

Further complicating the situation is the evolving nature of cybercrime. As criminals adapt and use new technologies, AI models may struggle to keep pace, rendering them less effective over time unless constantly updated and retrained (Dunsin et al., 2024).

2.4. Challenges in Real-Time Analysis

Another major challenge for black-box AI models is their ability to process and analyze data in real-time. In digital forensics, timely evidence collection and analysis can make the difference between solving a case and losing critical information (Mitchell, 2014). While AI models can analyze vast amounts of data, the computational resources required for real-time analysis are significant. Moreover, many black-box models are not optimized for rapid decision-making, making it challenging for investigators to act swiftly when dealing with fast-moving cyber threats (Iqbal, Debbabi, Fung, Iqbal, & Debbabi, 2020).

Additionally, in constrained environments where computational resources are limited (e.g., on-site or mobile investigations), AI systems may struggle to deliver timely and accurate results (Dunsin, Ghanem, & Ouazzane, 2024). This limits the practical application of AI in some forensic scenarios, especially those requiring immediate action.

2.5. Legal and Ethical Considerations

The opaque nature of black-box AI raises legal and ethical concerns. In many jurisdictions, the use of automated decision-making processes must comply with regulations regarding fairness, accountability, and transparency. AI systems that lack interpretability may be seen as "black-box systems" that do not adhere to these principles (Omar, M., 2024; Zangana, H. M., & Omar, M., 2025). This could lead to issues with evidence admissibility in court or potential challenges regarding the fairness of AI decisions, especially if they disproportionately impact certain individuals or groups.

Forensic investigators must also address the ethical implications of AI-driven forensic techniques, such as privacy violations or the potential for AI systems to be used maliciously (Jeong, 2020; Rizvi, Scanlon, Mcgibney, & Sheppard, 2022). AI models could be exploited to obscure evidence or manipulate investigations, highlighting the need for strict oversight and ethical guidelines in their application.

2.6. Integration with Existing Forensic Practices

Integrating AI models into existing forensic frameworks presents additional challenges. Traditional forensic methods often rely on human expertise and manual analysis, which may not always be compatible with the automated nature of AI systems. The friction between human-driven and AI-driven methodologies can lead to inefficiencies or resistance to adopting AI tools in forensic investigations (Irons & Lallie, 2014). Additionally, AI models may require specialized expertise to operate, which could limit their accessibility for some forensic teams (Tyagi, Kumari, & Richa, 2024).

For AI to be effectively integrated into digital forensics, a hybrid approach that combines AI's strengths with traditional forensic methods may be necessary. This requires careful design and training to ensure that human experts can effectively collaborate with AI tools, especially when making critical decisions in investigations (Zangana, H. M., & Omar, M., 2024).

2.7 Summary

While black-box AI models offer significant potential for enhancing digital forensic investigations, their application is fraught with challenges. The lack of transparency, potential for bias, dependency on large datasets, computational limitations, legal and ethical concerns, and integration difficulties all contribute to the complexity of adopting these technologies in forensic contexts. To overcome these obstacles, ongoing advancements in explainable AI (XAI) are critical to improving the trustworthiness and utility of AI in forensic investigations (Hall, Sakzad, & Choo, 2022). As the field continues to evolve, bridging the gap between AI capabilities and forensic practices will be essential for harnessing the full potential of AI in the fight against cybercrime.

3. EXPLAINABLE AI TECHNIQUES APPLICABLE TO FORENSIC ANALYSIS

The integration of Artificial Intelligence (AI) in digital forensics has grown significantly in recent years, providing enhanced capabilities for evidence analysis, investigation automation, and cybercrime prevention. However, as AI methods become more prevalent, the need for transparency and interpretability in decision-making processes has gained attention, especially in forensic contexts where results must be understandable and trustworthy. This is where Explainable AI (XAI) becomes crucial, offering insights into how AI models arrive at their conclusions, thus ensuring their reliability, accountability, and usability in forensic investigations.

The chart below demonstrates the distribution of common XAI techniques employed in digital forensics, such as local and global explanations, visualization methods, and rule extraction. This breakdown shows the diversity of approaches used to interpret complex models in forensic investigations.

Figure 2. Types of XAI Techniques Used in Forensic Analysis

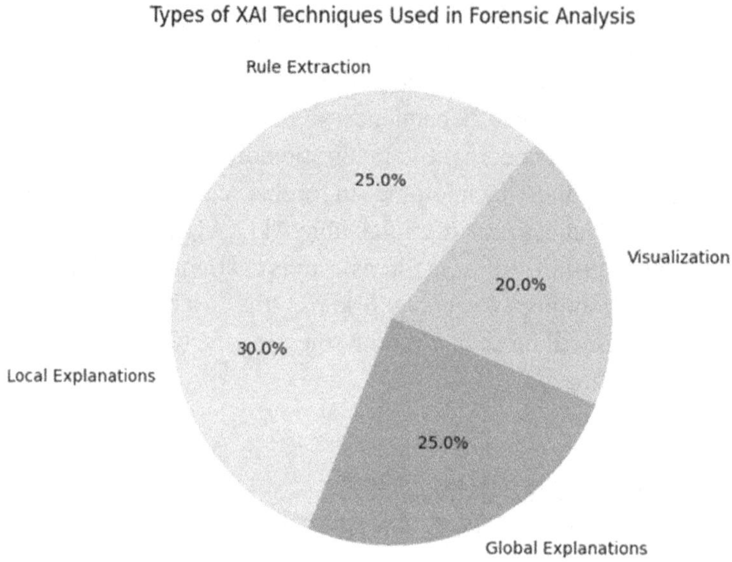

3.1. Overview of Explainable AI in Digital Forensics

Explainable AI refers to methods and techniques that make the results of machine learning models interpretable and transparent, allowing users to understand how and why decisions are made. In the context of digital forensics, the application of XAI is vital for ensuring that AI-driven evidence analysis is understandable to investigators, legal professionals, and other stakeholders. Traditional forensic tools, while effective, often lack the ability to explain why certain conclusions are drawn, which is a significant challenge in legal proceedings where transparency and accountability are essential (Costantini et al., 2019; Kelly et al., 2020).

In digital forensics, AI tools are commonly used to detect patterns, identify anomalies, or classify data in large-scale investigations. However, the complex nature of many AI models, especially deep learning models, can obscure the rationale behind these conclusions. As such, researchers and practitioners have focused on developing XAI techniques that bridge the gap between AI-driven analysis and human understanding (Hall et al., 2022).

3.2. Techniques of Explainable AI in Digital Forensics

Several explainable AI techniques have been developed and applied in digital forensics, including local and global explanation methods, model-agnostic tools, and visualization techniques. These methods provide insight into the workings of complex AI models, facilitating better decision-making and validation in forensic investigations.

a. **Local Explanation Methods:** These techniques explain individual predictions made by AI models. One popular approach is LIME (Local Interpretable Model-agnostic Explanations), which approximates complex models with interpretable ones for specific instances. LIME can be particularly useful in digital forensics for understanding how an AI model classified a particular piece of evidence, such as identifying whether a specific file is associated with criminal activity (Sikos, 2021). Similarly, SHAP (SHapley Additive exPlanations) values provide a more formal and game-theoretic explanation of the importance of different features in a model's prediction, offering a granular understanding of the AI's reasoning process (Jeong, 2020).
b. **Global Explanation Methods:** These techniques provide insight into the overall behavior of AI models across the entire dataset, offering a broader understanding of how models make decisions in general. For example, decision trees and rule-based models are often favored for their transparency in outlining the decision-making process (Bhawna & Mahajan, 2024). These methods can help investigators understand how an AI system arrives at its conclusions across different pieces of digital evidence, making them particularly valuable in criminal investigations.
c. **Visualization Techniques:** Visualization techniques are increasingly used to make complex AI models more interpretable by providing graphical representations of how models process data. Techniques like saliency maps and heatmaps are commonly used in image forensics to highlight the areas of an image or file that contributed most to the model's decision (Wright et al., 2012). These techniques help forensic analysts understand what aspects of the data are most relevant in detecting or classifying digital evidence.
d. **Rule Extraction:** In some cases, especially with neural networks, AI models can be too opaque for direct interpretation. In such instances, rule extraction techniques can be used to derive understandable decision rules from complex models (Ganesh, 2017). This process involves simplifying the AI model into a set of human-readable rules, which can then be validated and used in forensic investigations. This is crucial in situations where AI is used to analyze data from multiple sources, such as network traffic or smartphone logs, and investigators

need to ensure that the model's decision-making process is sound and legally defensible.

3.3. The Role of XAI in Forensic Investigations

Explainable AI is becoming an essential tool for ensuring that AI-based systems in forensic analysis remain trustworthy and legally defensible. In many cases, the results generated by AI systems must be presented in court, where they must be clearly understood by non-experts, such as judges and jurors. As noted by Hall et al. (2022), one of the key challenges in using AI for digital forensics is that traditional models often lack the ability to explain their decisions, making them difficult to justify in legal contexts.

By applying XAI techniques, forensic investigators can provide explanations for the AI's reasoning, helping to establish the reliability of evidence. For example, if an AI system classifies a set of email communications as part of a phishing scheme, XAI techniques can provide transparency on how the model identified specific features of the email, such as the sender's address, content patterns, and metadata (Zangana et al., 2024). This makes it easier for investigators to validate the results and demonstrate that the evidence was not only accurate but also arrived at through a process that can be understood and scrutinized.

The following flowchart illustrates the integration of Explainable AI (XAI) within digital forensic workflows. By identifying specific steps where XAI techniques can support forensic processes, such as evidence analysis, anomaly detection, and model validation, the flowchart highlights how XAI improves transparency and trustworthiness throughout the investigation.

Figure 3. XAI in Forensic Workflow

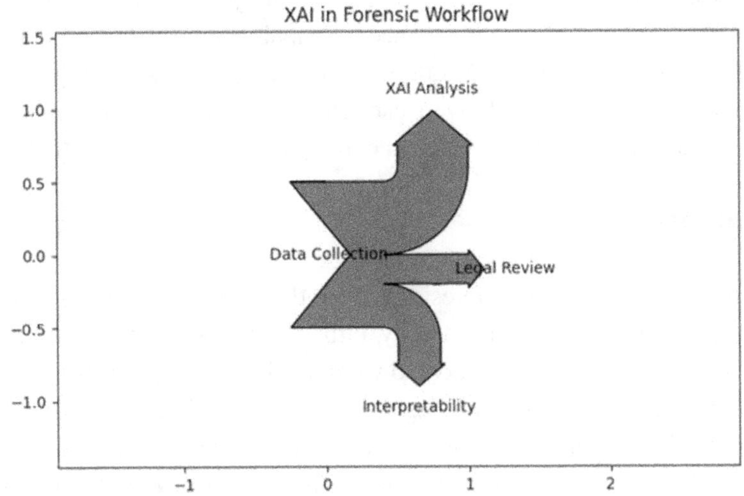

Furthermore, as digital forensics often involves dealing with large amounts of data, XAI can also improve the efficiency of investigations by highlighting the most critical aspects of evidence. This reduces the time spent on irrelevant or redundant data, allowing investigators to focus on the key elements that are most likely to yield useful information (Dunsin et al., 2022). The application of XAI ensures that the AI's decision-making aligns with the expectations of the judicial system and regulatory bodies, providing a solid foundation for forensic analysis.

3.4. Challenges and Future Directions

Despite its advantages, the implementation of XAI in digital forensics is not without challenges. One significant issue is the **complexity of models** used in digital forensics, especially in the case of deep learning models. These models often offer high accuracy but at the expense of interpretability, creating a trade-off between performance and explainability (Dunsin et al., 2024). Additionally, XAI techniques themselves are still evolving, and there remains a need for more sophisticated methods that can handle the intricacies of complex forensic datasets, such as network traffic logs or encrypted communications.

Moreover, ensuring that XAI techniques are both **scalable** and **adaptable** to different forensic contexts remains a critical challenge. As digital forensics expands into new domains such as blockchain analysis and Internet of Things (IoT) forensics, AI models and their explanations must adapt to new types of data and investigative requirements (Zangana & Omar, 2025).

In the future, a hybrid approach combining XAI with other advanced technologies such as blockchain for tamper-proof evidence storage or quantum computing for faster data processing may further enhance the capabilities of AI in forensic analysis (Jeong, 2020). Additionally, as AI continues to evolve, there is potential for creating more **user-friendly tools** that allow investigators to interact with and understand AI models without requiring deep technical expertise (Zangana et al., 2024).

3.5 Summary

Explainable AI techniques are essential for the successful application of AI in digital forensics. They offer transparency, build trust in AI models, and ensure that forensic evidence can be understood and validated by non-experts, which is critical for both criminal investigations and legal proceedings. While challenges remain in implementing XAI, continued advancements in AI transparency, along with the integration of other technologies, promise to further strengthen the role of AI in digital forensics and cybersecurity. As the field evolves, the focus on explainability will ensure that AI systems remain a powerful, reliable, and legally defensible tool in the forensic domain.

4. APPLICATIONS OF XAI IN FORENSIC INVESTIGATIONS

Explainable Artificial Intelligence (XAI) plays a critical role in the realm of digital forensics, where the need for transparency, accountability, and trust in automated systems is paramount. Forensic investigations require a combination of high accuracy, efficiency, and interpretability in data processing and analysis. XAI, with its capacity to offer transparent decision-making processes, has the potential to greatly enhance the field by providing clear, interpretable insights into automated decision systems.

The graph below presents a timeline of the rising adoption of XAI in digital forensic case studies over recent years. It reflects the expanding relevance of explainability in supporting reliable and legally defensible forensic AI applications.

Figure 4. Growth of XAI in Forensic Case Studies (2015-2024)

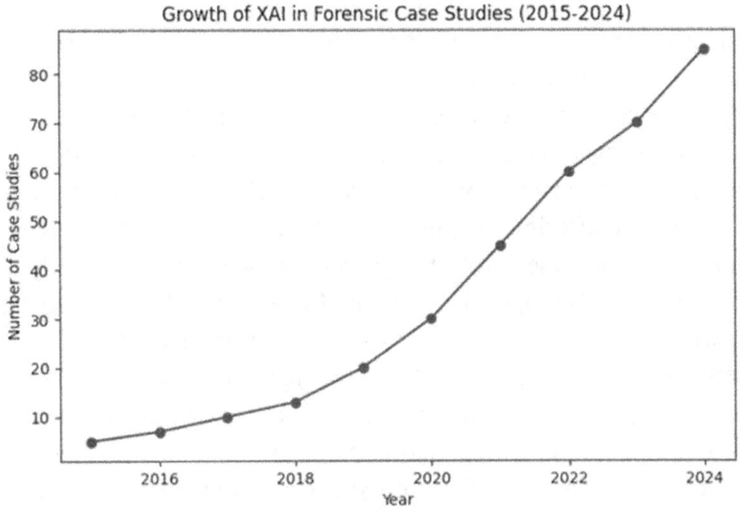

4.1. Enhancing Evidence Interpretation and Analysis

Digital forensics often involves the analysis of large volumes of data, such as network traffic, system logs, and digital devices. The incorporation of AI models, including machine learning (ML) algorithms, can help automate the identification of anomalies and potential evidence, thus streamlining the investigative process. However, one of the challenges is the black-box nature of many AI models, which can be difficult for investigators to interpret. XAI addresses this challenge by offering explainability features that allow forensic analysts to understand how AI models arrived at their conclusions, ultimately improving trust and decision-making in legal contexts (Costantini, De Gasperis, & Olivieri, 2019; Jarrett & Choo, 2021).

XAI facilitates the interpretation of complex patterns within data by generating human-understandable explanations for its findings. For instance, when AI identifies an anomaly in a network traffic log, XAI can provide an explanation of which factors contributed to the anomaly, such as unusual traffic patterns, specific time frames, or particular types of data exchanges (Jeong, 2020). This transparency is crucial when the results are presented in court, as it ensures that forensic experts can effectively communicate their findings to non-technical stakeholders (Zangana, H. M., & Omar, M., 2020).

4.2. AI-Driven Automation in Incident Response

Forensic investigators often need to respond quickly to security incidents, especially in cases of cybercrimes like data breaches or malware attacks. AI-powered systems are increasingly used to detect, analyze, and respond to such threats. However, without explainability, relying solely on AI systems in these high-stakes scenarios could lead to errors or misinterpretations of critical evidence. XAI methods help mitigate this risk by offering insights into why a certain response was triggered, which improves the accuracy and accountability of automated incident responses.

Dunsin et al. (2022) emphasize the significance of XAI in constrained environments, where computational resources may limit the use of traditional digital forensics methods. By incorporating XAI, investigators are better able to understand and validate the AI's decision-making process, ensuring that the right steps are taken based on the correct interpretation of the evidence. Additionally, XAI can help reduce the time taken to perform investigations by automating processes while maintaining transparency, which is crucial for rapid response and accurate evidence gathering (Bhawna & Mahajan, 2024).

4.3. Improving Cybersecurity Forensics with AI and XAI

The integration of AI and XAI into cybersecurity forensics has led to significant improvements in the detection and attribution of cyber-attacks. With the growing sophistication of cyber threats, traditional forensic methods often fall short in identifying complex attack patterns. AI, particularly machine learning, can uncover hidden patterns in large datasets, which human analysts may overlook. However, without XAI, these findings could remain opaque and unverifiable, potentially leading to misinterpretations.

Incorporating explainability into AI-driven cybersecurity systems ensures that investigators can trace the reasoning behind threat detection algorithms. For example, XAI can help explain the characteristics of malicious behavior detected within network traffic, providing investigators with a clearer understanding of the nature of the attack and how it correlates with known attack patterns (Rizvi, Scanlon, Mcgibney, & Sheppard, 2022). This is essential for refining security measures and preventing future attacks.

4.4. AI-Based Pattern Matching in Digital Forensics

Pattern matching is a fundamental aspect of digital forensics, especially when it comes to identifying traces of illicit activities or recovering digital evidence from compromised systems. AI models, particularly those based on deep learning, have shown promising results in automating this task. However, the lack of transparency in how these models identify patterns could limit their adoption in forensic investigations. XAI helps overcome this limitation by providing interpretable visualizations of how the AI models recognize specific patterns in the data.

For instance, AI models can be trained to detect malware signatures or other malicious patterns in large datasets. XAI can then highlight which features were most influential in the identification process, such as particular code sequences or system behavior anomalies (Mitchell, 2014). This not only enhances the forensic process but also ensures that the evidence is both verifiable and legally admissible (Ganesh, 2017).

4.5. Reducing Bias in Forensic Decision-Making

Forensic investigations, particularly in the context of digital forensics, are heavily reliant on the objective analysis of data. However, biases in forensic decision-making can arise from the tools and methods used during investigations. AI systems can sometimes inherit or exacerbate biases, leading to potentially flawed conclusions. XAI can reduce this risk by making the decision-making process more transparent, allowing forensic experts to identify and address any biases present in the AI model.

By understanding how AI systems make decisions, forensic investigators can ensure that their conclusions are not influenced by flawed or biased reasoning. This is particularly important in cases where the stakes are high, such as in criminal investigations or regulatory audits. Zangana et al. (2024) highlight the importance of unbiased AI models in forensic investigations, ensuring that AI's contribution is both accurate and fair.

4.6. Legal and Ethical Implications of AI in Forensics

As AI technologies continue to evolve, their use in forensic investigations raises important legal and ethical considerations. The need for explainability is critical, as it ensures that AI-generated evidence can be scrutinized and understood by courts, legal professionals, and forensic experts. Without transparency, there is a risk that AI systems could be used to make decisions that cannot be explained or challenged, undermining trust in the judicial system.

XAI enables forensic experts to defend their findings by providing clear, logical justifications for their conclusions. This becomes particularly important in legal proceedings, where the integrity and reliability of digital evidence are often scrutinized. The development of robust XAI systems that adhere to ethical guidelines will be crucial in shaping the future of AI in forensic investigations (Hall, Sakzad, & Choo, 2022; Sikos, 2021).

4.7 Summary

The integration of XAI into forensic investigations represents a significant advancement in the field, offering more efficient, transparent, and accountable methods for evidence analysis and incident response. By ensuring that AI-driven decisions are interpretable and explainable, XAI enhances the credibility of forensic investigations and supports the legal acceptance of AI-generated evidence. As digital threats continue to evolve, XAI will play a pivotal role in ensuring that forensic investigators are equipped with the tools and insights needed to tackle complex cybercrimes effectively.

5. CASE STUDIES DEMONSTRATING XAI IN FORENSIC PRACTICE

Explainable Artificial Intelligence (XAI) has garnered increasing attention in forensic practices, particularly in digital forensics, where transparency and interpretability of AI-based decisions are paramount. The integration of XAI in digital forensics serves to enhance the reliability, accuracy, and accountability of forensic investigations, especially when dealing with cybercrimes, incidents, and attacks. Below, we explore a series of case studies that illustrate how XAI is being applied in real-world forensic scenarios.

5.1 Case Study 1: AI-Powered Incident Response in Constrained Environments

In a case study conducted by Dunsin et al. (2022), artificial intelligence (AI) was used to automate incident response in digital forensics under resource-constrained environments. The research focused on integrating machine learning and AI models to enhance the efficiency of digital forensic investigations, particularly in settings with limited computational resources. XAI principles were applied to ensure the interpretability of AI-generated responses. This was critical in a situation where forensic experts had to make informed decisions based on the AI's analysis of suspicious network traffic. The incorporation of XAI allowed the forensic team to trace the origin of cyberattacks and malware propagation patterns, providing clear explanations of how the AI reached its conclusions. This transparency in AI decision-making ensured the reliability of the findings in a courtroom setting, where forensic evidence needs to be verifiable.

5.2 Case Study 2: Artificial Intelligence for Phishing Detection

Zangana et al. (2024) explored the application of XAI in detecting email phishing threats through a case study that focused on cybernetic deception. In this case, AI models were trained to identify phishing attacks by analyzing email metadata, content, and patterns. XAI was integrated into the process to provide a transparent explanation of how the model identified potential phishing attempts. By applying interpretable machine learning algorithms, the forensic team was able to explain the model's reasoning in a way that non-technical stakeholders, including legal experts, could understand. This was crucial for presenting the results of the investigation in legal proceedings where the chain of evidence must be clear.

5.3 Case Study 3: AI in Digital Forensic Investigations of Cybercrime

A study by Costantini, De Gasperis, and Olivieri (2019) examined the intersection of digital forensics and AI in the investigation of cybercrimes. The researchers developed a system that utilized AI to analyze large datasets from compromised systems. The XAI framework provided forensic experts with clear insights into the decision-making processes of the AI system, which was necessary for validating the forensic conclusions. For example, when AI was used to analyze encrypted communication, XAI allowed experts to visualize how specific features within the data—such as cryptographic patterns or metadata—led to the detection of illegal activity. The transparency of the AI model's output played a significant role in ensuring that the evidence could be presented and interpreted effectively in court.

5.4 Case Study 4: AI in Automated Forensic Investigation of Malware

Ganesh (2017) documented the use of AI techniques in the forensic investigation of malware in a case study involving an enterprise network breach. In this study, AI systems were deployed to autonomously identify and classify malicious software samples, categorizing them based on behavior patterns rather than traditional signature-based methods. By utilizing XAI, the system provided detailed, step-by-step explanations of how malware was detected, including the specific characteristics that led to its classification as malicious. These transparent outputs allowed forensic experts to verify the accuracy of the AI's findings and understand the rationale behind the AI's decisions in order to prevent false positives and enhance the overall reliability of the investigation.

5.5 Case Study 5: AI in Digital Forensics for Cloud Computing Security

The rise of cloud computing has presented unique challenges for digital forensics. Hamza and Omar (2013) conducted a case study exploring AI's role in cloud computing security, particularly forensics in the event of an attack. AI techniques were employed to automatically analyze logs, system states, and user activity to detect abnormal behaviors that may indicate a security breach. In this case, the use of XAI was instrumental in providing detailed insights into the AI model's analysis process, enabling forensic experts to understand how specific actions were classified as suspicious. XAI also helped trace the attack's origin, revealing how attackers exploited vulnerabilities within the cloud environment. The ability to provide clear, interpretable explanations ensured that the evidence gathered could be used effectively in forensic investigations and legal proceedings.

5.6 Case Study 6: AI in Forensic Analysis of Cyber Threats in Biotechnology

In the biotechnology sector, cybersecurity threats have become a growing concern. Huff et al. (2023) focused on applying AI in the forensic analysis of cybersecurity threats targeting biotechnology companies. The study utilized AI to monitor and analyze network traffic to detect and mitigate cyber threats. The incorporation of XAI allowed the forensic team to understand the AI's reasoning behind identifying specific threats, such as unauthorized access to sensitive research data or abnormal network behaviors. By using explainable AI techniques, forensic professionals could trace the steps of an attacker and provide clear explanations of how the threat was identified and neutralized, thereby improving the overall effectiveness of the investigation and ensuring its admissibility in legal contexts.

5.7 Case Study 7: Network Forensics and Machine Learning

Rizvi et al. (2022) highlighted a case study involving network forensics, where AI and machine learning algorithms were applied to analyze network traffic data for signs of a cyberattack. The researchers utilized a combination of deep learning models to identify anomalous patterns in the traffic, but they also integrated XAI methods to ensure the AI's decisions were interpretable. By applying techniques such as feature attribution and decision trees, the network forensic team was able to visually present how the AI arrived at its conclusions, explaining why certain patterns in the data were flagged as suspicious. This transparency was vital in helping forensic experts defend the validity of their findings in court, where understanding the model's reasoning process is crucial for credibility.

5.8 Summary

These case studies illustrate the crucial role of XAI in enhancing the effectiveness and transparency of AI applications in digital forensics. From phishing detection to malware analysis, the integration of XAI ensures that AI-driven decisions can be understood, verified, and communicated clearly to stakeholders, including forensic experts, law enforcement, and legal professionals. As AI continues to evolve, the application of XAI in forensic investigations will likely expand, enabling more reliable and interpretable outcomes in the detection, analysis, and resolution of cybercrimes.

6. LEGAL AND ETHICAL CONSIDERATIONS FOR XAI IN FORENSICS

Explainable Artificial Intelligence (XAI) has become a critical tool in the field of digital forensics, allowing investigators to interpret and understand the decision-making processes behind AI-driven conclusions. However, the application of XAI in forensic investigations presents a unique set of legal and ethical challenges. These considerations range from maintaining privacy and upholding the integrity of legal processes to addressing potential biases embedded within AI models. This section explores the primary legal and ethical issues surrounding the use of XAI in digital forensics, with a focus on privacy, accountability, transparency, and the ethical implications of AI-generated evidence.

6.1 Legal Considerations

1. **Admissibility of AI-Generated Evidence** One of the primary legal concerns in applying XAI to forensics is the admissibility of AI-generated evidence in court. Digital forensics often involves the collection, analysis, and presentation of data in legal proceedings, where the evidence must be legally sound and provable beyond a reasonable doubt. Courts require that forensic evidence, including AI-generated conclusions, be both reliable and understandable by legal professionals. This includes ensuring that the AI models used are trained on valid data and that their processes can be explained clearly to non-experts, such as jurors or judges (Adam & Varol, 2020). Without sufficient transparency into the AI decision-making process, the credibility of the evidence could be questioned, and it may be excluded from court proceedings.

2. **Data Privacy and Protection** AI-based forensic investigations often involve processing large amounts of personal data. Legal frameworks such as the General Data Protection Regulation (GDPR) in the European Union and similar regulations in other jurisdictions impose strict guidelines on the handling of sensitive personal information. The use of XAI must be compliant with these regulations, ensuring that the privacy of individuals is not compromised. For example, AI models trained on private data must be designed to avoid unauthorized access or the misuse of personal information (Bhawna & Mahajan, 2024). Furthermore, investigators must be cautious about the potential overreach of AI tools, ensuring that they do not collect or analyze data beyond what is necessary for the investigation.
3. **Accountability and Liability** As AI systems are increasingly used in forensic investigations, questions surrounding accountability and liability have become more prominent. In the event of errors or biases in AI-driven forensic findings, determining responsibility becomes complex. Who should be held accountable if an AI system misinterprets evidence or makes a faulty prediction? Should the developers of the AI system, the investigators using it, or the organizations that deployed it be held liable? This issue becomes especially relevant in cases where AI models are used to make critical decisions, such as identifying suspects or determining the cause of an event (Dunsin et al., 2024). The legal system must evolve to establish clear lines of accountability in the context of AI-driven forensic investigations.

6.2 Ethical Considerations

1. **Bias and Fairness in AI Models** One of the most significant ethical challenges in the use of XAI for forensics is ensuring that the AI systems do not perpetuate or amplify biases. AI systems, including those used in forensic investigations, can inadvertently reflect biases present in the data they are trained on. This can result in discriminatory outcomes that disproportionately affect certain groups of people, such as minority communities. For example, if an AI system is trained on biased datasets, it may make inaccurate or unjust conclusions about suspects or victims, leading to potential miscarriages of justice (Zangana et al., 2024). Ethical considerations must guide the development of AI models to minimize these biases, and robust auditing processes should be in place to identify and correct any biases that emerge.
2. **Transparency and Explainability** One of the core tenets of XAI is its ability to provide explanations for its decisions. However, ensuring that these explanations are understandable to humans, particularly in a forensic context, presents a significant ethical challenge. If an AI system's decision-making process is opaque,

it could undermine trust in the technology and raise ethical concerns about its use in high-stakes environments like criminal investigations (Hall et al., 2022). Forensics investigators, legal professionals, and the public must be able to trust that AI-generated evidence is not only accurate but also explainable in a way that is comprehensible and justifiable within the legal framework. As a result, the development and use of XAI systems in forensics must prioritize clear and interpretable explanations of AI-driven findings (Jarrett & Choo, 2021).

3. **Informed Consent and Autonomy** In forensic investigations, AI systems are often employed to examine data collected from individuals without their explicit consent. This raises concerns about autonomy and the right to privacy. While AI systems can potentially improve the efficiency and accuracy of investigations, ethical principles of informed consent must be considered, especially when the use of AI extends to personal or sensitive data. Investigators must ensure that individuals whose data is being analyzed are aware of how their information will be used and that they have the opportunity to provide consent where appropriate (Jeong, 2020).
4. **Impact on the Role of Human Investigators** Another ethical consideration is the potential displacement of human investigators. While AI has the potential to automate and augment many tasks in digital forensics, it should not entirely replace human judgment, especially when it comes to interpreting complex situations or understanding the nuances of human behavior. The reliance on AI-driven conclusions could lead to an erosion of human expertise and the devaluation of human oversight in forensic investigations. Therefore, it is essential to ensure that AI serves as a tool to assist, rather than replace, human forensic professionals (Mitchell, 2014).

6.3 Summary

The use of XAI in digital forensics holds significant promise for enhancing investigative capabilities, but it also introduces a host of legal and ethical challenges. The admissibility of AI-generated evidence, privacy concerns, accountability, and the need for transparency must be carefully addressed to ensure the integrity of forensic processes. Ethical considerations surrounding bias, fairness, and the role of human investigators are equally important to maintain justice and equity in AI-driven investigations. As XAI continues to evolve, both legal and ethical frameworks must adapt to the growing reliance on artificial intelligence in digital forensics, ensuring that these technologies are used responsibly and justly.

7. LIMITATIONS AND CHALLENGES OF IMPLEMENTING XAI IN FORENSIC INVESTIGATIONS

Explainable Artificial Intelligence (XAI) holds considerable promise for enhancing the transparency, reliability, and decision-making processes in digital forensics. However, its integration into forensic investigations is accompanied by a number of limitations and challenges. These challenges must be addressed to fully harness the potential of XAI for improving the effectiveness and accuracy of digital forensic processes.

7.1. Complexity of Models and Interpretability

XAI models are designed to provide clear explanations of their decision-making processes, but the complexity of many machine learning algorithms, particularly deep learning models, can make them difficult to interpret. In digital forensics, where the stakes are high, having an understandable rationale behind an AI decision is crucial for validating evidence in court. However, the inherently complex nature of AI models often results in "black-box" behavior that is difficult for forensic investigators to comprehend and communicate effectively (Hall, Sakzad, & Choo, 2022). This is particularly problematic when forensic experts are required to provide clear, concise explanations for their findings during legal proceedings. The inability to easily explain certain outcomes may undermine the credibility of AI-driven conclusions (Costantini, De Gasperis, & Olivieri, 2019).

7.2. Data Quality and Availability

The performance of XAI in digital forensics is highly dependent on the quality and availability of data. For AI models to make accurate and reliable predictions, they require vast amounts of high-quality training data, which is often not readily available in the forensic domain. Many digital forensics investigations involve incomplete or corrupted datasets, which may affect the accuracy of AI-driven conclusions (Dunsin, Ghanem, & Quazzane, 2022). Furthermore, historical data for training AI systems may not always be representative of current cybercrime trends, leading to model bias and reduced performance in real-world scenarios (Tyagi, Kumari, & Richa, 2024).

7.3. Integration with Existing Forensic Tools and Workflows

Integrating XAI into the existing digital forensics workflows is a significant challenge. Forensic investigators often rely on specialized software tools and procedures that are not always compatible with AI-based solutions. The integration of XAI systems requires seamless interaction with these tools while ensuring that forensic protocols, such as chain-of-custody and evidence integrity, are maintained (Bhawna & Mahajan, 2024). The implementation of AI-driven systems also requires significant changes to current workflows, which may encounter resistance from practitioners who are accustomed to traditional methods (Jarrett & Choo, 2021).

7.4. Ethical and Legal Implications

The use of AI in digital forensics raises several ethical and legal concerns. One significant issue is the potential for biased decision-making. AI models are often trained on historical data, which may contain biases reflecting previous investigative practices. These biases could lead to unfair or incorrect conclusions, particularly in high-stakes investigations. For example, biases in AI could disproportionately affect marginalized groups, leading to concerns about fairness and discrimination (Zangana, Omar, & Mohammed, 2024). Additionally, the legal system has yet to fully embrace AI as an acceptable tool in criminal investigations. While courts increasingly recognize the role of AI in forensics, there are still concerns about the transparency, fairness, and accountability of AI-driven decisions (Ganesh, 2017). In particular, the legal acceptance of AI explanations in court is still under scrutiny, as traditional forensics are based on expert testimony that AI models may struggle to replicate.

7.5. Security and Privacy Risks

The use of AI in forensics can also introduce security and privacy risks. As AI systems process sensitive forensic data, there is the potential for this information to be exposed or manipulated by cybercriminals. Ensuring the confidentiality and integrity of data while using AI for forensic purposes is a critical challenge (Jeong, 2020). Moreover, as XAI is integrated into forensic tools, the possibility of adversarial attacks against these systems increases. Cybercriminals may attempt to manipulate AI models to produce false conclusions, thus undermining the investigation (Sikos, 2021). Safeguarding against such attacks requires sophisticated security measures and continuous monitoring of AI models.

7.6. Lack of Standardization and Regulation

The field of digital forensics is still developing, and there is currently no widely accepted set of standards for the use of AI in forensic investigations. This lack of standardization makes it difficult to implement XAI in a consistent manner across different cases and jurisdictions. Without clear guidelines, it is challenging to assess the effectiveness and reliability of AI-driven forensic tools, and investigators may struggle to justify their use in legal contexts (Zangana, 2024). Regulatory frameworks for AI in digital forensics are still in their infancy, and significant work is needed to establish best practices and legal standards.

7.7. Resource Constraints

Implementing XAI in digital forensics requires significant computational resources, which may not always be available in all investigative environments. Forensic investigators often operate under tight budgets and time constraints, making it difficult to implement complex AI systems that demand substantial hardware and software infrastructure (Dunsin, Ghanem, Ouazzane, & Vassilev, 2024). Furthermore, the training of AI models can be time-consuming and expensive, particularly when large datasets are required. Smaller forensic teams may struggle to meet these resource demands, limiting the broader adoption of AI technologies.

7.8 Summary

While XAI has the potential to revolutionize digital forensics, its implementation is not without significant challenges. These challenges range from technical issues such as model complexity and data quality to ethical, legal, and resource-related concerns. As digital forensics continues to evolve, addressing these limitations will be crucial for the successful adoption of XAI in investigative processes. Developing standardized frameworks, improving data quality, and ensuring that AI systems are transparent, explainable, and secure will be essential steps towards making XAI a reliable tool in digital forensics (Mitchell, 2014; Hall et al., 2022).

8. FUTURE DIRECTIONS AND RESEARCH OPPORTUNITIES

The integration of Artificial Intelligence (AI) in digital forensics presents significant advancements and new challenges that open up numerous research opportunities. As cyber threats continue to evolve, the application of AI in digital forensics is critical to addressing emerging complexities. This section outlines key areas where research can further explore the potential of AI to enhance digital forensics practices and improve cybersecurity resilience.

8.1. Artificial Intelligence in Cybercrime Investigation and Digital Forensics

AI's role in digital forensics continues to expand, particularly in automating the analysis of digital evidence. AI systems can expedite traditional forensic processes such as evidence collection, analysis, and reporting. Machine learning (ML) algorithms, especially those focused on pattern recognition, have shown potential in improving the identification of suspicious activities, such as unusual network traffic or anomalies in digital files. However, a major challenge lies in the development of AI models capable of distinguishing between benign and malicious activities with high accuracy. Research is required to improve the explainability of AI systems in forensic applications, ensuring that results are interpretable and trustworthy for legal and investigative purposes (Adam & Varol, 2020; Dunsin, Ghanem, & Quazzane, 2022).

Furthermore, as AI algorithms become more integrated into forensic tools, the need for explainable AI (XAI) to clarify AI-driven conclusions becomes essential, especially for use in legal proceedings. Hall, Sakzad, and Choo (2022) highlighted the importance of incorporating XAI to ensure that investigators can clearly understand the decision-making processes of AI tools. This approach is vital in establishing the credibility of AI-driven investigations in court settings.

8.2. Enhancing Incident Response and Forensic Investigations

The evolution of AI in incident response is a significant area of research. AI can automate the detection, classification, and analysis of security breaches, minimizing human intervention and enabling faster response times. Dunsin et al. (2024) provided an in-depth review of AI and ML's potential in improving incident response, which is crucial for mitigating threats such as cyber-attacks, phishing, and data breaches. As AI continues to evolve, exploring its integration with blockchain technology for secure and immutable evidence collection can be a promising direction. Zangana and Omar (2024) discussed the application of blockchain-based timestamping tools in securing digital evidence, making it tamper-proof and enhancing the integrity of forensic investigations.

In addition to leveraging AI for incident detection, a more proactive approach is needed to prevent attacks before they occur. Research can focus on the development of predictive models that utilize AI to forecast potential threats based on patterns and trends in digital data. By combining AI with network forensics, it is possible to monitor and analyze large-scale network traffic for early signs of intrusions (Rizvi et al., 2022).

8.3. Synthetic Data for Training AI Models in Forensics

The use of synthetic data to train AI models in forensics is an area ripe for exploration. Gholami and Omar (2023) discussed the potential benefits of synthetic data in improving the efficiency of AI models, especially when real-world data is scarce or difficult to obtain due to privacy concerns. Synthetic datasets can simulate various cybercrime scenarios, providing a broad range of conditions under which AI algorithms can be trained. This could significantly enhance the performance of forensic tools in recognizing complex attack patterns or unusual behaviors. Research is needed to refine synthetic data generation techniques to ensure that it accurately represents real-world conditions and adversarial strategies.

8.4. AI-Based Pattern Matching in Security and Forensics

Pattern matching is fundamental to both digital forensics and cybersecurity. Mitchell (2014) outlined the role of AI in pattern recognition and matching within a digital forensic context. AI can be used to identify patterns that may go unnoticed by human investigators, such as rare malware signatures or subtle signs of unauthorized access. Enhancing pattern recognition capabilities using AI can lead to faster identification of attack vectors and security vulnerabilities. Future research can explore the application of AI-driven pattern matching in detecting new and sophisticated attack methods, including zero-day exploits, as discussed by Jones and Omar (2024).

8.5. AI and Privacy Concerns in Digital Forensics

While AI can enhance digital forensics capabilities, it also raises privacy concerns, especially regarding the collection, storage, and use of personal data. The application of AI in forensics necessitates the creation of stringent ethical guidelines to ensure that privacy rights are respected during investigations. Tyagi, Kumari, and Richa (2024) emphasized the need for a balanced approach that allows AI to enhance forensics without compromising individuals' privacy. Future research should focus on developing AI algorithms that can process and analyze data without violating privacy or breaching legal standards. This includes investigating ways to anonymize sensitive data while still deriving meaningful insights.

8.6. Improving Digital Evidence Handling and Chain of Custody

A critical aspect of digital forensics is maintaining the integrity and authenticity of digital evidence. As AI becomes more integrated into forensic tools, research should focus on improving evidence handling systems to ensure the preservation of the chain of custody. One avenue for research is the development of AI-powered solutions that can automatically document and track digital evidence from collection to presentation in court, ensuring that every step in the chain is auditable and tamper-resistant. Zangana et al. (2024) discussed the use of blockchain to secure timestamps, and similar technologies can be applied to maintain a robust chain of custody for digital evidence.

8.7. Advancing the Use of AI in Mobile and Cloud Forensics

Mobile devices and cloud computing platforms have become primary sources of digital evidence in forensic investigations. As mobile forensics becomes increasingly complex, AI can help in parsing data from various applications, systems, and cloud services. Omar (2021) and Hamza & Omar (2013) explored the security challenges related to cloud computing and mobile threats, noting the significant gaps in existing forensic methodologies. Future research can investigate AI tools designed specifically for mobile and cloud environments, capable of handling encrypted data, proprietary formats, and dynamic cloud-based architectures. These tools could include advanced algorithms that can sift through large datasets quickly and with minimal resource consumption.

8.8. AI-Enhanced Threat Intelligence

AI-powered threat intelligence platforms can provide valuable insights into emerging threats by analyzing vast amounts of data. Bhawna and Mahajan (2024) have explored the application of AI in threat intelligence, which could be applied to digital forensics for real-time identification of threat actors and attack strategies. Future research should focus on integrating threat intelligence into digital forensic investigations, enabling forensic experts to act more proactively rather than reactively. The combination of AI and threat intelligence can help develop systems that predict potential future threats based on evolving attack patterns.

8.9 Summary

The convergence of AI with digital forensics represents an exciting frontier in cybersecurity. While numerous advancements have been made, significant challenges remain in making AI-driven forensic investigations more accurate, interpretable, and secure. Research in synthetic data generation, explainable AI, privacy concerns, and cloud and mobile forensics will be essential in shaping the future of AI in digital forensics. By addressing these challenges, the digital forensics community can better equip itself to handle the increasingly sophisticated cyber threats of tomorrow.

The application of AI in digital forensics is a dynamic and evolving field, where continuous innovation and research are essential for maintaining the effectiveness and trustworthiness of forensic investigations.

9. CONCLUSION

The integration of Artificial Intelligence (AI) into digital forensics is reshaping how cybercrime investigations are conducted, offering unprecedented capabilities in data analysis, pattern recognition, and threat detection. AI tools can process vast amounts of data at high speeds, significantly enhancing the efficiency of forensic investigations. The ability of AI to identify patterns in digital evidence that might be invisible to traditional methods is one of its most promising advantages. As digital crimes become more complex, AI's role in automating repetitive tasks and providing predictive insights is becoming invaluable.

Furthermore, AI's application in digital forensics presents a dual opportunity to strengthen both preventive and reactive measures. By leveraging machine learning algorithms, forensics professionals can not only trace and investigate cyber-attacks but also anticipate potential threats and fortify defenses. In this rapidly evolving field, AI offers an essential advantage by enabling forensics teams to respond to incidents faster and with more precision, which is crucial in the face of increasingly sophisticated cyber threats.

However, while AI offers significant potential, challenges remain in its adoption. Issues related to data privacy, the explainability of AI models, and the integration of AI systems with existing forensic frameworks need to be addressed. Additionally, ethical concerns, including the risk of bias in AI algorithms, remain a significant consideration. As technology evolves, it is crucial that regulatory frameworks and best practices keep pace to ensure AI is used responsibly and effectively in forensic investigations.

Looking ahead, the future of AI in digital forensics is bright, with many exciting advancements on the horizon. Continued innovation in AI techniques and collaboration between industry experts will drive further integration of AI in cybercrime investigation processes. As we move into an era of greater connectivity and complexity, AI will continue to be a crucial tool in enhancing the security and integrity of digital environments worldwide.

REFERENCES

Adam, I. Y., & Varol, C. (2020, June). Intelligence in digital forensics process. In 2020 8th International Symposium on Digital Forensics and Security (ISDFS) (pp. 1-6). IEEE. DOI: 10.1109/ISDFS49300.2020.9116442

Costantini, S., De Gasperis, G., & Olivieri, R. (2019). Digital forensics and investigations meet artificial intelligence. *Annals of Mathematics and Artificial Intelligence*, 86(1), 193–229. DOI: 10.1007/s10472-019-09632-y

Dunsin, D., Ghanem, M. C., Ouazzane, K., & Vassilev, V. (2024). A comprehensive analysis of the role of artificial intelligence and machine learning in modern digital forensics and incident response. *Forensic Science International Digital Investigation*, 48, 301675. DOI: 10.1016/j.fsidi.2023.301675

Dunsin, D., Ghanem, M. C., & Quazzane, K. (2022). The use of artificial intelligence in digital forensics and incident response in a constrained environment. *International Journal of Information and Communication Engineering*, 16(8), 280–285.

Ganesh, V. (2017). Artificial intelligence applied to computer forensics. *International Journal (Toronto, Ont.)*, 5(5).

Gholami, S., & Omar, M. (2023). Does Synthetic Data Make Large Language Models More Efficient? arXiv preprint arXiv:2310.07830.

Gholami, S., & Omar, M. (2024). Can a student large language model perform as well as its teacher? In Innovations, Securities, and Case Studies Across Healthcare, Business, and Technology (pp. 122-139). IGI Global. DOI: 10.4018/979-8-3693-1906-2.ch007

Hall, S. W., Sakzad, A., & Choo, K. K. R. (2022). Explainable artificial intelligence for digital forensics. *Wiley Interdisciplinary Reviews: Forensic Science*, 4(2), e1434.

Hamza, Y. A., & Omar, M. D. (2013). Cloud computing security: Abuse and nefarious use of cloud computing. *International Journal of Computer Engineering Research*, 3(6), 22–27.

Huff, A. J., Burrell, D. N., Nobles, C., Richardson, K., Wright, J. B., Burton, S. L., Jones, A. J., Springs, D., Omar, M., & Brown-Jackson, K. L. (2023). Management Practices for Mitigating Cybersecurity Threats to Biotechnology Companies, Laboratories, and Healthcare Research Organizations. In Applied Research Approaches to Technology, Healthcare, and Business (pp. 1-12). IGI Global.

Iqbal, F., Debbabi, M., Fung, B. C., Iqbal, F., Debbabi, M., & Fung, B. C. (2020). Artificial intelligence and digital forensics. Machine Learning for Authorship Attribution and Cyber Forensics, 139-150.

Irons, A., & Lallie, H. S. (2014). Digital forensics to intelligent forensics. *Future Internet*, 6(3), 584–596. DOI: 10.3390/fi6030584

Jarrett, A., & Choo, K. K. R. (2021). The impact of automation and artificial intelligence on digital forensics. *WIREs Forensic Science*, 3(6), e1418. DOI: 10.1002/wfs2.1418

Jeong, D. (2020). Artificial intelligence security threat, crime, and forensics: Taxonomy and open issues. *IEEE Access : Practical Innovations, Open Solutions*, 8, 184560–184574. DOI: 10.1109/ACCESS.2020.3029280

Jones, R., & Omar, M. (2024). Revolutionizing Cybersecurity: The GPT-2 Enhanced Attack Detection and Defense (GEADD) Method for Zero-Day Threats. International Journal of Informatics [INJIISCOM]. *Information System and Computer Engineering*, 5(2), 178–191.

Jones, R., Omar, M., Mohammed, D., Nobles, C., & Dawson, M. (2023). *Harnessing the Speed and Accuracy of Machine Learning to Advance Cybersecurity. In 2023 Congress in Computer Science, Computer Engineering, & Applied Computing (CSCE)*. IEEE.

Karthikeyan, P., Pande, H. M., & Sarveshwaran, V. (Eds.). (2023). *Artificial intelligence and blockchain in digital forensics*. CRC Press.

Kelly, L., Sachan, S., Ni, L., Almaghrabi, F., Allmendinger, R., & Chen, Y. (2020). *Explainable artificial intelligence for digital forensics: opportunities, challenges and a drug testing case study*. Digital Forensic Science.

Manasa, S., & Kumar, K. P. (2022). Digital forensics investigation for attacks on artificial intelligence. *ECS Transactions*, 107(1), 19639–19645. DOI: 10.1149/10701.19639ecst

Mitchell, F. R. (2014). An overview of artificial intelligence based pattern matching in a security and digital forensic context. Cyberpatterns: Unifying Design Patterns with Security and Attack Patterns, 215-222.

Mohammed, D., Omar, M., & Nguyen, V. (2018). Wireless sensor network security: Approaches to detecting and avoiding wormhole attacks. Journal of Research in Business. *Economics and Management*, 10(2), 1860–1864.

Moustafa, N. (2022). *Digital Forensics in the Era of Artificial Intelligence*. CRC Press. DOI: 10.1201/9781003278962

Nguyen, V., Mohammed, D., Omar, M., & Banisakher, M. (2018). The Effects of the FCC Net Neutrality Repeal on Security and Privacy. [IJHIoT]. *International Journal of Hyperconnectivity and the Internet of Things*, 2(2), 21–29. DOI: 10.4018/IJHIoT.2018070102

Omar, M. (2021). New insights into database security: An effective and integrated approach for applying access control mechanisms and cryptographic concepts in Microsoft Access environments.

Omar, M. (2022). Machine Learning for Cybersecurity: Innovative Deep Learning Solutions. Springer Brief. https://link.springer.com/book/978303115

Omar, M. (2024). From Attack to Defense: Strengthening DNN Text Classification Against Adversarial Examples. In Innovations, Securities, and Case Studies Across Healthcare, Business, and Technology (pp. 174-195). IGI Global.

Omar, M. (2024). Revolutionizing Malware Detection: A Paradigm Shift Through Optimized Convolutional Neural Networks. In Innovations, Securities, and Case Studies Across Healthcare, Business, and Technology (pp. 196-220). IGI Global. DOI: 10.4018/979-8-3693-1906-2.ch011

Omar, M., & Zangana, H. M. (Eds.). (2024). *Redefining Security With Cyber AI*. IGI Global., DOI: 10.4018/979-8-3693-6517-5

Omar, M., & Zangana, H. M. (Eds.). (2025). *Application of Large Language Models (LLMs) for Software Vulnerability Detection*. IGI Global., DOI: 10.4018/979-8-3693-9311-6

Rizvi, S., Scanlon, M., Mcgibney, J., & Sheppard, J. (2022). Application of artificial intelligence to network forensics: Survey, challenges and future directions. *IEEE Access : Practical Innovations, Open Solutions*, 10, 110362–110384. DOI: 10.1109/ACCESS.2022.3214506

Rughani, P. H. (2017). Artificial Intelligence Based Digital Forensics Framework. *International Journal of Advanced Research in Computer Science*, 8(8), 10–14. DOI: 10.26483/ijarcs.v8i8.4571

Sikos, L. F. (2021). AI in digital forensics: Ontology engineering for cybercrime investigations. *WIREs Forensic Science*, 3(3), e1394. DOI: 10.1002/wfs2.1394

Tyagi, A. K., Kumari, S., & Richa. (2024). Artificial Intelligence-Based Cyber Security and Digital Forensics: A Review. Artificial Intelligence-Enabled Digital Twin for Smart Manufacturing, 391-419.

Wright, J., Dawson, M. E.Jr, & Omar, M. (2012). Cyber security and mobile threats: The need for antivirus applications for smartphones. *Journal of Information Systems Technology and Planning*, 5(14), 40–60.

Zangana, H. M. (2024). Exploring Blockchain-Based Timestamping Tools: A Comprehensive Review. Redefining Security With Cyber AI, 92-110.

Zangana, H. M. (2024). Exploring the Landscape of Website Vulnerability Scanners: A Comprehensive Review and Comparative Analysis. Redefining Security With Cyber AI, 111-129.

Zangana, H. M., Mohammed, A. K., Sallow, A. B., & Sallow, Z. B. (2024). Cybernetic Deception: Unraveling the Layers of Email Phishing Threats. [INJURATECH]. *International Journal of Research and Applied Technology*, 4(1), 35–47.

Zangana, H. M., & Mohammed, D. (2025). Foundations of Large Language Models in Software Vulnerability Detection. In Omar, M., & Zangana, H. (Eds.), *Application of Large Language Models (LLMs) for Software Vulnerability Detection* (pp. 41–74). IGI Global., DOI: 10.4018/979-8-3693-9311-6.ch002

Zangana, H. M., & Omar, M. (2020). Threats, Attacks, and Mitigations of Smartphone Security. *Academic Journal of Nawroz University*, 9(4), 324–332. DOI: 10.25007/ajnu.v9n4a989

Zangana, H. M., & Omar, M. (2025). Harnessing the Power of Large Language Models for Cybersecurity: Applications, Challenges, and Future Directions. In Omar, M., & Zangana, H. (Eds.), *Application of Large Language Models (LLMs) for Software Vulnerability Detection* (pp. 1–40). IGI Global., DOI: 10.4018/979-8-3693-9311-6.ch001

Zangana, H. M., Omar, M., Al-Karaki, J. N., & Mohammed, D. (2024). Comprehensive Review and Analysis of Network Firewall Rule Analyzers: Enhancing Security Posture and Efficiency. Redefining Security With Cyber AI, 15-36.

Chapter 3
Anti-Forensics:
The Art of Deceiving and Evading Cybersecurity Analysts

Robert John Mapa Soler
https://orcid.org/0009-0006-2466-5412
Illinois Institute of Technology, USA

ABSTRACT

Today's world has seen rapid advancements in technology. With that comes even more rapid advancements in cybersecurity. And to combat that, criminals and adversaries have also developed even more advanced techniques to combat cybersecurity. Many of these techniques fall under the field of anti-forensics. Digital forensics is the branch of cybersecurity that deals with investigating incidents in cyberspace. So, to hide themselves even more, cybercriminals have come up with very created anti-forensic techniques to evade these investigators and make it harder to prove that they actually committed a crime. This paper highlights published and proven anti-forensic techniques across different devices. It covers the technical details of these techniques, as well as the forensic techniques that they evade. Although many of the techniques in this paper can be used for malicious purposes, forensic investigators should nevertheless know these so that they can continue to perform their jobs effectively despite the rapid growth of techniques that are used against them.

DOI: 10.4018/979-8-3373-0857-9.ch003

I. INTRODUCTION

A. Background and Significance

This is the digital age. Everything makes use of technology. All technology makes use of information. In short, everything we do today relies on information technology. And that includes cybercrime and cyberwarfare.

The field of cybersecurity is like a game of cat and mouse. It's a never-ending cycle of opposing sides getting better than each other. Attackers find a clever way to get past the defenses of systems, then the defenders find a clever solution to prevent that, then the attackers yet again find a more advanced way to hack into those systems, and then the defenders find an even more advanced solution to that problem, and so on and so forth. The same thing happens with forensics and anti-forensics. Investigators have found ways to extract data that should not be extractable by normal means, then people made tools to cleverly hide that information even further so that investigators can't find them, then investigators made their own tools to counter that, and then other people made even more advanced tools that are harder to counter, and so on and so forth. With that being said, it's clear that the field of cybersecurity is only getting more and more advanced.

This paper will focus on two branches of cybersecurity: forensics and anti-forensics. In this context, forensics is the science of retrieving and recovering data from a machine for further purposes. In law and crime, this information can be used as evidence admissible in court (Slonopas, 2024). In cyberwarfare, this information can be used to gain intelligence on the adversary (ADF Solutions, 2023) and even reverse-engineer their own technology.

On the other hand, anti-forensics is the science of evading forensics. Criminals use this to make themselves harder to track and harder to be proven guilty in court. In warfare, militaries use this on their technology to make it harder for their opponents to gain information about them and the technology they use (ADF Solutions, 2023). All this is done in the name of hiding information that would give their opposition an edge against them.

However, anti-forensics has only recently been acknowledged as a legitimate field of study, and because of this, there is a general lack of knowledge on anti-forensics techniques. Therefore, the aim of this paper is to fill that gap and provide knowledge to everyone in the technology sector, especially the people in the field of cybersecurity.

Though it would seem that this paper mostly helps criminals or people trying to hide suspicious information, it is also actually true the other way around. As stated in the previous paragraph, the information in this paper can be used to enlighten cybersecurity professionals as well, so that they may be aware of the possible anti-forensic techniques they may come across in their jobs. It can also be applied in military operations and projects, ensuring national safety by hiding information from potential adversaries.

B. Scope of the study

Each electronic device that stores data and information can be subject to forensic analysis. Each electronic device subject to forensic analysis can also be subject to anti-forensic techniques. However, there are countless kinds of electronic devices that exist today. The most popular ones are personal computing devices such as laptops, desktops, tablets, and cell phones; and even among these devices, there are hundreds of kinds of operating systems that run on them, each one requiring different approaches in forensic and anti-forensic techniques. With all the different kinds of electronic devices and possible operating systems that run on them, it is impossible to cover all the possible anti-forensic techniques that can be done on computers.

To address the sheer number of different electronic devices and operating systems, this paper will only explore anti-forensic techniques on two of the three most popular operating systems as of today (Stat Counter, 2024):

- Windows – makes up 26.6% of the global market share of operating systems
- iOS – makes up 18.12% of the global market share of operating systems

The reason for this is that Windows and iOS are two almost completely different operating systems. Windows is a desktop/laptop operating system developed by Microsoft. It uses the New Technology File System for storage and allows open-source applications to run on it. On the other hand, iOS is a mobile operating system developed by Apple. It uses the Macintosh Hierarchical File System for storage and does not allow open-source applications in its system. Because of these differences, forensic and anti-forensic approaches are very different between the two operating systems.

Figure 1. Leading shares of operating systems worldwide

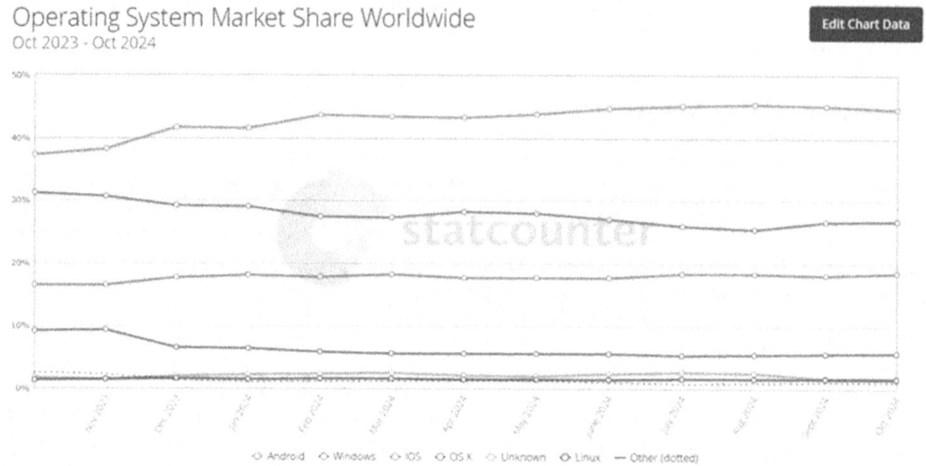

Additionally, this paper will also cover a technique that is applicable to Windows XP. Released in 2001, it is an old version of windows that is no longer being updated and supported by Microsoft and most of the services being used today. Despite that, it still plays a major role in today's world, with the US Navy still relying on this operating system in all of its operations and daily tasks (Goldman, 2015). For this reason, this old operating system will also be discussed in this paper.

II. <u>LITERATURE REVIEW</u>

A. An Overview of Digital Forensics

According to the website Computer Forensics World, "computer forensics is considered to be the use of analytical and investigative techniques to identify, collect, examine, and preserve evidence/information which is magnetically stored and encoded." This is its general purpose in the field of technology, and because of its investigative nature, it is often used for criminal investigations. These cases can range anywhere from a mere corporate breach in user agreement policy, to drug or human trafficking, to international-scale cybercrimes. Basically, any crime that relies on technology and the storage of digital information is subject to digital forensic analysis.

Additionally, because digital forensics plays a huge role in investigating criminal cases, it also plays a huge role in court proceedings. In a more legal context, its objective is to recover, analyze, and present computer-based material such that it can be admissible in court. Therefore, it is not enough to just casually extract data from an electronic device under investigation; it should follow a proper procedure to make sure that the evidence is not tampered with or corrupted before further investigation and presentation is done.

B. An Overview of Anti-Forensics

Anti-forensics, on the other hand, is exactly what its name entails: it is the art and science of opposing forensic investigations and analysis. The goal of anti-forensics isn't just to evade and hide information from forensic tools and analysis. According to Gül and Kugu (2024), the main goal of anti-forensics is to force forensic investigations to add more man-hours and spend more money, and to frustrate and mislead forensic tools and investigators so that it becomes harder for them to find meaningful evidence or catch the culprit behind the given investigation.

Grugq (2005) states that anti-forensic techniques generally have three strategies: data hiding, data destruction, and data contraception. Data hiding involves hiding important data in such a manner that digital forensic analysis won't find it. Data destruction also aims to prevent forensic analysis from finding the data by completely and physically eliminating the data from wherever it is stored. Some ways of doing this are by overwriting it with random data or by just physically burning the storage device that contains the data. The only difference between the two is that data hiding makes it possible for the culprit/s to access the data again and again, while data destruction removes the data forever. On the other hand, data contraception is defined as the effort to limit the quantity of information and evidence that investigators can find (Gurgq, 2005).

Furthermore, Franco et al. (2016) divides anti-forensic techniques into six different categories:

- Hiding, obfuscation, and Data Encryption
- Deletion or Data Destruction
- Data Falsification
- Analysis Prevention
- Obstruction of Traces Collection
- Tools Subversion

Classical anti-forensics consists of HDD and File Wiping, encryption, and steganography. However, over the years, the side of forensic analysts have advanced in their tools and technologies, making the classical anti-forensic techniques obsolete. To address this, anti-forensics have also advanced in their methodologies and have developed more modern and sophisticated approaches to combating digital forensic analysis. Below are a list of these modern approaches (Gül & Kugu, 2024):

1. *Data Pooling* – Pertains to the culprits using lots of media for their digital data. If an investigation about their case is conducted, then the investigators would have to search through all of the concerned media and would therefore take a lot of time and money.

Figure 2. Redundant Array of Independent disk in a server rack

2. *Non-Standard RAID'ed Disks* – Redundant Array of Independent Disks (RAID) is a technology that combines multiple physical drives to function as one logical disk for a computer (Wikipedia, n.d). This anti-forensic technique consists of using uncommon settings like disk order, stripe order and size, block size, and endianness for the purpose of making it harder for common tools to retrieve meaningful data using default settings based on widely known standards.
3. *Manipulating File Signatures* – A file signature is a small block of hex code that signifies what kind of file a file is. Manipulating file signatures makes it possible for tools to detect a file as a .exe file (Windows executable file) when it actually is a .txt file (text file). That way, it can trick tools and investigators into thinking that a file is something that it isn't.
4. *Restricted Filenames* – culprits can use tools or special commands to create files or directories with restricted names. For example, the string "aux" is normally not allowed to be a filename or directory name for most operating systems, but with the simple command "md \\.\c:\aux", it is possible to create a folder named

"aux" in a windows machine. Then, when forensic tools find this folder, analysts won't be able to open it because it will return an error.

Figure 3. File Signature for a PNG file

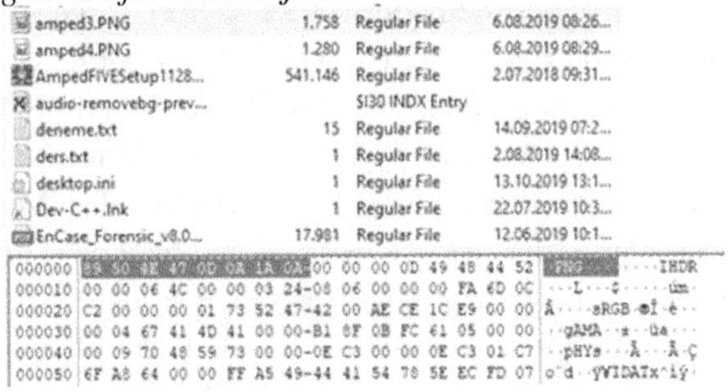

5. *Manipulating MACE Times* – This technique involves the criminal changing metadata of files such as timestamps when the file was created, deleted, or modified. This is done to mislead forensic investigators when making a timeline of events.
6. *Loop References* – The Windows API only allows file path lengths to be a maximum of 260 characters. However, third-party tools like the Long Path Tool make it possible to create file paths longer than that. Most forensic tools won't discover a file like this, and when they do, it will show an error saying that the file name cannot be resolved or the file path is too long.
7. *Dummy HDDs* – This is a very simple yet effective way to fool forensic investigators. In this technique, criminals simply replace the computer's HDD with one that has absolutely nothing to do with the crime they commit. When the investigators arrive at the scene, they take the computer thinking that the HDD in it was used in whatever the criminals were doing, when it actually wasn't. As long as the given hard disk has "recent" entries, investigators will think that it is significant evidence (Perklin, 2012).

III. ANTI-FORENSICS IN WINDOWS

This section will cover various anti-forensic techniques in Windows operating systems. However, before proceeding, it is important to first discuss the nature of how storage systems in Windows machines work.

The New Technology File System, or NTFS for short, is the file system that the Windows NT OS uses for storing and fetching files from storage (Lutkevich, 2021). This storage can either be a Hard Disk Drive (HDD) or a Solid-State Drive (SSD), which are hardware components that physically store clusters of file data within them. Within the NTFS is the Master File Table, or MFT. The MFT is a table that stores the records of all the files that are being stored by the NTFS. These records include the file name, an indicator whether it is deleted or not, metadata about it, and file data's physical location in the HDD or SSD if the file size is greater than 1KB. If the file is less than 1KB in size, then the MFT record would just store the file data itself, rather than its location in storage (Kai et al., 2010).

All the indexes in the MFT are arranged alphanumerically based on the file-names being stored. When a file is created, an index for this file is created in the MFT. When a file is deleted from the user's directories and moved to the recycle bin, its index remains in the MFT, but it is marked as deleted. This explains why it is still possible to recover a deleted file that is still in the recycling bin. When a file is removed from the recycling bin as well, the MFT gets rid of the file's index and all the indexes under it are shifted upward to fill in the space that it left behind (Cho, 2015). However, the deleted index is not actually physically removed from storage. Rather, it remains in the same location until it is overwritten by new data.

Since Windows operating systems have changed over the years, the following anti-forensic techniques will only be feasible on specific versions of the Windows operating system, particularly Windows XP, and 7+.

A. Using the MFT of the NTFS to hide data

One of the most well-known ways of hiding data is using the slack space of a hard disk. Slack space is defined by Chuck Easttom (2022) as "the unused space between the logical end of file and the physical end of file." This means that if 4KB of space is allocated for a file, but the file contents only total up to 3KB, then the remaining 1KB of space after the file's contents is the slack space. Furthermore, if a 4KB file got deleted, but the file that replaced it in storage only overwrote 3.5KB of data, then the remaining 0.5KB of data from the deleted file will remain in the new file's slack space. Whatever is in this space is not part of the file, but this space also cannot be used for other files since it is part of the said file's allocated space.

Many anti-forensic techniques involve hiding data in these slack spaces to avoid detection by common tools.

Since this technique is a very basic and common one, many tools have been made to automatically check the slack space of disks for data that might be significant. However, Korean researcher Gyu-Sang Cho (2015) has cleverly found a way to evade these tools as well by finding a way to reuse the data in the slack space and assign it to an existing file. In his work, he creates a software tool that hides a message in the directory index of the NTFS file system of Windows. The tool follows a 10-step algorithm:

1. Input the working directory name, message to hide, and block size *b*.
2. Preprocess unsuitable characters for a file name.
3. Divide the message into *n* fragments. Each fragment has block size *b* and is not larger than 255 bytes.
4. Attach a header to each message fragment. This takes advantage of the fact that the MFT stores file names in alphabetical order. The attached header makes sure that the fragments are arranged in the correct order.
5. Create a file named "$fixedFile.txt" to keep it to the first slot in the working directory.
6. Create a file for each *n*-sized fragment with their attached headers on their filenames.
7. Delete the first message file both from the working directory and the recycling bin. This removes its entry from the MFT, but the data of the entry itself still exists in unallocated storage.
8. Create a new file in such a way that it uses the deleted fragment's data in storage as its own file data. This involves intricate, low-level programming to directly manipulate the MFT to use the slack space (which contains the deleted fragment) for the new file. The new file's name should also be seemingly innocent (i.e. a long integer).
9. Delete the disguised file.
10. Repeat everything from step 7 for all the remaining file fragments. The names for the newly created files should make it possible for them to be arranged alphabetically or numerically.

There are two facts to remember about how the MFT works. First, filenames are arranged in alphabetical order. If a new file is added, it will be inserted in the table according to alphabetical order, and the rest of the table indexes will be adjusted accordingly. Second, when a file is deleted from the MFT, all the file indexes under it get shifted "upwards" to fill in the "gap" that the deleted index left behind. However, though this index is removed from the MFT, it still remains in unallocated storage.

Therefore, the act of deleting an entry from the MFT and then creating another entry using the same data it left behind creates the illusion of file data moving around in the MFT, something that should normally not be possible. This, combined with the seemingly innocent file names, makes it very difficult for forensic investigators to find all the message fragments and piece them up together to get the information they are looking for.

Overall, this tool makes use of the data in slack space as the file data for the new files that get created. It hides data makes it harder for forensic investigators to reconstruct the original message because it splits the message into fragments and "moves" them around in the MFT. Not only that, but the naming convention of the new files (alphanumerical order) makes it possible for the intended recipient to easily piece up all the fragments and recreate the original message. So not only is the data hidden and obfuscated, but it is also retained for future reconstruction by the intended recipient.

B. Using Alternate Data Streams

Another way to hide information is to use Alternate Data Streams, or ADS. ADS is a feature in Windows machines that use the NTFS file system. This feature was created to support compatibility with the Macintosh Hierarchical File System (HFS), the file system of Macintosh machines (Shamblin, 2008). Basically, the engineers at Microsoft wanted the NTFS to be able to seamlessly store files that were originally stored in HFS. However, because of the structural differences between NTFS and HFS, the files stored in HFS would have different sets of metadata compared to the ones stored in NTFS. To address this difference, they created ADS so that when a file is transferred from a Macintosh machine to a Windows machine, the NTFS could store the HFS-exclusive metadata while storing the actual file data without any problems. And then, if that same file is transferred back to a Macintosh machine, the HFS-exclusive metadata would still be there in the original file.

The problem with this is that people have found out that it is actually very easy and simple to just hide information and even malware in ADS. It is highly effective as well. In fact, nowadays, ADS is more known as a means by which data can be hidden in the Windows OS (Hermon et al., 2022), rather than a feature for cross-system support, which is what it was intended for.

Doing it is very simple too. In the Windows command line, the command to use ADS to attach a file called malware.exe to a seemingly innocent file called readme.txt would be "type malware.exe > readme.txt:malware.exe". So, when a user opens readme.txt, malware.exe would automatically get executed without the user manually running it. To make this even more discrete, the file size of readme.txt will not change no matter what the file size of malware.exe is. If readme.txt is

427 bytes, then File Explorer will show that its file size is only 427 bytes even if there is an 800-byte malware.exe file attached to its ADS. This is because in the NTFS, the ADS is stored in a different and separate location from the actual file data. This makes it even harder for the average user to detect that something is not normal with the file that they are opening.

Since this technique is a very old and common one, many tools have been made to detect this already. But the major problem is that the vast majority of Windows users are not aware of this feature (Hermon et al., 2022). Therefore, it is easy to hide malware from them and trick them into running it without them knowing.

Figure 4. Initial file sizes of readme.txt and malware.exe

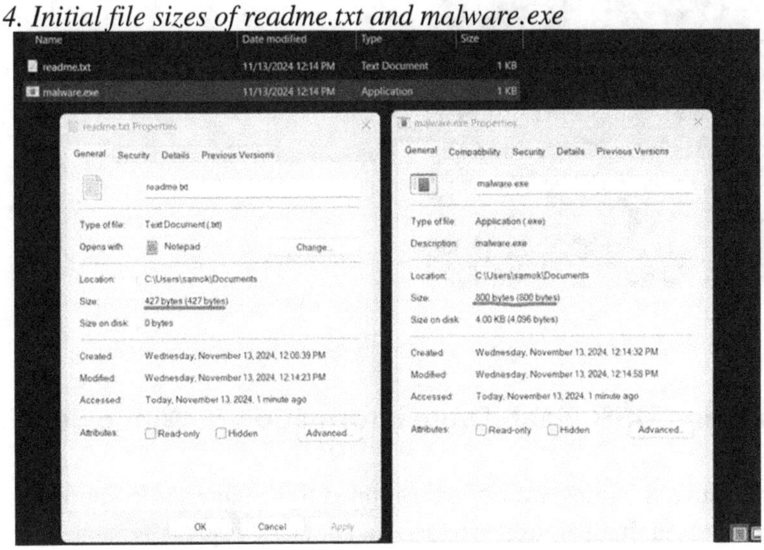

Figure 5. Command used to hide malware.exe within readme.txt

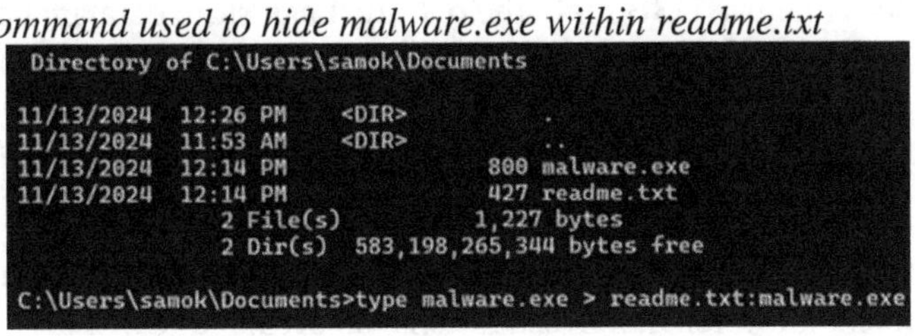

Figure 6. Even after hiding malware.exe within readme.txt, the latter's file size still stays the same.

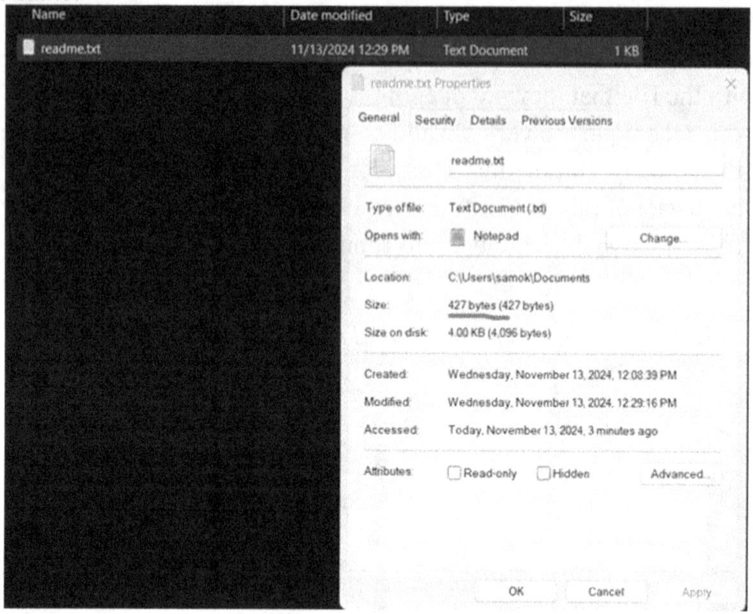

C. Obscuring USB Flash Drive Information in Windows XP

Forensic investigations are not only limited to the internal components of the computer involved. It also extends to external devices, especially those that use the Universal Serial Bus, or more commonly known as USB. In fact, USB devices are one of the most efficient and effective ways for a hacker to deliver his payload and execute an attack. Researchers Paula Thomas and Alun Morris (2008) argue that of all the devices that use USB, only the ones that can store data are considered to be the most dangerous in terms of security. Furthermore, 51% of malware attacks against critical infrastructure are designed for USB devices (Honeywell, 2024). These statistics prove that USB devices are not to be undermined when investigating the aftermath of a cyber-attack or cybercrime. Because of this, USB drives are subject to digital forensics, which in turn also makes them subject to anti-forensics.

In the context of forensic investigations involving a USB drive, the most information-rich places in a Windows machine are the registry and the log file "Setupapi.log" (Thomas & Morris, 2008). Once a USB device gets plugged into the computer, its device ID and serial number are saved in the registry. The device ID can be used to figure out the manufacturer, vendor, or device type of the USB device. On the other hand, "Setupapi.log" will log the date and time when this device was installed. For this reason, analysts check these two first when investigating an incident that had to do with a USB drive. Of course, any adversary that knows this will find a way to modify the data in the registry and the log file in an effort to make it harder for investigators to track them down.

To further emphasize their statement about USB drives being one of the biggest threats in cybersecurity, Thomas and Morris (2008) showcase a tool they created that automatically obscures, modifies, or deletes significant information about a given USB device once it is plugged into a Windows Machine. This tool is a program that resides on a USB memory stick and will automatically run as soon as it is inserted into the victim device. The user will also be able to decide beforehand which keys will be modified or left unchanged.

Once the USB stick is inserted, the tool is capable of running the following tasks in quick succession:

1. Add (fake) Device – Writes fake details of a USB device in the registry.
2. Delete Key – Removes the key of the USB stick from the registry.
3. Remove Traces – Modifies Setupapi.log and removes the installation data and time for the USB device.
4. Mounted Devices – Gives the user an option to overwrite the existing key values of the mounted devices.
5. USB Timeline – Lets the user input a fake timeline of the USB installation to be put in the Setupapi.log file.

Figure 7. The tool developed for anti-forensic techniques using a USB stick.

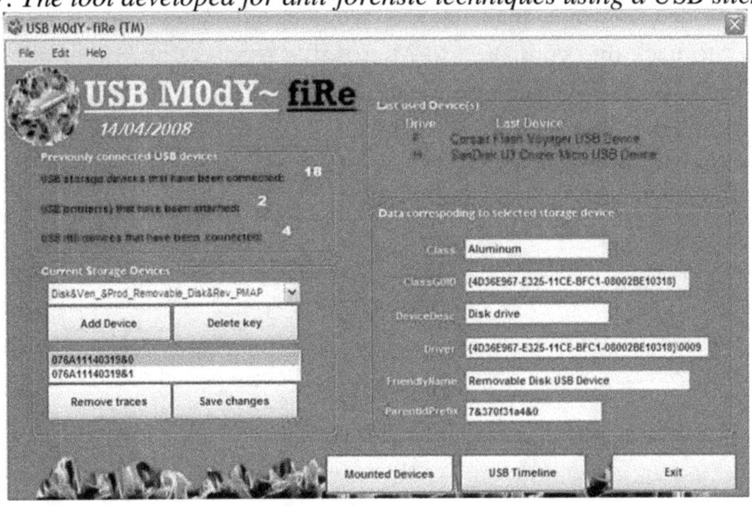

With a tool like this proven to work, not only does a USB stick become an ideal medium to deliver an attack, but it also becomes the prefect device to hide this attack from incident responders and forensic investigators.

IV. ANTI-FORENSICS IN IOS

The third most popular operating system today is the iOS. It is Apple's proprietary mobile operating system that runs on iPhones and iPads. Its approach to security is very different from those of Android and Windows devices. Simply put, there are two characteristics that separate this OS from the previous two mentioned in this paper.

The first characteristic is its highly closed ecosystem (Nesbo, 2021). Apple maintains tight control over hardware and software integration in their products. This means that the iOS can only run on any particular device they make, and any device they make is engineered in such a manner that iOS is the only OS that can run on them. This makes it a lot harder for people to experiment with Apple's operating systems and hardware features.

The second characteristic is its extremely restrictive policy on open-source software. Before Apple allows a particular application to be downloadable for their devices, this application undergoes very strict app reviews within the company (Nesbo, 2021). Then, it undergoes a highly secure distribution process. This means that open-source software is not allowed in Apple products. Because of this, getting any form of malware or malicious code in an iOS machine is many times more difficult and complex than doing it in a Windows or Android machine.

Because of Apple's highly closed ecosystem and extremely restrictive policy on open-sourced software, their devices are generally known to be more secure and harder to hack into compared to Microsoft's products and other devices that run Android. And for this same reason, there is not a lot of material covering anti-forensic techniques on iOS devices. However, this doesn't mean that anti-forensics is impossible in their machines.

Figure 8. Overview of the iOS file decryption process (as taken directly from the source paper)

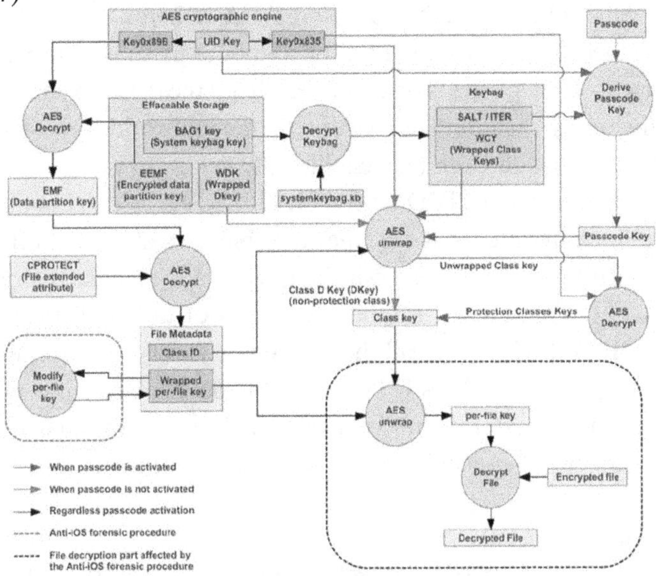

Before discussing anti-forensics in iOS devices, it is important to first discuss how iOS protects the privacy of files in its operating system. Each file in an iOS device is encrypted using a 256-bit per-file key, meaning each file has its own key. This key is also encrypted by a Class D key (Class D keys are for non-protected files). The Class D key in turn is encrypted using the device key, which is based on the device's Unique ID (UID), and is then stored in the device's effaceable storage. The UID and device key are unique for every single device. All the encryption and decryption that happens uses the Advanced Encryption Standard (AES). During a forensic investigation, one of the first steps would be to retrieve the Class D key and then use it to decrypt all the files in the iOS device.

Given the iOS encryption mechanism, it only makes sense for anti-forensic techniques to revolve around the Class D key and the encryption process that follows it. That is exactly what researchers Christian D'Orazio, Aswami Ariffin, and Kim-Kwang Raymond Choo (2014) proposed in their paper. Their work details how one can conceal, delete, and insert fake data in iPhones after getting the Class D key.

To start the process of concealing, deleting, or modifying data, the iOS machine has to be in a tethered jailbroken state first. Jailbreaking an iOS system means breaking through the security mechanisms and limitations that the operating system imposes on the device (Liu et al., 2016). If done on a machine that runs iOS, the user gets root privileges and permissions to read or write data directly into memory and storage, something that wouldn't be possible otherwise. This means that the user would be able to run open-source or unapproved software on the device, effectively bypassing Apple's restrictions on those kinds of software. There are two kinds of jailbreaks: tethered and untethered jailbreak. A tethered jailbreak requires the phone to be connected to a desktop unit for it to boot up in a jailbroken state. It is only temporary, so if the phone is disconnected from the desktop and then rebooted again, it will no longer be jailbroken. An untethered jailbreak simply means that the phone is permanently jailbroken (Zdziarski, 2012).

The process in the work of D'Orazio et al. (2014) starts with booting an iPhone in a tethered jailbroken state. That way, they are able to establish an SSH connection over USB, have full root privileges over the device, and can use their own custom tools in the process. Then, they use their custom tool called "SetKey" to retrieve the device key from the kernel, read the effaceable storage and retrieve the Class D key, and then unwrap the Class D key using the device key. Now with the Class D key, they are able to perform anti-forensic techniques on the files in the iPhone.

These are the steps to conceal data in the jailbroken iPhone:

1. Choose a file to conceal.
2. Obtain its encrypted per-file key and decrypt it using the Class D key.
3. Apply a bitwise XOR operation on it using a secret 256-bit value. This alters the key without permanently damaging it while making the file unreadable.
4. The modified per-file key is then re-encrypted using the Class D key and placed back where it was taken from.
5. The file is now unreadable. To recover it, simply decrypt the output in step 4 to obtain the modified per-file key, then XOR it with the secret value used in step 3. This will give the original per-file key that can make the files readable again.

These are the steps to insert data in the jailbroken iPhone, for the purpose of misleading investigators:

1. On the desktop unit, prepare a file in such a way that it follows iOS's naming convention. For example, if images are stored as IMG_XXXX.JPG in the /mobile/Media/DCIM/100/APPLE/ directory, where XXXX is the image's sequential number.
2. The external file is then transferred from the desktop to the iPhone via SSH over USB and stored in the correct location in the iPhone's HFS file system.
3. From the desktop, the researchers modify the metadata of the external file that just got inserted into the iPhone. They use the chmod command to update the permissions on the file to make it match the permissions on the other files in the device (usually -rw-r--r--).

4. The researchers then use their own custom tool "SetDate" to ensure that the external file's timestamps are consistent with the timestamps of the other existing files in the device.

These are the steps to permanently delete data in an effort to make it completely unrecoverable for forensic investigators:

1. Choose a file to delete.
2. Obtain its encrypted per-file key and decrypt it using the Class D key.
3. Replace the per-key file with a 256-bit string of zeroes. This effectively wipes the correct per-file key permanently.
4. The modified per-file key is then re-encrypted using the Class D key and placed back where it was taken from.
5. Because the per-file key has been completely wiped, it is now impossible to recover the file that was encrypted by it. Thus, the data is permanently deleted.

V. CONCLUSION

At the end of this paper, several conclusions can be made. This paper has discussed the modern ways of hiding information in Windows and iOS devices such that regular forensic techniques won't be able to find them. The possible applications of the contents of this paper are countless, with most of them being useful in the field of cybercrime investigations and cyberwarfare.

It is without doubt that cybersecurity is a game of cat and mouse, with both sides finding ways to get better than each other indefinitely. This is why over the last few years, cybersecurity has advanced drastically and opened more possibilities in the technology industry. This rapid advancement is the reason why the demand for cybersecurity professionals has increased so much that many believe there is a shortage of cybersecurity professionals.

It is also worth noting that the differences between Windows systems and iOS systems cause widely different approaches to anti-forensics in their respective machines. Because of these differences, anti-forensics are a lot easier to perform in Windows machines but significantly more tedious for iOS devices. This also gives forensic investigators an advantage because if they know the operating system of the device they are trying to investigate, they can narrow down the possible anti-forensic techniques that they have to look out for. If they are investigating a Windows machine, then they can stop worrying about anti-forensic techniques that would only work on an iOS machine. The same can be said the other way around.

Lastly, this paper is further proof that forensics and anti-forensics are forcing each other to advance as fast as possible. With that, one could say that in the near future, the techniques used in forensics and anti-forensics won't be as we know it today.

REFERENCES

Cho, G.-S. (2015). Development of an anti-forensic tool for hiding message in a directory index of NTFS. *2015 World Congress on Internet Security (WorldCIS)*, 144–145. https://doi.org/DOI: 10.1109/WorldCIS.2015.7359431

Cybersecurity in 2024: USB devices continue to pose major threat. Honeywell. (2024). https://www.honeywell.com/us/en/news/2024/04/cybersecurity-in-2024-usb-devices-continue-to-pose-major-threat

D'Orazio, C., Ariffin, A., & Choo, K.-K. R. (2014). iOS Anti-forensics: How can we securely conceal, delete, and insert data? *2014 47th Hawaii International Conference on System Sciences*, 460, 4838–4847. https://doi.org/DOI: 10.1109/HICSS.2014.594

Easttom, C. (2022). *Digital forensics, investigation, and response* (4th ed.). Jones & Bartlett Learning.

Franco, D., Fuschini, D., & Rodrigues, T. (2016). How to detect anti-forensic techniques. *eForensics*, 45-69.

Goldman, D. (2015). Navy pays Microsoft $9 million a year for Windows XP. CNN Business. https://money.cnn.com/2015/06/26/technology/microsoft-windows-xp-navy-contract/index.html

Grugq. (2005). The art of defiling: Defeating forensic analysis. *Blackhat Briefings*.

Gul, M., & Kugu, E. (2017). A survey on anti-forensics techniques. *2017 International Artificial Intelligence and Data Processing Symposium (IDAP)*, 10 2, 1–6. https://doi.org/DOI: 10.1109/IDAP.2017.8090341

Hermon, R., Singh, U., & Singh, B. (2022). Anti-forensic technique using alternate data streams for data hiding in NTFS. *2022 International Conference on Futuristic Technologies (INCOFT)*, 1, 1–5. https://doi.org/DOI: 10.1109/INCOFT55651.2022.10094445

Kai, Z., En, C., & Qinquan, G. (2010). Analysis and implementation of NTFS file system based on computer forensics. *2010 Second International Workshop on Education Technology and Computer Science*, 27, 325–328. https://doi.org/DOI: 10.1109/ETCS.2010.434

Liu, F., Liu, K.-S., Chang, C., & Wang, Y. (2016). Research on the technology of iOS jailbreak. *2016 Sixth International Conference on Instrumentation & Measurement, Computer, Communication and Control (IMCCC)*, 644–647. https://doi.org/DOI: 10.1109/IMCCC.2016.178

Long Path Tool. (n.d.). Long Path Tool. Retrieved from https://longpathtool.com/

Lutkevich, B. (2021, April 21). What is NTFS and how does it work? TechTarget. https://www.techtarget.com/searchwindowsserver/definition/NTFS

Nesbo, E. (2021, June 11). 5 ways Apple is securing your device right now. MUO. https://www.makeuseof.com/apple-more-secure-than-android/

Operating system market share worldwide. StatCounter Global Stats. (2024, September). https://gs.statcounter.com/os-market-share

Perklin, M. (2012). *Def Con*. In Anti-forensics and anti-anti-forensics. Las Vegas, Nevada; Def Con.

Shamblin, Q. (2024, October 4). Alternate data streams overview. *SANS Digital Forensics and Incident Response Blog*. https://www.sans.org/blog/alternate-data-streams-overview/

Slonopas, A. (2024, March 15). What is digital forensics? A closer examination of the field. American Public University. https://www.apu.apus.edu/area-of-study/information-technology/resources/what-is-digital-forensics/

Solutions, A. D. F. Inc. (2023, July 28). Digital forensics: The military's secret to combating cyber threats. ADF. https://www.adfsolutions.com/adf-blog/digital-forensics-the-militarys-secret-weapon-to-combat-cyber-threats?srsltid=AfmBOooUar16dGj-mMR09kYxzt8zKU_4Ar0d1AnyLcQ9f-q6KmK40jeH

Thomas, P., & Morris, A. (2008). An investigation into the development of an anti-forensic tool to obscure USB flash drive device information on a Windows XP platform. *2008 Third International Annual Workshop on Digital Forensics and Incident Analysis*, 60–66. https://doi.org/DOI: 10.1109/WDFIA.2008.13

Wikimedia Foundation. (2024, July 28). RAID. Wikipedia. https://en.wikipedia.org/wiki/RAID

Zdziarski, J. (2012). *Hacking and securing iOS applications*. O'Reilly Media.

Chapter 4
Cybercrime Investigation and Fraud Detection With AI

Yara Shamoo
https://orcid.org/0009-0004-2459-0807
Saint Leo University, USA

ABSTRACT

The rapid evolution of artificial intelligence (AI) has introduced transformative possibilities for cybercrime investigation and fraud detection, enabling enhanced accuracy, efficiency, and adaptability. AI-powered tools such as machine learning algorithms, natural language processing, and computer vision offer robust solutions for detecting fraudulent activities, tracing digital evidence, and identifying anomalous behaviors across diverse platforms. This chapter explores the fundamental technologies that underlie AI applications in digital forensics, discussing key methodologies, challenges, and case studies that illustrate AI's role in combating cybercrime. Emphasis is placed on how AI techniques support law enforcement in recognizing sophisticated fraud schemes, performing predictive analysis, and adapting to ever-changing cyber threats. Additionally, we address ethical and privacy concerns related to AI-driven surveillance and investigation processes, underscoring the need for a balanced approach in leveraging AI for crime prevention. This chapter provides valuable insights for cybersecurity professionals, digital forensics experts, and law enforcement agencies on the effective deployment of AI to counteract fraud and secure digital ecosystems.

DOI: 10.4018/979-8-3373-0857-9.ch004

1. INTRODUCTION TO CYBERCRIME AND FRAUD IN THE DIGITAL AGE

The digital era has transformed not only the means by which information is shared and businesses operate but has also created new opportunities for criminal activity. Cybercrime and fraud have evolved significantly alongside technological advances, leading to sophisticated, complex, and often globalized threats. The rise of the internet, social media, cloud computing, and mobile technologies has provided unprecedented avenues for cybercriminals to exploit vulnerabilities and target individuals, organizations, and even nation-states. With each advancement, cybercriminals have adopted more intricate methods, posing significant challenges for traditional investigative approaches. This section explores the nature of cybercrime and fraud in today's digital landscape, the critical need for enhanced detection and prevention mechanisms, and the transformative role of artificial intelligence (AI) in tackling these issues.

The escalating trends in cybercrime, highlighted by a surge in cases over recent years, underscore the critical need for advanced technological interventions. The chart below illustrates this growth and emphasizes the urgency of robust detection mechanisms.

Figure 1. Rising Threats Over Time

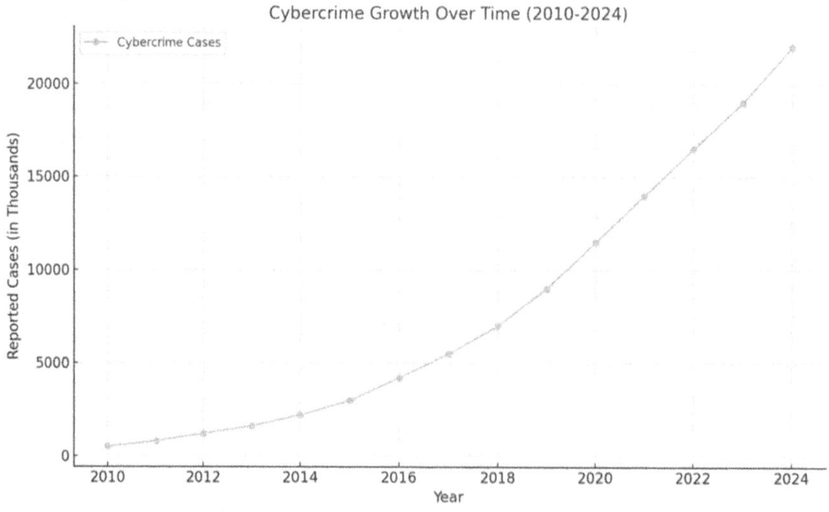

1.1 Cybercrime Defined and the Broad Scope of Digital Fraud

Cybercrime encompasses a wide array of illegal activities conducted via digital means. This includes hacking, identity theft, cyber espionage, ransomware, phishing, and online financial fraud (Irons & Lallie, 2014). Often financially or politically motivated, cybercriminals use advanced tools to infiltrate systems, extract sensitive data, and disrupt operations. Cyber fraud, a subset of cybercrime, typically involves deception to achieve financial gain, such as phishing, credit card fraud, and cryptocurrency scams (Moustafa, 2022). The proliferation of interconnected devices and networks, along with the growth of e-commerce and online banking, has significantly increased exposure to these crimes, requiring novel investigative methods and detection technologies (Jeong, 2020).

1.2 Key Challenges in Cybercrime Investigation

Traditional digital forensics methods face limitations when applied to modern cybercrime. The vast amount of data generated from multiple sources, including social media, emails, and network logs, can overwhelm investigators (Rizvi et al., 2022). Moreover, cybercriminals leverage anonymizing technologies like the Dark Web and encrypted communications, further complicating efforts to trace their activities (Costantini, De Gasperis, & Olivieri, 2019). The international nature of cybercrime also creates legal and jurisdictional obstacles, as crimes often involve perpetrators, victims, and servers located in different countries (Zangana et al., 2024).

Another significant challenge in digital forensics is evidence tampering. Cybercriminals may alter digital evidence to hinder investigations, a practice that complicates the process of tracing their actions and identifying key data points (Hamza & Omar, 2013). These factors necessitate the adoption of innovative tools and approaches, such as artificial intelligence, which offers new capabilities in automating and enhancing cybercrime investigations (Bhawna & Mahajan, 2024).

1.3 The Emergence of AI in Fraud Detection and Cyber Forensics

Artificial intelligence and machine learning have emerged as powerful tools in combating cybercrime. AI's capacity to analyze large volumes of data at high speeds makes it invaluable in identifying suspicious patterns, detecting anomalies, and predicting potential threats. With AI, forensic investigators can move from manual analysis to automated systems that flag unusual behavior in real-time, facilitating faster responses to cyber incidents (Dunsin et al., 2022).

Fraud detection has particularly benefited from AI advancements. Machine learning algorithms can process historical transaction data to learn normal behavior patterns and flag deviations that may indicate fraud. Such systems are especially valuable in sectors like banking and e-commerce, where rapid detection is essential to minimize financial losses and protect customers' data (Adam & Varol, 2020). Further, AI-enabled predictive models assist in profiling cybercriminals' behaviors, thereby aiding in preemptive measures (Hall, Sakzad, & Choo, 2022).

1.4 AI-Driven Techniques in Cybercrime Prevention and Detection

Several AI-driven techniques are revolutionizing the field of cybercrime prevention and fraud detection. These include anomaly detection, natural language processing (NLP), and deep learning-based image and pattern recognition (Mitchell, 2014). For example, anomaly detection algorithms use machine learning to identify deviations from typical behavior in network traffic, helping to uncover unauthorized access or unusual system activities. NLP techniques are valuable in parsing large amounts of textual data, such as social media posts or emails, to detect phishing attempts and other types of digital fraud (Iqbal et al., 2020).

Deep learning models, including convolutional neural networks (CNNs) and recurrent neural networks (RNNs), have also been applied in image and audio analysis, useful for investigating digital evidence like video footage or voice recordings (Ganesh, 2017). These advancements represent a significant leap from traditional forensics, where manual review of digital evidence was time-consuming and often error-prone (Sikos, 2021).

1.5 Ethical and Privacy Considerations in AI-Driven Forensics

Despite the advantages of AI in cybercrime investigation, there are ethical and privacy concerns related to its application. AI models rely heavily on personal data for training and improvement, raising questions about data privacy and consent (Kelly et al., 2020). The use of facial recognition technology, for instance, has sparked debates over surveillance, as it can potentially infringe on individual privacy rights if used improperly (Jarrett & Choo, 2021). Balancing the need for robust cybercrime detection with the protection of civil liberties remains a critical consideration in the integration of AI into digital forensics (Tyagi, Kumari, & Richa, 2024).

1.6 The Future of Cybercrime and Fraud Detection

The future of cybercrime and fraud detection lies in increasingly sophisticated AI and machine learning models capable of self-learning, real-time response, and adaptation to emerging threats (Zangana & Mohammed, 2025). As AI continues to evolve, it will likely facilitate even greater automation in digital forensics, including the integration of blockchain for data integrity and the use of large language models for advanced threat analysis (Gholami & Omar, 2023). This progression underscores the importance of continued research, development, and collaboration among cybersecurity experts, data scientists, and law enforcement agencies to create more resilient systems against the ever-evolving landscape of cyber threats (Omar, 2024).

Through these innovations, AI not only holds the potential to transform digital forensics but also to redefine how we understand, prevent, and respond to cybercrime in the digital age. As such, developing AI-centric frameworks and protocols will be essential in creating a robust defense against increasingly sophisticated digital threats and ensuring the safety and security of digital infrastructures worldwide (Dunsin, Ghanem, Ouazzane, & Vassilev, 2024).

2. AI TECHNIQUES IN CYBERCRIME INVESTIGATION

The integration of artificial intelligence (AI) in cybercrime investigations has transformed digital forensics, facilitating swift data analysis, threat detection, and incident response. These AI techniques enhance the efficiency and accuracy of cybercrime investigations by automating complex processes, reducing human error, and enabling forensic experts to analyze vast datasets in real-time. This section examines various AI applications in cybercrime investigation, including machine learning, deep learning, natural language processing, and large language models, as well as their impact on digital forensics and cybersecurity.

2.1 Machine Learning and Pattern Recognition in Cybercrime Investigation

Machine learning (ML) is extensively utilized in cybercrime investigations for identifying patterns and anomalies within large datasets. Through supervised and unsupervised learning models, ML algorithms can recognize malicious activities and unusual behavior patterns that may indicate cyber threats (Ganesh, 2017). These techniques are especially useful for network forensics, where rapid detection of anomalies can prevent potential cyber attacks (Rizvi et al., 2022). For example, ML models trained on historical cybercrime data can detect new instances of similar attacks, supporting forensic investigators in identifying both known and emerging threats (Dunsin, Ghanem, & Quazzane, 2022).

ML models also play a crucial role in identifying attack vectors and developing defensive mechanisms against cyber intrusions. This capability is essential in network security, where AI models like those discussed by Zangana, Omar, Al-Karaki, and Mohammed (2024) analyze firewall rules to improve security postures and optimize threat detection. By using pattern recognition and anomaly detection, ML contributes to building predictive models that anticipate cybercrime tactics and assist investigators in adapting their methodologies.

Understanding the comparative advantages of machine learning and deep learning techniques is essential for selecting the appropriate tool in forensic applications. The following diagram visualizes key differences and overlaps in their capabilities.

Figure 2. ML and DL Techniques in Forensics: Comparative Analysis

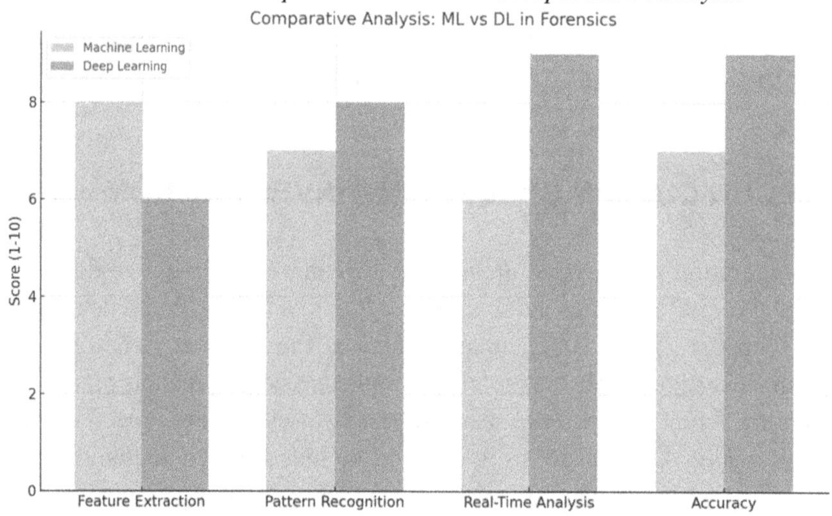

2.2 Deep Learning for Image and Speech Analysis

Deep learning (DL) techniques are valuable in the context of cybercrime investigations, particularly for tasks like image recognition, speech analysis, and document classification. Convolutional neural networks (CNNs), a type of DL model, are effective in analyzing images, which can be useful in cases involving digital evidence in the form of photos or videos (Omar, 2024). In cyber forensics, DL models can analyze digital artifacts, such as screenshots of malicious emails or phishing websites, to determine their authenticity and origins (Zangana et al.,

2024). This capability allows forensic analysts to identify visual cues associated with fraudulent websites and malicious actors.

DL also extends to speech analysis, aiding investigations that require analyzing audio recordings or voice messages. These models assist in identifying individuals, interpreting context, and verifying authenticity, especially in social engineering and cyber fraud cases (Iqbal, Debbabi, & Fung, 2020). This capability is particularly relevant in investigations where covert communications or identity verification are involved, supporting digital forensics with automated and accurate analysis.

2.3 Natural Language Processing (NLP) for Cybercrime Analysis

Natural language processing (NLP) enables forensic investigators to analyze text-based data such as emails, chat logs, and social media messages. This is critical in detecting instances of cyberbullying, hate speech, or criminal communication that often occur in plain text formats. AI-driven NLP tools are capable of detecting hidden meanings, sentiment, and intent in these communications, thus identifying cybercriminal behavior or intent (Jones & Omar, 2024). For example, NLP models can analyze patterns of phishing language in emails, supporting proactive phishing detection (Zangana, Mohammed, Sallow, & Sallow, 2024).

Additionally, NLP plays a pivotal role in analyzing large corpuses of digital evidence. As detailed by Hall, Sakzad, and Choo (2022), explainable AI (XAI) and NLP algorithms aid investigators by highlighting relevant sections within vast text datasets, thereby simplifying the extraction of critical information from digital evidence. This capability significantly enhances the efficiency of forensic investigations by pinpointing suspicious language patterns without requiring manual reviews of extensive datasets.

2.4 Large Language Models (LLMs) in Digital Forensics

The recent advancements in large language models (LLMs), such as GPT, have revolutionized digital forensics by enabling sophisticated analysis of textual data in cyber investigations. LLMs can understand context, detect nuanced communication patterns, and generate insights from unstructured data sources, making them valuable tools in cybercrime investigations (Omar & Zangana, 2025). For example, LLMs can be used to identify complex fraud schemes or organized cyber attacks that rely on encoded language, allowing investigators to decode such communications and uncover criminal networks (Gholami & Omar, 2023).

Moreover, LLMs support forensic investigators by performing sentiment analysis on digital conversations to detect malicious intent and predict potential threats. The ability of LLMs to generate coherent summaries from vast datasets enables forensic experts to gain insights quickly and respond to cyber threats more efficiently (Bhawna & Mahajan, 2024). Their implementation in digital forensics not only enhances data processing speed but also contributes to investigative precision.

2.5 AI in Malware and Phishing Detection

AI techniques are crucial in identifying and mitigating phishing and malware attacks, two prominent cyber threats in today's digital landscape. By analyzing vast databases of email and web data, AI algorithms can detect phishing emails based on linguistic patterns, link characteristics, and sender information (Zangana et al., 2024). Similarly, malware detection tools powered by AI can identify malicious software by analyzing executable code, network traffic, and behavior patterns (Mohammed, Omar, & Nguyen, 2018). These AI-powered detection methods allow investigators to prevent the spread of malware and identify phishing attempts with high accuracy.

AI's ability to recognize even subtle variations in malware and phishing techniques makes it a formidable tool for cybercrime investigation. Techniques such as cybernetic deception, as explored by Zangana et al. (2024), are also being developed to counter phishing threats, leveraging AI to identify evolving tactics used by cybercriminals. These capabilities improve the resilience of cybercrime investigations, providing investigators with adaptive tools that evolve alongside cyber threats.

2.6 Challenges and Ethical Considerations

While AI-driven techniques significantly enhance cybercrime investigations, they also pose challenges and ethical considerations. One major challenge is the interpretability of complex AI models, often referred to as the "black box" problem. This challenge complicates the validation of AI-driven findings in a legal context, where transparent and explainable results are necessary (Kelly et al., 2020). The importance of interpretability in forensic AI applications has led to the development of explainable AI (XAI) techniques, allowing investigators to understand and justify AI outputs in court settings (Irons & Lallie, 2014).

Another challenge relates to privacy concerns, as the use of AI in digital forensics involves analyzing potentially sensitive personal data. Legal frameworks must balance the need for comprehensive forensic analysis with individuals' privacy rights, preventing misuse of forensic data (Hamza & Omar, 2013). Additionally, ethical considerations arise regarding the potential biases in AI algorithms, which could lead to unfair treatment or wrongful accusations if not carefully managed (Jeong, 2020).

In conclusion, AI techniques are indispensable in cybercrime investigation, offering powerful tools for pattern recognition, text analysis, malware detection, and much more. However, the application of AI in this field requires careful consideration of interpretability, privacy, and ethical issues to ensure fair and effective investigations.

3. AI IN FRAUD DETECTION

Artificial Intelligence (AI) is playing an increasingly central role in fraud detection, enhancing capabilities to detect and prevent fraudulent activities with greater precision and speed. AI-driven approaches for fraud detection leverage machine learning, deep learning, and natural language processing (NLP) to identify patterns, anomalies, and suspicious behaviors that may indicate fraudulent actions. The integration of AI into fraud detection is especially crucial as traditional, rule-based methods struggle to keep up with sophisticated fraud tactics and large volumes of transactional data.

3.1 Machine Learning for Fraud Detection

Machine learning (ML) algorithms can analyze vast datasets to detect unusual patterns that indicate potential fraud. Supervised learning models, which are trained on labeled data, allow the system to learn from historical instances of fraud to identify similar occurrences in real time (Dunsin et al., 2022). For instance, classification algorithms such as decision trees and neural networks can distinguish between legitimate and fraudulent transactions by recognizing specific transaction attributes. Moreover, unsupervised learning models, which do not rely on labeled data, are adept at anomaly detection, a common approach in fraud detection where the model identifies transactions that deviate significantly from typical patterns (Bhawna & Mahajan, 2024).

The adaptability of ML in fraud detection enables continuous improvement in fraud detection mechanisms, making them robust against evolving fraud tactics. As noted by Rizvi et al. (2022), one of the key advantages of AI in this context is the ability to process large volumes of data in real-time, allowing for proactive detection of fraud. Additionally, models can be optimized and fine-tuned for different types of fraud, from financial fraud to online identity theft (Adam & Varol, 2020).

3.2 Deep Learning and Natural Language Processing in Fraud Detection

Deep learning (DL), an advanced subset of machine learning, is highly effective for complex data structures and patterns, such as those encountered in fraud detection. Convolutional neural networks (CNNs) and recurrent neural networks (RNNs) can capture intricate details in the data that traditional algorithms may miss, providing a nuanced analysis of transaction behaviors and user activities (Mitchell, 2014). Furthermore, NLP techniques enhance fraud detection by analyzing textual data, such as emails, messages, and other communications, to detect fraud-related language patterns (Gholami & Omar, 2023).

The utilization of NLP for fraud detection has become increasingly relevant with the rise in online scams and phishing attacks. NLP can detect subtle linguistic cues in fraudulent communications, such as the use of urgency, grammatical inconsistencies, and other psychological manipulation tactics often found in scam messages (Zangana et al., 2024). As Zangana and Omar (2025) suggest, NLP models can even be trained to detect particular phrases or sentence structures commonly associated with fraudulent intent.

3.3 Real-Time Fraud Detection Systems

AI-based real-time fraud detection systems enable organizations to identify and respond to potential fraud as it occurs. These systems utilize advanced algorithms capable of processing large data streams in real time, enabling them to flag suspicious transactions almost instantly (Jones et al., 2023). According to Rughani (2017), such systems are critical for industries like banking and e-commerce, where rapid responses to fraud can minimize financial losses and protect customer trust.

Real-time fraud detection often incorporates both predictive and prescriptive analytics to assess risk levels and recommend actions. For instance, if a credit card transaction is flagged as suspicious, the system might immediately freeze the account or notify the customer for verification. This approach minimizes the time window for fraudulent activities, thereby reducing potential damages (Hall et al., 2022).

The AI-driven fraud detection pipeline integrates multiple steps, from data collection to anomaly detection and decision-making, to ensure real-time responses. The flowchart below delineates the workflow.

Figure 3. AI Pipeline for Fraud Detection

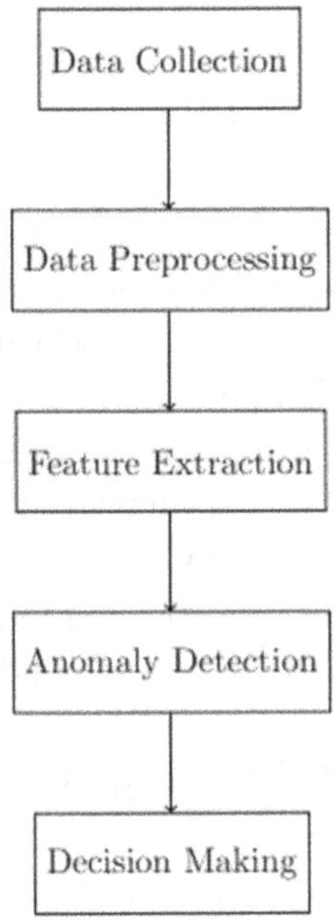

3.4 Explainable AI in Fraud Detection

One of the significant challenges in AI-driven fraud detection is ensuring that these systems are transparent and understandable, especially for non-technical stakeholders. Explainable AI (XAI) addresses this challenge by providing insights into how AI models reach their decisions. In fraud detection, XAI can help investigators and auditors understand why a particular transaction was flagged, supporting regulatory compliance and enhancing trust in AI systems (Costantini et al., 2019; Kelly et al., 2020).

For example, XAI techniques can highlight the specific features or transaction attributes that led to a fraud classification, such as unusual transaction locations or atypical purchase patterns (Dunsin et al., 2024). As noted by Sikos (2021), this transparency is essential for both improving model performance and satisfying regulatory standards that mandate accountability in automated decision-making.

3.5 AI in Digital Forensics for Fraud Investigation

In the event of confirmed fraud, AI extends beyond detection into digital forensics, where it aids in investigating the incident. AI tools can assist forensic experts in gathering and analyzing digital evidence, reconstructing events, and identifying the parties involved in the fraud (Irons & Lallie, 2014; Jeong, 2020). Techniques such as data mining, behavior analysis, and network analysis help to map out fraudulent networks and trace the flow of transactions, which is crucial for building a case against the perpetrators (Jarrett & Choo, 2021).

AI-based forensics can significantly reduce the time required to complete fraud investigations, as it automates the labor-intensive tasks of data sorting and pattern recognition. As Moustafa (2022) explains, AI tools can rapidly filter through large datasets to pinpoint relevant evidence, providing forensic investigators with actionable insights that lead to quicker resolution of fraud cases.

3.6 Future Directions and Challenges

While AI has demonstrated substantial benefits in fraud detection, challenges remain in areas such as data privacy, model interpretability, and the risk of adversarial attacks. AI models must be safeguarded against manipulation by fraudsters who might attempt to reverse-engineer detection systems. Additionally, as fraud tactics continue to evolve, so too must AI systems; they require regular updates and retraining to remain effective (Hamza & Omar, 2013; Omar, 2022).

Future advancements in AI, particularly in areas like reinforcement learning and autonomous agents, are expected to further enhance fraud detection systems. These technologies could enable models to adapt in real time, learning from each new instance of fraud to improve their predictive accuracy continuously (Zangana & Mohammed, 2025).

In conclusion, AI has transformed fraud detection, offering sophisticated, adaptive, and scalable solutions to combat various types of fraud. The integration of machine learning, deep learning, NLP, and digital forensics capabilities into fraud detection systems equips organizations with robust tools to protect against fraudulent activities while also paving the way for future innovations in this critical field of cybersecurity.

4. AI-POWERED TOOLS FOR CYBERCRIME INVESTIGATION

The application of artificial intelligence (AI) in digital forensics has transformed cybercrime investigation, enabling faster, more accurate, and more efficient analyses of complex datasets and crime patterns. These AI-powered tools are becoming indispensable in law enforcement and forensic science, enhancing the detection and prevention of cybercrimes by automating tasks, improving pattern recognition, and facilitating predictive insights.

4.1. Machine Learning for Data Analysis in Digital Forensics

Machine learning algorithms play a pivotal role in cybercrime investigation by analyzing large volumes of digital evidence, such as logs, network traffic, and files. These tools can identify suspicious patterns, anomalies, or trends that might indicate malicious activity. For instance, clustering and classification algorithms are utilized to group similar files, detect outliers, and prioritize leads based on likelihood of relevance to a case (Iqbal et al., 2020; Jones & Omar, 2024). Moreover, deep learning models, especially Convolutional Neural Networks (CNNs), are used to analyze image data, such as screen captures or incriminating photos, which may contain evidence of cybercrime (Omar, 2024).

4.2. AI-Driven Automation in Digital Forensics Processes

AI-driven automation is significantly improving efficiency in digital forensic processes. Automation of repetitive or labor-intensive tasks, such as data triage and filtering irrelevant data, frees up human analysts to focus on complex aspects of an investigation. According to studies, automation tools utilizing machine learning can reduce investigation times considerably by eliminating noise and identifying key pieces of evidence faster (Ganesh, 2017; Hall et al., 2022). For example, AI systems can automatically categorize digital content (text, images, audio) and recognize file types, significantly accelerating the data review process (Jarrett & Choo, 2021).

4.3. Explainable AI for Transparency in Investigations

Explainable AI (XAI) models are increasingly adopted to provide transparency and accountability in digital forensics. These models allow investigators to understand the reasoning behind AI-driven insights, thereby making the forensic process more reliable and legally defensible. XAI offers an added layer of trust and interpretability, which is crucial in court cases where evidence must be clearly explainable (Kelly et al., 2020; Hall et al., 2022). Explainable AI frameworks enable investigators to view decision pathways and uncover hidden connections between data points, enhancing the accuracy of forensic conclusions (Hamza & Omar, 2013; Dunsin et al., 2022).

4.4. AI for Malware and Phishing Detection

The rise in cybercrimes involving malware and phishing has driven the development of AI-based tools designed specifically for their detection. Neural networks and deep learning models are widely used to identify malicious files and phishing links by analyzing characteristics of known threats and detecting similar traits in new data. These AI systems learn from extensive datasets, continuously improving their accuracy in spotting and preventing emerging threats (Dunsin et al., 2024; Zangana et al., 2024). For instance, recent advancements in AI-powered malware detection leverage CNNs for pattern recognition and anomaly detection, significantly enhancing the identification of sophisticated attack vectors (Omar, 2024; Wright et al., 2012).

4.5. Natural Language Processing in Forensic Analysis

Natural Language Processing (NLP) is another powerful tool used to process vast amounts of textual data in cybercrime investigations. NLP can analyze chat logs, emails, and social media messages, identifying linguistic patterns and behaviors associated with fraudulent or malicious activities. Large Language Models (LLMs), such as GPT, have been used to detect phishing scams by recognizing linguistic cues and generating reports on potential threats (Jeong, 2020; Huff et al., 2023). Additionally, LLMs can be trained to flag offensive language, threats, or abnormal activity in online communications, thereby supporting investigators in identifying suspects or locating criminal networks (Omar & Zangana, 2025; Zangana & Mohammed, 2025).

4.6. AI in Behavioral Analysis and Predictive Policing

Behavioral analysis in digital forensics is another area where AI tools prove essential. By analyzing data on user behaviors, AI can help predict potential security breaches and cybercrimes. Behavioral analysis models consider factors such as browsing patterns, login times, and communication styles, which can indicate unauthorized access or suspicious activity (Irons & Lallie, 2014; Manasa & Kumar, 2022). Predictive policing is a related application, using AI to forecast potential cyber threats and suggest proactive measures for law enforcement (Adam & Varol, 2020; Tyagi et al., 2024).

4.7. Blockchain-Based Timestamping and Integrity Verification

Ensuring data integrity and maintaining accurate timestamps are critical in digital forensics. Blockchain technology, combined with AI, is increasingly applied to enhance data integrity and establish reliable timelines. Blockchain's immutable record-keeping properties make it well-suited for securely timestamping digital evidence, allowing investigators to verify that data has not been tampered with throughout the investigative process (Zangana, 2024). AI algorithms can work alongside blockchain to create secure, timestamped logs that are virtually tamper-proof, providing a transparent and trustworthy digital audit trail (Omar & Zangana, 2024).

4.8. Challenges and Future Directions

While AI-powered tools offer significant benefits in cybercrime investigation, they also present challenges. One concern is the potential for AI biases that could impact investigations if the models are not trained on diverse and representative datasets (Bhawna & Mahajan, 2024). Additionally, AI models require extensive computational resources, which may be a constraint in resource-limited environments (Dunsin et al., 2022). However, research is advancing to address these issues, focusing on improving algorithm transparency, reducing biases, and developing lightweight AI models for broader applicability (Sikos, 2021; Rizvi et al., 2022).

In summary, AI-powered tools are revolutionizing cybercrime investigation, making forensic analysis faster, more efficient, and more reliable. As these technologies continue to evolve, they will undoubtedly play an even greater role in combating cybercrime and enhancing digital forensic capabilities (Zangana et al., 2024; Mohammed et al., 2018). Future developments will likely focus on enhancing AI transparency, reducing computational demands, and integrating emerging technologies like blockchain to further strengthen cybersecurity measures.

5. CASE STUDIES OF AI IN CYBERCRIME AND FRAUD DETECTION

The integration of artificial intelligence (AI) in cybercrime detection and fraud prevention has shown promising results, facilitating the identification and mitigation of malicious activities across various digital platforms. AI-based tools have transformed traditional approaches to digital forensics by enabling more efficient and accurate analysis of vast data sets, thereby enhancing capabilities in cybercrime and fraud detection. This section explores several real-world applications and studies where AI played a significant role in combating cybercrime and improving fraud detection mechanisms.

5.1 AI-Driven Digital Forensics and Incident Response

AI-enhanced digital forensics tools enable investigators to analyze complex data patterns, detect anomalies, and link digital evidence more effectively, particularly in constrained environments. Dunsin et al. (2022) explore the deployment of AI models in incident response, highlighting how these models streamline forensic investigations by automating repetitive tasks and accelerating the detection of potential threats. Such automation reduces manual intervention, allowing forensic teams to focus on more strategic tasks within their investigations (Dunsin, Ghanem, & Quazzane, 2022; Dunsin et al., 2024). Additionally, the application of AI in constrained environments demonstrates the versatility and adaptability of these models, which are essential in remote or resource-limited settings.

In another study, Rizvi et al. (2022) present a survey on AI's role in network forensics, identifying how AI-based techniques such as machine learning (ML) improve the detection of network-based cybercrimes, including phishing and malware attacks. The researchers note that AI models can rapidly analyze network traffic, distinguish normal patterns from anomalies, and trigger alerts in real-time, a vital function for preventing extensive damage in cases of cyber attacks. This capability underscores AI's critical role in enhancing the responsiveness of network forensic systems (Rizvi, Scanlon, McGibney, & Sheppard, 2022).

5.2 Applications of Machine Learning in Fraud Detection

AI models, particularly those utilizing machine learning, have been instrumental in fraud detection across various sectors, including banking and e-commerce. For instance, Omar (2022) highlights how deep learning solutions are applied to detect fraudulent activities in financial transactions by identifying irregular spending patterns and detecting anomalies. By employing sophisticated algorithms, these models can differentiate between legitimate transactions and suspicious ones with high accuracy, effectively reducing false positives and improving customer experience.

Fraud detection models have also evolved to counter increasingly sophisticated fraudulent techniques. As Hall, Sakzad, and Choo (2022) note, explainable AI (XAI) methods have made these fraud detection models more transparent, enhancing trust and reliability in AI-driven forensic systems. XAI provides clear, interpretable insights into how specific transactions are flagged as fraudulent, aiding human investigators in understanding and verifying the decisions made by AI models (Hall, Sakzad, &

Choo, 2022). This interpretability is crucial in sectors like finance and e-commerce, where regulatory compliance and customer trust are paramount.

5.3 Case Studies of AI in Phishing and Email Fraud Detection

Email phishing remains one of the most prevalent methods of cyber fraud, and AI has significantly improved detection accuracy for this type of attack. Zangana et al. (2024) discuss how AI-based models can detect patterns in email metadata, such as the sender's behavior and content structure, to classify and flag potential phishing emails. These AI systems analyze linguistic cues, sender reputation, and other contextual indicators to predict whether an email is fraudulent, often in real-time. This capability has proven essential for businesses that rely heavily on digital communication, as it minimizes the risk of data breaches stemming from phishing attacks (Zangana, Mohammed, Sallow, & Sallow, 2024).

Moreover, large language models (LLMs) have demonstrated potential in detecting phishing attempts by analyzing and generating responses that can simulate human judgment. For example, the GPT-2 Enhanced Attack Detection and Defense (GEADD) method, developed by Jones and Omar (2024), utilizes an LLM to assess and classify textual elements in digital communications. This method not only enhances phishing detection but also supports training for users to identify phishing attempts, thus building organizational resilience against social engineering attacks (Jones & Omar, 2024).

5.4 AI in Network Security and Rule Analysis

Network security heavily relies on firewalls and intrusion detection systems, which need frequent updates to counter new types of cyber threats. Zangana et al. (2024) present a comprehensive review of network firewall rule analyzers, which use AI to assess and optimize security rules, thus enhancing the efficiency of network defenses. These AI-based analyzers identify redundant or conflicting rules that could compromise network security, ensuring that the firewall remains resilient against emerging threats (Zangana, Omar, Al-Karaki, & Mohammed, 2024).

Furthermore, Adam and Varol (2020) discuss the importance of intelligence in the digital forensic process, emphasizing how AI's predictive capabilities support proactive threat detection. By analyzing previous cyber incidents, AI models can identify trends and patterns that aid in predicting future attacks, providing a proactive layer of defense that traditional methods lack. This approach enables cybersecurity professionals to preemptively address vulnerabilities and minimize the likelihood of successful cyber attacks (Adam & Varol, 2020).

5.5 Advanced Threat Detection and Countermeasures Using AI

One notable advancement in AI for cybercrime prevention is the development of sophisticated models for identifying zero-day vulnerabilities. These are previously unknown security flaws that hackers can exploit before they are patched. Omar (2024) introduces an optimized convolutional neural network (CNN) model designed to detect zero-day malware through anomaly detection, marking a paradigm shift in malware detection by focusing on behavior-based rather than signature-based detection. This AI-driven approach allows security teams to mitigate threats even in the absence of prior knowledge about the specific malware (Omar, 2024).

Additionally, Costantini, De Gasperis, and Olivieri (2019) provide insights into how AI enhances digital forensic investigations by integrating with existing forensic tools to facilitate the automated collection and analysis of digital evidence. This integration reduces the time required for evidence processing and increases the accuracy of findings, making AI an invaluable asset in high-stakes cybercrime investigations (Costantini, De Gasperis, & Olivieri, 2019).

5.6 Summary

The case studies discussed illustrate the profound impact AI has on cybercrime detection and fraud prevention, demonstrating how AI-driven solutions enhance the efficiency and effectiveness of digital forensics and fraud detection. AI not only accelerates response times and improves detection accuracy but also supports transparency and interpretability through XAI, providing a robust framework for combating sophisticated cyber threats. With continued advancements in AI, digital forensic teams and cybersecurity professionals can expect more powerful and adaptive tools, ensuring that they stay ahead in the ongoing battle against cybercrime and fraud.

6. CHALLENGES IN APPLYING AI TO CYBERCRIME AND FRAUD INVESTIGATIONS

The integration of artificial intelligence (AI) into cybercrime and fraud investigations presents transformative opportunities for efficiency and insight. However, numerous challenges also arise, many of which are technical, legal, and ethical. Addressing these obstacles requires a nuanced understanding of both AI technologies and the complexities inherent to digital forensics and cybersecurity.

6.1. Data Privacy and Legal Constraints

One of the primary challenges in applying AI to cybercrime investigations is the need to protect data privacy while collecting evidence. AI tools used in digital forensics must operate under strict legal standards to avoid infringing on individuals' rights to privacy (Hall et al., 2022). AI algorithms analyze vast amounts of data, which often include sensitive personal information, posing potential risks if this data is mishandled. Legal frameworks, such as the General Data Protection Regulation (GDPR), impose strict rules on data processing, which can complicate the integration of AI in investigations (Jarrett & Choo, 2021). Additionally, the cross-jurisdictional nature of cybercrime further complicates data sharing, as each region has its own legal requirements (Adam & Varol, 2020).

6.2. Lack of Standardization in Digital Forensics

Digital forensics currently lacks a universal standard for methodologies and practices, leading to inconsistencies in AI application across investigations. As AI technologies continue to evolve, this lack of standardization hinders interoperability among different forensic tools, limiting their effectiveness in investigations (Costantini et al., 2019). Bhawna and Mahajan (2024) emphasize that, to maximize AI's potential in this field, standard protocols must be established that enable AI-based forensic tools to operate uniformly across different cases and agencies.

6.3. Technical Complexity and Reliability of AI Algorithms

AI models, particularly those used in cybercrime investigations, are often complex and difficult to interpret, raising concerns about their reliability and transparency. Investigations frequently rely on black-box models, which can make it challenging for forensic analysts to justify AI-derived conclusions in court. Explainable AI (XAI) has been suggested as a solution to this issue, aiming to make AI's decision-making process more transparent (Kelly et al., 2020). However, achieving transparency without compromising the performance of the models is still an ongoing research area, with limited success so far (Hall et al., 2022).

Explainable AI (XAI) is pivotal for ensuring transparency and reliability in forensic investigations. The diagram below outlines a framework for integrating XAI into forensic workflows.

Figure 4. Explainable AI Framework in Forensics

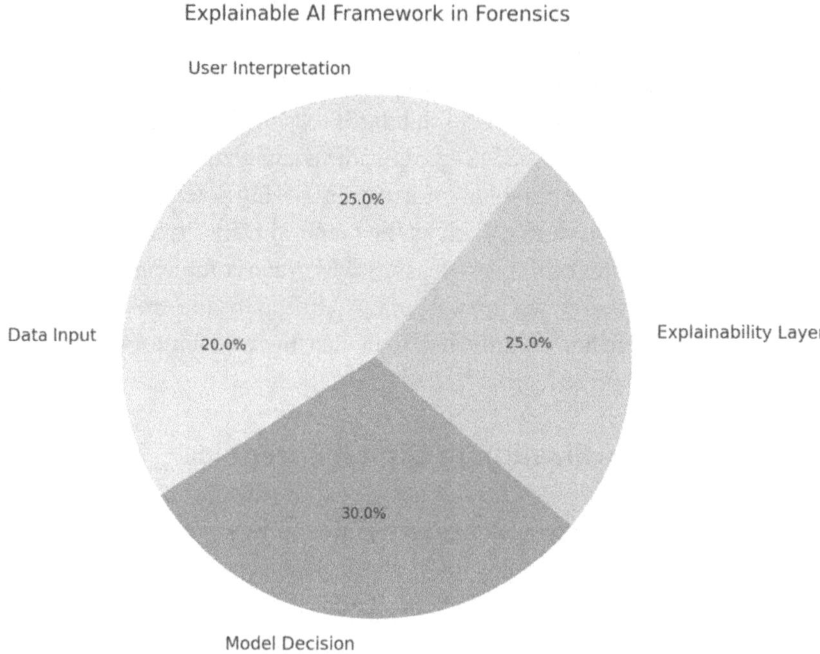

6.4. Scalability and Resource Requirements

AI applications in cybercrime investigations require considerable computational power and large datasets to function effectively. In resource-constrained environments, such as small law enforcement agencies, implementing sophisticated AI systems may be impractical due to the lack of infrastructure (Dunsin et al., 2022). Additionally, cybercriminals often use advanced technologies that evolve rapidly, requiring forensic tools that can scale and adapt to these advancements. Dunsin et al. (2024) discuss the importance of developing lightweight, scalable AI solutions tailored to environments with limited resources.

6.5. Evasion Tactics Employed by Cybercriminals

Cybercriminals are increasingly aware of the capabilities of AI-powered forensic tools and have begun developing methods to evade detection. These tactics include encryption, data obfuscation, and the use of advanced malware that adapts to evade AI detection (Ganesh, 2017). Zangana et al. (2024) highlight that as AI models become more adept at identifying certain patterns, criminals adapt their methods, creating a continuous cycle of evasion and detection. Developing AI models that can anticipate and counteract these evolving tactics is a significant challenge.

6.6. Ethical and Bias Concerns in AI-Driven Investigations

Ethical considerations are critical when deploying AI in cybercrime investigations, especially concerning bias within AI algorithms. Biases can unintentionally emerge in AI models due to the data they are trained on, leading to unfair or inaccurate results (Jeong, 2020). For instance, if a dataset used to train an AI model is unrepresentative, the model may produce biased outcomes, potentially leading to wrongful accusations or overlooked evidence (Rizvi et al., 2022). Efforts to address these issues involve developing more inclusive datasets and implementing ethical guidelines for AI in forensic investigations (Sikos, 2021).

6.7. Dependence on Specialized Expertise

AI-based forensic tools often require specialized knowledge to interpret and operate, creating a skills gap in many investigative teams. Forensic analysts may lack the technical expertise needed to leverage AI fully, which limits the technology's utility in investigations (Moustafa, 2022). Programs aimed at training forensic analysts in AI, as well as the development of user-friendly interfaces, are essential for overcoming this obstacle (Irons & Lallie, 2014).

6.8. Data Quality and Integrity Issues

Data quality is crucial in any AI-driven analysis, and digital forensics is no exception. Poor data quality or corruption can significantly impact the accuracy of AI models, leading to false positives or negatives in investigations. In digital forensics, ensuring the integrity of collected data is vital, as corrupted data can invalidate an entire case. Costantini et al. (2019) underscore the importance of maintaining rigorous standards for data collection, storage, and processing to ensure reliable AI outputs.

In conclusion, while AI holds significant promise for enhancing cybercrime and fraud investigations, addressing these challenges is essential to ensure its effective, ethical, and lawful application. Solutions to these challenges require collaborative efforts among AI developers, digital forensic experts, legal professionals, and policymakers to establish frameworks that balance technological advancements with privacy, transparency, and ethical considerations.

7. LEGAL, ETHICAL, AND PRIVACY CONSIDERATIONS

The integration of artificial intelligence (AI) into digital forensics introduces complex legal, ethical, and privacy challenges that demand careful consideration. As digital forensic investigations leverage AI for efficiency and accuracy, they must address issues concerning data protection, transparency, accountability, and adherence to legal frameworks to maintain public trust.

7.1 Legal Implications of AI in Digital Forensics

AI-driven digital forensics is governed by various laws and regulations, which aim to protect individuals' privacy and rights during investigations. Legally, forensic professionals must handle digital evidence in a manner compliant with laws such as the General Data Protection Regulation (GDPR) in Europe, which mandates the minimization of personal data collection and ensures transparency in data processing (Adam & Varol, 2020). The GDPR's "right to be forgotten" poses a challenge for forensic processes, as investigators may need to retain certain data to support future investigations. Forensic professionals must be trained to navigate this legal landscape to balance investigative efficacy with compliance (Costantini et al., 2019; Hall et al., 2022).

Furthermore, the increasing use of automated processes raises questions about liability and accountability, especially when AI algorithms make critical forensic decisions. For example, biases embedded in AI algorithms could lead to errors in evidence analysis, potentially affecting the outcomes of legal cases. Legal systems currently struggle to address who is accountable for such biases and errors – the developers of AI systems, forensic professionals, or the institutions deploying them (Jeong, 2020). Laws addressing AI accountability in forensic applications are crucial to resolving these ambiguities (Omar, 2024; Irons & Lallie, 2014).

7.2 Ethical Challenges in AI-Driven Forensics

Ethical issues in AI-enabled forensics are profound. AI can analyze vast datasets from various sources, raising ethical concerns about privacy invasion and consent. Collecting and analyzing personal information without individuals' explicit consent can lead to privacy violations, especially in cases involving sensitive information. It is ethically imperative for forensic professionals to adhere to guidelines ensuring that data collection respects individuals' privacy rights (Ganesh, 2017; Bhawna & Mahajan, 2024).

Another ethical concern is algorithmic transparency and fairness. AI models used in forensics often operate as "black boxes," making it challenging for forensic experts to understand how certain decisions were made. This opacity can lead to unintentional biases, particularly if datasets used to train AI models do not represent diverse populations. Ethical guidelines for AI in forensics call for transparent model design and thorough testing to minimize biases that could disproportionately affect certain demographic groups (Huff et al., 2023; Sikos, 2021).

7.3 Privacy Considerations in AI-Enhanced Forensic Investigations

The application of AI in digital forensics raises significant privacy concerns due to the large-scale processing of personal and often sensitive data. AI systems can access and analyze vast quantities of information, including private communications, location data, and personal identifiers. This extensive data processing can potentially infringe on individuals' privacy rights, especially in cases where data is collected without explicit consent (Jeong, 2020; Jarrett & Choo, 2021). Digital forensic investigators must employ strict privacy-preserving practices, ensuring that only data necessary for an investigation is processed, in compliance with privacy regulations.

Privacy-preserving AI techniques, such as federated learning and differential privacy, offer promising solutions by enabling collaborative model training across decentralized data sources without directly accessing sensitive information. Such methods can enhance privacy protections while maintaining the effectiveness of forensic investigations (Dunsin et al., 2024; Tyagi et al., 2024). Furthermore, blockchain-based timestamping tools provide a method to track data handling and access securely, ensuring transparency and traceability in forensic investigations (Zangana, 2024).

7.4 Balancing Security with Legal, Ethical, and Privacy Requirements

The use of AI in digital forensics necessitates a delicate balance between maintaining security and upholding legal, ethical, and privacy principles. AI-enhanced forensic tools must be designed to comply with existing laws and ethical standards, minimizing privacy intrusions while achieving investigative goals (Dunsin et al., 2022). In particular, explainable AI (XAI) methodologies offer transparency by making AI decision-making processes interpretable, thereby enhancing accountability and trustworthiness in digital forensics (Hall et al., 2022; Kelly et al., 2020).

Organizations implementing AI in digital forensics should establish ethical guidelines and provide comprehensive training for forensic professionals. This training should emphasize adherence to ethical practices, legal compliance, and privacy protection, ensuring that investigators can responsibly use AI tools without compromising individuals' rights (Rizvi et al., 2022; Gholami & Omar, 2024). Additionally, regulatory bodies must continuously update legal frameworks to address the evolving landscape of AI in digital forensics, ensuring that the legal system keeps pace with technological advancements.

In conclusion, AI's role in digital forensics introduces numerous legal, ethical, and privacy considerations. Effective solutions require collaboration between policymakers, forensic professionals, and AI developers to create frameworks that support responsible AI use. By prioritizing transparency, accountability, and compliance, the forensic community can harness AI's potential while upholding the rights and privacy of individuals involved in digital investigations.

8. FUTURE DIRECTIONS IN AI FOR CYBERCRIME AND FRAUD DETECTION

Artificial Intelligence (AI) holds vast potential to reshape the fields of cybercrime and fraud detection. Emerging technologies in AI—particularly large language models (LLMs), explainable AI (XAI), and advanced machine learning techniques—offer novel ways to address increasingly complex cyber threats and support digital forensic investigations.

8.1. Enhanced Explainability in AI Models

Future advancements in AI for cybercrime detection will likely focus on increasing the transparency of machine learning models. Explainable AI (XAI) techniques enable investigators and security experts to better understand AI-driven decisions, providing insights into the reasoning behind anomaly detection or fraud alerts (Hall, Sakzad, & Choo, 2022). Improved transparency is critical for forensic analyses where interpretability can determine the admissibility of AI-generated evidence in legal proceedings (Kelly et al., 2020).

8.2. Integration of LLMs for Fraud and Threat Detection

LLMs like GPT-3 and its successors, which demonstrate strong contextual understanding, are expected to play a greater role in cybersecurity and fraud detection. These models can process vast amounts of textual data, identify patterns, and flag potential threats in real-time. They could assist investigators in tracing digital footprints or interpreting coded language often used by cybercriminals (Omar & Zangana, 2025). Furthermore, studies indicate that the effectiveness of LLMs can be enhanced with synthetic data, which can increase the models' capacity to detect fraud and adapt to evolving cyber threats (Gholami & Omar, 2023).

Emerging trends in AI and their potential applications signify the next frontier in cybersecurity. The following chart highlights these key advancements and their anticipated impact.

Figure 5. Future Prospects in AI-Enhanced Cybersecurity

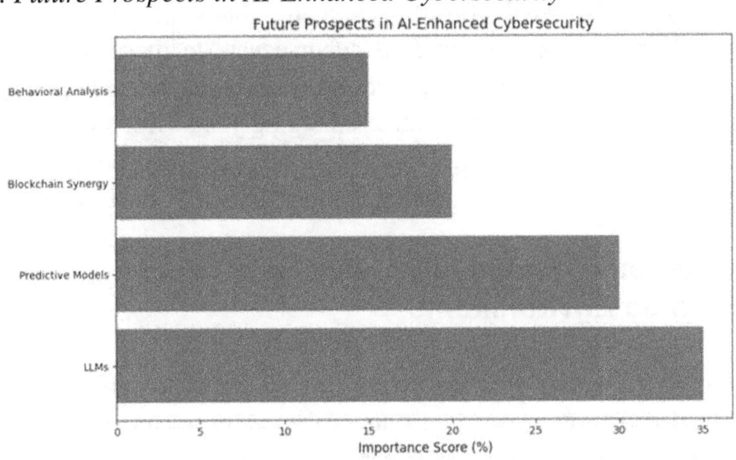

8.3. Application of AI in Digital Forensics for Evidence Collection and Analysis

Digital forensics is increasingly dependent on AI to gather, analyze, and interpret data from digital devices. AI can automate the identification and preservation of digital evidence, reducing the time needed for investigations and helping analysts manage the increasing volume and variety of data (Costantini, De Gasperis, & Olivieri, 2019). For example, digital forensic tools enhanced with machine learning capabilities can more quickly identify patterns indicative of cybercrimes, such as phishing or identity theft (Dunsin, Ghanem, & Quazzane, 2022). By employing these tools, forensic analysts can streamline evidence collection and focus on interpreting high-priority leads.

8.4. AI-Driven Deception Detection Techniques

A promising area for AI research is cyber deception detection, such as identifying phishing schemes or social engineering attacks. AI can analyze communication patterns and identify subtle cues that may indicate fraudulent intentions (Zangana et al., 2024). For instance, email filtering systems enhanced with AI can detect deceptive patterns in messaging, potentially reducing successful phishing attacks and mitigating the risks associated with fraud.

8.5. Behavioral Analysis for Enhanced Cybersecurity Measures

AI can analyze user behavior to detect anomalies that suggest fraudulent activity. By applying AI-driven behavioral analysis, cybersecurity teams can implement more proactive measures in fraud detection, creating systems that not only react to known threats but also anticipate and neutralize emerging risks (Irons & Lallie, 2014). These techniques help in profiling typical user behaviors and flagging deviations that may indicate compromised accounts or unauthorized activities (Sikos, 2021).

8.6. Automation of Forensic Processes in Constrained Environments

AI can support digital forensics in constrained environments, such as mobile devices and IoT ecosystems, where resources like processing power and storage are limited. Automated AI solutions can streamline data processing, enabling efficient evidence collection and analysis even in low-resource settings (Dunsin et al., 2024). This capability is critical as IoT devices are increasingly targeted by cybercriminals, and they often lack robust security measures (Jeong, 2020).

8.7. AI-Enhanced Network Forensics

AI can advance network forensics, particularly for real-time threat detection on corporate or public networks. Network forensic analysis often involves parsing large datasets to identify potential intrusions, suspicious patterns, or anomalies. AI-based solutions that specialize in network forensics can detect complex attack patterns, such as Advanced Persistent Threats (APTs), and provide a more accurate assessment of cybersecurity risks (Rizvi et al., 2022). For instance, AI can track unusual traffic patterns across networks, enabling more effective mitigation strategies and improved situational awareness (Zangana, Omar, Al-Karaki, & Mohammed, 2024).

8.8. AI in Predictive Analysis for Cybersecurity Preparedness

Predictive AI models may become essential tools in cybersecurity, helping organizations anticipate and prepare for potential cyber threats before they occur. These models can analyze historical data and simulate attack scenarios to predict vulnerabilities within an organization's infrastructure (Jarrett & Choo, 2021). Predictive analytics could help reduce the impact of cyber threats and optimize incident response strategies.

8.9. Blockchain and AI Synergy for Forensic Integrity

The intersection of AI and blockchain technology could improve the integrity and verifiability of digital forensic processes. Blockchain's immutability and AI's analytical power could be combined to ensure data integrity during evidence handling, enabling tamper-proof records and enhancing the credibility of forensic findings in legal contexts (Zangana, 2024).

8.10. Continued Development of AI Ethics and Regulations

As AI becomes increasingly integrated into cybersecurity, the need for regulatory frameworks and ethical guidelines will also grow. Addressing potential biases in AI models, ensuring privacy, and establishing industry standards will be essential to ensure that AI is used responsibly and fairly in detecting and combating cyber threats (Hamza & Omar, 2013). Ethical considerations are critical for the continued development of AI systems that are both effective and trustworthy in the fight against cybercrime (Adam & Varol, 2020).

In conclusion, future advancements in AI hold the potential to revolutionize cybercrime and fraud detection. As AI technology evolves, it will enable more sophisticated, proactive, and scalable solutions to mitigate cyber threats, making the digital space more secure for individuals, organizations, and societies. Continued research and development, combined with responsible implementation practices, will be essential to fully realize AI's promise in these critical areas of cybersecurity.

9. CONCLUSION

The integration of artificial intelligence into cybercrime and fraud detection represents a transformative advancement in the field of digital forensics. AI's capability to analyze vast quantities of data in real-time allows it to identify patterns and anomalies far beyond the reach of traditional forensic methods. These advancements are reshaping the approach to identifying cyber threats, enhancing the precision of investigations, and enabling proactive measures against evolving cyber threats. AI has not only accelerated the pace of forensic analysis but also introduced new methods for detecting and mitigating threats through predictive analytics and behavioral analysis, which were previously unavailable to cybersecurity professionals.

As cyber threats become more sophisticated, AI's role in digital forensics will continue to evolve. The complexity of cybercrime requires innovative, adaptable solutions that AI provides, from machine learning-based intrusion detection systems to large language models that assist in understanding and predicting attacker tactics. Despite the remarkable capabilities AI brings, challenges such as data privacy, ethical considerations, and ensuring the transparency of AI-driven processes remain critical. Addressing these challenges is essential to building trust in AI systems, especially in sensitive forensic investigations where the stakes are high.

The continued refinement of AI models, as well as their integration with existing cybersecurity frameworks, holds significant potential for advancing digital forensics. By leveraging AI's potential, forensic experts are better equipped to counter cyber threats in an increasingly interconnected digital world. However, as AI continues to shape the future of cybersecurity, the need for continuous learning, robust regulatory frameworks, and ethical practices in AI implementation becomes ever more pressing. These efforts will be essential to harnessing the full potential of AI in digital forensics and establishing a secure digital ecosystem for future generations.

REFERENCES

Adam, I. Y., & Varol, C. (2020, June). Intelligence in digital forensics process. In *2020 8th International Symposium on Digital Forensics and Security (ISDFS)* (pp. 1-6). IEEE. DOI: 10.1109/ISDFS49300.2020.9116442

Costantini, S., De Gasperis, G., & Olivieri, R. (2019). Digital forensics and investigations meet artificial intelligence. *Annals of Mathematics and Artificial Intelligence*, 86(1), 193–229. DOI: 10.1007/s10472-019-09632-y

Dunsin, D., Ghanem, M. C., Ouazzane, K., & Vassilev, V. (2024). A comprehensive analysis of the role of artificial intelligence and machine learning in modern digital forensics and incident response. *Forensic Science International Digital Investigation*, 48, 301675. DOI: 10.1016/j.fsidi.2023.301675

Dunsin, D., Ghanem, M. C., & Quazzane, K. (2022). The use of artificial intelligence in digital forensics and incident response in a constrained environment. *International Journal of Information and Communication Engineering*, 16(8), 280–285.

Ganesh, V. (2017). Artificial intelligence applied to computer forensics. *International Journal (Toronto, Ont.)*, 5(5).

Gholami, S., & Omar, M. (2023). Does Synthetic Data Make Large Language Models More Efficient? *arXiv preprint arXiv:2310.07830.*

Gholami, S., & Omar, M. (2024). Can a student large language model perform as well as its teacher? In *Innovations, Securities, and Case Studies Across Healthcare, Business, and Technology* (pp. 122-139). IGI Global. DOI: 10.4018/979-8-3693-1906-2.ch007

Hall, S. W., Sakzad, A., & Choo, K. K. R. (2022). Explainable artificial intelligence for digital forensics. *Wiley Interdisciplinary Reviews: Forensic Science*, 4(2), e1434.

Hamza, Y. A., & Omar, M. D. (2013). Cloud computing security: Abuse and nefarious use of cloud computing. *International Journal of Computer Engineering Research*, 3(6), 22–27.

Huff, A. J., Burrell, D. N., Nobles, C., Richardson, K., Wright, J. B., Burton, S. L., Jones, A. J., Springs, D., Omar, M., & Brown-Jackson, K. L. (2023). Management Practices for Mitigating Cybersecurity Threats to Biotechnology Companies, Laboratories, and Healthcare Research Organizations. In *Applied Research Approaches to Technology, Healthcare, and Business* (pp. 1-12). IGI Global.

Iqbal, F., Debbabi, M., Fung, B. C., Iqbal, F., Debbabi, M., & Fung, B. C. (2020). Artificial intelligence and digital forensics. *Machine Learning for Authorship Attribution and Cyber Forensics*, 139-150.

Irons, A., & Lallie, H. S. (2014). Digital forensics to intelligent forensics. *Future Internet*, 6(3), 584–596. DOI: 10.3390/fi6030584

Jarrett, A., & Choo, K. K. R. (2021). The impact of automation and artificial intelligence on digital forensics. *WIREs Forensic Science*, 3(6), e1418. DOI: 10.1002/wfs2.1418

Jeong, D. (2020). Artificial intelligence security threat, crime, and forensics: Taxonomy and open issues. *IEEE Access : Practical Innovations, Open Solutions*, 8, 184560–184574. DOI: 10.1109/ACCESS.2020.3029280

Jones, R., & Omar, M. (2024). Revolutionizing Cybersecurity: The GPT-2 Enhanced Attack Detection and Defense (GEADD) Method for Zero-Day Threats. *International Journal of Informatics* [INJIISCOM]. *Information System and Computer Engineering*, 5(2), 178–191.

Jones, R., Omar, M., Mohammed, D., Nobles, C., & Dawson, M. (2023). Harnessing the Speed and Accuracy of Machine Learning to Advance Cybersecurity. In *2023 Congress in Computer Science, Computer Engineering, & Applied Computing (CSCE)* (pp. 418-421). IEEE. DOI: 10.1109/CSCE60160.2023.00074

Karthikeyan, P., Pande, H. M., & Sarveshwaran, V. (Eds.). (2023). *Artificial intelligence and blockchain in digital forensics*. CRC Press.

Kelly, L., Sachan, S., Ni, L., Almaghrabi, F., Allmendinger, R., & Chen, Y. (2020). *Explainable artificial intelligence for digital forensics: opportunities, challenges and a drug testing case study*. Digital Forensic Science.

Manasa, S., & Kumar, K. P. (2022). Digital forensics investigation for attacks on artificial intelligence. *ECS Transactions*, 107(1), 19639–19645. DOI: 10.1149/10701.19639ecst

Mitchell, F. R. (2014). An overview of artificial intelligence based pattern matching in a security and digital forensic context. *Cyberpatterns: Unifying Design Patterns with Security and Attack Patterns*, 215-222.

Mohammed, D., Omar, M., & Nguyen, V. (2018). Wireless sensor network security: Approaches to detecting and avoiding wormhole attacks. *Journal of Research in Business. Economics and Management*, 10(2), 1860–1864.

Moustafa, N. (2022). *Digital Forensics in the Era of Artificial Intelligence*. CRC Press. DOI: 10.1201/9781003278962

Nguyen, V., Mohammed, D., Omar, M., & Banisakher, M. (2018). The Effects of the FCC Net Neutrality Repeal on Security and Privacy. [IJHIoT]. *International Journal of Hyperconnectivity and the Internet of Things*, 2(2), 21–29. DOI: 10.4018/IJHIoT.2018070102

Omar, M. (2021). New insights into database security: An effective and integrated approach for applying access control mechanisms and cryptographic concepts in Microsoft Access environments.

Omar, M. (2024). From Attack to Defense: Strengthening DNN Text Classification Against Adversarial Examples. In *Innovations, Securities, and Case Studies Across Healthcare, Business, and Technology* (pp. 174-195). IGI Global.

Omar, M. (2024). Revolutionizing Malware Detection: A Paradigm Shift Through Optimized Convolutional Neural Networks. In *Innovations, Securities, and Case Studies Across Healthcare, Business, and Technology* (pp. 196-220). IGI Global. DOI: 10.4018/979-8-3693-1906-2.ch011

Rizvi, S., Scanlon, M., Mcgibney, J., & Sheppard, J. (2022). Application of artificial intelligence to network forensics: Survey, challenges and future directions. *IEEE Access : Practical Innovations, Open Solutions*, 10, 110362–110384. DOI: 10.1109/ACCESS.2022.3214506

Rughani, P. H. (2017). Artificial Intelligence Based Digital Forensics Framework. *International Journal of Advanced Research in Computer Science*, 8(8), 10–14. DOI: 10.26483/ijarcs.v8i8.4571

Sikos, L. F. (2021). AI in digital forensics: Ontology engineering for cybercrime investigations. *WIREs Forensic Science*, 3(3), e1394. DOI: 10.1002/wfs2.1394

Tyagi, A. K., Kumari, S., & Richa. (2024). Artificial Intelligence-Based Cyber Security and Digital Forensics: A Review. Artificial Intelligence-Enabled Digital Twin for Smart Manufacturing, 391-419.

Wright, J., Dawson, M. E.Jr, & Omar, M. (2012). Cyber security and mobile threats: The need for antivirus applications for smartphones. *Journal of Information Systems Technology and Planning*, 5(14), 40–60.

Zangana, H. M., & Mohammed, D. (2025). Foundations of Large Language Models in Software Vulnerability Detection. In Omar, M., & Zangana, H. (Eds.), *Application of Large Language Models (LLMs) for Software Vulnerability Detection* (pp. 41–74). IGI Global., DOI: 10.4018/979-8-3693-9311-6.ch002

Chapter 5
Machine Learning in IoT and Mobile Device Forensics

Mahmoud Basharat
https://orcid.org/0009-0000-1859-5485
Capitol Technology University, USA

ABSTRACT

The increasing integration of the Internet of Things (IoT) and mobile devices in everyday life has led to significant advancements in the field of digital forensics. However, the complexity and volume of data generated by these devices pose challenges for traditional forensic methods. Machine learning (ML) has emerged as a powerful tool to address these challenges by enabling the automation of data analysis, anomaly detection, and pattern recognition in IoT and mobile device forensics. This chapter explores the role of machine learning in enhancing forensic investigations, with a focus on its application to IoT devices and mobile phones. It highlights various machine learning techniques, including supervised and unsupervised learning, deep learning, and reinforcement learning, and examines their potential in solving complex forensic cases. The chapter also discusses the ethical and legal considerations surrounding the use of machine learning in forensics, as well as its limitations and future prospects in the evolving landscape of digital forensics.

1. INTRODUCTION TO IOT AND MOBILE DEVICE FORENSICS

In recent years, the proliferation of Internet of Things (IoT) devices and mobile technologies has radically transformed how individuals and organizations interact with the digital world. With the increasing integration of smart devices into daily

DOI: 10.4018/979-8-3373-0857-9.ch005

life, ranging from smartphones and wearables to IoT-enabled appliances, the volume and complexity of digital data generated have expanded significantly. These developments present new challenges and opportunities in the field of digital forensics, particularly in the investigation of cybercrimes, data breaches, and other illegal activities. IoT and mobile devices serve as both sources and targets of digital forensics investigations, making it imperative to understand their unique characteristics and how they influence the forensic process.

IoT forensics pertains to the collection, analysis, and interpretation of digital evidence from interconnected devices that communicate over networks. These devices, which include smart home systems, industrial sensors, wearable health devices, and vehicles, often store and transmit sensitive data such as user behaviors, location information, and communication logs. Mobile device forensics, on the other hand, focuses on smartphones, tablets, and other portable devices that are commonly used for personal and business purposes. These devices hold critical evidence such as call logs, text messages, multimedia content, and application data, which are valuable in criminal investigations. Both IoT and mobile device forensics require specialized techniques for data extraction, preservation, and analysis, considering the proprietary nature of many devices and the constantly evolving technologies used in their design.

The complexities of IoT and mobile device forensics are compounded by issues such as encryption, data storage across cloud systems, and the sheer variety of devices and operating systems involved. Additionally, the sheer volume of data generated by IoT devices, combined with the frequent lack of standardization, makes it difficult for forensic experts to apply traditional digital forensics methodologies. For instance, IoT systems often lack the same level of logging and evidence-collection capabilities that are common in computer systems, necessitating the development of new tools and techniques for forensic investigation (Zangana et al., 2024; Zangana & Omar, 2020).

Recent advancements in artificial intelligence (AI) and machine learning (ML) have shown great potential in transforming IoT and mobile device forensics. AI techniques, such as machine learning-based anomaly detection, can help forensic investigators identify suspicious activities, correlate disparate data sources, and predict potential areas of interest for deeper investigation (Dunsin et al., 2024). These AI-powered tools can also automate tedious tasks such as data parsing, pattern recognition, and the extraction of valuable evidence from raw data, significantly reducing the time required for investigation and increasing accuracy.

The application of AI in digital forensics is not without challenges. Issues such as data integrity, the privacy of individuals, and the ethical implications of using AI-based tools in sensitive investigations must be considered (Bhawna & Mahajan, 2024; Jarrett & Choo, 2021). Furthermore, as AI and ML algorithms become more integrated into the forensic process, it is essential to ensure transparency and explainability, particularly when these technologies are used to make decisions that may affect legal proceedings (Hall et al., 2022; Costantini et al., 2019).

The process of IoT forensics involves various stages, including data collection, analysis, and interpretation. The following flowchart illustrates the key steps in handling forensic data from IoT devices, emphasizing the role of machine learning in automating these processes.

Figure 1. IoT Forensics Data Flow

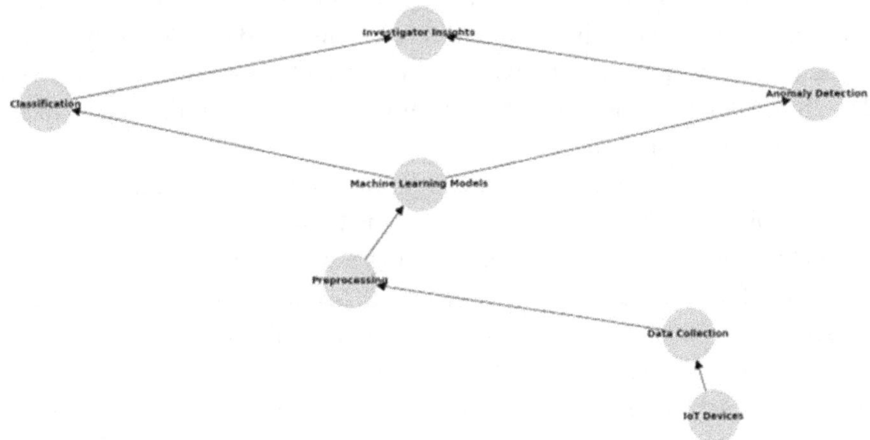

Ultimately, the intersection of IoT, mobile device forensics, and AI presents a dynamic landscape where traditional forensic methods must adapt to the challenges posed by new technologies. This chapter aims to explore the role of AI and ML in enhancing the capabilities of forensic investigators working with IoT and mobile devices, while also discussing the various issues and future directions for research in this emerging area of digital forensics.

2. ROLE OF MACHINE LEARNING IN IOT AND MOBILE DEVICE FORENSICS

In recent years, the convergence of **machine learning (ML)** with **digital forensics** has significantly enhanced the capabilities and effectiveness of investigations in IoT and mobile device environments. The pervasive integration of smart devices in daily life has led to an explosion of data, much of which is often critical for digital forensic investigations. Machine learning offers a robust framework for automating, optimizing, and scaling forensic processes, making it indispensable in the context of IoT and mobile device forensics.

2.1 Enhancing Data Analysis with Machine Learning

The core challenge in **IoT forensics** lies in the massive and heterogeneous datasets generated by interconnected devices, such as sensors, smart appliances, and wearable technologies. These devices produce varied data types, ranging from network logs to device-specific events, all of which must be meticulously examined to uncover evidence of cybercrime or policy violations. Traditional forensic methods are often too slow and error-prone to handle such large volumes of data effectively. Machine learning (ML) algorithms, particularly those related to **classification**, **clustering**, and **anomaly detection**, have proven to be invaluable tools for identifying relevant patterns and outliers in this data.

For instance, machine learning techniques such as **random forests**, **support vector machines (SVMs)**, and **deep learning networks** can classify vast amounts of raw data from IoT devices to quickly identify incidents like unauthorized access or device malfunctions (Bhawna & Mahajan, 2024). Moreover, anomaly detection models, trained on normal behavioral data, can automatically flag suspicious activities, enabling faster responses to potential threats (Dunsin, Ghanem, & Quazzane, 2022).

Different machine learning techniques play distinct roles in digital forensics, ranging from supervised learning for classification to deep learning for complex pattern recognition. The chart below provides a comparative analysis of these techniques and their applications in forensics.

Figure 2. Machine Learning Techniques for Forensics

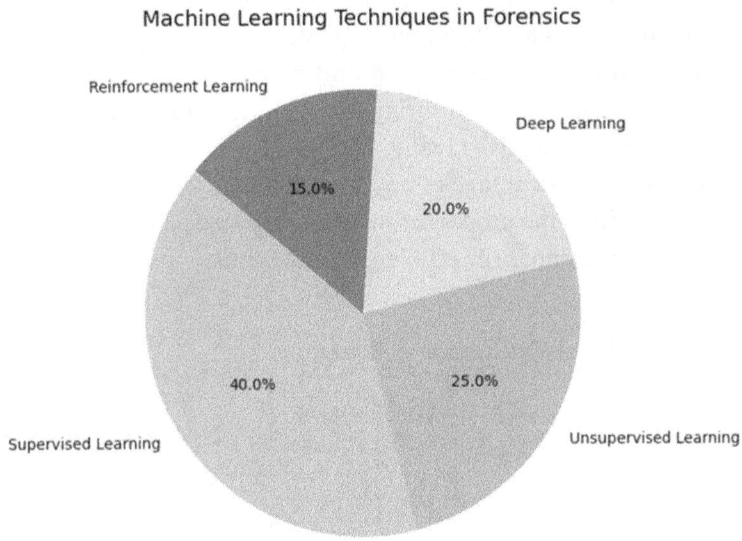

In **mobile device forensics**, the integration of machine learning allows investigators to efficiently process and analyze data from smartphones, which often includes call records, messaging history, location data, and app interactions. By applying natural language processing (NLP) models, investigators can retrieve valuable information from unstructured data, such as text messages or emails, in a much more streamlined manner (Jarrett & Choo, 2021).

2.2 Automating Forensic Investigations in IoT and Mobile Devices

One of the most significant advantages of incorporating machine learning into digital forensics is the automation of labor-intensive tasks. Investigating mobile device or IoT-related incidents often involves sifting through thousands of logs, files, and records manually, which is both time-consuming and prone to human error. ML algorithms can be trained to automatically parse and sort these data sets, identifying key pieces of evidence much faster than manual methods would allow.

For instance, in the context of mobile device forensics, machine learning can automate the identification of **malware** by analyzing the behavioral patterns of apps, detecting anomalies that are indicative of malicious intent (Wright, Dawson Jr., & Omar, 2012). This level of automation not only speeds up the investigation process but also ensures that the analysis is consistent and unbiased, which is crucial for maintaining the integrity of forensic procedures (Hall, Sakzad, & Choo, 2022).

Similarly, in IoT forensics, machine learning can be used to monitor network traffic and **device interactions** for signs of compromise. Using a combination of **supervised** and **unsupervised learning** approaches, machine learning can detect patterns of **data exfiltration, command-and-control** communications, or **compromised firmware** on devices, ensuring that incidents are detected early and that investigations are more effective (Jeong, 2020).

Automation is a key advantage of applying machine learning in forensics. The workflow below outlines the process of incident response using ML models, showcasing how automation enhances efficiency and accuracy.

Figure 3. Automated Incident Response Workflow

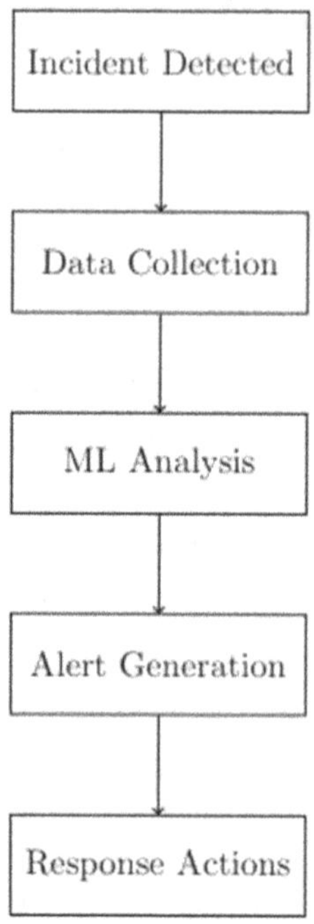

2.3 Handling the Unique Challenges of IoT and Mobile Forensics

Despite the promise of machine learning, several challenges remain when applying ML to IoT and mobile forensics. First, the diversity of IoT devices presents a challenge for forensic investigations. Devices come with varying levels of security, firmware versions, and data collection methods, making it difficult to apply a one-size-fits-all approach to forensic analysis. As noted by Zangana (2024), researchers are working on creating more **robust ML models** capable of adapting to this diverse environment by training on a wide range of device data and evolving attack patterns.

Moreover, the **privacy concerns** associated with mobile device forensics are heightened when applying machine learning. Sensitive data, such as personal communications, location information, and financial records, are often critical to investigations. This raises significant concerns about **data privacy** and the ethical use of machine learning in sensitive contexts (Sikos, 2021). It is essential that the application of ML in digital forensics adheres to strict privacy guidelines, ensuring that personal information is not unnecessarily exposed or misused.

Finally, the **evolving nature of cyber threats** means that machine learning models need to be continually updated to detect new and emerging forms of attack. As stated by **Omar & Zangana** (2024), keeping forensic algorithms up to date is crucial to maintaining their effectiveness in the face of increasingly sophisticated cybercrime tactics.

2.4 Future Directions and Research

Looking ahead, machine learning's role in IoT and mobile device forensics will continue to grow as the technology matures and the landscape of cybercrime evolves. Future research will likely focus on developing more **explainable AI** (XAI) models that can provide clear, interpretable reasoning behind the predictions made by machine learning systems (Costantini, De Gasperis, & Olivieri, 2019). This is especially important in forensic investigations, where transparency and the ability to validate AI-driven decisions are paramount.

Moreover, researchers are exploring the integration of machine learning with other **emerging technologies** such as **blockchain** and **cloud forensics**, which could enhance the ability to preserve the integrity of digital evidence (Zangana & Omar, 2025). With these advancements, the future of digital forensics promises to be more efficient, secure, and capable of handling the complexities of modern cyber threats across IoT and mobile ecosystems.

In conclusion, machine learning offers immense potential for advancing **IoT and mobile device forensics** by improving automation, scalability, and efficiency in investigations. As the field continues to evolve, it will be essential to address the privacy, ethical, and technical challenges to fully leverage its benefits in the quest for digital justice.

3. APPLICATIONS OF MACHINE LEARNING IN IOT FORENSICS

The integration of **Machine Learning (ML)** in **Internet of Things (IoT) forensics** has emerged as a promising solution to tackle the complexity of investigating cybercrimes involving IoT devices. These devices, which range from smart home systems to industrial equipment, generate vast amounts of data that can be invaluable in forensic investigations. However, the sheer volume, diversity, and dynamic nature of IoT data present significant challenges. By applying machine learning techniques, forensics experts can automate data analysis, enhance detection accuracy, and improve investigative workflows.

The data sources in IoT and mobile forensics vary significantly in terms of volume, structure, and analysis requirements. The bar chart below compares the characteristics of key data sources in these domains.

Figure 4. Comparison of Data Sources in IoT and Mobile Forensics

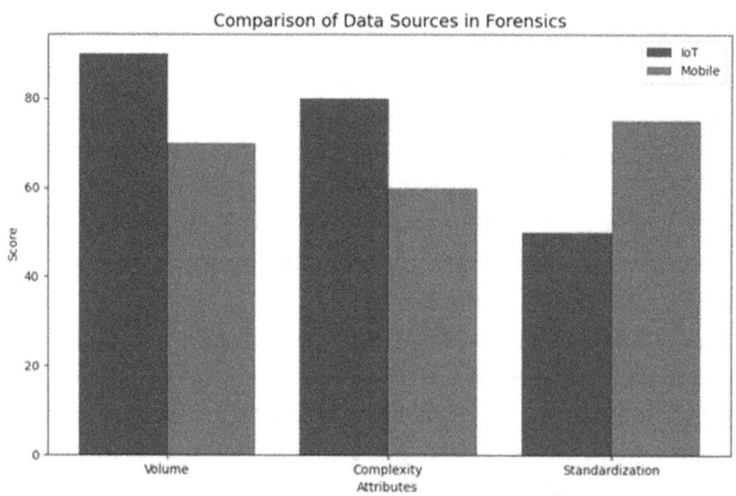

3.1. Data Classification and Anomaly Detection

One of the key challenges in IoT forensics is efficiently classifying and analyzing the massive amounts of data generated by IoT devices. Machine learning models, particularly **supervised learning** techniques, have been successfully employed to classify IoT data based on predefined categories. For example, **classification algorithms** such as decision trees, random forests, and support vector machines (SVM) can categorize data from IoT devices into normal and suspicious activities. These algorithms can also help in detecting unauthorized access or abnormal behavior that could indicate a security breach.

In addition, **unsupervised learning** techniques, like clustering and anomaly detection, are vital for uncovering unknown threats. By analyzing the behavior of devices in a network, ML can detect anomalous patterns that deviate from typical usage, which might be indicative of malicious activity. For example, **autoencoders** and **k-means clustering** can be used to identify outliers in IoT device behavior, assisting forensic investigators in detecting hidden attacks or devices that have been compromised (Zangana et al., 2024).

3.2. Automated Incident Response

The use of ML in automating incident response is a key advancement in the realm of IoT forensics. With the ability to analyze data in real time, ML models can identify and respond to security incidents much faster than traditional methods. For instance, when an IoT device exhibits suspicious activity, such as unexpected data transmission or control signals, machine learning systems can automatically trigger predefined responses, such as isolating the affected device, alerting security teams, or even initiating corrective actions like resetting the device or blocking specific communication channels.

This approach significantly reduces the time required to detect and respond to potential threats, which is crucial in minimizing damage during an attack. By utilizing reinforcement learning, ML models can continuously improve their response strategies based on the outcomes of previous incidents (Dunsin et al., 2024).

3.3. Digital Evidence Extraction and Analysis

Machine learning models have also found applications in extracting valuable digital evidence from IoT devices. Given the wide range of devices and platforms in the IoT ecosystem, manual data collection and analysis can be tedious and error-prone. ML algorithms can automate the extraction of logs, communication patterns, and configuration settings from devices and aggregate this data for analysis.

Furthermore, **natural language processing (NLP)** techniques are increasingly used in IoT forensics to analyze textual data from devices like voice assistants, smart cameras, and messaging platforms. This allows for the extraction of insights from logs, text messages, or even audio recordings, which can be crucial for understanding the context of an incident (Omar & Zangana, 2024).

3.4. IoT Forensic Evidence Correlation

Correlating evidence from various IoT devices is a complex task, as IoT systems often consist of heterogeneous devices communicating over different protocols. Machine learning models, especially **graph-based models** and **neural networks**, can assist in connecting disparate pieces of forensic data across IoT devices. These models can uncover hidden relationships between devices and identify suspicious communication channels or behaviors that may otherwise go unnoticed.

For example, **graph neural networks (GNNs)** can be used to model the interactions between IoT devices in a network and analyze how they influence each other during an incident. This technique can help trace the origin of a cyber attack by identifying compromised devices and the path the attacker took within the network (Zangana et al., 2024).

3.5. Predictive Forensics and Cyber Threat Intelligence

ML techniques also enable predictive forensics, where the system learns from historical data and trends to forecast potential security incidents. By analyzing patterns from past cyber attacks and incidents, machine learning models can identify emerging threats and predict the likelihood of similar attacks in the future. These predictive capabilities can inform proactive security measures and help investigators focus on high-risk areas.

Moreover, **cyber threat intelligence (CTI)** platforms powered by ML can gather, correlate, and analyze data from multiple IoT sources, providing real-time intelligence on emerging threats. This assists investigators in staying ahead of potential threats and enables more efficient resource allocation during forensic investigations (Bhawna & Mahajan, 2024; Zangana et al., 2024).

3.6. Explainable AI (XAI) for Forensic Investigations

As machine learning models become more integrated into IoT forensics, ensuring that these systems remain interpretable is critical. **Explainable AI (XAI)** techniques are increasingly being adopted to make ML models' decision-making processes transparent to forensic investigators. In IoT forensics, XAI can provide clear explanations of why a particular IoT device or behavior is flagged as suspicious, helping investigators trust and act on the results produced by ML models.

This transparency is particularly important in legal settings, where forensic findings may need to be presented as evidence in court. The integration of XAI ensures that decisions made by machine learning models can be understood and justified, enhancing the credibility of forensic investigations (Hall et al., 2022; Costantini et al., 2019).

3.7. Challenges and Future Directions

Despite the significant advantages of applying machine learning in IoT forensics, several challenges remain. These include the complexity of IoT ecosystems, data privacy concerns, the need for large labeled datasets for training ML models, and the difficulty of ensuring the explainability of ML models. Future research should focus on developing more robust and adaptable machine learning algorithms that can handle the dynamic and diverse nature of IoT data while addressing these challenges.

In particular, advances in **federated learning**, which allows for decentralized model training without sharing sensitive data, could provide a solution to privacy concerns in IoT forensics. Additionally, **transfer learning** may help in overcoming the scarcity of labeled data, enabling models to generalize across various IoT environments (Dunsin et al., 2022).

3.8 Summary

The application of machine learning in IoT forensics represents a major leap forward in how cybercrimes involving IoT devices are investigated and resolved. By automating data analysis, enhancing detection capabilities, and enabling predictive forensics, ML is revolutionizing the way digital forensic experts approach IoT-related incidents. As IoT ecosystems continue to evolve, the ongoing integration of machine learning techniques will be crucial in ensuring that forensic investigators can effectively combat new and emerging threats in this complex and rapidly changing domain.

4. APPLICATIONS OF MACHINE LEARNING IN MOBILE DEVICE FORENSICS

Mobile device forensics is a critical aspect of digital forensics that involves the recovery, analysis, and investigation of data stored on mobile devices such as smartphones and tablets. With the growing prevalence of mobile devices in our daily lives, they have become essential tools for communication, financial transactions, and data storage. As a result, mobile devices are often key sources of evidence in criminal investigations and cybercrime analysis. The advent of machine learning (ML) and artificial intelligence (AI) has significantly transformed mobile device forensics, enabling more efficient, accurate, and scalable investigative techniques.

4.1. Data Extraction and Classification

Machine learning has revolutionized the extraction and classification of data from mobile devices. Traditionally, forensic investigators relied on manual methods to recover data, which were time-consuming and prone to human error. However, ML models can be trained to automatically identify and classify various types of data, such as images, messages, app data, and call logs, from mobile devices. This automation helps investigators process large volumes of data quickly and accurately.

Techniques such as supervised learning have been applied to classify data based on pre-labeled examples. For instance, a machine learning model can be trained to identify suspicious files or behaviors on a mobile device based on patterns found in previous investigations (Dunsin et al., 2024). Furthermore, deep learning approaches, such as convolutional neural networks (CNNs), are capable of recognizing more complex patterns in multimedia files, improving the accuracy of data classification (Omar, 2024). These techniques streamline the investigation process, allowing forensic experts to focus on analyzing critical evidence rather than sorting through massive amounts of data.

4.2. Detection of Malicious Software and Malware

Mobile devices are prime targets for cybercriminals, who often use malware to gain unauthorized access to sensitive information. The detection of malicious software and malware on mobile devices is a challenging task due to the constantly evolving nature of these threats. However, machine learning techniques, particularly anomaly detection and pattern recognition, have proven effective in identifying malicious activity on mobile devices.

By training models on known malware samples and normal device behavior, machine learning algorithms can detect anomalies indicative of malware infections. For example, if a mobile device exhibits behavior that deviates from typical usage patterns, such as excessive data transmission or unusual app permissions, an ML model can flag this as suspicious (Tyagi et al., 2024). In this context, ML not only assists in identifying known threats but also helps in the detection of previously unknown malware through behavioral analysis (Rizvi et al., 2022).

4.3. Forensic Data Reconstruction

Reconstructing deleted or hidden data is a significant challenge in mobile device forensics. While traditional methods may recover deleted files using techniques like file carving or data fragment reconstruction, these approaches are limited in their ability to reconstruct fragmented data that may have been overwritten. Machine learning offers a more advanced approach to this problem by enabling predictive models to infer deleted or hidden data based on existing patterns.

For instance, using unsupervised learning, a model can be trained to recognize the structure of data within a file system. This approach has been successful in recovering fragmented files or identifying hidden files that are not easily accessible through traditional methods (Gholami & Omar, 2024). Machine learning models can also be used to predict the likelihood of data being overwritten and estimate the potential for successful data recovery, providing forensic investigators with valuable insights into the integrity of mobile device data.

4.4. Analysis of Mobile Application Behavior

Mobile applications are ubiquitous on smartphones, and they can serve as a source of digital evidence in investigations. However, mobile applications often collect sensitive user data, such as location information, contacts, and browsing history, which may not be easily accessible through conventional forensic tools. Machine learning has proven useful in analyzing mobile application behavior to identify data leakage or other suspicious activities.

By employing behavioral analysis techniques, machine learning models can identify anomalous behaviors in mobile apps. For example, if an app is transmitting data to a server without the user's knowledge or consent, ML models can flag such activities as suspicious, alerting forensic investigators to potential security breaches (Bhawna & Mahajan, 2024). Additionally, ML algorithms can be applied to analyze the interactions between different applications on a mobile device to uncover hidden relationships between apps, users, and potentially malicious actors (Kelly et al., 2020).

4.5. Automated Reporting and Evidence Interpretation

One of the most significant advantages of machine learning in mobile device forensics is its ability to automate the reporting and interpretation of forensic evidence. Traditional forensic methods often involve extensive manual analysis, which can be time-consuming and error-prone. Machine learning models, particularly natural language processing (NLP) techniques, can be used to generate automated forensic reports, making it easier for investigators to interpret large datasets quickly.

For example, NLP can be used to extract relevant information from messages, emails, and social media posts on mobile devices. These techniques can summarize key events, identify correlations between different pieces of evidence, and even suggest possible criminal activities (Hall et al., 2022). Additionally, machine learning can assist in ranking evidence by relevance, enabling investigators to prioritize their analysis and identify critical data faster.

4.6. Privacy and Ethical Concerns

While the application of machine learning in mobile device forensics brings numerous benefits, it also raises privacy and ethical concerns. The use of AI and ML to analyze mobile devices may inadvertently expose sensitive personal information, leading to potential violations of privacy. Furthermore, the effectiveness of machine learning models depends on the quality of the data used to train them, which can lead to biased results if not carefully managed.

To address these concerns, it is essential to implement robust privacy protection measures and ensure that machine learning models are transparent and explainable. Explainable AI (XAI) techniques can be employed to provide investigators with clear explanations of how the models arrived at their conclusions, which is critical for maintaining the integrity of the forensic process (Jeong, 2020; Jarrett & Choo, 2021).

4.7. Future Directions and Challenges

Despite the promising applications of machine learning in mobile device forensics, there are several challenges that need to be addressed. One major issue is the need for more advanced models that can handle the complexity and diversity of mobile devices and their operating systems. As mobile technology continues to evolve, so too must the machine learning techniques used to analyze mobile devices. Additionally, the increasing use of encryption and privacy-enhancing technologies in mobile devices presents new hurdles for forensic investigators, requiring the development of novel techniques to access and analyze encrypted data.

Looking ahead, the integration of machine learning with other emerging technologies, such as blockchain and quantum computing, may offer new opportunities for enhancing mobile device forensics. For example, blockchain could provide an immutable and transparent ledger for forensic investigations, while quantum computing could potentially accelerate the processing of large datasets (Zangana & Omar, 2025).

4.8 Summary

Machine learning has become a powerful tool in mobile device forensics, enhancing the capabilities of forensic investigators in areas such as data extraction, malware detection, forensic reconstruction, and evidence interpretation. However, challenges related to privacy, ethics, and technological advancements remain. As mobile devices continue to play a central role in modern life, the role of machine learning in mobile forensics will undoubtedly grow, offering new opportunities and solutions for digital investigators.

5. KEY MACHINE LEARNING TECHNIQUES USED IN FORENSICS

Machine learning (ML) has become an essential tool in modern digital forensics, enhancing the capabilities of forensic experts to investigate cybercrimes efficiently and accurately. Various machine learning techniques are being integrated into forensic tools to analyze vast amounts of digital evidence, detect anomalies, and provide actionable insights. Below, we explore several key ML techniques that are transforming the field of digital forensics.

5.1. Supervised Learning

Supervised learning is one of the most widely applied ML techniques in digital forensics. This technique involves training a model on labeled data, where the input data and corresponding output labels are provided to the model during the training phase. The model then learns the relationship between the inputs and outputs and can make predictions on new, unseen data.

In the context of digital forensics, supervised learning has been used for tasks such as intrusion detection, malware classification, and digital evidence classification. For example, Costantini, De Gasperis, and Olivieri (2019) discuss the application of supervised learning in identifying known patterns in cyber-attacks, enabling quicker detection and classification of malicious activities. In network forensics, supervised learning models are trained to identify patterns of network traffic that match previous attack vectors, which can significantly reduce the time spent on manual investigations.

5.2. Unsupervised Learning

Unsupervised learning, in contrast to supervised learning, does not require labeled data. Instead, the algorithm identifies hidden patterns or structures within the data. This technique is particularly useful in scenarios where labeled datasets are unavailable or incomplete.

Unsupervised learning has been effectively applied in anomaly detection, where it is used to identify unusual patterns that may indicate a security breach or cybercrime activity. Zangana et al. (2024) highlight how unsupervised learning techniques such as clustering and anomaly detection are utilized to detect new and unknown attack types by analyzing deviations from normal system behavior. By clustering similar incidents, forensic experts can prioritize their investigations, focusing on those that appear to be most anomalous or malicious.

5.3. Deep Learning

Deep learning, a subset of machine learning, utilizes neural networks with many layers (hence "deep") to model complex relationships within data. Deep learning techniques, particularly Convolutional Neural Networks (CNNs) and Recurrent Neural Networks (RNNs), have shown remarkable success in analyzing large-scale data, making them valuable for digital forensic applications.

Deep learning is widely used for tasks like image analysis, voice recognition, and text analysis within the forensic domain. For instance, in image forensics, CNNs are employed to detect alterations or tampering in digital images, which can be crucial in verifying the authenticity of digital evidence. Hall, Sakzad, and Choo (2022) emphasize the use of explainable deep learning models for forensic analysis, where the process and results can be understood and validated by forensic experts. This transparency is essential when dealing with legal investigations.

5.4. Natural Language Processing (NLP)

Natural Language Processing (NLP), a field of artificial intelligence that focuses on the interaction between computers and human languages, is another key ML technique utilized in digital forensics. NLP can process and analyze large volumes of textual data, such as emails, social media posts, or chat logs, to identify evidence of criminal activity.

In digital forensics, NLP is used for tasks such as sentiment analysis, text classification, and authorship attribution. Tools powered by NLP techniques can help forensic experts identify threats such as phishing attacks, social engineering, and other forms of online fraud. Dunsin et al. (2024) explore how NLP algorithms are applied to email forensics, analyzing the language used to detect potential phishing attempts or fraud.

5.5. Reinforcement Learning

Reinforcement learning (RL) is a type of ML where agents learn to make decisions by interacting with an environment and receiving feedback through rewards or punishments. While still an emerging area in digital forensics, RL shows great potential for automating investigative processes.

RL can be used to develop systems that autonomously learn optimal investigation strategies by interacting with various types of data. For instance, RL-based models could help automate the process of incident response, suggesting the most effective methods for handling specific types of security incidents. Zangana et al. (2024) suggest that reinforcement learning could significantly enhance the efficiency of digital forensics tools by continuously improving their detection and response capabilities based on past experiences.

5.6. Generative Adversarial Networks (GANs)

Generative Adversarial Networks (GANs) are a class of machine learning techniques in which two neural networks (the generator and the discriminator) compete against each other. While GANs are widely used in data generation tasks such as creating realistic images, they can also play a role in digital forensics.

In digital forensics, GANs can be used for data augmentation, where they generate synthetic data that can be used to train forensic models when real data is limited or difficult to acquire. Gholami and Omar (2024) suggest that GANs could be employed to simulate various forensic scenarios, providing forensic experts with diverse datasets to improve their models' generalization capabilities. Furthermore, GANs can assist in improving the robustness of forensic systems against adversarial attacks by learning to identify and counteract manipulated data.

5.7. Explainable AI (XAI)

Explainable Artificial Intelligence (XAI) is a subfield of AI that focuses on creating models whose decisions and actions can be easily understood by humans. XAI is especially important in digital forensics, as forensic investigators need to trust and understand the decisions made by AI-powered systems.

Hall, Sakzad, and Choo (2022) argue that XAI is crucial in ensuring that AI-driven forensic tools provide transparent and interpretable results. In legal contexts, the ability to explain how an AI model arrived at a conclusion is essential for ensuring the validity of evidence. In the case of automated analysis of digital evidence, XAI helps forensic experts verify the findings and determine the relevance of specific evidence.

5.8. Support Vector Machines (SVMs)

Support Vector Machines (SVMs) are supervised learning algorithms that are particularly effective in classification and regression tasks. SVMs have been applied in digital forensics to classify data, such as identifying whether a specific file or network packet is benign or malicious.

SVMs have been used in intrusion detection systems to classify network traffic as normal or abnormal, helping forensic investigators identify potential breaches or attacks. Dunsin et al. (2022) highlight how SVMs are applied to network forensics to classify different types of cyber threats based on traffic patterns and other relevant features.

5.9 Summary

Machine learning techniques have revolutionized the field of digital forensics by automating and enhancing various aspects of forensic investigations. From supervised and unsupervised learning to deep learning and reinforcement learning, these techniques enable forensic experts to process and analyze large volumes of data, detect new attack patterns, and make more informed decisions. As technology continues to evolve, the integration of advanced machine learning techniques will undoubtedly play a pivotal role in the future of digital forensics.

6. CASE STUDIES OF MACHINE LEARNING IN IOT AND MOBILE FORENSICS

The intersection of machine learning (ML) and digital forensics has become increasingly pivotal, especially within the domains of Internet of Things (IoT) and mobile forensics. These fields generate vast amounts of data that require sophisticated methods for analysis and investigation. Machine learning techniques provide automated, scalable solutions to detect anomalies, predict potential threats, and even reconstruct digital events. In this section, we delve into case studies that demonstrate the application of machine learning in IoT and mobile forensics, highlighting their capabilities, challenges, and future potential.

6.1. Enhancing IoT Forensics through Machine Learning: A Case Study on Smart Home Devices

IoT devices, particularly those in smart homes, continuously collect and transmit sensitive data, making them lucrative targets for cybercriminals. In a case study conducted by Zangana et al. (2024), machine learning techniques were deployed to analyze network traffic generated by smart home devices, identifying potential security breaches. Through anomaly detection algorithms, such as unsupervised learning techniques, the system was able to flag suspicious activities that could indicate unauthorized access or tampering. Machine learning algorithms like clustering and decision trees were used to classify network behaviors into normal and anomalous categories, improving the response time to security incidents.

Moreover, the study by Dunsin et al. (2022) explored the use of supervised learning models to predict IoT device vulnerabilities. By training classifiers on historical data of IoT breaches, the system could identify high-risk devices before they were compromised. This proactive approach allowed for timely interventions, ensuring the integrity of IoT ecosystems in connected environments.

6.2. Mobile Forensics and Machine Learning: Extracting Critical Evidence from Smartphones

Smartphones are a rich source of evidence in digital forensics, containing communications, location data, application usage history, and much more. Machine learning has been effectively applied in extracting and analyzing this data in various forensic investigations. In a case study by Bhawna and Mahajan (2024), machine learning algorithms were utilized to analyze smartphone data to detect fraudulent activities. By applying classification algorithms such as support vector machines (SVM) and deep learning models, investigators were able to identify suspicious patterns of app usage and communication that indicated illegal activities.

In mobile forensics, the vast volume of data poses a significant challenge in extracting relevant evidence efficiently. Jarrett and Choo (2021) highlighted the adoption of natural language processing (NLP) techniques, an area within machine learning, to analyze text messages and social media interactions on smartphones. This allowed for the quick extraction of critical communication evidence, even from encrypted or partially corrupted files. The application of NLP not only speeds up the forensic analysis but also ensures that no crucial detail is overlooked.

6.3. AI-Powered Automated Digital Forensics in Constrained Environments

Dunsin et al. (2024) examined the application of machine learning in digital forensics within constrained environments, such as low-resource IoT devices or smartphones with limited storage capacity. Traditional forensic tools often struggle to work effectively in these settings due to the lack of computational resources. The case study introduced an AI-powered forensic tool that utilized lightweight machine learning models to analyze data from such constrained devices. By leveraging feature selection techniques, the system could prioritize relevant data points and reduce the computational overhead required for analysis, making it possible to conduct forensic investigations in resource-limited environments.

6.4. The Role of Machine Learning in Email Phishing Detection: A Case Study in Mobile Forensics

Mobile devices are a common platform for phishing attacks, which are often carried out through fraudulent emails or text messages. Zangana et al. (2024) explored the use of machine learning to detect phishing attempts in mobile forensics. In their study, they used a combination of supervised learning and natural language processing to analyze email metadata and content. The system was able to accurately classify phishing emails based on features such as suspicious URLs, email addresses, and linguistic patterns typical of phishing attempts.

This approach has significant implications for mobile forensics, where investigators often encounter phishing-related evidence that requires swift analysis to prevent further damage. The use of machine learning models that continuously learn and adapt to new phishing techniques ensures the system's effectiveness in identifying novel threats.

6.5. Predicting Cybersecurity Threats in IoT Networks Using ML Algorithms

The increasing interconnectivity of IoT devices exposes networks to a wide range of cyber threats. In the case study by Rizvi et al. (2022), machine learning models were implemented to predict and mitigate potential security risks in IoT networks. By analyzing historical data from IoT networks, the system used predictive modeling techniques such as time series forecasting to identify potential vulnerabilities before they could be exploited. The study demonstrated that machine learning could significantly reduce the time required for threat detection and response, thus strengthening the overall security posture of IoT networks.

6.6. AI-Driven Forensics in Network Security: Analyzing Firewall Logs with ML

In the context of network forensics, firewalls play a crucial role in protecting against unauthorized access. Zangana et al. (2024) conducted a study on using machine learning to analyze network firewall logs, which are often voluminous and challenging to manually examine. The researchers applied clustering and classification algorithms to identify patterns in the data that indicated potential security incidents, such as intrusion attempts or unauthorized data exfiltration. By automating the analysis of these logs, the system could detect emerging threats much faster than traditional methods, allowing security teams to respond proactively.

6.7. Exploring Blockchain and AI Integration for IoT Forensics

Blockchain technology, when integrated with AI, offers a novel solution for preserving the integrity of digital evidence in IoT forensics. Zangana (2024) reviewed the application of blockchain-based timestamping tools to track the provenance of digital evidence in IoT environments. Machine learning was used to verify the authenticity of the data recorded on the blockchain, ensuring that the evidence had not been tampered with. This combination of blockchain and AI helps investigators maintain a reliable chain of custody, which is critical in legal contexts.

6.8 Summary

Machine learning is revolutionizing digital forensics in IoT and mobile environments, providing investigators with powerful tools to automate the analysis of large and complex datasets. From enhancing security in IoT networks to detecting phishing attempts on mobile devices, machine learning algorithms enable faster, more accurate investigations. However, challenges such as data privacy concerns, algorithmic bias, and the need for continual adaptation to new threats must be addressed to ensure the reliability and effectiveness of these systems. As machine learning continues to evolve, its integration with other technologies like blockchain promises to further strengthen the capabilities of digital forensics in the future.

7. CHALLENGES AND LIMITATIONS OF MACHINE LEARNING IN IOT AND MOBILE FORENSICS

The integration of machine learning (ML) into the domains of Internet of Things (IoT) and mobile forensics has brought significant advancements in enhancing digital investigation capabilities. However, this transformation also introduces a series of challenges and limitations that must be addressed for these technologies to reach their full potential.

7.1 Data Complexity and Volume

One of the primary challenges in IoT and mobile forensics is the enormous amount of data generated by these systems. IoT devices, by their nature, produce vast quantities of real-time data, often at high velocities, which can overwhelm traditional forensic analysis methods (Adam & Varol, 2020). Mobile devices, similarly, store a diverse array of data types including multimedia files, location data, and system logs. The sheer volume and heterogeneity of this data make it difficult for ML models to effectively identify, classify, and analyze relevant information without requiring extensive computational resources (Bhawna & Mahajan, 2024). Machine learning algorithms must be trained to handle these large datasets, which often involve noisy, incomplete, or unstructured data, leading to potential inaccuracies in forensic investigations (Zangana, Omar, Al-Karaki, & Mohammed, 2024).

7.2 Feature Selection and Model Interpretability

The success of ML applications in IoT and mobile forensics heavily relies on accurate feature selection. Identifying which features of the data are most relevant to the forensic investigation process is crucial, as irrelevant or redundant features can degrade the performance of ML models (Costantini, De Gasperis, & Olivieri, 2019). Additionally, machine learning models, particularly deep learning models, often operate as "black boxes," meaning they provide results without clear explanations of the decision-making process. This lack of interpretability is a significant barrier in forensic environments where transparency is crucial for validating evidence in legal proceedings (Dunsin, Ghanem, & Quazzane, 2022). Forensic professionals must be able to understand the rationale behind the decisions made by machine learning systems, especially in cases where the findings are pivotal for legal outcomes (Hall, Sakzad, & Choo, 2022).

7.3 Ethical and Privacy Concerns

Another pressing issue is the ethical implications and privacy concerns associated with using machine learning in IoT and mobile forensics. The data collected from these devices can be highly personal, encompassing private communications, location histories, and sensitive health or financial information. Ensuring that ML techniques are employed in a manner that respects privacy while still enabling effective forensic analysis is a delicate balance. For example, the use of AI and ML in identifying and analyzing smartphone data could potentially violate privacy rights if not handled appropriately (Zangana, Mohammed, Sallow, & Sallow, 2024). Strict adherence to ethical guidelines and regulatory frameworks is required to prevent the misuse of these technologies in forensic investigations (Zangana & Omar, 2020).

7.4 Resource Constraints and Scalability

In forensic settings, especially in constrained environments like mobile and IoT devices, the processing power and storage capacity available for deploying machine learning models are limited. This limitation poses a significant challenge for real-time forensic analysis, as complex ML algorithms often require substantial computational resources, which may not be available in resource-constrained environments (Dunsin, Ghanem, Ouazzane, & Vassilev, 2024). Additionally, scalability remains a concern, as forensic investigations involving large-scale IoT networks or mobile device ecosystems require ML models that can effectively scale without compromising performance or accuracy (Jeong, 2020).

7.5 False Positives and Accuracy

Machine learning systems, despite their advantages, are not infallible. In the context of IoT and mobile forensics, the accuracy of ML models can be undermined by high rates of false positives or negatives. These errors can significantly affect the outcome of forensic investigations. For instance, a false positive may identify benign activity as malicious, leading to incorrect conclusions, while a false negative may fail to detect crucial evidence (Ganesh, 2017). The performance of ML models is highly dependent on the quality of training data, and if the data is biased, unbalanced, or incomplete, the model's accuracy can be severely compromised (Iqbal, Debbabi, Fung, Iqbal, & Debbabi, 2020).

7.6 Lack of Standardization

A further challenge to the widespread adoption of ML in digital forensics is the lack of standardization across the industry. Different IoT and mobile devices employ varying protocols, data formats, and encryption techniques, making it difficult to develop universal forensic tools based on machine learning (Irons & Lallie, 2014). The absence of standardized practices and guidelines for implementing machine learning models in forensic investigations further complicates their integration into established forensic workflows (Sikos, 2021). This lack of consistency can hinder the reliability and repeatability of forensic analyses, which are essential qualities in legal contexts (Zangana & Omar, 2025).

7.7 Evolving Nature of Threats

Finally, the constantly evolving nature of threats in the IoT and mobile environments presents an additional challenge for machine learning models. As cyber threats evolve, forensic investigators must continuously update and retrain their machine learning models to detect new forms of attacks and cybercrimes (Jarrett & Choo, 2021). This dynamic landscape means that models trained on historical data may struggle to identify new attack vectors, requiring ongoing investment in model refinement and updating (Mitchell, 2014). Furthermore, adversarial attacks on ML models themselves can be used to manipulate forensic outcomes, potentially leading to the misinterpretation of digital evidence (Zangana & Mohammed, 2025).

7.8 Summary

While machine learning offers powerful tools for enhancing the capabilities of IoT and mobile forensics, its integration comes with significant challenges. Issues such as data complexity, model interpretability, privacy concerns, and the need for continuous adaptation to new threats must be carefully considered. Addressing these challenges requires ongoing research, improved standards, and ethical frameworks to ensure that the use of machine learning in forensic investigations is both effective and responsible.

8. FUTURE DIRECTIONS IN MACHINE LEARNING FOR IOT AND MOBILE FORENSICS

As we move into an era dominated by the Internet of Things (IoT) and mobile technology, the scope of digital forensics is expanding rapidly. With the proliferation of smart devices and the complexity of mobile ecosystems, traditional forensic techniques are being challenged to keep pace with emerging technologies. Machine learning (ML) has emerged as a powerful tool in enhancing forensic investigations in these domains, providing new methods for data analysis, anomaly detection, and pattern recognition. This section explores future directions in machine learning for IoT and mobile forensics, emphasizing the role of AI in enhancing digital investigations.

8.1. Advancements in Data Acquisition and Preservation

The process of collecting and preserving evidence in IoT and mobile forensics is increasingly complex due to the sheer volume and diversity of data sources. Devices often generate vast amounts of data in various formats (sensor data, location tracking, communication logs, etc.), making traditional data collection methods inefficient. Machine learning can be leveraged to automate data extraction from different IoT devices and mobile platforms, ensuring that critical evidence is preserved accurately and efficiently.

In the context of IoT, devices may be connected to a variety of networks, leading to challenges in acquiring data from distributed systems. Machine learning techniques, such as deep learning models, can help in filtering and prioritizing the most relevant data, reducing the burden of manually sifting through terabytes of information (Zangana, H. M., & Omar, M., 2024).

8.2. Enhancing Data Analysis through AI-driven Techniques

Machine learning offers significant potential to improve the analysis of forensic data. In IoT and mobile forensics, investigators are often faced with unstructured and noisy data that requires sophisticated processing to identify meaningful patterns. AI and machine learning algorithms, particularly deep learning models, are capable of detecting anomalies, classifying data, and identifying correlations that might not be immediately obvious to human analysts (Jeong, 2020).

For instance, AI-powered tools can automatically identify suspicious activities or irregularities in sensor data from IoT devices, such as unusual patterns of device communication or abnormal energy consumption, which may indicate tampering or hacking attempts. These techniques can significantly enhance the speed and accuracy of investigations (Bhawna & Mahajan, 2024).

8.3. Integrating Explainable AI (XAI) for Forensic Transparency

While machine learning models are highly effective in detecting patterns and anomalies, they are often considered "black boxes" due to their lack of transparency. This is a particular concern in forensics, where it is essential to understand the reasoning behind a model's decision-making process. Future developments in explainable AI (XAI) will be crucial for providing transparency in forensic investigations, ensuring that the results of AI-driven analysis can be easily interpreted and verified by forensic experts (Hall et al., 2022; Costantini, De Gasperis, & Olivieri, 2019).

For example, in mobile forensics, an XAI approach could help investigators understand why a particular device log was flagged as suspicious, providing a clearer trail of evidence for courtroom proceedings. As forensic investigators rely more on machine learning models, the integration of explainable AI will enhance trust in these systems and ensure their accountability (Kelly et al., 2020).

8.4. Leveraging Synthetic Data for Enhanced Model Training

One of the challenges in training machine learning models for IoT and mobile forensics is the lack of high-quality, labeled datasets. Many forensic investigations involve rare or novel events, making it difficult to gather sufficient real-world data to train accurate models. Synthetic data generation techniques offer a promising solution by creating realistic, but artificially generated, datasets that can be used to train machine learning algorithms.

In the context of mobile forensics, synthetic data can simulate device behavior, network traffic, and potential cyberattacks, allowing for more robust model training (Gholami & Omar, 2023). This approach can help improve the efficiency of anomaly detection systems, even when real-world data is scarce.

8.5. Real-Time Forensic Analysis for IoT Networks

IoT devices are constantly generating real-time data streams that require immediate analysis in the event of a security breach or criminal activity. Machine learning can play a pivotal role in real-time data analysis by enabling faster identification of potential threats. For example, AI models could continuously monitor IoT devices for signs of compromise, such as unauthorized access attempts or unusual network traffic patterns, triggering immediate alerts for forensic investigation (Rizvi et al., 2022).

Moreover, real-time analysis of mobile devices could help detect malware or unauthorized access on a smartphone or tablet as soon as it occurs, enabling rapid intervention and minimizing damage (Zangana et al., 2024).

8.6. Privacy-Preserving Machine Learning Models

As digital forensics increasingly involves sensitive personal data, privacy concerns must be addressed. Future directions will see the rise of privacy-preserving machine learning models, which can perform forensic analysis without compromising data privacy. Techniques such as federated learning and differential privacy are being explored to enable machine learning models to learn from data without needing access to the raw data itself, thus ensuring compliance with data protection regulations (Jarrett & Choo, 2021).

For instance, a federated learning approach could allow investigators to collaborate across jurisdictions without sharing sensitive data, thereby enhancing the security of the forensic process while ensuring privacy (Omar & Zangana, 2025).

8.7. Adversarial Machine Learning in Forensics

The threat landscape in digital forensics is evolving, with attackers increasingly using adversarial machine learning techniques to evade detection. As machine learning models become more prevalent in forensic investigations, criminals may attempt to exploit vulnerabilities in these systems. Researchers are beginning to explore methods for strengthening machine learning models against adversarial attacks, ensuring that forensic tools remain effective even in the face of sophisticated threats (Dunsin, Ghanem, Ouazzane, & Vassilev, 2024).

By applying robust training techniques, such as adversarial training or model ensembling, future forensic systems can become more resilient to manipulation, ensuring their integrity during investigations (Sikos, 2021).

8.8. AI-Driven Legal and Ethical Implications

The growing reliance on AI in digital forensics raises important legal and ethical questions. As machine learning models are used to process and analyze potentially incriminating data, there is a need for frameworks that ensure AI systems are used responsibly. Issues such as algorithmic bias, fairness, and transparency will need to be addressed to ensure that machine learning-driven investigations are conducted ethically and that the rights of individuals are protected (Bhawna & Mahajan, 2024).

Future research in this area will focus on developing guidelines for the ethical use of AI in digital forensics, ensuring that forensic investigators are equipped with tools that are not only effective but also legally and ethically sound (Mitchell, 2014).

8.9 Summary

Machine learning holds great promise for the future of IoT and mobile forensics, offering advanced capabilities in data acquisition, analysis, real-time detection, and privacy-preserving technologies. As the field continues to evolve, ongoing research into explainable AI, synthetic data generation, and adversarial robustness will be essential to overcome the challenges presented by new technologies. With the increasing integration of AI into forensic investigations, the next generation of forensic tools will be more efficient, accurate, and transparent, helping investigators stay one step ahead in the fight against cybercrime.

9. CONCLUSION

The integration of machine learning (ML) in digital forensics, especially in the context of Internet of Things (IoT) and mobile devices, is transforming the way forensic investigations are conducted. Machine learning techniques offer the ability to process large volumes of data rapidly, uncover hidden patterns, and identify anomalies that may go unnoticed using traditional methods. As digital forensic tools evolve, the incorporation of artificial intelligence (AI) and ML promises more efficient and accurate results in tracing cybercrimes, recovering data, and analyzing evidence across diverse digital environments.

However, the journey towards fully harnessing AI and ML in digital forensics is not without challenges. Issues related to data quality, privacy concerns, ethical dilemmas, and the need for specialized knowledge in handling complex systems remain critical hurdles. Despite these obstacles, the continued development of AI-based frameworks is proving invaluable in addressing the increasing volume and sophistication of cyber threats, particularly those targeting IoT and mobile ecosystems.

Looking ahead, the future of digital forensics lies in the ongoing refinement of AI models and algorithms, which can adapt to the constantly changing landscape of digital crimes. The combination of explainable AI, real-time processing capabilities, and advanced anomaly detection tools will enhance forensic investigations, making them more agile and comprehensive. As IoT devices become ubiquitous and mobile technology continues to evolve, the importance of leveraging ML for digital forensics will only grow, promising a more secure and resilient digital future.

REFERENCES

Adam, I. Y., & Varol, C. (2020, June). Intelligence in digital forensics process. In 2020 8th International Symposium on Digital Forensics and Security (ISDFS) (pp. 1-6). IEEE. DOI: 10.1109/ISDFS49300.2020.9116442

Costantini, S., De Gasperis, G., & Olivieri, R. (2019). Digital forensics and investigations meet artificial intelligence. *Annals of Mathematics and Artificial Intelligence*, 86(1), 193–229. DOI: 10.1007/s10472-019-09632-y

Dunsin, D., Ghanem, M. C., Ouazzane, K., & Vassilev, V. (2024). A comprehensive analysis of the role of artificial intelligence and machine learning in modern digital forensics and incident response. *Forensic Science International Digital Investigation*, 48, 301675. DOI: 10.1016/j.fsidi.2023.301675

Dunsin, D., Ghanem, M. C., & Quazzane, K. (2022). The use of artificial intelligence in digital forensics and incident response in a constrained environment. *International Journal of Information and Communication Engineering*, 16(8), 280–285.

Ganesh, V. (2017). Artificial intelligence applied to computer forensics. *International Journal (Toronto, Ont.)*, 5(5).

Gholami, S., & Omar, M. (2023). Does Synthetic Data Make Large Language Models More Efficient? arXiv preprint arXiv:2310.07830.

Gholami, S., & Omar, M. (2024). Can a student large language model perform as well as its teacher? In Innovations, Securities, and Case Studies Across Healthcare, Business, and Technology (pp. 122-139). IGI Global. DOI: 10.4018/979-8-3693-1906-2.ch007

Hall, S. W., Sakzad, A., & Choo, K. K. R. (2022). Explainable artificial intelligence for digital forensics. *Wiley Interdisciplinary Reviews: Forensic Science*, 4(2), e1434.

Hamza, Y. A., & Omar, M. D. (2013). Cloud computing security: Abuse and nefarious use of cloud computing. *International Journal of Computer Engineering Research*, 3(6), 22–27.

Huff, A. J., Burrell, D. N., Nobles, C., Richardson, K., Wright, J. B., Burton, S. L., Jones, A. J., Springs, D., Omar, M., & Brown-Jackson, K. L. (2023). Management Practices for Mitigating Cybersecurity Threats to Biotechnology Companies, Laboratories, and Healthcare Research Organizations. In Applied Research Approaches to Technology, Healthcare, and Business (pp. 1-12). IGI Global.

Iqbal, F., Debbabi, M., Fung, B. C., Iqbal, F., Debbabi, M., & Fung, B. C. (2020). Artificial intelligence and digital forensics. Machine Learning for Authorship Attribution and Cyber Forensics, 139-150.

Irons, A., & Lallie, H. S. (2014). Digital forensics to intelligent forensics. *Future Internet*, 6(3), 584–596. DOI: 10.3390/fi6030584

Jarrett, A., & Choo, K. K. R. (2021). The impact of automation and artificial intelligence on digital forensics. *WIREs Forensic Science*, 3(6), e1418. DOI: 10.1002/wfs2.1418

Jeong, D. (2020). Artificial intelligence security threat, crime, and forensics: Taxonomy and open issues. *IEEE Access : Practical Innovations, Open Solutions*, 8, 184560–184574. DOI: 10.1109/ACCESS.2020.3029280

Jones, R., & Omar, M. (2024). Revolutionizing Cybersecurity: The GPT-2 Enhanced Attack Detection and Defense (GEADD) Method for Zero-Day Threats. International Journal of Informatics [INJIISCOM]. *Information System and Computer Engineering*, 5(2), 178–191.

Jones, R., Omar, M., Mohammed, D., Nobles, C., & Dawson, M. (2023). *Harnessing the Speed and Accuracy of Machine Learning to Advance Cybersecurity. In 2023 Congress in Computer Science, Computer Engineering, & Applied Computing (CSCE)*. IEEE.

Karthikeyan, P., Pande, H. M., & Sarveshwaran, V. (Eds.). (2023). *Artificial intelligence and blockchain in digital forensics*. CRC Press.

Kelly, L., Sachan, S., Ni, L., Almaghrabi, F., Allmendinger, R., & Chen, Y. (2020). *Explainable artificial intelligence for digital forensics: opportunities, challenges and a drug testing case study*. Digital Forensic Science.

Manasa, S., & Kumar, K. P. (2022). Digital forensics investigation for attacks on artificial intelligence. *ECS Transactions*, 107(1), 19639–19645. DOI: 10.1149/10701.19639ecst

Mitchell, F. R. (2014). An overview of artificial intelligence based pattern matching in a security and digital forensic context. Cyberpatterns: Unifying Design Patterns with Security and Attack Patterns, 215-222.

Mohammed, D., Omar, M., & Nguyen, V. (2018). Wireless sensor network security: Approaches to detecting and avoiding wormhole attacks. Journal of Research in Business. *Economics and Management*, 10(2), 1860–1864.

Moustafa, N. (2022). *Digital Forensics in the Era of Artificial Intelligence.* CRC Press. DOI: 10.1201/9781003278962

Nguyen, V., Mohammed, D., Omar, M., & Banisakher, M. (2018). The Effects of the FCC Net Neutrality Repeal on Security and Privacy. [IJHIoT]. *International Journal of Hyperconnectivity and the Internet of Things*, 2(2), 21–29. DOI: 10.4018/IJHIoT.2018070102

Omar, M. (2021). New insights into database security: An effective and integrated approach for applying access control mechanisms and cryptographic concepts in Microsoft Access environments.

Omar, M. (2022). Machine Learning for Cybersecurity: Innovative Deep Learning Solutions. Springer Brief. https://link.springer.com/book/978303115

Omar, M. (2024). From Attack to Defense: Strengthening DNN Text Classification Against Adversarial Examples. In Innovations, Securities, and Case Studies Across Healthcare, Business, and Technology (pp. 174-195). IGI Global.

Omar, M. (2024). Revolutionizing Malware Detection: A Paradigm Shift Through Optimized Convolutional Neural Networks. In Innovations, Securities, and Case Studies Across Healthcare, Business, and Technology (pp. 196-220). IGI Global. DOI: 10.4018/979-8-3693-1906-2.ch011

Omar, M., & Zangana, H. M. (Eds.). (2024). *Redefining Security With Cyber AI.* IGI Global., DOI: 10.4018/979-8-3693-6517-5

Omar, M., & Zangana, H. M. (Eds.). (2025). *Application of Large Language Models (LLMs) for Software Vulnerability Detection.* IGI Global., DOI: 10.4018/979-8-3693-9311-6

Rizvi, S., Scanlon, M., Mcgibney, J., & Sheppard, J. (2022). Application of artificial intelligence to network forensics: Survey, challenges and future directions. *IEEE Access : Practical Innovations, Open Solutions*, 10, 110362–110384. DOI: 10.1109/ACCESS.2022.3214506

Rughani, P. H. (2017). Artificial Intelligence Based Digital Forensics Framework. *International Journal of Advanced Research in Computer Science*, 8(8), 10–14. DOI: 10.26483/ijarcs.v8i8.4571

Sikos, L. F. (2021). AI in digital forensics: Ontology engineering for cybercrime investigations. *WIREs Forensic Science*, 3(3), e1394. DOI: 10.1002/wfs2.1394

Tyagi, A. K., Kumari, S., & Richa. (2024). Artificial Intelligence-Based Cyber Security and Digital Forensics: A Review. Artificial Intelligence-Enabled Digital Twin for Smart Manufacturing, 391-419.

Wright, J., Dawson, M. E.Jr, & Omar, M. (2012). Cyber security and mobile threats: The need for antivirus applications for smartphones. *Journal of Information Systems Technology and Planning*, 5(14), 40–60.

Zangana, H. M. (2024). Exploring Blockchain-Based Timestamping Tools: A Comprehensive Review. Redefining Security With Cyber AI, 92-110.

Zangana, H. M. (2024). Exploring the Landscape of Website Vulnerability Scanners: A Comprehensive Review and Comparative Analysis. Redefining Security With Cyber AI, 111-129.

Zangana, H. M., Mohammed, A. K., Sallow, A. B., & Sallow, Z. B. (2024). Cybernetic Deception: Unraveling the Layers of Email Phishing Threats. [INJURATECH]. *International Journal of Research and Applied Technology*, 4(1), 35–47.

Zangana, H. M., & Mohammed, D. (2025). Foundations of Large Language Models in Software Vulnerability Detection. In Omar, M., & Zangana, H. (Eds.), *Application of Large Language Models (LLMs) for Software Vulnerability Detection* (pp. 41–74). IGI Global., DOI: 10.4018/979-8-3693-9311-6.ch002

Zangana, H. M., & Omar, M. (2020). Threats, Attacks, and Mitigations of Smartphone Security. *Academic Journal of Nawroz University*, 9(4), 324–332. DOI: 10.25007/ajnu.v9n4a989

Zangana, H. M., & Omar, M. (2025). Harnessing the Power of Large Language Models for Cybersecurity: Applications, Challenges, and Future Directions. In Omar, M., & Zangana, H. (Eds.), *Application of Large Language Models (LLMs) for Software Vulnerability Detection* (pp. 1–40). IGI Global., DOI: 10.4018/979-8-3693-9311-6.ch001

Zangana, H. M., Omar, M., Al-Karaki, J. N., & Mohammed, D. (2024). Comprehensive Review and Analysis of Network Firewall Rule Analyzers: Enhancing Security Posture and Efficiency. Redefining Security With Cyber AI, 15-36.

Chapter 6
Legal and Ethical Challenges in Digital Forensics Investigations

Ngozi Tracy Aleke
https://orcid.org/0009-0005-2328-5680
Illinois Institute of Technology, USA

Mohamed Trigui
https://orcid.org/0009-0007-7442-0656
Illinois Institute of Technology, USA

ABSTRACT

Digital forensics has become an essential part of modern investigative work. The main goal of this field is to analyze electronic evidence while ensuring its integrity and reliability. Digital forensics is used in a variety of cases, from identity theft to homicide and corporate disputes, often through electronic discovery, or eDiscovery. However, digital forensics faces many legal and ethical challenges. This chapter aims to answer questions about evidence admissibility, jurisdiction conflicts, privacy concerns, and compliance with search and seizure laws that create legal difficulties. Ethical concerns, such as protecting the integrity of evidence, respecting privacy, and avoiding digital bias, will be addressed. As reliance on data-driven algorithms grows, transparency and ethical oversight are needed to prevent unfair outcomes. Balancing the goals of law enforcement with the protection of basic human rights is critical to maintaining fairness, credibility, and trust in digital forensic investigations in today's rapidly advancing technological world.

DOI: 10.4018/979-8-3373-0857-9.ch006

INTRODUCTION

As technology advances, it has also brought about disputes and disagreements that require court interventions. Digital forensics refers to the processes and procedures involved in the collection and analysis of digital evidence to maintain its integrity, credibility, and admissibility in court or during a legal investigation. The aim of digital forensics is to support cases, either civil or criminal, by uncovering electronically stored relevant information. Ken Zatyko, in *Forensic Magazine*, defines digital forensics as "the application of computer science and investigative procedure for a purpose involving the analysis of digital evidence after proper search authority, chain of custody, validation with mathematics, use of validation tools, repeatability, reporting and possible expert presentation" (Zatyko, 2007). Contrary to popular belief, digital forensics transcends investigations carried out on a laptop or desktop computer. Digital forensics encompasses mobile devices, network and cloud systems, and the analysis of both digital and analog copies of images, videos, and audio files (Sammons, 2014).

During investigations that relate to digital forensics, evidence is carefully retrieved, assessed, preserved, and documented to support the investigation at hand. When the use of digital forensics is discussed, the majority of individuals tend to associate it with criminal matters relating to child pornography and identity theft only. However, the use of digital forensics also spans homicide investigations, sexual assaults, robbery, stalking, harassment, and rape, to mention just a few. Apart from criminal investigations, digital forensics is also used in civil litigation cases through a process known as electronic discovery or eDiscovery. According to TechTarget, eDiscovery refers to "any process in which electronic data is sought, located, secured, and searched with the intent of using it as evidence in a civil or criminal legal case" (TechTarget, 2005). Digital forensics is also utilized by intelligence agencies, as the proliferation of digital technologies has led to a wave of terrorist and threat actors moving their activities online. Many of these threat actors communicate online using coded methods such as cryptography and steganography tools to encrypt and decrypt information relating to their operations. For example, the US Army, through a process known as Document and Media Exploitation (DOMEX), exploits intelligence collected from digital devices recovered from the battlefield in Iraq and Afghanistan during the war in these countries in the early 2000s.

HISTORY OF DIGITAL FORENSICS

Digital forensics was first introduced in the 1970s when digital data was first becoming prevalent in the technological field. During this period, computers were mostly mainframe and minicomputers. However, the field did not gain traction until the 1980s when the use of personal computers became more rampant. During this period, apart from using computers for legitimate personal purposes, criminal actors also saw the proliferation of this new technology as a way of carrying out criminal activities. This gave rise to law enforcement devising ways to investigate computer-related crimes. During this period, there was no standardized procedure in place for collecting or handling digital evidence.

In 1984, the FBI created Magnetic Media, the first digital forensics program developed to find child pornography. Since that time, the National Cyber Workforce Framework has recorded 31 different specialty areas in the field. Another pivotal period associated with the history of cybersecurity is the 1990s when foundational techniques and standards for digital forensics were established. During this period, law enforcement and cybersecurity experts developed protocols and methodologies for digital forensics investigations.

Figure 1. Evolution of Digital Forensics.

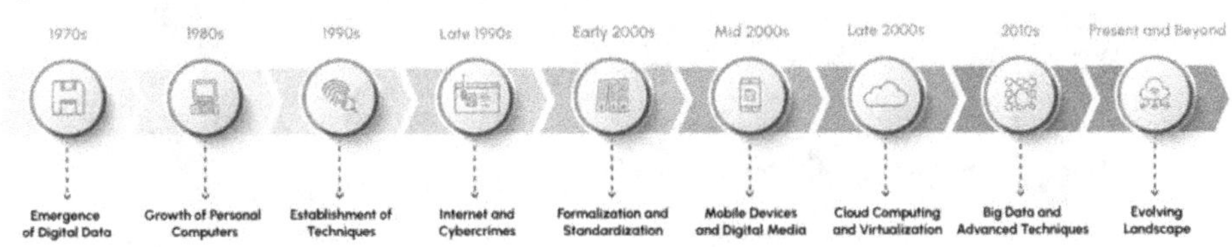

The first Computer Analysis and Response Team was created, and early digital forensics tools such as *IMDUMP, SafeBack, DIBS* (a hardware and software solution), and *Fix Disk Image* were developed. These tools can be regarded as the foundation for later commercial tools like *EnCase* and *FTK*, which are currently being widely used in the field. As more and more people gained access to computers and the internet became generalized, the need for greater formalization and standardization of forensic tools was emphasized. The widespread cybercrime created the need for law enforcement to act. The International Association of Computer Investigative Specialists (IACIS) and the National Institute of Standards and Technology (NIST) were established, and these organizations became the custodians of digital forensics best practices.

The field of digital forensics and the techniques used for investigation have evolved since the late 1990s and early 2000s. The increase in mobile devices and digital media storage, including cloud computing, virtualization, machine learning, and artificial intelligence, has expanded the scope of digital forensics. Experts have had to devise new ways and techniques for extracting evidence from a variety of environments, including cell phones, flash drives, memory cards, and cloud storage. The complexities associated with these new environments that digital forensics experts have to work with can pose both legal and ethical challenges, which will be further addressed in this chapter.

Figure 2. Types of Digital Forensics

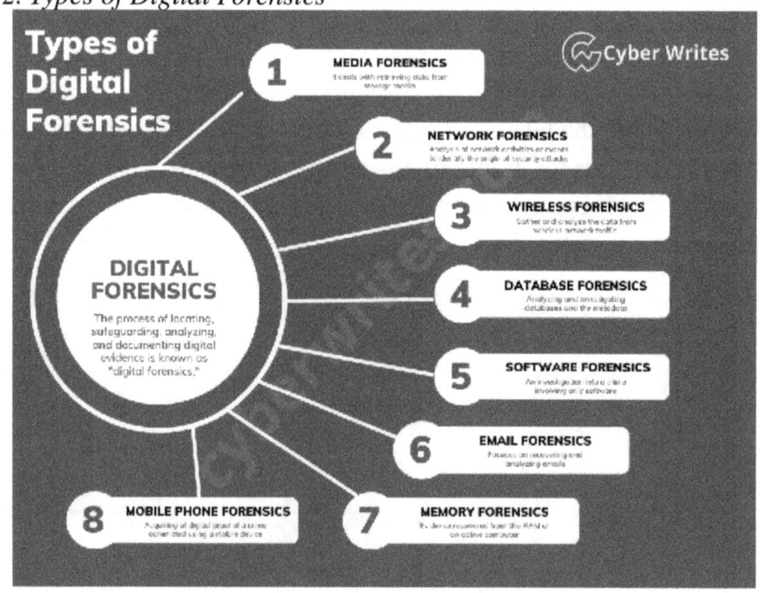

PROCESS OF DIGITAL FORENSICS

One major theme of this chapter is to outline the legal and ethical framework associated with Digital Forensics. However, to delve into this discussion, key attention must be given to what the acceptable best practices for a digital forensics process are. NIST 800-86 provides a general step for forensic examination, including acquisition, examination, analysis, and reporting. However, Ken Zatyko, in 2007, expanded these steps and laid out an eight-phase process that a digital forensics analyst must follow to comply with legal and ethical rules in carrying out their investigative activities.

Figure 3. The Digital Forensics Process

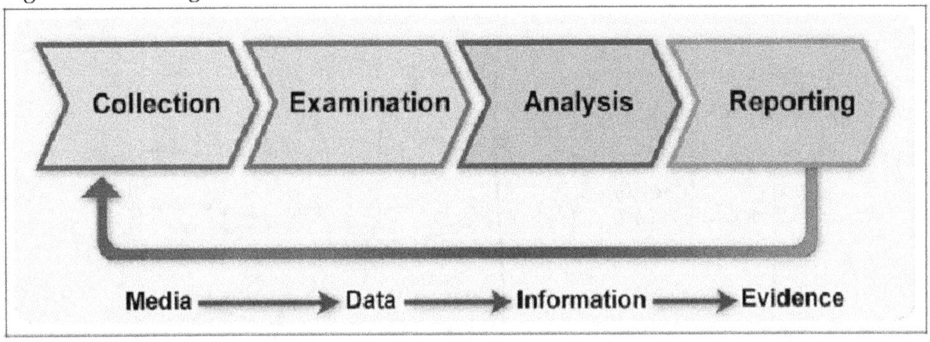

Search Authority

This is usually the first step that must be taken in order to be compliant with digital forensics best practices. A search authority can take different forms starting from a search warrant issued by a competent judge or a search order, subpoena, or consent by the party to be searched. It must be noted that lack of a proper search authority can lead to the suppression and inadmissibility of any evidence recovered from such illegal search.

Chain of Custody

A well-documented chain of custody is required to preserve the integrity of any retrieved evidence. This chain of custody must account for the evidence from the time of its initial retrieval to its presentation before the court. The chain of custody can be documented in forms, reports, notes, evidence receipts, or by marking the actual evidence to indicate the chain of events whenever such evidence changes hands during the investigation process.

Figure 4. Broken Chain of Custody

Imaging and Hashing

It is usually advisable for examiners to carry out their investigations on a copy of the original data to ensure the security and protection of the original data. Data imaging involves creating a duplicate or replica of the original data provided for investigation to preserve its integrity and security. Hashing, on the other hand, generates a fixed-length string of bits, like a digital fingerprint, that can be used to verify the authenticity of the data. A hash value changes whenever the data is altered or manipulated. In the imaging process, a hash value is created for the original data before imaging is performed. Then, another hash value is generated after imaging is completed and compared with the original hash. If both hashes are the same, it can be concluded that the data was not altered during the imaging phase, and as such, the evidence obtained from the investigation is authentic.

Validating Tools

All tools, both hardware and software, used during a forensic investigation must be tested and trusted. Validation is the process of confirming that a tool, technique, or procedure works as intended and produces correct results. This validation process should be documented whenever it is carried out. As a best practice, examiners should only use tools that are recognized and accepted within the forensics field. New tools should only be used when they have gone through the validation process.

Analysis

This is the process of examining and interpreting digital data to extract evidence for use in criminal investigations, civil litigation, internal investigations, and data breaches. During this process, examiners use their skills and tools to extract artifacts found in the data being examined. The premise of analysis will be based on the facts and circumstances of the investigation at hand.

Repeatability (Quality Assurance)

The hallmark of an efficient forensics process is accuracy in the results. For evidence that has passed through a forensic examination to be admissible, the index score for its accuracy must be high (forensic examiners aim for 100%). This score can be obtained by passing the evidence through more than one forensic tool and aiming for the same result, getting the opinion and vetting of a separate examiner after repeating the same process, and making sure proper quality assurance is performed on the result to maintain the integrity and accuracy of the result.

Reporting

The purpose of an investigation will be defeated if no proper reporting is done. Reports can take various forms and lengths; some are short and straight to the point, while others are long and detailed. Whatever shape or form a report may take, the underlying factor behind its creation is the desires and goals of the organization or client requesting the investigation (Sammons, 2014). Whichever form of report is needed for a particular investigation, an executive summary should be added to provide the audience with a quick summary of what the investigation entails, along with the results and findings. Additionally, a well-written report should include a list of all items examined, a list of methods and tools used during the investigation, findings, recommendations (if requested), and conclusions.

Expert Presentation

There will be a need for an expert presentation if the investigation carried out by digital forensics was conducted based on a legal matter before a court or even a panel. Because of the complexity involved in forensics and the fact that a judge may not understand some of the concepts and terminologies used in a report, an expert presentation will be necessary to help the audience better understand the technical findings in the report.

Addressing the complex legal and ethical challenges in digital forensics is essential to maintaining the integrity of investigations and protecting individual rights, requiring balanced regulatory frameworks, rigorous ethical standards, and advanced protocols that prioritize both justice and privacy.

LEGAL CHALLENGES IN DIGITAL FORENSICS

It has been established that the technological advancements of this new age have led criminals to find new ways of carrying out their activities, and law enforcement has responded by devising new methods of investigating these activities and enforcing the law. However, these new methods are usually faced with complex legal challenges that, if not addressed, may render the evidence recovered during such investigations inadmissible. The implications of this would include getting a not guilty verdict against the accused, even when they actually committed the offense for which they are before the court, and also resulting in a waste of time, money, and resources for all those who have participated in the investigation.

Fourth Amendment and Search and Seizure

The Fourth Amendment to the Constitution of the United States provides: "The right of the people to be secure in their persons, houses, papers, and effects, against unreasonable searches and seizures, shall not be violated, and no Warrants shall issue, but upon probable cause, supported by Oath or affirmation, and particularly describing the place to be searched, and the persons or things to be seized." This provision, in a nutshell, protects citizens from unreasonable searches and seizures. A search will be considered reasonable if it meets the following conditions:

- An unbiased judge or magistrate must issue the warrant.
- The warrant must be supported by probable cause.
- The warrant must be supported by an oath or affirmation.
- The warrant must describe in detail the place to be searched and the objects to be seized.

Even though the term "privacy" is not explicitly defined in the United States Constitution, the Fourth Amendment can be considered a key contributor to the protection of privacy. The application of the Fourth Amendment is usually straightforward when the place to be searched or the person to be searched is tangible, as in traditional evidence. However, a gray area arises when the evidence to be investigated is digital. The Fourth Amendment has been challenged by the advent of the internet and other digital technologies.

Some questions that have arisen include: When must police obtain a warrant? What must support the warrant? And what must the warrant specify? Kerr (2010) opined that applying existing Fourth Amendment principles to digital evidence is a challenging endeavor. He argued that searching through a computer is roughly analogous to searching for a needle in a haystack. The implication in relation to the Fourth Amendment is this: How can a warrant describe the place or the system in a digital forensics case if investigators often do not even know what they are looking for during these investigations? Commentators have recommended that new rules must be developed to regulate how investigators look through the haystack to find the needle (Kerr, 2010).

Case study: Carpenter v. United States

This case stemmed from a criminal investigation in 2011. The premise of the case was that four men were arrested for multiple robberies at RadioShack and T-Mobile stores in the U.S. One of the arrestees provided the cell phone numbers of other accomplices involved in the robbery. These cell phone numbers were further used by federal prosecutors to apply for the cell phone records of the accomplices under the SCA without the accomplices' consent or a valid warrant under the Fourth Amendment. The FBI obtained CSLI records of 16 individuals, including the petitioner Timothy Carpenter. The cell-site location information (CSLI) provided time-stamped records and location points accurately reflecting Carpenter's movements over 127 days. Carpenter, through a motion, moved to suppress the admissibility and use of the CSLI information obtained by the prosecutor on the grounds that the acquisition of the evidence breached his Fourth Amendment rights. The District Court denied the motion and allowed prosecutors to use the evidence to substantiate their charge, based on which Carpenter was convicted of aiding and abetting robbery. On appeal to the Sixth Circuit, the court dismissed the appeal.

However, on further appeal to the Supreme Court, the court held that for investigators to obtain weeks-long information generated by a cell phone showing a record of the individual, a warrant must first be obtained. The prosecution pleaded the third-party exception, which provides that people have no reasonable expectation of privacy in information held by a third party. The court refused to apply this exception to Carpenter's case and further ruled that people have a reasonable expectation of privacy in their movements over a several-week period because the information creates a revealing portrait of the person's daily life.

Challenges in obtaining proper warrants for electronic data

One of the challenges associated with obtaining a search warrant in this new digital era is jurisdiction. Many digital services span across jurisdictions. For example, services related to social media or cloud storage are stored in locations across different countries, and obtaining or accessing that data can be tricky, as a court in the United States may not have the authority to issue a warrant for a server hosted in another country. Additionally, there may be a conflicting legal framework between one jurisdiction and another, in the sense that what is applicable and legal in one jurisdiction may not be legal in another. For example, the European Union's General Data Protection Regulation (GDPR) imposes stringent privacy requirements, which are not applicable in other countries; these requirements may hinder access to information requested by a non-EU country.

Another challenge to obtaining a proper warrant is the volatility of some data. Data that was present when the warrant was sought may no longer be available when the warrant is obtained, and this may impact the rule that a warrant must specify the name of the place and the item to be searched.

Data Privacy and Protection Laws

Data privacy and protection laws establish the legal framework for how data is obtained, used, and stored. These laws give individuals the right to control who has access to their data and what that data is used for. To begin, many jurisdictions have incorporated legal frameworks that safeguard individual data, privacy, and user rights. According to the *World Bank Identification for Development Practitioner's Guide*, many countries have not only adopted data protection and privacy laws that relate to identification systems but also frameworks that apply to other government or private sector activities involving the processing of personal data. Most data protection laws, in line with international standards, typically stipulate broad provisions and specific principles relating to the collection, storage, use, and disposal of personal information.

- Purpose of collection: Must be limited to the purpose stated in the law and must be known to the individual at the time of collection, and the individual must have consented to the collection.
- Proportionality to the purpose of collection: The method of collection and use must be lawful.
- Fairness and transparency: Data collected must be accurate and up to date.
- Data should not be kept longer than necessary for the purpose for which it was collected.

- Requirements to use technologies that protect privacy.
- Accountability.

Some laws are crucial in data privacy and protection, such as the European Union General Data Protection Regulation (GDPR), the California Consumer Privacy Act (CCPA), and the Health Insurance Portability and Accountability Act (HIPAA).

GDPR: The GDPR is one of the most comprehensive data privacy laws in recent years. It sets new standards for international data protection practices. Built on principles like those of the OECD, it has become a global benchmark. In digital forensics, the GDPR affects investigations by limiting the collection, processing, and retention of personal data for EU citizens. Investigators are required to collect only the minimum data necessary for their work.

HIPAA: HIPAA creates strict rules around accessing and analyzing patient health information (PHI) during investigations. Investigators must get proper authorization before working with sensitive medical data, which can limit the scope of forensic examinations. Compliance with HIPAA ensures patient privacy is respected while investigations into healthcare systems proceed within legal boundaries.

CCPA: The CCPA gives individuals more control over their personal data by providing rights to access, delete, and manage how their information is collected and shared. Companies must clearly explain how they use customer data and offer opt-out options. These rules aim to improve transparency and ensure organizations handle personal data responsibly.

With these laws in place, it can be tricky for organizations and providers to ascertain when an individual's or a patient's (in cases relating to HIPAA) privacy is being compromised and when they are merely adhering to law enforcement requests. The good thing, though, is that most of these laws, GDPR and HIPAA inclusive, provide for situations when it is permissible for personal information or protected health information (PHI) to be released. For example, HIPAA Privacy Rules allow the use and disclosure of PHI without the authorization of the owner if "12 national priority purposes" are met, such as protecting public health, supporting law enforcement investigations, or addressing threats to national security. These exceptions are designed to strike a balance between protecting individual privacy and enabling crucial public and governmental functions.

Table 1. CCPA vs. GDPR: Comparative Analysis

Aspect	CCPA	GDPR
Consumer Rights	• Opting Out: Allows consumers to prohibit the sale of their PII to third parties. • Non-Retaliation: Businesses cannot penalize consumers for challenging their data handling. • Legal Representation: Consumers can appoint an attorney for disputes. • Incentives: Must notify consumers if financial incentives were offered for data.	• Right to Correct Errors: Consumers can request corrections to inaccurate personal data. • Restrict Processing: Consumers can stop processing of their data, not just its sale. • Profiling Restrictions: Prohibits automated profiling of individuals unless explicitly authorized.
Usage and Processing of Data	• Broad Usage: Businesses have broader latitude to use data but must provide written notification and allow opt-outs.	• Explicit Consent: Data usage requires informed, explicit approval. • Purpose Limitation: Data can only be used for the intended purpose. • Legal Basis: Must meet one of six legal bases, including public interest or contractual necessity.
Ethical Considerations	• Does not explicitly address ethical implications of AI/ML but requires transparency in data processing.	• AI/ML Accountability: Strictly limits profiling and decision-making by automated systems. • Transparency and Oversight: Requires human over-sight for decisions impacting individuals (e.g., credit, employment).
Enforcement and Penalties	• Enforced by the California Attorney General and Privacy Protection Agency. • Fines up to $7,500 per intentional violation. • Consumers can sue for breaches.	• Enforced by Data Protection Authorities (DPAs) across EU member states. • Fines up to C20 million or 4% of global revenue, whichever is higher. • Comprehensive rights to file complaints with DPAs.
Compliance and Digital Forensics	• Digital forensic tools help ensure compliance by proac-tively scanning datasets and supporting audit readiness. • In case of breaches, forensics enables rapid evidencecollection and response.	• Digital forensics tools are critical for maintainingGDPR's strict accountability and ensuring audit readiness. • Tools facilitate incident response and adherence to dataprotection standards during breaches.

General Data Protection Regulations

Under the GDPR, accessing and processing data without explicit consent from the data owner amounts to a regulation violation, even if such data is critical to the investigation. The implication of this is that investigators must carefully assess the scope and authority they must ensure compliance with GDPR regulations. This may slow down or even stop the investigation as permissions and justification for use are sought. Other GDPR restrictions, such as "the right to data erasure" and "profiling restrictions," may place limitations on an investigation that may require extra intervention for effective compliance with the laws.

California Consumer Privacy Act

The opt-out and data usage limitations imposed by the CCPA empower a consumer with the right to opt out of their data being used without their consent. For example, in a data breach investigation under the CCPA, a company must respect a customer's opt-out request unless there is a legal exception applicable to the case. When this is the case, the investigators must exclude certain datasets from the investigation, thereby complicating the entire process and reducing the breadth of available evidence. Other CCPA restrictions, such as the transparency requirement, which requires an investigator to notify California residents about how their data is being processed and used in the investigation, could lead to delays. This is because forensic teams must carefully document and disclose the process of their investigation while also managing the investigation.

While the CCPA focuses on transparency and consumer rights related to the sale and distribution of data, the GDPR imposes stricter controls over data usage, processing, and ethical concerns for emerging technologies like AI and ML. The GDPR's emphasis on consent, purpose limitation, and accountability reflects its broad approach to data protection. Both frameworks mirror evolving standards for privacy and data protection. By incorporating digital forensic tools and maintaining compliance, businesses can navigate the complex regulatory landscape, protect consumer rights, and ensure ethical data practices.

Jurisdictional Issues

This is usually considered to be the toughest challenge in forensic investigations (Buyya et al., 2013). These issues are mostly related to the jurisdiction where specific data needed for an investigation is located and the governing laws in that location. Cloud service providers (one of the widely used storage services) mostly locate their data centers in various locations that span across jurisdictions. Even though some argue that the placement of data in these various locations is for the reduction of operational costs, it is also so that these service providers can serve customers on a global scale. However, specific issues arise from various laws applicable to these different locations. For example, as earlier noted, the GDPR, which is peculiar to the EU, places a major restriction on the movement of EU citizens' personal data outside of the EU. This may become challenging for a cloud provider who needs to move data between data centers located in different countries (Buyya et al., 2013).

To curtail these issues, service-level agreements are entered into by providers within the context of a specific governing law. However, there is no guarantee that these agreements are adequate to absolve providers from breach due to the mobility of data.

Another jurisdictional issue relates to conflicts of laws, that is, when laws are in opposition to each other. A transaction leading to an investigation may be subject to laws from different states or countries, and the issue would be what law to apply. In such instances, the general rule is that since each nation is sovereign within its own territory, the laws of a country will affect all the people and property therein, including contracts made and actions carried out within its borders. This can be addressed if a service-level agreement (SLA) specifies the governing law as well as any other potential jurisdictions that may be involved in delivering the service to the end user (Buyya et al., 2013).

Admissibility of Evidence

Legal standards for the admissibility of digital evidence in court:

For evidence to be admissible, it must meet legal requirements. The court would usually consider whether the evidence meets these stipulated requirements. Antwi-Boasiako and Venter (2017) created a framework, the Harmonized Model for Digital Evidence Admissibility Assessment (HMDEAA), that sought to encapsulate these standards. These standards include:

- Legal Authorization: This deals with the authority vested in an investigator to obtain particular evidence. Such authority can be a proper warrant, consent, or authorization. Legal authorization grants judicial legitimacy to any evidence backed by that authorization.
- Relevance: Evidence will be deemed relevant if it is sufficiently related to the fact in issue (Mason, 2012). Irrelevant evidence will not be admissible by the court. In this context, relevance means that the evidence must tend to prove or disprove the facts in issue (Brobbey, 2014). Evidence with probative value must make the fact in issue more (or less) probable than it would be without the evidence (Antwi-Boasiako and Venter, 2017).
- Authenticity: The authenticity of evidence significantly impacts its reliability and, ultimately, its admissibility. For evidence to be admissible, there must be proof that it is what it purports to be and that it relates to the issues at hand (Mason, 2012).
- Integrity: The integrity of evidence is one of its cornerstones. Evidence that is sought to be admitted must be shown to be whole, sound, complete, and unaltered. One rule of the court is that all evidence must be established and guaranteed to have integrity and not have been obtained through coercion or

other improper means. Such evidence must remain untainted throughout its lifecycle (Antwi-Boasiako and Venter, 2017).

- Reliability: The Daubert standard (Daubert v. Merrell Dow Pharmaceuticals Inc., 1993) provides the framework for assessing the reliability of any evidence. The standard outlines five factors that a judge must consider before relying on evidence:

1. Is the method used for collecting evidence based on a scientific methodology, including creating hypotheses and conducting experiments to disprove them?
2. Was the theory or technique used to obtain the evidence peer-reviewed?
3. Does the expert know, or can they identify the known or potential error rate of the methodology used?
4. Is the technique or theory used by the investigator a generally accepted procedure in the scientific community?
5. Does the investigator's testimony fit the facts in the dispute?

Once all these questions are answered in the affirmative, the evidence obtained from the investigation can be considered reliable.

Chain of custody issues and ensuring the integrity of the digital evidence:

The chain of custody must remain unbroken throughout the lifecycle of the evidence for it to be considered reliable. This can pose a major problem for investigators, as a simple mistake can render a tedious investigation a waste. The chain of custody must remain intact from the acquisition of the evidence, through the preservation stage, transportation, and finally the analysis stage. At every stage of the process, investigators must be able to account for the custody of the evidence. Every detail of the evidence, including information about everyone who handled it and the time it was handled, must be documented. This ensures that the evidence is reliable and therefore admissible (Prayudi, 2015).

Legal Precedent: Daubert v. Merrell Dow Pharmaceuticals (1993):

The Daubert v. Merrell Dow Pharmaceuticals (1993) case established the standard for determining the admissibility of expert scientific testimony in federal courts.

In this case, the court ruled that an expert may testify about scientific knowledge that helps the jury understand evidence or determine a fact in dispute. However, the judge must first evaluate several factors: whether the expert's theory can be tested or has been tested, whether it has been subject to peer review and publication, the known or potential error rate, the existence and maintenance of standards for its operation, and whether the theory is widely accepted in the relevant scientific community.

The petitioners were two minor children and their parents, who alleged that the children's serious birth defects were caused by the mothers' prenatal ingestion of Bendectin, a prescription drug marketed by the respondent. The District Court granted summary judgment in favor of the respondent, relying on a well-qualified expert's affidavit. This expert reviewed extensive published scientific literature and concluded that Bendectin had not been shown to pose a risk for human birth defects.

The petitioners countered with testimony from eight other qualified experts who argued that Bendectin could cause birth defects. Their conclusions were based on animal studies, chemical structure analyses, and unpublished reanalysis of previously published human statistical studies. However, the court ruled that this evidence did not meet the "general acceptance" standard required for expert testimony. The Court of Appeals affirmed this decision, stating that expert opinions based on scientific techniques are inadmissible unless those techniques are "generally accepted" as reliable in the relevant scientific community.

ETHICAL CHALLENGES IN DIGITAL FORENSICS

With the rise of technology, digital forensics has become faster and more precise, making investigations more effective. Yet, these advancements also raise several important ethical issues. First, digital forensics often involves processing vast amounts of personal and sensitive information, making privacy a critical concern (Roux & Falgoust, 2012). In addition to privacy, data integrity is vital in forensic investigations, as any manipulation or bias in evidence handling can compromise the process (Balogun & Zuva, 2017). Ethical concerns also surround the dual-use capability of some forensic tools, which may often be applied outside of criminal investigations, such as in employee monitoring or corporate espionage, further blurring ethical boundaries. Moreover, investigators must uphold high levels of competence and integrity, as any mistake or exaggeration in their findings could lead to wrongful convictions or diminish public confidence in the legal system (Balogun & Zuva, 2017). Balancing each of these aspects is essential to protect individual rights to ensure that digital forensics remains both accurate and fair.

The Selective Reporting Problem

One major challenge within digital forensics comes from the possibility of bias, or selective reporting by forensic analysts themselves. Forensic results cannot be considered valid just because they are technically correct, they also depend on the ethical integrity of the analysts who interpret and present this evidence. According to Nance and Ryan (2011), forensic investigators have a responsibility to eliminate any hint of selective reporting because even unconscious bias may affect findings and lead to unfair resolutions in some legal cases. This issue is particularly relevant in a field where evidence can be intricate and complex, and small details may not be interpreted objectively.

Additionally, there is often pressure related to the expectations of the investigation or organization, which can sometimes lead to the minimization of certain findings, and therefore increasing the potential for bias in digital forensics. Clear documentation and adherence to standards are essential to maintaining objectivity since even minor biases can significantly influence judicial decisions. Objectivity is not only a technical skill, but also an ethical commitment to truth, and the credibility of the judicial system itself relies on this fact.

Data Integrity and Manipulation

What comes to mind when thinking about data integrity is something presentable to a court of law—after all, this is the backbone of any credible investigation or judicial process. The need for evidence to remain in its original state is more of an ethical responsibility than a technical one, as even a slight alteration can compromise the integrity of the case. This is especially important when considering the methods of digital evidence collection and preservation. Forensic algorithms, much like the digital evidence collection process itself, incorporate strict controls to prevent even unintentional manipulation of evidence. Maratsi et al. (2022) indicate that, in digital forensics, protocols must be rigorous to ensure that digital evidence remains unaltered. Any tampering can change findings and even invalidate judicial proceedings due to inadequate handling or storage. Techniques like cryptographic hashing, chain-of-custody protocols, and secure storage mechanisms help ensure the reliability of evidence from acquisition to presentation, and therefore maintaining the ethical and legal standards essential in this field.

Cryptographic hashing plays a crucial role in preserving the integrity of digital evidence by protecting it from tampering and corruption. Hashing operates by processing any data—such as a document, image, or piece of code—through a specialized algorithm to produce a unique fixed length output known as a hash value. This hash value uniquely represents the original data, and therefore it is a digital fingerprint. Even the slightest alteration to the data results in a completely different hash value, making any tampering immediately detectable. For instance, if a file is edited in any way, the new hash value will differ from the original, clearly indicating interference. Kumar et al. (2012) emphasizes the importance of hashing in digital forensic examinations, as it ensures data remains unchanged from the moment it is first collected.

By comparing the hash values of evidence at various stages of collection, storage, and analysis, investigators can confirm the data's integrity. This process is not just a technical safeguard but also an ethical responsibility. Maintaining evidence integrity prevents errors or misconduct that could compromise an investigation or jeopardize justice. Thus, hashing is both a functional tool and a testament to the commitment to trust and credibility in digital investigations.

The SSL Store illustrates how hashing ensures data integrity through an image demonstrating that even a minor alteration to an email result in a completely different hash value, highlighting the precision and reliability of the process:

Figure 5. How Hashing Ensures Data Integrity.

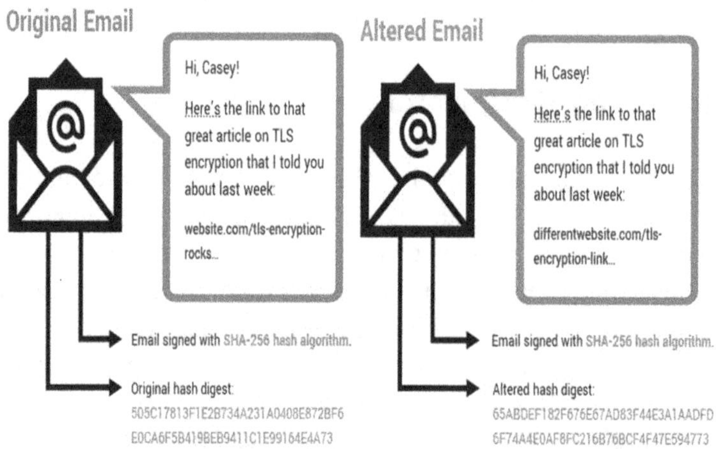

Ethical Implications of Dual-Use Forensic Tools

The dual-use capability of forensic tools raises serious ethical concerns. Most tools developed for criminal investigations can also be used outside these contexts, such as in employee monitoring or corporate surveillance. Casino et al. (2022) discuss these ethical issues, noting that while such tools are immensely useful in criminal cases, their application outside legitimate investigative contexts violates privacy and autonomy. The dual nature of these tools increases the ethical burden on investigators who must ensure that such tools remain strictly confined to criminal investigations and do not fall into the wrong hands. Misusing forensic tools leads to privacy violations and can erode public confidence in forensic science. Investigators should, therefore, balance their duty to uncover the truth with a commitment to individual privacy.

Tools like password crackers, disk imaging software, and network analyzers are essential in a forensic setting to recover data, analyze breaches, and track malicious activity. For example, password crackers, such as *John the Ripper*, allow forensic experts to recover lost or encrypted data, but can also be exploited to access protected systems if used unethically. This dual-use nature means that while these tools are critical to forensic work, they also introduce risks if their power is misapplied, potentially harming privacy and data integrity (Stauffacher, 2022).

Figure 6. John The Ripper.

Erbacher & Swart (2006) highlight that dual-use tools can easily "identify weaknesses and cover up tracks left by an intrusion," underscoring the ethical dangers if these tools fall into the wrong hands. Disk imaging software like *FTK Imager* allows investigators to create exact copies of digital evidence, preserving data for analysis. However, these tools can also be used to alter or erase information, and therefore risk the manipulation of evidence if not properly safeguarded. Similarly, network analyzers like *Wireshark* are valuable for tracing and documenting network intrusions, but can also be misused to intercept private data, such as passwords and confidential information, leading to severe privacy breaches. These examples stress the importance of embedding ethical considerations directly into the forensic curriculum (Bradbury, 2011).

Case Study: United States v. Nghia Hoang Pho

In 2015, former NSA employee Nghia Hoang Pho pleaded guilty to illegally storing highly classified documents on his personal workstation. His actions exposed top-secret information to Russian hackers through a compromised personal computer (Khandelwal, 2017).

Pho worked in the NSA's Tailored Access Operations (TAO), a specialized hacking unit responsible for cyber operations and intelligence gathering. On his personal computer, Pho had previously installed *Kaspersky Lab antivirus software*, which inadvertently became a vulnerability. The antivirus software scanned the system, flagged the classified NSA documents as malicious software, and uploaded them to its cloud for further analysis by a team of researchers. Once the documents were uploaded to the cloud, the classified information became available to Russian hackers, who stole the top-secret information. Pho was sentenced to 66 months in prison, as well as the forfeiture of all property, both real and personal, derived from or used in connection with the offense, to the U.S. government (Schenning, 2017).

This case shows how tools like antivirus software, which are meant to protect systems, can unintentionally cause serious harm when dealing with classified information. It highlights the dangers of not following strict security rules, especially when handling sensitive data. The incident reminds us that dual-use tools can have unintended consequences, and it is critical to carefully manage and secure systems to prevent such risks. It also underscores the need for stronger cybersecurity practices and greater responsibility, especially when dealing with national security information.

Ethical Principles for AI in Digital Investigations

Another major issue that is continuously growing in today's digital world is the heavy reliance on Artificial Intelligence (AI), particularly in digital investigations, where the use of AI systems that are not ethically grounded can lead to significant risks. Since 2012, private companies, research institutions, and public organizations have begun to express concerns about ethical guidelines for Artificial Intelligence (Jobin et al., 2019). In digital investigations, ethical concerns are especially important as AI tools often handle sensitive personal data, assist in decision-making, and analyze patterns that could impact individuals' rights and privacy.

Today, there is widespread agreement on the need for ethical AI systems. However, debates still persist about what constitutes an ethical AI system and how to implement them effectively. Jobin et al. (2019) identified five key ethical principles for Artificial Intelligence systems: "transparency, justice and fairness, non-maleficence, responsibility, and privacy." These principles are particularly relevant to digital investigations, providing a foundation for addressing the ethical challenges posed by AI in this sensitive field.

In this section, we will focus on the five ethical principles mentioned above.

- Transparency: Transparency means that there must be "openness" in AI systems, meaning their decisions must be explainable, traceable, and accessible to stakeholders. For example, if an AI system is used to provide insight on a particular matter, such as a chatbot answering a question, the decisions that system took must be clear and traceable, ultimately explaining why it made that decision or gave that answer. Transparency addresses issues like the "black box" problem in AI, where users do not have access to or cannot trace the inner workings of the system. Therefore, transparency enables users and developers to understand how decisions are made and fosters trust in the system.
- Justice and Fairness: AI systems must ensure fairness by avoiding bias and discriminatory outcomes. This particular principle is arguably the most delicate because bias can arise from the initial training of the AI and the data it was initialized with (Wong, 2020). Developers must ensure that the data and training phase are bias-free. Justice involves both procedural fairness (fair procedures) and substantive fairness (fair impacts) (Kazim & Koshiyama, 2021).
    - Procedural fairness refers to the fairness of the procedures and methods used to make decisions, which means designing algorithms that treat inputs equitably and free of bias. For example, an AI hiring tool should evaluate all candidates based on the same criteria to avoid favoritism or discrimination in the process.
    - Substantive fairness refers to the fairness of the outcomes of those decisions. It examines whether the results of a system are equitable and just for individuals and groups affected by it. For example, an AI credit scoring system may be procedurally fair but still produce substantively unfair outcomes if historical data reflect societal biases, resulting in higher loan rejections for marginalized groups. Substantive fairness ensures that such outcomes do not perpetuate inequality.

These two aspects ensure that fairness is not only built into the design and operation of AI systems but also reflected in their real-world consequences.

- Non-Maleficence: Non-maleficence is essentially the ethical principle of "do no harm." It involves preventing adverse effects on individuals and society. This includes mitigating risks like malicious use, design flaws, or any unintended consequences of an AI system. Ensuring robustness, safety, and proper testing in AI design helps uphold this principle.

- Responsibility: Responsibility involves assigning accountability for the development, deployment, and impacts of AI systems. This principle emphasizes that human oversight is central to ensure that humans remain accountable for AI decisions. It includes mechanisms like impact assessments, auditing, and thorough documentation to maintain responsibility throughout the AI lifecycle.
- Privacy: Respecting personal data and maintaining individual autonomy are fundamental to AI ethics. This principle is not only an ethical concern but also a legal one in the United States and other countries. The legality of privacy was discussed earlier, especially in the context of the Fourth Amendment. Privacy is tied to ethics because it is directly connected to human dignity and autonomy.
  - Dignity: Privacy prevents the exposure or misuse of personal details, and violating privacy can dehumanize individuals by reducing them to data points or objects. Disclosing personal information allows intimate access to the individual, and safeguarding this information is important to maintain respect (McFarland, 2012).
  - Autonomy: Ethically, respecting an individual's privacy means acknowledging their right to control personal information and make autonomous decisions without undue interference. This respect is essential to maintain trust and enable individuals to realize their potential.

In summary, these five ethical principles—transparency, justice and fairness, non-maleficence, responsibility, and privacy—serve as the foundation for guiding the development and use of Artificial Intelligence systems. They ensure that AI operates in a way that is understandable, fair, safe, accountable, and respectful of individual rights. By addressing these principles, developers and organizations can build AI systems that not only advance technology but also uphold ethical standards and protect societal values.

Case Study: AI Misuse and Justice on Trial

In 2021, two men were arrested in Akron, Ohio, for an alleged crime of murder. At the time, law enforcement in the area relied on an artificial intelligence tool called CyberCheck that claimed to help "investigate, charge, and convict suspects accused of serious crimes." The use of this tool later raised significant ethical concerns about the blind reliance on AI technologies in criminal justice (Stelloh, 2024).

CyberCheck was created by Adam Mosher, who promoted it as a powerful investigative instrument. It was claimed that the tool could analyze massive amounts of digital data to identify suspects with high accuracy. As CyberCheck was relied on for investigation, the results from this tool claimed to place the suspects near the crime scene using Wi-Fi network data from a nearby security camera, which was an important piece of evidence in the case to charge the defendants as guilty. The defense lawyers, however, argued that the CyberCheck report was flawed and unreliable:

- The software didn't preserve the raw data it analyzed, so the findings couldn't be verified.
- Social media profiles mentioned in the report couldn't be traced or confirmed.
- It wasn't clear how CyberCheck obtained or verified the Wi-Fi data it used to link the sus-pects to the scene.

Adam Mosher, the creator of CyberCheck, testified that the software's findings were 98.2% accurate. However, he also admitted that the tool had never been peer-reviewed (Stelloh, 2024). He wouldn't share the software's code or methodology, claiming it was proprietary. The defense requested that Mosher disclose the software's workings, but he refused. The judge, therefore, barred CyberCheck evidence because Mosher wouldn't provide this information.

Mosher's refusal to show the inner workings of this AI tool raises more questions than answers about its accuracy and reliability ("CyberCheck AI", 2024). The fact that the creator of the tool refused to share more information on how the evidence was obtained already breaks two ethical principles discussed in the previous sections:

- Transparency: The decisions of this system were not explainable, traceable, or accessible to stakeholders.
- Justice and fairness: The fact that the tool was never peer-reviewed suggests that the results could also be biased and break both procedural fairness and substantive fairness.

This is an example of why there must be adherence to key ethical principles when developing AI systems, especially if used in criminal justice.

BEST PRACTICES FOR ENSURING COMPLIANCE

Finding a balance between legal and ethical considerations when carrying out a forensics investigation can be sometimes hard. There is usually no room for mistake during an investigation as decisions may be solely based on the report of an investigator. As such an investigator is expected to act legally and uphold ethical values but there may be some instances where a legally permissible action may not be ethical and vice versa. In such instances investigators are usually faced with a dilemma as to what to do. In cases like that, the legal requirement may set the minimum standard for the investigation; however, the ethical requirements will help the investigator exceed the minimum requirements set out by the laws and foster building trust, accountability, and long-term success. For an investigator to succeed during a digital forensics investigation, it is important to:

- Know the applicable laws and regulatory framework. For example, ISO standards for digital forensics.
- Understand applicable ethical values.
- Seek guidance from both legal expert and ethical committees.
- Consider the consequence of every legal, financial, reputational, and ethical action before taking them.
- Reflect on the potential impact of the decisions on individual stakeholders involved in the investigation. Always make choices that prioritize fairness, integrity and well-being of all parties involved.
- There is also the need for close collaboration between digital forensic experts and legal professionals to ensure that both legal requirements and ethical considerations are met.
- Continuous education for digital forensic professionals to keep up with evolving legal frameworks and ethical standards.

FUTURE IMPLICATIONS

As digital technologies continue to evolve, the field of digital forensics is experiencing rapid growth and increasing complexity (Ghonge et al., 2022). This advancement brings forth numerous legal and ethical challenges that must be addressed to ensure that investigations remain fair, just, and in alignment with the rights of individuals (Cohen, 2010). One of the most significant developments in digital forensics is the growing reliance on advanced technologies such as artificial intelligence (AI) and machine learning. These tools are invaluable for processing large volumes of data quickly; however, they also introduce issues of transparency and accountability. When AI systems are used to analyze digital evidence, there is a potential for biases that could affect the outcomes of investigations, leading to wrongful conclusions (Malik et al. 2024). This concern raises the need for clear ethical standards and rigorous validation of AI tools to ensure their reliability and impartiality.

The increasing use of Internet of Things (IoT) devices and cloud services adds another layer of complexity to digital forensics. Evidence is often distributed across multiple devices and may span international jurisdictions, making it difficult to establish a clear chain of custody. These challenges highlight the urgent need for standardized global legal frameworks to facilitate evidence collection and ensure compliance across different jurisdictions.

Data privacy regulations are also evolving, and digital forensic practices must keep pace. Laws such as the General Data Protection Regulation (GDPR) in the European Union and the California Consumer Privacy Act (CCPA) in the United States are reshaping the way digital evidence is collected and managed. Future legislation may impose even stricter rules, further complicating the process of gathering evidence. Additionally, emerging digital rights, like the right to be forgotten, could limit what forensic analysts can legally access, requiring a shift in traditional methods of evidence collection. Ethical considerations are becoming increasingly significant in the realm of digital forensics. The debate between public safety and individual privacy is intensifying, particularly as technology advances. Investigators must strike a balance between uncovering criminal activities and respecting personal rights, a task that requires robust ethical guidelines and careful decision-making.

As public awareness of data privacy issues increases, so does the demand for greater transparency and accountability in digital forensic investigations. The public expects clearer explanations of how digital evidence is collected and analyzed, putting pressure on forensic analysts to justify their methods and findings. This heightened scrutiny underscores the need for investigators to maintain rigorous standards of professionalism and integrity. In conclusion, the future of digital forensics will be shaped by the rapid advancement of technology, evolving legal frameworks, and growing ethical concerns. To remain effective and just, the field must adapt by embracing new legal standards, investing in continuous training, and implementing strong ethical guidelines. By addressing these challenges proactively, digital forensics can continue to be a vital tool in the pursuit of justice, while also protecting individual rights and maintaining public trust.

CALL FOR REGULATORY REFORMS

The complexity surrounding digital forensics investigation will only continue to rise. Investigators are encouraged to properly equip themselves to withstand the changes that come with these complexities. Some proposed regulations are needed to support and guide investigators in navigating this ever-changing field. One such regulation is standardization. Regulators should establish clear legal and ethical standards for evidence collection, including handling evidence and updating search and seizure laws. Reforms should also address balancing privacy laws and investigative needs while minimizing data exposure. Jurisdictional issues are also crucial, requiring an international legal framework with treaties and agreements for transborder investigations and data protection. Finally, the increasing use of artificial intelligence and machine learning in digital forensics introduces new concerns. Regulatory reforms addressing algorithmic accountability and certification of forensic tools are vital. Rules ensuring tools meet legal and ethical standards would help reduce the risk of biased or unreliable results.

CONCLUSION

Digital forensics plays an important role in uncovering and analyzing electronic evidence for legal cases, investigations, and cybersecurity incidents. However, the practice faces several legal issues related to the admissibility of evidence, privacy laws and regulations, jurisdictional issues and the fourth amendment search and seizure laws. Ethical challenges that bedevil forensics investigations include ensuring the integrity and accuracy of the evidence, respect for privacy and professional conduct. Furthermore, the growing reliance on data-driven algorithms raises concerns about digital bias, which could disproportionately impact marginalized communities if not carefully managed. Ensuring fairness and equity in forensic analysis will require transparency and ethical oversight. Addressing these challenges is crucial to the legitimacy and integrity of a digital forensics investigation. By adhering to legal and ethical standards, investigators uphold the principles of fairness, credibility and protection of individuals balancing the need for investigation with fundamental human rights.

REFERENCES

Aaron, W. C., Irekponor, O., Aleke, N. T., Yeboah, L., & Joseph, J. E. (2024). *Machine learning techniques for enhancing security in financial technology systems.*

Aleke, N. (2024). *Combatting deep fakes: Ethical frameworks and technological solutions for preserving integrity in digital media.* Retrieved from https://doi.org/.DOI: 10.4018/979-8-3693-93116.ch010

Antwi-Boasiako, A., & Venter, H. (2017). *A model for digital evidence admissibility assessment.* Advances in Digital Forensics XIII. DOI: 10.1007/978-3-319-67208-3_2

Balogun, A. M., & Zuva, T. (2017). *Open ethical issues in digital forensic systems.* International Journal of eBusiness and eGovernment Studies, 9(1), 55–71.

Bradbury, D. (2011). Point to own: The problem with hacking tools. *Computer Fraud & Security*, 2011(11), 12–14. DOI: 10.1016/S1361-3723(11)70114-2

Buyya, R., Vecchiola, C., & Selvi, S. T. (2013). *Mastering cloud computing: foundations and applications programming.* Newnes.

Casino, F., Dasaklis, T. K., Spathoulas, G. P., Anagnostopoulos, M., Ghosal, A., Borocz, I., Solanas, A., Conti, M., & Patsakis, C. (2022). Research trends, challenges, and emerging topics in digital forensics: A review of reviews. *IEEE Access : Practical Innovations, Open Solutions*, 10, 25464–25493. DOI: 10.1109/ACCESS.2022.3154059

Cohen, F. B. (2010). *Digital forensic evidence examination.* Asp Press.

Cyber Writers Team. (2023) *What is Digital Forensics? Tools, Types, Phases & History* Cybersecuritynews. Retrieved from https://cybersecuritynews.com/what-is-digital-forensics/

Experts question opaque Cybercheck AI crime fighting tool. (2024). AIAAIC. Retrieved from Ghonge, M. M., Pramanik, S., Mangrulkar, R., & Le, D. N. (2022). *Cyber security and digital forensics: Challenges and future trends.* John Wiley & Sons. Github. John The Ripper. Retrieved from https://github.com/magnumripper/

Forensics, O. History of Digital Forensics. Retrieved from https://www.oxygenforensics.com

Gubanov, Y. (2022). *Preserving chain of custody in digital forensics.* Belkasoft, LinkedIn. Retrieved from https://www.linkedin.com/pulse/preserving-chain-custody-digital-forensics-belkasoft/

Hawaii International Conference on System Sciences, Kauai, HI, USA, January 4–7, 2011, 1–6. Retrieved from .DOI: 10.1109/HICSS.2011.282

Jobin, A., Ienca, M., & Vayena, E. (2019). The global landscape of AI ethics guidelines. *Nature Machine Intelligence*, 1(9), 389–399. https://www.nature.com/articles/s42256019-0088-2. DOI: 10.1038/s42256-019-0088-2

Kazim, E., & Koshiyama, A. S. (2021). A high-level overview of AI ethics. *Patterns (New York, N.Y.)*, 2(10), 100333. https://www.cell.com/patterns/fulltext/S2666-3899(21)00157-4 PMID: 34553166

Kerr, O. (2010). The Fourth Amendment and Digital Evidence. *The Journal of Legal Studies.*

Khan, A. A., Shaikh, A. A., Laghari, A. A., Dootio, M. A., Rind, M. M., & Awan, S. A. (2022). Digital forensics and cyber forensics investigation: Security challenges, limitations, and future directions. *International Journal of Electronic Security and Digital Forensics*, 14(2), 124–150. DOI: 10.1504/IJESDF.2022.121174

Khandelwal, S. (2017). *Here's the NSA employee who kept top secret documents at home.* The Hacker News. Retrieved from https://thehackernews.com/2017/12/nghia-hoang-pho-nsa.html/

Kumar, K., Sofat, S., Jain, S. K., & Aggarwal, N. (2012). *Significance of hash value generation in digital forensics: A case study.* CiteSeerX.

Malik, P., Dawar, H., Patel, P., Ahuja, D., & Jain, A. (2024). *Enhancing forensic analysis of digital evidence using machine learning: Techniques, applications, and challenges.* International Journal of Innovative Research in Multidisciplinary Perspectives and Studies (IJIRMPS), Sep-Oct 2024, 1–8. Retrieved from www.ijirmps.org

Maratsi, M. I., Popov, O., Alexopoulos, C., & Charalabidis, Y. (2022). Ethical and legal aspects of digital forensics algorithms: The case of digital evidence acquisition. In *Proceedings of the 15th International Conference on Theory and Practice of Electronic Governance (ICEGOV '22)* (pp. 32–40). Association for Computing Machinery. DOI: 10.1145/3560107.3560114

Mason, S. (Ed.). (2012). *Electronic evidence* (3rd ed.). LexisNexis Butterworths.

McFarland, M. (2012). *Why we care about privacy.* Markkula Center for Applied Ethics at Santa Clara University. Retrieved from https://www.scu.edu/ethics/focus-areas/internet-ethics/resources/whywe-care-about-privacy/

Nance, K., & Ryan, D. J. (2011). Legal aspects of digital forensics: A research agenda. 2011 44th

NIST 800-86. Guide to Integrating Forensic Techniques into Incident Response. Retrieved from https://www.researchgate.net/figure/NISTs-4-phases-forensic-model fig2 263619846/

Prayudi, Y., & Sn, A. (2015). Digital Chain of Custody: State of the Art. *International Journal of Computer Applications*, 114(5), 1–9. DOI: 10.5120/19971-1856

Roux, B., & Falgoust, M. (2012). Ethical issues raised by data acquisition methods in digital forensics research. *Journal of Information Ethics*, 21(1), 40–60. DOI: 10.3172/JIE.21.1.40

Sammons, J. (2014). *The Basics of Digital Forensics: The Primer for Getting Started in Digital Forensics*. Syngress.

Stelloh, T. (2024). *An AI tool used in thousands of criminal cases is facing legal challenges.* NBCNews. Retrieved from https://www.nbcnews.com/news/crime-courts/ai-tool-used-thousandscriminal-cases-facing-legal-challenges-rcna149607

The SSL Store. What Is a Hash Function in Cryptography? A Beginner's Guide. Retrieved from https://www.thesslstore.com/blog/what-is-a-hash-function-in-cryptography-a-beginners-guide/

U.S. Supreme Court, Daubert v. Merrell Dow Pharmaceuticals Inc., United States Reports, vol. 509, pp. 579–601, 1993.

Wong, H. (2020). *Siri, Alexa and unconscious bias: The case for designing fairer AI assistants.* Design Week. Retrieved from https://www.designweek.co.uk/issues/13-19-january-2020/unconsciousbias-ai-voice-assistants/

Zatyko, K. (2007). *Commentary: Defining Digital Forensics*. Forensics Magazine.

Chapter 7
Understanding File System Forensics: FAT, NTFS, HFS, and EXT

Henil Sanjaykumar Gandhi
https://orcid.org/0009-0009-0121-3255
Illinois Institute of Technology, USA

Aryan Dinesh Deshmukh
Illinois Institute of Technology, USA

ABSTRACT

In the following paper, we look at file system forensics intricacies for four dominant ones: EXT, FAT, NTFS and HFS. In this book, each of the system is discussed with its structure, operational characteristics and forensic challenge to collect evidence against it. The EXT family (EXT2, EXT3, EXT4) gets its turn on being evolutionary and providing tons of improvements around journaling and data integrity. It describes the FAT file system for its simplicity and great acceptance, then it presents common forensic techniques such as metadata examination and cluster chain analysis. Although NTFS has some advanced features of its own, such as the Master File Table (MFT) and strong journaling system that it uses to recover both resident and non-resident files, it's really not too much different from other file systems. Now comes to its proprietary nature with the analysis of HFS file system including Catalog file corruption, encryption handling, and more details about the entire structure of its Cloud.

DOI: 10.4018/979-8-3373-0857-9.ch007

INTRODUCTION

File systems are fundamental operations of computers that govern how data is stored and retrieved from the computer. They manage attributes like file properties, including the date and time of creation, file type, name, and last modification. Over the years, numerous file systems have been developed, but some of the most widely used include NTFS, which is an appropriate file system for Windows (Sterniczuk (2022)), and Linux file systems like ext4, XFS, Btrfs, and ZFS (Sterniczuk (2022)). File system forensics is an essential branch of cyber forensics, particularly when dealing with recovering deleted files, corrupt files, hidden files, and metadata from disks during forensic investigations. NTFS (New Technology File System), HFS (Hierarchical File System), FAT (File Allocation Table), and Ext (Extended File System) are among the prominent file systems discussed in this paper. FAT and Ext cater to different types of computing environments, but NTFS remains the default file system for Windows, while HFS is primarily used in macOS (Craiger & Burke (2005)). FAT and NTFS have always been of major significance in forensic analysis and investigation over the years. Microsoft developed both of these systems during different eras of computing. NTFS stands for New Technology File System. NTFS was developed on the evolutionary basis from FAT, and it has more advanced features in comparison, with improvements in reliability, file system structure, and security combined with user-friendliness. Currently, the Windows operating system has over 90% market share, and FAT32 and NTFS are common file systems used on a variety of Windows operating systems (Zhang, N., Jiang, Y., & Wang, J.2020).

File Allocation Table [FAT] File System

One of the oldest file systems is known as File allocation table (FAT) which was developed by Microsoft to use in floppy disks. It got utilized in hard drives & other equipment. FAT filesystem gets its moniker from the structure (array) of indexes to clusters (groups of contiguous disk sectors) with annotations (Li, Q., Zhang, Q., Tan, Y. A., Li, Y., & Zheng, J. (2016)) FAT, which stands for File Allocation Table, was first implemented back in 1977 as the standard filesystem of MS-DOS and Windows 9x operating systems.

FAT File System Structure:

Figure 1. FAT file system

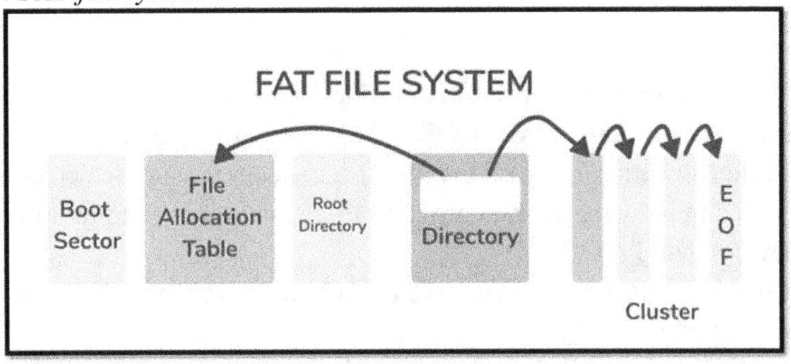

FAT file system breakdown the disk and divide it into clusters in order to manage & organize data on storage devices. To keep track of in-use, free or linked with other files the status of FAT table cluster (File System Comparison: NTFS, FAT32, exFAT, and EXT). A file is created, and the FAT allocates clusters & links to them in order. EOF (End of File) flag will be set in the last cluster. The boot sector would bootstrap the system while FAT could handle data access efficiency & crash recovery (File System Comparison: NTFS, FAT32, exFAT, and EXT). The root directory contains metadata such as names, attributes, timestamps & starting cluster no of the file.

FAT has various version as below:

1. FAT12:

FAT12 was the first version of FAT file system in 1977, introduced by Microsoft for the use of floppy disk. It uses 12-bit entries in allocation table in order to track file clusters (Microsoft Original DOS File system).

As it has 12-bit entries in the file allocation table, it has only 4096(2^12) possible clusters. It seems like a very small volume of capacity it contains. It supports a maximum of 32 MB disk size. It uses small cluster size; it means it is not suitable for large volume disks (Microsoft Original DOS File system).

Forensics Implication:

FAT12 is mostly found in floppy disks only as it has a very small volume size (32 MB), which makes it rare in forensic investigation. While looking for file recovery, it is easy to recover file because when deleting it just marked as deleted in FAT, but system does not delete it from the storage devices (Microsoft Original DOS File system). It makes space free when deleted from the system.

2. FAT16:

FAT16 is the second version of the FAT (File Allocation Table) file system developed by Microsoft in 1984 for MS-DOS and early Windows versions (FAT16, F., & FATX, F. File Allocation Table). This file system keeps track of which clusters the files are stored in by using 16-bit entries in FAT, thus supporting more enormous storage devices than FAT12.

16-bit Entries: Supports up to 65,536 (2^16) clusters because FAT uses 16 bits for each cluster entry.

Maximum Disk Size: FAT16 supports disk sizes up to 4 GB, with cluster sizes from 512 bytes to 64 KB (FAT16, F., & FATX, F. File Allocation Table). However, it was not uncommon for practical implementations (e.g. Windows 95) to limit the size of a disk used in an unexpended partition to a few gigabytes at most (FAT16, F., & FATX, F. File Allocation Table).

Cluster Size: By using larger clusters (up to 64 KB) it was able with bigger disk sizes, but they did this by wasting so much space would be inefficient for lot of smaller files because there'd always be slack.

FAT16 was widely implemented on hard drives, USB flash drives and memory cards through the 80s and mid-90s as one of Microsoft's main file systems.

Forensics Implications:

Similar to FAT12, when files are deleted in FAT16, only the first character of the filename is replaced with the E5 special marker and the space is marked as free, but the rest of the data remains until overwritten. Consequently, deleted files can be recovered during the forensics examination. Slack space is prevalent in FAT16 due to large cluster sizes that may contain parts of previously deleted files or fragment content, which can be critical for forensics. Unlike modern systems, FAT16 lacks newer features such as journaling of file permissions, allowing adversaries to modify or delete critical files undetected.

3. FAT32:

FAT32 is a widely used file system developed in the 1990s. It was designed to overcome the limitations of FAT 12 & FAT 16. FAT 32 supports larger volumes & files which makes it compatible for trending storage devices (Bhat, W. A., & Quadri,

S. M. K. (2010)). FAT32 is popular in USB drive, SD card & legacy systems due to its cross-platform compatibility.

FAT32 can manage up to 2 TB partition & 4 GB of files. Its simple design makes it easy to implement & compatible with a every OS & other device which has systems like DOS & windows 95 (Bhat, W. A., & Quadri, S. M. K. (2010)). It reduces the unused disk space by utilizing smaller size of cluster. Its wide adaptation across multiple OS makes it useful for various storage mediums.

Forensic Implication:

In FAT32, when the actual file is deleted, the actual data remains on the disk until it overwritten by other files. It would be helpful in forensic investigation to recover the deleted evidence files (Li, Q., Zhang, Q., Tan, Y. A., Li, Y., & Zheng, J. (2016). Unlike NTFS, there is no journaling capabilities in FAT32 which makes it more inclined to data loss from unexpected system crashes.

FAT32 maintains timestamps for file creation, modification & access. However, it can be altered with manipulation (Li, Q., Zhang, Q., Tan, Y. A., Li, Y., & Zheng, J. (2016)). Its compatibility across devices lead the fragments of modified files can be found on multiple systems which offers broader scope for collecting the evidence.

Tools for Forensic Investigation in FAT:

There are multiple tools used in forensic investigation of FAT file system for different purposes. **Autopsy & Sleuth** Kit is mostly used to recover deleted files & in analysis of directory structure of system. Where **FTK Imager** examines & acquires FAT based storage drives to extract the evidence from the disk. **X-Ways Forensics** performs cross-platform analysis to inspect FAT file system on USB drives & other old devices.

New Technology File System [NTFS] File System

The New Technology File System (NTFS) is a file system that originated from Microsoft in 1993 as part of the Windows NT 3.1 operating-system It was created as an improved file system alternative to FAT, which restored stability and security needed for more advanced features in PCs (Chow, K. P., Law, F. Y., Kwan, M. Y., & Lai, P. K. (2007)). Exclusive to major Windows operating systems, such as Windows 10 and now also used in Microsoft's latest upgrade; Window 11, NTFS remains the file system technology of choice for today's applications.

NTFS File System Structure:

Figure 2. NTFS File System

NTFS Boot Sector	Master File Table	File System Storage	Master File Table Copy

NTFS Boot Sector contains the BIOS parameter for booting the system includes file system structure, cluster size & information of volume layout (NTFS File system Guide). It also includes the executable code of the booting process. NTFS uses a structure called Master File Table to store metadata and file locations (NTFS File system Guide). MFT is the container for metadata of every file, including name, size, permissions and access times along with all data location. The MFT contains one entry for each file or directory. NTFS includes system files such as $LogFile, $Bitmap & $BadClus for internal operation of records of changes in file system, tracks allocation of cluster & stores the info about bad clusters respectively (NTFS File system Guide).

Key Features:

NTFS is a journaling file system, it records changes made to files in a transaction log (File System Comparison: NTFS, FAT32, exFAT, and EXT). This feature is useful in order to avoid data corruption on power failures or if the system crashes. It further offers several advanced features like file permissions, encryption, compression and large storage volumes support that also makes it the most flexible of all.

1. **Size of Files and Volume**: Compared with FAT systems, NTFS allows significantly larger volumes and files. An NTFS volume has a maximum theoretical size of 16 exabytes, almost the same as for ReFS or ext4 and significantly less than ZFS and Btrfs. The actual practical limit is dependent upon various selectable options such as sector size (default 4096 bytes), although in many cases above well over one yottabyte (Chow, K. P., Law, F. Y., Kwan, M. Y., & Lai, P. K. (2007)). Each file can be up to 16 terabytes (while this technically far beyond the limits of FAT16 and surpassed depending on version), which is another notable difference from traditional disk operating systems (Chow, K. P., Law, F. Y., Kwan, M. Y., & Lai, P. K. (2007)). This means that NTFS is well-suited to modern large storage drives and corporate environments.

2. **File Compression and Encryption:** It supports native file compression as well as encryption (EFS or Encrypted File System). Cupping mechanisms use compression to make the tape occupy less space on disk, and encryption ensures that sensitive data is not readable. This is not the case in older file systems such as FAT.

Forensic Implications:

NTFS faced several forensic implications due to its advanced features. It has a great journaling capability through $LogFile, which records the change in metadata (Alazab, M., Venkatraman, S., & Watters, P. (2009)). It can help forensics experts to backtrack into the log file with its creation, updating, deletion & modification in the file system when it is tempered by other.

Another element, $MFT (Master File Table) used to keep every file and directory on the volume including its size, timestamps & access permissions (NTFS File system Guide). It also maintains the record of ADS (alternate data system) which allows multiple data streams associated with a single file only. It can be exploited for hiding malicious file, makes it critical to work on it in running investigation.

NTFS supports encryption & compression through its EFS (Encrypting File System). Though it complicates the forensics recovery while decryption key would be missing or inaccessible, Forensic experts can uncover some traces by analyzing windows registry or $MFT (Alazab, M., Venkatraman, S., & Watters, P. (2009).

NTFS maintain the detailed time stamp of file creation, modification & entry-modified times (MAC times) which implied to important evidence for the forensics investigator to work on the case, offer insights of unauthorized user activities & anti-forensics efforts.

Tools for Forensic Investigation in NTFS File Systems

In NTFS, forensic investigator required advanced tool to perform analysis on complex file system structure. **EnCase & Autopsy** are used to parse the NTFS metadata which includes MFT & details information recovery (Alazab, M., Venkatraman, S., & Watters, P. (2009)). **FTK Imager** is generally used to retrieve the disk image of file system. In addition, **Paraben E3 & AccessData FTK** is mainly used to examine NTFS features like Encrypted file system. On the other side, **Sleuth Kit** can be used to identify hidden or deleted files & track the user activities on the windows operating system (Alazab, M., Venkatraman, S., & Watters, P. (2009)).

DIFFERENCES BETWEEN THE FILE SYSTEMS

Table 1. Differences Between the File Systems

File System	Max File Size	Max Volume Size	Operating System
NTFS	• 16EB - 1KB • 16TB - 64KB • 256TB - 64KB • 8PB - 2MB	• 256TB - 64KB • 8PB - 2MB	• Windows NT3.1 and later • macOS X 10.3 and later (Read-only) • Linux kernel 2.6 and later (read-only) • FreeBSD, NetBSD, OpenBSD(read-only), Chrome OS, Solaris, ReactOS(read-only)
FAT32	• 4GB	• 2TB - 512 byte • 8TB - 2KB • 16TB - 4KB	• Windows 95OSR2, Windows 98, XP, 7, 8, 10, and 11. • macOS • Linux
EXT2/3/4	• 4TB - 1KB • 8TB - 2KB • 16TB - 4KB • 256PB - 64KB	• 4TB - 1KB • 8TB - 2KB • 16TB - 4KB • 256PB - 64K	• Linux kernel 0.96 and later
exFAT	• 128 PB	• 128 PB	• Windows XP, Vista, 1/8/10/11, Windows Server 2003/2008/2008 R2 • Linux kernal 5.4 and later, FUSE • Mac OS X 6.5 and later
HFS	• 2 GB	• 2 TB	• Classic Mac OS (System 3.2 to Mac OS 9.2.2) • Early macOS versions (Mac OS X 10.0 to 10.4)

HIERARCHICAL FILE SYSTEM [HFS] FILE SYSTEM

The Hierarchical File System (HFS) is the default file system used by macOS systems developed by Apple Inc. HFS is a bit more proprietary in nature and organizes the data hierarchically through Volume Header, Catalog File, Extent Overflow File, Attributes File and Allocation File. Together, they serve the purpose of data management, retrieval and forensic analysis providing a strong framework to handle complex file system operations. If your work and investigations happen to cover macOS this knowledge becomes even more crucial: HFS is the centre of navigation for digital forensics.

HFS File System Structure:

Central to macOS is the Hierarchical File System (HFS), which was designed by Apple Inc. The root of FAT is Volume Header, which stores information such as file system size, location, and allocation block size (File System Forensics: No Longer the Gold Standard). You find this header is an entry point for accessing the file system which is important to both normal usage and forensic examination. The location is essential because it plays a role in the efficient navigation and management of the file system. The second part is the Catalog File, which is an indexed (B-tree) file that stores all files and directories available in the system (Hard Disks and File Systems). Catalog File entries contain metadata such as the name, type, and size, as well as pointers to data blocks that aid in retrieval. It plays an important role in forensic investigations, as it allows a lift of the directory structure and enables deleted files to be recovered by accessing and manipulating the content of the file at high speed.

HFS uses a Extent Overflow File to handle extents that overflow the main Catalog entries (File System Forensics: No Longer the Gold Standard). In HFS, however, the data can be stored in multiple extents as opposed to contiguous blocks. In order to cover these extra extents, the Extent Overflow File assigns them so that all pieces of a fragmented file are visible in a forensic examination. This is especially for forensic situations where you will need to reconstruct files correctly. Attributes File — This file contains additional attributes of files and directories, including extended metadata, security information, and identification tags not involved in the standard metadata (File System Forensics: No Longer the Gold Standard). This is important information for forensic investigators, as it helps in understanding file access controls and ownership, in order to maybe better understand how users behave with files or what kind of system history you may have. Allocation File: Bitmap representation of blocks allocated or not within the volume; allows forensic investigators to locate portions of a volume that are unused (free space) which may be examined for remnants or deleted data (File System Forensics: No Longer the Gold Standard).

Figure 3. HFS File System

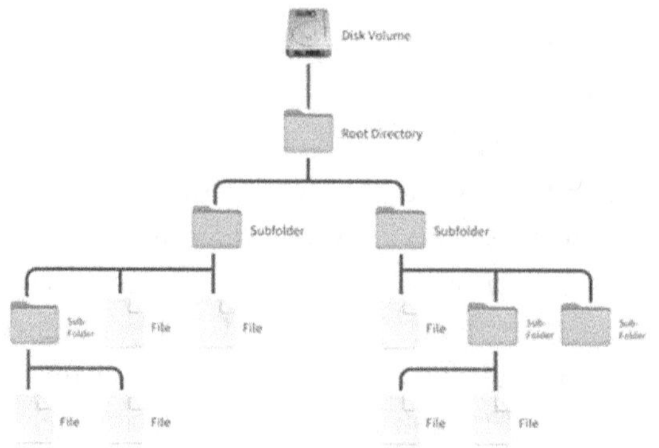

Finally, the Startup File has important information about booting the operating system (File System Forensics: No Longer the Gold Standard). It contains bootstrap code and params needed for hardware initialization and OS kernel loading. In the cases where a system is tampered or malware activity is taking place, forensic analysis of the Startup File provides useful information about boot order and its changes (Computer Forensics: Media & File System Forensics). Each part of the HFS is important in both its operation and forensic capability, but it is clear that it operates solely to manage as much data as possible.

Forensic Analysis Techniques

There are a handful of key techniques to HFS forensic analysis. The first step is Imaging, which creates a copy of the HFS volume, bit by bit to maintain data integrity (Computer Forensics: Media & File System Forensics). This process uses tools like dd and EnCase (Computer Forensics: Media & File System Forensics). Imaging involves taking bit-for-bit copies of hard drives and then using file recovery to obtain the files which have been deleted because these still exist even after deletion (Understanding Hard Disks and File Systems). We can mark it as available for future such that tools like Autopsy and The Sleuth Kit can recover deleted files (Autopsy Digital Forensics) as HFS, Table 2: Some parameters for data in the Catalog File (File System Forensics: No Longer the Gold Standard) Metadata, when examined, gives history of file Such metadata is extracted and interpreted by tools like mac_apt (Computer Forensics: Media & File System Forensics), PlistViewer. MacOS-specific functionalities, such as Spotlight and Time Machine, can be utilized to make investigations more robust; while Spotlight indexes the files on MacOS (Hard Disks and File Systems), Time machine takes snapshots of the file system (Hard

Disks and File Systems). Finding your way through these backups is made easier with something like BackupLoupe (Understanding Hard Disks and File Systems). HFS logs modifications for integrity purposes during a crash, so journal analysis (via tools such as X-Ways Forensics and BlackLight) is essential (WinHex).

Challenges in HFS Forensics

Due to its proprietary nature, forensic analysis in HFS are multifaceted challenges (File System Forensics: No Longer the Gold Standard), as the availability of forensic tools is sparse, and folks will need to update incessantly. Corruption in a file system, especially crucial files like the Catalog File, may obstruct the processing of analysis and thus make it impossible for correct data recovery (Hard Disks and File Systems) Additional complexity arises from the possible encryption, where for example analysts might be faced with encrypted HFS volumes that they cannot access without a decryption key, which can take time and through specialist means (WinHex). The need of carrying out continuous training and adaptation in digital forensics to deal with the complications involved in HFS investigations is highlighted by these factors (Hard Disks and File Systems).

Tools Used in HFS Forensics

There are multiple tools used in forensic art of HFS. **Autopsy** supports analysis of HFS volume (Autopsy Digital Forensics) and provides a graphical user interface (GUI) for file recovery and metadata analysis. The **Sleuth Kit** offers strong command-line tools for the deeper analysis of file systems (The Sleuth Kit). A hexadecimal editor for in depth HFS volume analysis — **WinHex** (WinHex) **FileXray**, an advanced command-line based tool for file-system examination and deleted file recovery (FileXray). **DiffFork** is a comparison of changes made to the file system, it tracks modifications over time and identifies their differences (DiffFork).

Extended File System [EXT] File System

The EXT (Extended File System) family which includes EXT2, EXT3, and EXT4 is the backbone of Linux OS. These file systems date back to 1993 with the arrival of EXT2 and have incorporated additional features like journaling in EXT3 and performance enhancements since then within EXT4. Core elements of EXT file systems, which include the Superblock, Inode Table and Data blocks to name a few, are utilized for the purpose of data persistence. Knowledge of EXT is critical in the digital forensic realm, as it allows forensic analysts to carry out all aspects from file recovery to performing detailed analyses that aid their investigation on a Linux box.

File System Structure:

1. **EXT2:** The EXT family of file systems began in 1993 with the original EXT2. Its design is straightforward, minimalist and functional, prioritizing performance and compatibility. The key elements of EXT2 are composed of a Superblock that holds metadata on the file system, an Inode Table which defines both files and directories (Understanding Ext4 Disk Layout), and data blocks where the actual data is stored (DiffFork). Although EXT2 is a very efficient disk system, it does not have journaling capability (Lu, L., Arpaci-Dusseau, A. C., Arpaci-Dusseau, R. H., & Lu, S. (2013)) which increases the chance of corruption in case of crashes.
2. **EXT3**: Released in 2001, EXT3 is an extension of EXT2 which includes journaling functionality. Journaling maintains a log of changes that make file system recovery cheaper after crashes (An analysis of Ext4 for digital forensics). This feature mitigates the chances of corruption to the file system and enhances recovery time (Lee, S., Jo, W., Eo, S., & Shon, T. (2020)). Tracing the evolution of EXT2, EXT3 has kept its basic pattern for backward compatibility with better data integrity (Journaling the Linux ext2fs Filesystem).
3. **EXT4:** The most recent version of EXT was developed in 2008 and includes many new features. Larger file sizes and volumes support, faster performance and a better journaling support (Comparative Study on Various File System Implementations). EXT4 reduces fragmentation and introduces new functionality, such as extents (a linear chunk of storage), delayed allocation for performance and checksums to ensure data integrity (Understanding Ext4 Disk Layout). All the above enable ext4 to be a reliable and flexible file system which can be used for contemporary computing requirements (Linux File Systems: ext3 vs. ext4).

Figure 4. EXT File System

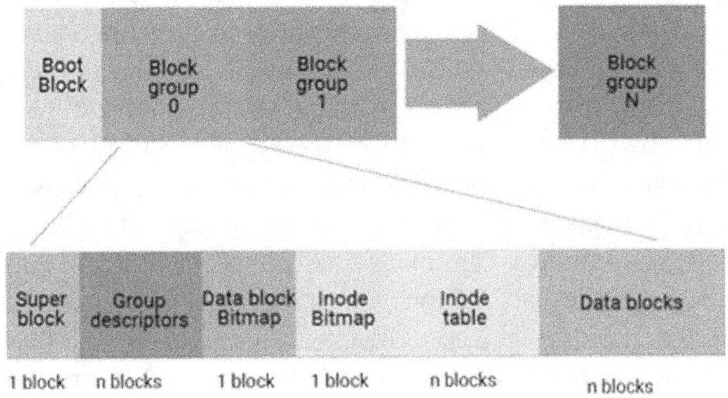

Forensic Analysis Techniques for EXT

Key forensic analysis techniques for EXT file systems Using tools like dd and FTK Imager based on imaging and data acquisition to create a bit-by-bit copy of the EXT volume (Lu, L., Arpaci-Dusseau, A. C., Arpaci-Dusseau, R. H., & Lu, S. (2013) is used to preclude modification of original data. After imaging, deleted files can also be recovered using tools such as extundelete or TestDisk through the examination of inodes and file allocation tables (Lee, S., Jo, W., Eo, S., & Shon, T. (2020)). Tools like Autopsy and Sleuth Kit are deployed for the examination of metadata (DiffFork), which is essential for understanding user activity and extracting information regarding inodes. 8147242.0378Journal analysis using Instruments such as X-Ways Forensics and Rekall, reconstructs the previous state of the file system before incidents (Journaling the Linux ext2fs Filesystem). There are powerful tools like Ext4magic, capable of recovering fragmented files and Bulk Extractor able to extract useful information in a forensic context [25, 31].

Challenges in EXT Forensics

Challenges of Forensic Analysis on EXT file systems (EXT2, EXT3, and EXT4) The main problem relates to file system corruption, especially on EXT2 that does not support journaling and is therefore more likely to get corrupted during a crash or power failure (Lu, L., Arpaci-Dusseau, A. C., Arpaci-Dusseau, R. H., & Lu, S. (2013)). Though EXT3 and EXT4 operates journaling to avoid this problem, under some circumstances it is still possible that the journal itself proves to be corrupted, making it difficult for forensic analyst to reconstruct a file and directory structures (Lee, S., Jo, W., Eo, S., & Shon, T. (2020)). Challenges in dealing with Encrypted data - One biggest challenge As data security is getting more and more attention, EXT file systems are now often encrypted. Analysts may be faced with encrypted files (that is, one or more files encrypted) or even an entire system where he/she needs to have decryption keys (Understanding Ext4 Disk Layout). That is the case because without valuate keys on hand, data analysis cannot be accomplished, which would culminate in further steps as obtaining legal consent to read that information and/or an extra cryptographic process consuming time (Linux File Systems: ext3 vs. ext4).

Another major hurdle that EXT forensic analysis faces is fragmentation. Due to this structure of EXT file systems, heavy fragmentation occurs on large files and write operations (Understanding Ext4 Disk Layout). Because the files are stored within non-contiguous blocks, fragmented files demand labour intensive, time-consuming techniques to piece them together accurately, making recovery and analysis difficult. In addition, the availability and compatibility of forensic tools for EXT file systems varies as some tools are designed to work with specific versions (EXT2, EXT3, EXT4) (The Filer - Linux Magazine) File system forensics can be complicated by the widely adopted nature of prepend extension. Thus, a comprehensive understanding regarding the tool capability (The Filer - Linux Magazine).

Tools Used in EXT Forensics

To understand EXT file systems, a forensic analysis involves a few key tools. **Autopsy** provides an easy-to-use interface for deleted file recovery, metadata analysis, and file structure examination that supports EXT system analysis (An analysis of Ext4 for digital forensics). The **Sleuth Kit** is well-known for its command line tools designed for disk imaging, file recovery and metadata analysis, providing a fine-tuned control (Lee, S., Jo, W., Eo, S., & Shon, T. (2020)). **Extundelete** and **TestDisk** are also made to recover deleted files by scanning inodes and file allocation tables. X-Ways Forensics specializes in features for disk imaging and file recovery (An analysis of Ext4 for digital forensics), whereas Ext4magic focuses on reconstructing fragmented files (Comparative Study on Various File System Implementations). **Rekall** works for both memory and disk analysis (An analysis of Ext4 for digital forensics), similarly **Bulk Extractor** extracts pattern-based information from disk images.(Understanding Ext4 Disk Layout)

CONCLUSION

File system is one of the important parts of every operating system and also very helpful in forensic analysis. Easy and cross-platform compatible, FAT is mostly found in removable devices such as USB media. It's missing many more advanced capabilities that would help forensics professionals perform a thorough analysis. NTFS, on the other hand provides an elaborate structure containing journaling, encryption and MFT creating a rich source of forensic data for evidence collection in modern days systems. These file systems depict changes in technology and its impact on digital forensics. Another important one that needs to be understood for appropriate investigative work is the Hierarchical File System (HFS) and EXT file systems (EXT2, EXT3 and EXT4). HFS is built on a proprietary basis over very heavy structures, requiring special tools and procedures. Crucial techniques for reconstructing the digital jigsaw that is HFS volumes include imaging, recovery of relevant files by examining the metadata and utilizing macOS features such as Spotlight and Time Machine, in addition to journal analysis.

With EXT's iterations comes new challenges and features for forensic analysis. The simplistic structure of EXT2 stands in stark disparity with the sophisticated journaling as well as performance improvements gained in both EXT3 and EXT4. Specialized tools and followed methods are leveraged such as imaging, file carving, Metadata analysis, journal analysis to extract the evidence. Forensic tools are making their way towards new horizons despite the challenges associated with file system corruption, encryption and fragmentation. Many tools such as Autopsy, The Sleuth Kit, extundelete and Ext4magic that implement complete solutions to the EXT file systems have been developed. The ongoing evolution of forensic techniques and tools ensures that forensic analysts have the best resources at their disposal to accommodate the increasing complexity of digital investigations, ultimately aiding in solving forensic cases.

REFERENCES

Alazab, M., Venkatraman, S., & Watters, P. (2009). Effective digital forensic analysis of the NTFS disk image. *Ubiquitous Computing and Communication Journal*, 4(1), 551–558.

Bhat, W. A., & Quadri, S. M. K. (2010). Review of FAT data structure of FAT32 file system. *Oriental Journal of Computer Science & Technology*, 3(1), 161–164.

Chow, K. P., Law, F. Y., Kwan, M. Y., & Lai, P. K. (2007, April). The rules of time on NTFS file system. In *Proceedings of the Second International Workshop on Systematic Approaches to Digital Forensic Engineering (SADFE)* (pp. 71–85). IEEE. DOI: 10.1109/SADFE.2007.22

Craiger, P., & Burke, P. K. (2005). Mac forensics: Mac OS X and the HFS+ file system. *Department of Engineering Technology, University of Central Florida*. Retrieved from https://stars.library.ucf.edu/etd/2167/

Digital Forensics Research Workshop. (n.d.). An analysis of Ext4 for digital forensics. Retrieved from https://dfrws.org/archives/papers/ext4-forensics.pdf

EaseUS. (n.d.). File system comparison: NTFS, FAT32, exFAT, and EXT. Retrieved from https://www.easeus.com/diskmanager/file-system.html

Forensics Community. (n.d.). DiffFork. Retrieved from https://github.com/forensics/difffork

InfoSec Institute. (n.d.). Computer forensics: Media & file system forensics. Retrieved from https://www.infosecinstitute.com/resources/digital-forensics/computer-forensics-media-file-system-forensics/

International Research Journal of Engineering and Technology. (2021). Comparative study on various file system implementations. *International Research Journal of Engineering and Technology, 8*(11), 123–130. Retrieved from https://www.irjet.net/archives/V8/i11/IRJET-V8I11190.pdf

IP with Ease. (n.d.). NTFS file system guide. Retrieved from https://ipwithease.com/ntfs-file-system/

Lee, S., Jo, W., Eo, S., & Shon, T. (2020). ExtSFR: Scalable file recovery framework based on an Ext file system. *Multimedia Tools and Applications*, 79(23), 16093–16111. DOI: 10.1007/s11042-019-7199-y

Li, Q., Zhang, Q., Tan, Y. A., Li, Y., & Zheng, J. (2016, January). Research on allocator strategy of FAT32 file system based on Linux & Windows. In *Proceedings of the 2016 International Conference on Intelligent Control and Computer Application (ICCA)* (pp. 248–252). Atlantis Press. DOI: 10.2991/icca-16.2016.58

Linux Careers Blog. (2022, May). Linux file systems: ext3 vs. ext4. Retrieved from https://linuxcareers.com/blog/2022/05/linux-file-systems-ext3-vs-ext4

Linux Magazine. (2022). The filer. *Linux Magazine, 255.* Retrieved from https://linux-magazine.com/Issues/2022/255/The-Filer

Lu, L., Arpaci-Dusseau, A. C., Arpaci-Dusseau, R. H., & Lu, S. (2013). A study of Linux file system evolution. In *Proceedings of the 11th USENIX Conference on File and Storage Technologies (FAST 13)* (pp. 31–44). USENIX Association.

Magnet Forensics. (n.d.). File system forensics: No longer the gold standard? Part 1. Retrieved from https://www.magnetforensics.com/blog/file-system-forensics-no-longer-the-gold-standard-part-1/

Microsoft. (n.d.). Original DOS file system. Princeton University. Retrieved from https://mirror.math.princeton.edu/pub/oldlinux/Linux.old/distributions/cnix/FAT.pdf

Microtek Learning. (n.d.). Understanding hard disks and file systems. Retrieved from https://www.microteklearning.com/pdf/CHFIv10%20Course%20Outline.pdf

Microtek Learning. (n.d.). Understanding hard disks and file systems. Retrieved from https://www.microteklearning.com/pdf/CHFIv10%20Course%20Outline.pdf

Oracle. (n.d.). Understanding Ext4 disk layout, part 1. Retrieved from https://blogs.oracle.com/linux/post/understanding-ext4-disk-layout-part-1

Oracle. (n.d.). Understanding Ext4 disk layout, part 2. Retrieved from https://blogs.oracle.com/linux/post/understanding-ext4-disk-layout-part-2

SourceForge. (n.d.). FileXray: Advanced file system analysis tool. Retrieved from https://filexray.sourceforge.net/

Sterniczuk, B. (2022). Comparison of EXT4 and NTFS filesystem performance: Porównanie wydajności systemu plików EXT4 i NTFS. *Journal of Computer Sciences Institute*, 25, 297–300. DOI: 10.35784/jcsi.3004

Tai, J. (n.d.). Hard disks and file systems. Retrieved from https://john.tai.dev/posts/chfi-notes/module-03/

The Sleuth Kit. (n.d.). Autopsy digital forensics. Retrieved from https://www.sleuthkit.org/autopsy/

The Sleuth Kit. (n.d.). Autopsy digital forensics. Retrieved from https://www.sleuthkit.org/autopsy/

The Sleuth Kit. (n.d.). The Sleuth Kit. Retrieved from https://www.sleuthkit.org/

Ts'o, T. Y. (n.d.). Journaling the Linux ext2fs filesystem. *Massachusetts Institute of Technology*. Retrieved from https://web.mit.edu/tytso/www/linux/ext2intro.html

X-Ways Software Technology AG. (n.d.). WinHex: Hexadecimal editor and disk forensics tool. Retrieved from https://www.winhex.com/

Zhang, N., Jiang, Y., & Wang, J. (2020, January). The research of data recovery on Windows file systems. In *Proceedings of the 2020 International Conference on Intelligent Transportation, Big Data & Smart City (ICITBS)* (pp. 644–647). IEEE. DOI: 10.1109/ICITBS49701.2020.00141

Chapter 8
A Survey on 5G Wireless Network Intrusion Detection Systems Using Machine Learning Techniques

Michael Chai Chon Yun
https://orcid.org/0009-0004-3256-2902
Curtin University, Malaysia

Sivaraman Eswaran
https://orcid.org/0000-0003-0858-148X
Curtin University, Malaysia

ABSTRACT

This survey explores the landscape of Intrusion Detection Systems (IDS) in 5G wireless networks, with a specific emphasis on those leveraging Machine Learning (ML) techniques. The deployment of 5G is poised to revolutionize telecommunications with unprecedented data rates, reduced latency, and enhanced capacity. However, the advanced infrastructure also brings heightened security challenges, necessitating robust and adaptive security measures. IDS have emerged as a key strategy to counteract these vulnerabilities, particularly those that exploit machine learning for anomaly detection and rapid response. This paper reviews several 5G IDS implementations across different domains, including the 5G Core Network, Internet of Things (IoT), and Smart Grids. Each domain's technical and cyber-security environment is explored for better context in understanding the different implementations available, which are scrutinised based on ML models used, datasets

DOI: 10.4018/979-8-3373-0857-9.ch008

for training and testing, and architecture.

INTRODUCTION

Fifth-generation wireless networks, commonly known as 5G, is the latest poster child in telecommunication innovation that introduces new features and exponentially superior performance against its predecessors (Flinders & Smalley, 2024). According to a global economic study by IHS Markit and Omdia (2020), the roll out of 5G is projected to generate 3.8 trillion US dollars' worth of added GDP, and create 22.8 million new jobs in the global value economy. Wang et al. (2021) also points out that the adoption of 5G into industry, agriculture, and infrastructure, can amplify process efficiency, and limit resource utilisation for better sustainability on the long run. With 5G adoption being inevitable, comes the need to ensure its implementation respects security and privacy.

5G infrastructure is a prime target by adversaries due to its hosting of abundant private data and high-value operations (Deloitte, 2020). Moreover, threat actors look forward to leveraging the larger attack landscape and new zero-days that comes with 5G (Cybersecurity and Infrastructure Security Agency (CISA), 2021). Network security solutions are diverse and multifaceted, but this survey shall focus on an industry favourite solution that has proven its effectiveness, the Intrusion Detection System (IDS). This survey looks into different IDS implementations in 5G networks across multiple areas, with an additional emphasis on 5G-IDS that utilise machine learning (ML) techniques. As more modern security solutions embrace machine learning for better efficiency, and effectiveness against zero-days and unknown attacks, which often evade legacy signature-based IDS (Ni, 2023).

This chapter also looks into the design and engineering of 5G, how it is implemented into different areas, its unique security vulnerabilities, and the different IDS solutions to address them. IDS implementations into the 5G Core, 5G Internet-of-Things (IoT), and 5G Smart Grids, are observed and compared. From its findings, there is an abundance of 5G IDS implementations that address these different application areas and possess fine performance. However, a gap found within the survey is the lack of privacy preserving features in these 5G IDS solutions, especially when the ML models employed collect and aggregate private network data for further training. Albeit this, some IDS implementations in 5G IoT and 5G Smart Grids manage to successfully integrate Federated Learning (FL) as a ML model mechanism to keep private network data local and not shared with other ML models in training. But rather ironically, there's a lack of FL utilisation, or any other privacy preserving features for that matter, in IDS for 5G Core, when 5G Core is the backbone of public 5G infrastructure that hosts the most private data and mission critical operations.

OVERVIEW OF 5G NETWORKS AND IDS

5G Technology and Applications

5G intuitively represents the fifth-generation standard of wireless mobile networks, that is now replacing its 4G predecessor. 5G technology brings forth exponential improvements in performance and new features to enable emerging technologies. Performance wise, 5G exhibits both better efficiency and scalability. In comparison to 4G, 5G commands 100 times higher user data rate, five times lower end-to-end latency, and 100 times higher connected device capacity (Mohyeldin, 2016). This performance is made possible by 5G's utilisation of the 5G New Radio standard which enhances the preexisting Orthogonal Frequency-Division Multiplexing (OFDM) model to increase scalability (Ghannam & Darwazeh, 2019). Moreover, 5G now deploys lower sub-6GHz bands and higher 24GHz and up mm-Wave, for an even wider bandwidth spectrum for different applications. Apart from performance improvements, 5G also introduces a new feature, network slicing. Network slicing allows for the creation of separate end-to-end virtual networks by pairing individual Radio Area Network (RAN) to Core Network (CN) slice (Sultan, 2022), following the edge-to-core framework of 5G as represented in Figure 1.

Figure 1. 5G Edge to Core Framework

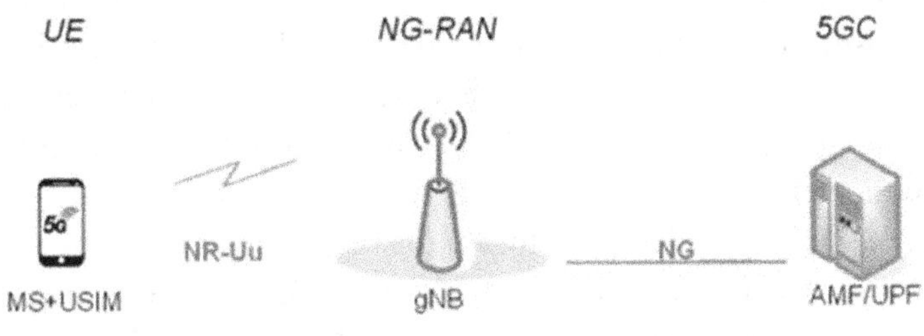

Source: Sultan (2022) breaks down 5G framework.

Application wise, 5G's stellar performance and new features do not stop at improving mobile broadband, but create opportunities for new applications and use cases. For instance, 5G's massive capacity can support vast sensor networks in an Internet-of-Things (IoT) Network (Altaleb & Zoltán, 2023). Potentially serving the growing interest in interconnected smart-infrastructure, such as electrical grids and industrial control systems. Meanwhile, 5G's network slicing can segregate the network into specific functions for mission-critical communications such as in transportation (Xue et al., 2023) and healthcare (Roddy et al., 2019), as illustrated in Figure 2.

Figure 2. Network Slicing for Mission Specific Functions

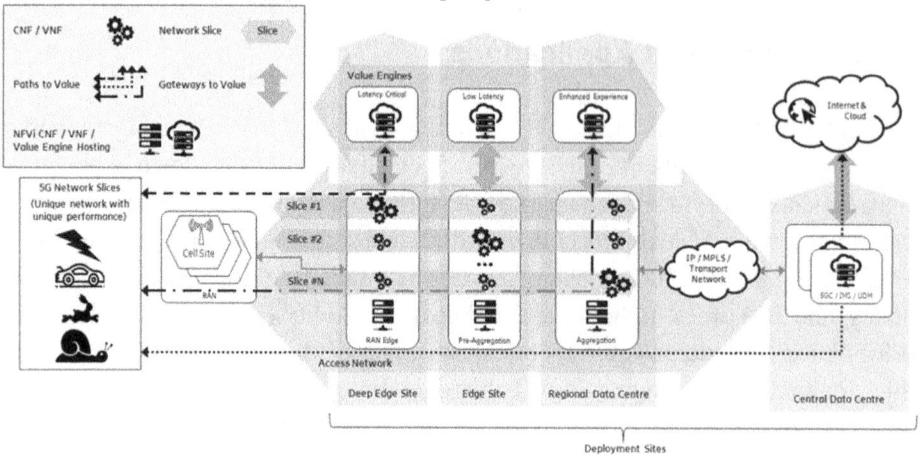

Source: Graphica (2020) illustrates using 5G network slicing for specific functions.

Vulnerabilities and IDS

As with all emerging technologies, comes emerging vulnerabilities and threats, and 5G is no exception. Following a Deloitte report (2020), wireless mobile networks, such as predeceasing 4G, have always been a prime target to cyberattacks due to their value in hosting communication infrastructure and transporting valuable data. Moreover, making it a target from a diverse range of attackers for social, political, and economic motivations. However, 5G may exacerbate this risk as it makes the network landscape increasingly complex and interconnected with other sectors and infrastructure, adding more attack vectors and a bigger bounty for threat actors.

According to a threat vector study by the CISA (2021), notable potential threat vectors of 5G infrastructure are through its Mobile Edge Computing (MEC), Spectrum Sharing, Network Slicing, and Software-Defined Networking (SDN) architecture. These unique 5G threat vectors are made more apparent in the context of the implementation areas of their respective underlying features. For instance, IoT and SG network utilisation of MEC and SDN, and CN utilisation of SDN. This paper will continue to dive deeper into the vulnerabilities these implementation areas.

Among the many mitigation and defensive solutions against these 5G vulnerabilities, this paper will focus on the implementation of Intrusion Detection Systems (IDS). An IDS is a software and/or hardware-based mechanism used to detect potential intrusions into a secured network, either based on a recognised malware signature or behavioural anomaly. Nonetheless, a rapidly innovating network requires an equally rapidly innovating IDS. As of late, IDS with integrated Machine

Learning (ML) or Deep Learning (DL) techniques have been showing promising results, as they can adequately address the increasingly larger and complex data plane posed by 5G, where traditional IDS may not suffice (Ni, 2023). Considering that, this paper will review different 5G IDS with integrated ML/DL, in the context of implementation areas. Those being as aforementioned, Core Network, Internet-of-Things, and Smart Grids.

CORE NETWORK (CN)

The backbone of 5G network infrastructure rests on the connection between User Equipment (UE) to the RAN and to the CN as illustrated in Figure 1, similarly to predeceasing 4G networks. The CN, or 5G Core (5GC), resembles the governing realm of the mobile network tasked with connection and user management. This makes it not only in charge of ensuring smooth and secure functioning of the network services, but also other network applications such as data and subscriber management. 5G sets CN apart from legacy systems by implementing it in a software-defined and cloud-native manner. This enhances CN capabilities by equipping it more programmable control and operability in cloud infrastructures (Ericsson, 2022).

According to 3GPP (Sultan, 2022), 5G CN utilises its newest capabilities by adopting a Service-Based-Architecture (SBA) approach. In the SBA, resources in the network are now defined as 'Network Functions' (NFs), instead of being lumped together with other network elements as 'Network Entities' as in legacy infrastructure. With SBA, CN has better control over the network by being able to assign NFs to authenticated and authorised users or even other NFs. This enables better segmentation or modulation of the network, which ultimately enables 5G's flagship network slicing feature. Examples of NFs on the 5GC control plane include Authentication Server Function (AUSF), Access and Mobility Management Function (AMF), Session Management Function (SMF), and more as shown in Figure 3.

Figure 3. Network Functions in 5GC

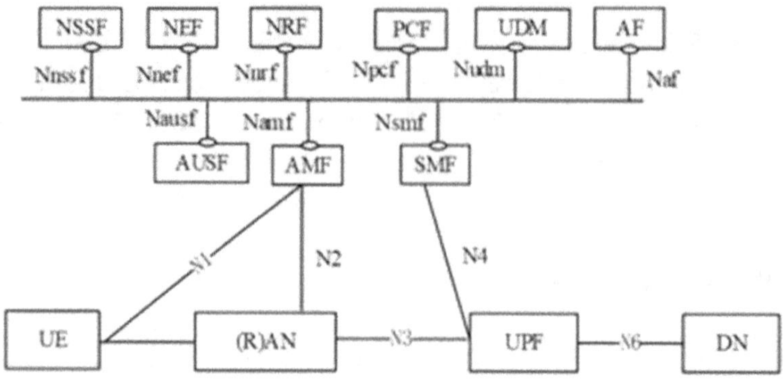

Source: Sultan (2022) details the network functions the in the 5G Core.

Vulnerabilities

CN are a prime target for attackers due to their value in network administrator privileges and access to data. Moreover, the complex architecture of CN introduces new vulnerabilities, primarily from its newer features such as network slicing. Network slicing is exposed to potential cross-slice disruption, which can pave the way for Man-in-the-Middle (MITM) and Side-Channel attacks that target one or more network slices (Vittal et al., 2023). Moreover, this is further exacerbated by third-party vendor dependencies in the CN. From here, attackers have access to additional attack vectors through this third-party equipment, that may not satisfy relevant security standards or lack in-sync updates with other elements in the network (Dixit et al., 2024).

The attack vector of CN becomes further complex by the proliferation of different and interconnected NFs. According to a systemic study on 5GC security by Dixit et al. (2024), the main vulnerability of NFs lies within their dependency architecture. As perpetrators can start by exploiting critical NFs and further attack its dependent NFs. For instance, a perpetrator with the aim of attacking the CN's session management may start by attacking the AMF, then proceed to attack the dependent SMF from there, allowing them to disrupt network services and carry out a denial-of-service (DoS) attack. Ultimately, the CN is predisposed to security vulnerabilities through its innovative features, exposing it to a myriad of multifaceted attacks that threaten all confidentiality, integrity, and availability aspects.

IDS Methods

This paper reviews two different IDS implementations for the 5G Core Network. Each implementation will be reviewed with a primary focus on their architecture, AI model, datasets used, results, performance in comparison to benchmarks (if any), as well as any other novel ideas proposed.

The first implementation follows Lu et al. (2023), where the authors proposed an IDS that analyses network slices for anomalies using the Convolution Neural Network (CNN) and Neural Architecture Search (NAS) models. The authors implemented the IDS as a Security Defined Software (SDS) to better suit the already software defined and cloud-native nature of 5GC. The proposed SDS detects anomalies from the backhaul link to the core network link, providing end-to-end coverage for network slice capture, as shown in Figure 4. The SDS will create copies of network data and process them into images for the CNN model to analyse for anomalies, and further train itself with optimisation from the NAS model. This SDS setup allows for IDS auto-detection and auto-update, as well as limited impact on network performance due to the traffic copying approach. The authors noted that the CNN model was trained using the IDS-2018 dataset, rather than the common KDD99 dataset which they claimed to be dated. The proposed method resulted in a detection accuracy of 97.9% for binary classification, and 94.9% in multiclass classification.

Figure 4. Security Defined Software System

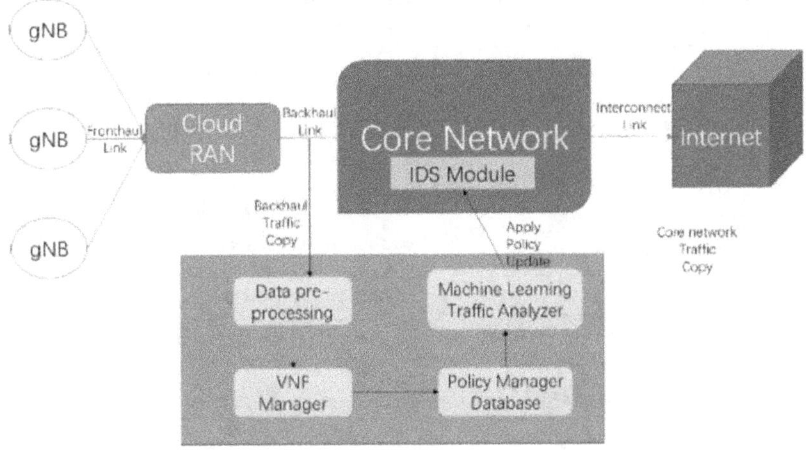

Source. Proposed IDS architecture of Lu et al. (2023) for the 5G core.

The second implementation follows Kalafatidis et al. (2024), where the authors experimented their proposed SDN-based IDS with both AI and simple statistical (SS) models. Akin to the first implementation, the authors stipulate that a SDN-based approach would provide more comprehensive security for the cloud-native 5GC, as it allows for a real-time global view of network topology, and centralised data collection for rapid AI analysis and security response. The authors set up the experimental environment with two main entities, the Attack Identification Engine (AIE), and the Network Environment, as illustrated in Figure 5. The authors deployed two types of detection mechanisms, a SS model-based IDS, and two AI model-based IDS. The two AI models in question are 1D Convolutional Neural Network (CNN), and Fully Connected Multilayer Perceptron (MLP). Both models were trained with 35GB of pcap file data, made up of 12GB of UDP DoS attacks, 10GB of SCTP DoS attack, and the remaining 13GB being normal traffic. For the experiment results, the authors focused on measuring IDS performance by the average response time by each detection mechanism. The SS model-based IDS yielded an average response time of more than four seconds, while the AI model-based IDS yielded more than five seconds. Despite the faster performance from SS models, the authors did note that the AI models performed better at identifying minor anomalies and more complex attack patterns, while the SS models significantly under-performed in attack instances that did not involve spikes in network traffic. Indicating that the AI models were more robust in detecting more advanced DoS attacks.

Figure 5. Architecture of proposed IDS byKalafatidis et al. (2024)

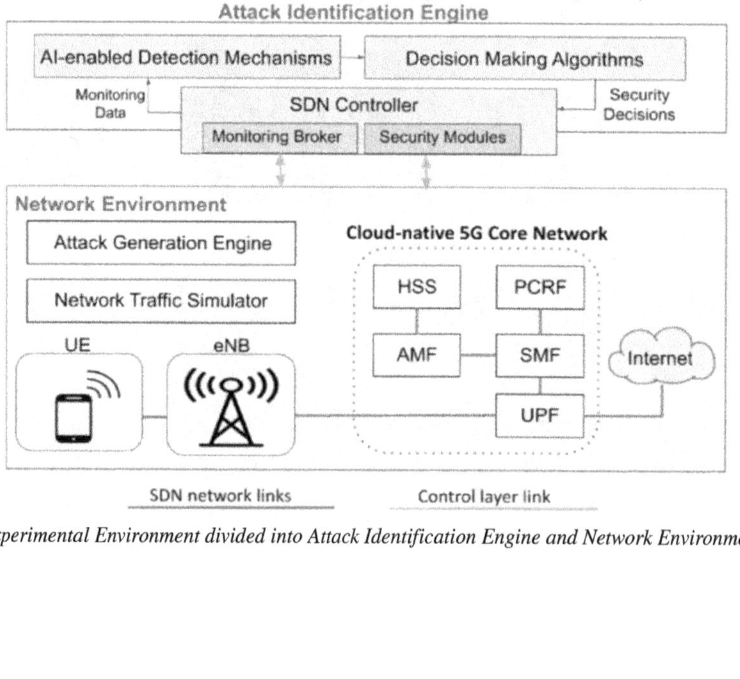

Note Experimental Environment divided into Attack Identification Engine and Network Environment.

INTERNET OF THINGS (IOT)

Internet of Things (IoT) resembles the expansive networks of interconnected physical devices equipped with sensors that collect data, and software that processes and communicates the data with the rest of the network. Presenting abundant use cases that revolve around massive data collection and system controls. As explained by Greengard (2023), IoT networks expand the technological environment by incorporating both already digital-first devices such as smartphones and computers, with physical-first analog devices such as basic sensors and home appliances. This new symbiotic relationship harnesses new data from physical devices, for smarter decision making and robust controls in digital devices. IoT architecture exists in varying forms, with no current standardisation or common convention. However, through a comparison of different architectures made by Al-Awami et al. (2023), the most basic and common components of almost all architectures are the perception layer, network layer, and application layer. Perception layer refers to the physical devices or nodes of the IoT that collect data, while network layer refers to the networking infrastructure and protocols that enable communication, which in this paper will focus on 5G. Lastly, application layer processes the data for specific services and use-cases for the user, this processing can be done in either a central IoT gateway, and or along the edge of the network, as supported by 5G.

The application areas of IoT are vast and diverse. Shehu Yalli et al. (2024) best described IoT applications as upgrading digital objects into intelligent objects by integrating object-oriented interface to harness their data for smart decisions and analysis. Ding et al. (2020) classified IoT applications by their data rate and end-user-type, being either human-oriented or machine-oriented applications. Human-oriented applications involve significant human interaction with the IoT network, such as security cameras or remote-controlled appliances in a smart home setting. Machine-oriented applications on the other hand are more independent of human involvement in order to operate normally, for instance fault detection sensors that control precision machinery in industrial environments. That being said, IoT can be applied to a vast multitude of domains, with 5G being an appropriate carrier due to compatible technologies. To be specific, 5G's vast networks to support massive IoT, support for edge-computing and high data rates, and interoperable software-defined infrastructure (Shafique et al., 2020).

Vulnerabilities

As with 5G's own vulnerabilities, IoT adds on its own unique security challenges to the stack. According to leading cybersecurity firm, Fortinet (2023), IoT possesses an even wider attack vector landscape with its abundant devices or nodes in the network, many of which are basic physical-first devices that are lack the computational power to run security features. Moreover, the lack of standardisation of IoT architecture further complicates security across different setups (Iqbal et al., 2020).

Siwakoti et al. (2023) analysed IoT attacks from the United States' National Vulnerability Database (National Institute of Standards and Technology, 2019), and classified them based on the levels of the IoT architecture that they attack, those being Perception, Network, Data, and Application layer as they opted for a 4-layer IoT architecture approach as shown in Figure 6. Perception layer attacks involve targeting the vulnerabilities posed from physical devices, such as spoofing attack to mimic nodes in the network, or sleep deprivation attacks that manipulate power mode to drain battery life. Attacks on network layer leverage networking protocols to either disrupt traffic through Distributed Denial of Service (DDoS) or Sybil attacks, or spy on traffic using MITM and Sniffing attacks. Data and Application layer attacks occur closer to the end-user environment such as malware injections and access control attacks to degrade Quality-of-Service. All in all, this paper will focus on IDS solutions to counter these IoT vulnerabilities in a 5G environment.

Figure 6. Attacks across IoT Architecture

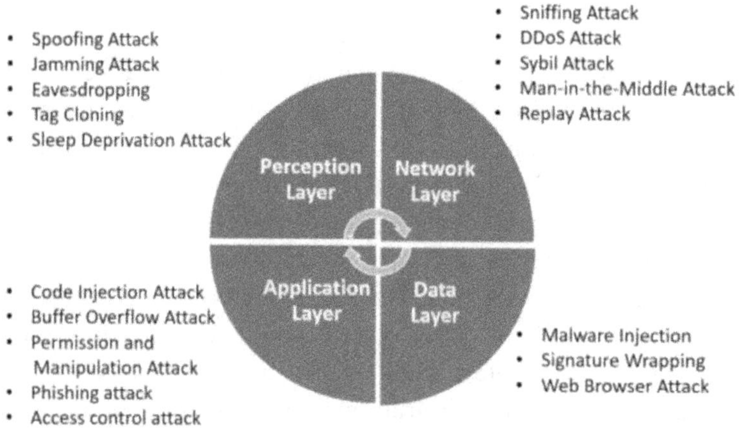

Source: Siwakoti et al. (2023) categorises various cyberattacks on IoT by layer.

IDS Methods

This paper reviews two different IDS implementations for the 5G IoT Networks. Each implementation will be reviewed with a primary focus on their architecture, AI model, datasets used, results, performance in comparison to benchmarks (if any), as well as any other novel ideas proposed.

Linh Le et al. (2023) proposes a novel 5G IoT IDS that exists as a NF within the 5G Core. The authors implemented the IDS as a NF to inspect IoT MQTT packets on the User Plane Network Function (UPF) using various ML algorithms, as shown in Figure 7. The novel IDS was implemented as a NF in strict compliance with 3GPP standards for ease of integration into pre-existing 5G infrastructure, which a lot of 5G IDS papers do not take into consideration. Moreover, with the IDS strategically placed in the 5G Core, it can carry out real-time monitoring of the UPF, and respond quickly through its connection with AMF and SMF on the control plane. ML algorithms used are Linear Support Vector (LSV), Stochastic Gradient Descent (SGD) Classifier, MLP, XGBoost, Decision Trees, and Random Forest. The ML models were trained via emulating a IoT network with a DoS attacker using the MQTT-malaria tool. The novel IDS was tested afterwards via two emulations, each consisting of a 200 IoT devices, and one or two attackers. The test concluded in satisfactory detection accuracy of over 95% for SGD Classifier, MLP, Random Forest, and XGBoost, but under performance of below 60% accuracy for LSV and Decision Trees.

Figure 7. Proposed 5G-IoT IDS byLe et al. (2023)

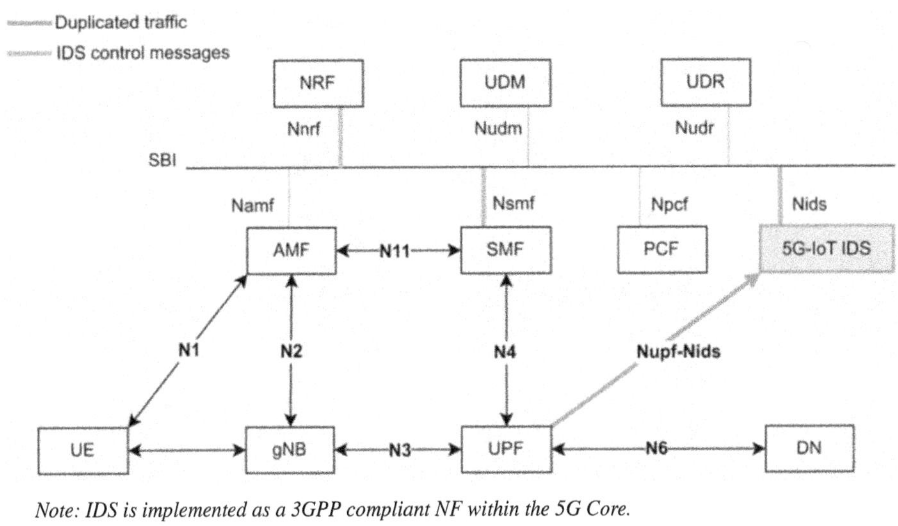

Note: IDS is implemented as a 3GPP compliant NF within the 5G Core.

Fan et al. (2020) presents IoTDefender, a federated transfer learning-based IDS for 5G IoT. In light of heterogeneous and personalised IoT networks supported by 5G, these 5G IoT networks exist as individual data islands that makes it difficult to implement a centralised IDS to protect all of them, and not to mention the privacy issues that arise from cross-sharing their data. To address this, IoTDefender leverages 5G edge computing capabilities to aggregate data in a privacy respecting manner with a federated learning (FL) model. IoTDefender's architecture is illustrated in Figure 8, where it is split up into three layers, cloud, Mobile Edge Computing (MEC), and IoT device layer. At the cloud layer, the 5G security cloud is tasked with training the server model, which distributes a public IDS dataset to all the MEC platforms. At the MEC layer, a local IDS is trained with the public IDS dataset from the server model, and continues to train itself with local network data using TL, fine tuning the local IDS to its IoT device layer. IoTDefender implemented CNN for its base model on both server model and MEC later, for better compatibility with TL. Rigorous testing resulted in IoTDefender being capable of detecting 91.93% of malicious packages on average, with improved performance at detecting unknown attacks or anomalies compared to traditional models.

Figure 8. IoTDefender byFan et al. (2020)

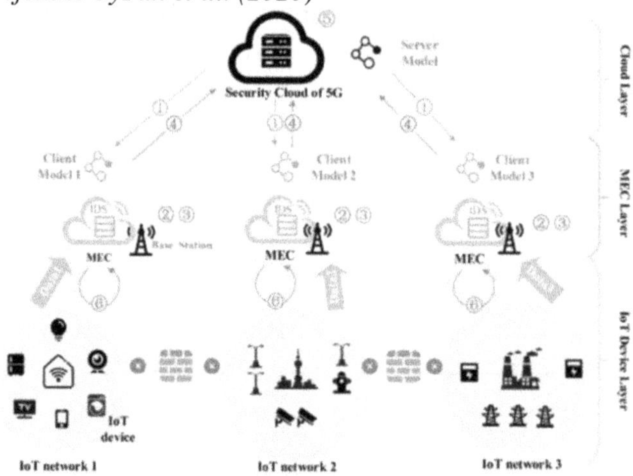

Note; Breakdown of FL-based IDS by cloud, MEC, and device layers.

SMART GRID

Smart grids (SG) refer to power grid infrastructure that employ digital solutions, such as software, sensors, and networking, for comprehensive monitoring and control capabilities. These newfound capabilities enable real-time monitoring of power supply and demand, and communicating it with power generation and distribution sides, thus enhancing communication for enhanced control (Abrahamsen et al., 2021). As highlighted by the International Energy Agency (2023), smart grids adoption continues to grow globally to meet the insatiable demand for electricity as part of the global effort to electrify the economy, and shift to renewable energy. Colak et al. (2021) compared SG to traditional power grids as more distributed, robust, and bi-directional in data flow across the grid, as detailed in Table 1.

Table 1. Comparison of Traditional and Smart Grids

Characteristic	Traditional Grid	Smart Grid
Information Flow	One-way	Two-way
Electricity Generation	Centralized	Distributed
Grid Topology	Radial	Network
Distributed Energy Sources	Seldom	Often
Monitoring	Usually Blind	Self-monitoring
Outage Recovery	Manual Restoration	Self-reconfiguration
Testing	Manual Check	Remote Check
Control Ability	Limited Control	Pervasive Control
Overall Efficiency	Low	High

Colak et al. (2021) compares the differences between traditional power grids and emerging smart grids.

According to an industry report by Ericsson (2024), SG may utilise a variety of wired and wireless communication technologies, however as SG become increasingly advanced and complex, they require high performance communication technologies which limit the best options to wired fibre and 5G. They further highlighted 5G being the preferred choice over wired fibre, citing better flexibility and cost efficiency, especially in rural settings. Besides the high performance of 5G networks, Esenogho et al. (2022) points to the unique features of 5G that makes it a good carrier for SG, those being its SDN controller and network slicing ability. As the SDN would enable the robust monitoring and controls employed by SG, and network slicing to isolate specific SG functions such as metering or fault detection.

Vulnerabilities

5G enabled SG will inevitably inherit the native security vulnerabilities of 5G, much of which has been covered earlier in this paper. Putting that aside, SG introduces new security vulnerabilities that may either be unique or leverage these 5G-native vulnerabilities. Zou et al. (2021) considers the widening attack surface from the introduction of SDN controller and network slicing, plus multitype access in SG, to be of major security concern. SDN controller and network slicing remove the hardware barrier between control and data plane that used to exist in legacy systems, potentially allowing cross-intrusions within these software defined planes. Furthermore, multi-type access due to the diverse set of devices in a SG may complicate or entirely prevent a unified security approach for the whole network, due to protocol mismatch or even lack thereof in lightweight devices.

Table 2. Attacks on SG by CIA triad

CIA	Attack
Confidentiality	Social Engineering, Eavesdropping, Traffic Analysis, Unauthorized Access, Password Pilfering, MITM, Sniffing, Replay, Masquerading, Data Injection
Integrity	Tampering, Replay, Wormhole, False Data Injection, Spoofing, Data Modification, MITM, Time Synchronization, Masquerading, Load-Drop
Availability	Jamming, Wormhole, Denial of Service, LDos, Buffer Overflow, Teardrop, Smurf, Puppet, Time Synchronization, Masquerading, MITM, Spoofing

Faquir et al. (2021) categorises the various cyberattacks on SG according to the CIA triad.

In regards to specific attacks, Faquir et al. (2021) conducted a literature review and compiled common attacks on SG, categorised by the Confidentiality, Integrity, Availability (CIA) triad, on Table 2. As a countermeasure to these 5G-SG vulnerabilities and potential attacks, Rakas et al. (2022) suggests that an IDS would be an effective one, considering it is well adapted to the unique SG environment. That involving limited computational power of SG devices such as meters and sensors, and integration into the distributed substations of SG.

IDS Methods

This paper reviews two different IDS implementations for the SG. Each implementation will be reviewed with a primary focus on their architecture, AI model, datasets used, results, performance in comparison to benchmarks (if any), as well as any other novel ideas proposed.

Mirzaee et al. (2021) proposes a Federated IDS (FIDS) using FL for 5G enabled SG. Their motivation comes from the lack of privacy considerations in conventional ML-based IDS, as implementing them in a SG would use and move data on users' energy consumption. FIDS equips each household's smart meter with its own local IDS (L-IDS) on a participant-side Host Area Network (HAN), which is connected to a central server-side Neighbourhood Area Network (NAN), illustrated in Figure 9.

Figure 9. SG over 5G and FIDS Architecture

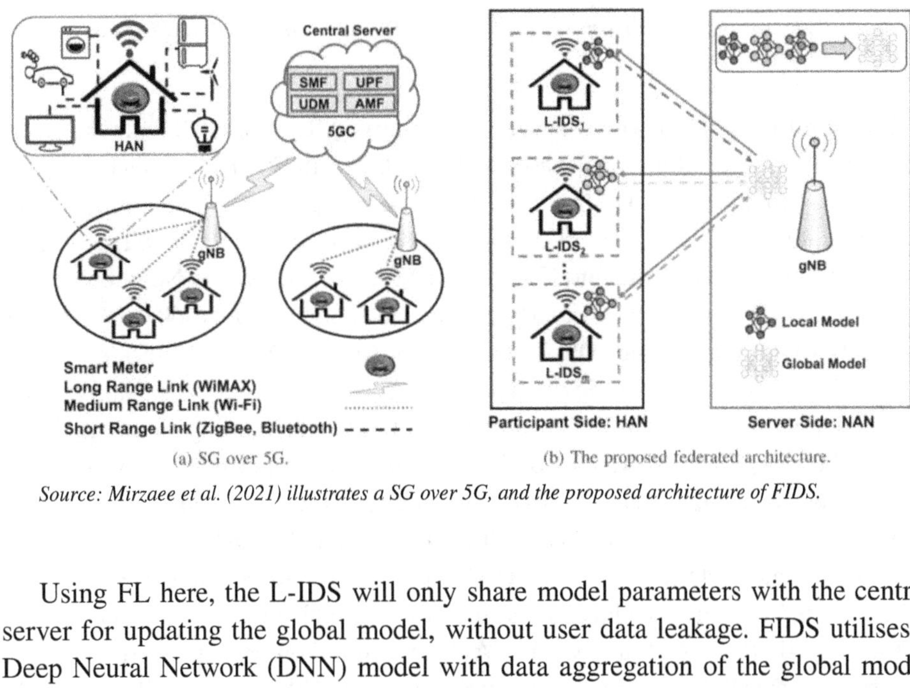

(a) SG over 5G. (b) The proposed federated architecture.

Source: Mirzaee et al. (2021) illustrates a SG over 5G, and the proposed architecture of FIDS.

Using FL here, the L-IDS will only share model parameters with the central server for updating the global model, without user data leakage. FIDS utilises a Deep Neural Network (DNN) model with data aggregation of the global model using Federated Averaging. The experiment is set up with 16 different host L-IDS trained with the NSL-KDD dataset, and is evaluated alongside other centralised ML models as a benchmark. The authors selected the NSL-KDD dataset citing its well-regarded usage for anomaly detection training, having include DoS, User to Root, Remote to Local, and Probe Scanning attacks. In the experiment, FIDS yielded a 99.55% detection accuracy, which is at par with its benchmark centralised models.

The authors concluded that FIDS is effective at detecting threats whilst preserving privacy.

Figure 10. Collaborative ML-IDS for SDN-based SG

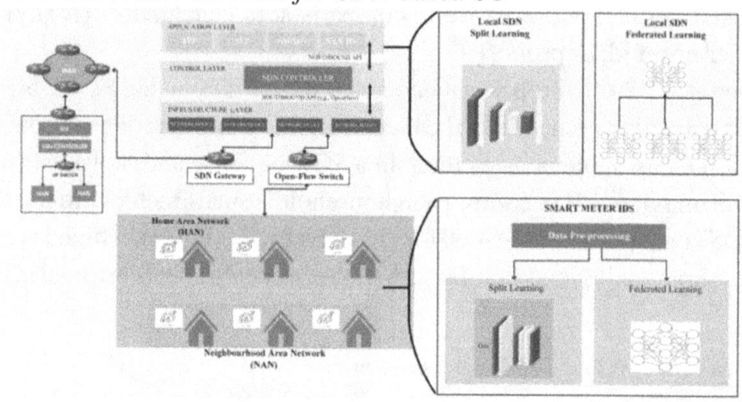

Source: Chatzimiltis et al. (2024) proposes a collaborative IDS that incorporates either FL or SL.

Chatzimiltis et al. (2024) presents a collaborative ML-based IDS that resides on the application layer of an SDN-based SG, illustrated in Figure 10. SDN splits up the SG's communication infrastructure into the control and data plane, similar to 5G infrastructure, centralising network control whilst streamlining data flow. The authors also segmented the SDN-SG into Home Area Network (HAN) and Neighbourhood Area Network (NAN) layers, similarly to Mirzaee et al. [39], but took two different approaches with placing the IDS. The first approach is a Smart Meter based IDS (SM-IDS), where the IDS resides on a smart meter in the HAN, that partially trains its model locally, and uses Split Learning (SL) to finish the training on a centralised server. The usage of SL solves the problem of limited computational power on the smart meters, by using resources on a centralised server without transferring private local data. The second approach places the IDS server at the NAN level, NAN-IDS, which aggregates data from multiple HAN clients. NAN-IDS employs either a FL or SL, where FL trains each local smart meter IDS which updates the global model on the NAN-IDS bidirectionally. SL NAN-IDS on the other hand partially trains each smart meter IDS, and finishes the training on the NAN-IDS, similarly to SM-IDS. The authors used Feed Forward Neural Network (FFNN) models trained and tested with the NSL-KDD dataset. Experimental results yielded an average detection accuracy rate of 80.3% for SM-IDS, 78.43% for FL-NAN-IDS, and 81.1% for SL-NAN-IDS. Concluding SL as an effective IDS method, that excels in performance, considers limited computational power on SG devices, and preserves data privacy.

COMPARATIVE ANALYSIS ACROSS AREAS

Table 3. Summarised comparison of different IDS methods

Paper	Area	ML Model	Dataset	Detection Results
Lu et al. (2023)	5GC	CNN & NAS	CIC-IDS2018	Accuracy: 97.9% (binary) 94.9% (multiclass)
Kalafatidis et al. (2024)	5GC	CNN, MLP, Statistical	UDP DoS 12GB, SCTP Dos 10GB	Response Time: Statistical= 4s ML Models= 5s
Le et al. (2023)	IoT	LSV, SGD, MLP, XGBoost, Decision Trees, Random Forest	MQTT-Malaria	Accuracy: >95% for SGD, MLP, XGBoost, Random Forest
Fan et al. (2020)	IoT	FLCNN & TL	CIC-IDS2017, NSL-KDD, 3x IoT Datasets	Accuracy: 91.39%, 2-3% higher than traditional models
Mirzaee et al. (2021)	SG	FLDNN	NSL-KDD	Accuracy: 99.55%
Chatzimiltis et al. (2024)	SG	FFNN & FL/SL	NSL-KDD	Accuracy: SM-IDS= 80.3% FL-NAN= 78.43% SL-NAN= 81.8%

Comparison of all six different implementations based on 5G application area, ML model(s) used, datasets used, and detection results.

Table 3 compares the key features of the six IDS methods in this literature review. Notable observations are that neural networks were the ML model of choice across all application areas for its robustness and performance, while NSL-KDD was the most common dataset used for its multi category attacks (Hong et al., 2021). Besides looking at ML models and datasets utilised, along with their results, there remains a few noteworthy novel ideas introduced. Linh Le et al. (2023) implemented their IDS as a 3GPP compliant NF for integration into the 5G Core, which could potentially aid in the ease of integration into common 5G infrastructure. While Fan et al. (2020), and both SG IDS (Mirzaee et al., 2021) (Chatzimiltis et al., 2024), implemented the Federated Learning approach in their IDS to protect private user data from exfiltration during model training. Differences aside, all approaches had shown stellar performance in terms of detection accuracy and time rates, plus additional capabilities in detecting zero-day threats. Suggesting that ML or AI is indeed a viable technology to bolster IDS.

POTENTIAL FUTURE DEVELOPMENTS

The evolution of IDS for 5G networks delivers not just better scalability and efficiency in handling 5G's massive networks, but also better zero-day detection capabilities. AI will play an important role in achieving this by leveraging techniques such as neural networks for high performance signature and anomaly detection, and federated learning in preserving data privacy during model training. 5G IDS will not only be built solely for mobile telecommunication service providers in mind, but also an increasingly diverse application base of IoT and Smart Infrastructure networks that introduce unique infrastructure challenges and a wider threat landscape. To which future IDS may have to increasingly rely on SDN and a cloud native approach for added flexibility to accommodate the demands.

REFERENCES

Abrahamsen, F. E., Ai, Y., & Cheffena, M. (2021). Communication technologies for Smart Grid: A comprehensive survey. *Sensors (Basel)*, 21(23), 8087. DOI: 10.3390/s21238087 PMID: 34884092

Al-Awami, S. H., Al-Aty, M. M., & Al-Najar, M. F. (2023). Comparison of IoT architectures based on the seven essential characteristics. *2023 IEEE 3rd International Maghreb Meeting of the Conference on Sciences and Techniques of Automatic Control and Computer Engineering (MI-STA)*. DOI: 10.1109/MI-STA57575.2023.10169289

Altaleb, H., & Zoltán, R. (2023, November 1). Addressing cybersecurity challenges in 5G-enabled IoT and critical infrastructures: A comprehensive overview. *2023 IEEE 27th International Conference on Intelligent Engineering Systems (INES)*. DOI: 10.1109/INES59282.2023.10297774

Chatzimiltis, S., Shojafar, M., Mashhadi, M., & Tafazolli, R. (2024). A collaborative Software Defined Network-Based Smart Grid Intrusion Detection System. *IEEE Open Journal of the Communications Society*, 5, 700–711. DOI: 10.1109/OJCOMS.2024.3351088

Colak, A., Guler, N., & Ahmed, K. (2021). Intelligent communication techniques for Smart Grid systems: A survey. *2021 9th International Conference on Smart Grid (IcSmartGrid)*. DOI: 10.1109/icSmartGrid52357.2021.9551027

Cybersecurity and Infrastructure Security Agency. (2021). *Potential Threat Vectors To 5G Infrastructure*. Cybersecurity and Infrastructure Security Agency. https://www.cisa.gov/sites/default/files/publications/potential-threat-vectors-5G- infrastructure_508_v2_0%2520%25281%2529.pdf

Deloitte. (2020, March 10). *Global cyber executive briefing*. Deloitte; Deloitte Global. https://www.deloitte.com/global/en/services/risk-advisory/research/Telecommunications.html

Ding, J., Nemati, M., Ranaweera, C., & Choi, J. (2020). IoT connectivity technologies and applications: A survey. *IEEE Access : Practical Innovations, Open Solutions*, 8, 67646–67673. DOI: 10.1109/ACCESS.2020.2985932

Dixit, U., Vittal, S., & A, A. F. (2024). A systematic study for understanding the security risks in 5G Core network. *2024 16th International Conference on COMmunication Systems & NETworkS (COMSNETS)*, 43–48. DOI: 10.1109/COMSNETS59351.2024.10427440

Ericsson. (2022). *5G Core (5GC) network: Get to the core of 5G*. Ericsson.com. https://www.ericsson.com/en/core-network/5g-core

Ericsson. (2024). *Study of 5G as enabler of new power grid architectures*. Ericsson.com. https://www.ericsson.com/en/reports-and-papers/industrylab/reports/bringing-5g-to-power

Esenogho, E., Djouani, K., & Kurien, A. (2022). Integrating Artificial Intelligence Internet of Things and 5G for Next-Generation Smartgrid: A survey of trends challenges and prospect. *IEEE Access : Practical Innovations, Open Solutions*, 10, 1–1. DOI: 10.1109/ACCESS.2022.3140595

Fan, Y., Li, Y., Zhan, M., Cui, H., & Zhang, Y. (2020). IoTDefender: A Federated Transfer Learning Intrusion Detection framework for 5G IoT. *2020 IEEE 14th International Conference on Big Data Science and Engineering (BigDataSE)*. DOI: 10.1109/BigDataSE50710.2020.00020

Faquir, D., Chouliaras, N., Sofia, V., Olga, K., & Maglaras, L. (2021). Cybersecurity in smart grids, challenges and solutions. *AIMS Electronics and Electrical Engineering*, 5(1), 24–37. DOI: 10.3934/electreng.2021002

Flinders, M., & Smalley, I. (2024, February 20). *What is 5G?* IBM. https://www.ibm.com/topics/5g

Fortinet. (2023). *Top IoT device vulnerabilities: How to secure IoT devices*. Fortinet. https://www.fortinet.com/resources/cyberglossary/iot-device-vulnerabilities

Ghannam, H., & Darwazeh, I. (2019, June 27). A proposal for scalable 5G new radio frames with enhanced throughput. *2019 IEEE 89th Vehicular Technology Conference (VTC2019-Spring)*. DOI: 10.1109/VTCSpring.2019.8746532

Graphica. (2020). *An introduction to 5G architecture*. Graphica. https://just.graphica.com.au/an- introduction-to-5g-architecture/

Greengard, S. (2023, April 28). *Internet of Things | electronic network*. Encyclopedia Britannica. https://www.britannica.com/science/Internet-of-Things

Hong, R.-F., Horng, S.-C., & Lin, S.-S. (2021, November 1). *Machine learning in cyber security analytics using NSL-KDD dataset*. IEEE Xplore. DOI: 10.1109/TAAI54685.2021.00057

IHS Markit, & Omdia. (2020). *The 5G economy in a post-COVID-19 era*. IHS Markit. https://www.qualcomm.com/content/%20dam/qcomm-martech/dm- assets/documents/qualcomm_5g_economy_in_%20a_post-pandemic_era_report_2020.pdf

International Energy Agency. (2023, July 11). *Smart Grids*. IEA. https://www.iea.org/energy- system/electricity/smart-grids

Iqbal, W., Abbas, H., Daneshmand, M., Rauf, B., & Abbas, Y. (2020). An in-depth analysis of IoT security requirements, challenges and their countermeasures via software defined security. *IEEE Internet of Things Journal*, 7(10), 1–1. DOI: 10.1109/JIOT.2020.2997651

Kalafatidis, S., Agrafiotis, G., Giapantzis, K., Lalas, A., & Votis, K. (2024). Experiments with digital security processes over SDN-based cloud-native 5G Core networks. *2024 27th Conference on Innovation in Clouds, Internet and Networks (ICIN)*. DOI: 10.1109/ICIN60470.2024.10494481

Le, L., Salem, B., Ahad, E., Aitsaadi, N., & Du, X. (2023). 5G-IoT-IDS: Intrusion Detection System for CIoT as Network Function in 5G Core network. *GLOBECOM 2023 - 2023 IEEE Global Communications Conference*. DOI: 10.1109/GLOBECOM54140.2023.10437158

Lu, C., Tao, Z., & Yuanyuan, M. (2023). A 5G slice traffic anomaly detection method based on convolution neural network. *2022 7th International Conference on Signal and Image Processing (ICSIP), 34*, 963–967. DOI: 10.1109/ICSIP57908.2023.10270927

Mirzaee, P., Shojafar, M., Pooranian, Z., Asefy, P., Cruickshank, H., & Tafazolli, R. (2021). FIDS: A Federated Intrusion Detection System for 5G Smart Metering network. *2021 17th International Conference on Mobility, Sensing and Networking (MSN)*. DOI: 10.1109/MSN53354.2021.00044

Mohyeldin, E. (2016). *Minimum technical performance requirements for IMT-2020 radio interface(s)*. International Telecommunication Union. https://www.itu.int/en/ITU-R/study- groups/rsg5/rwp5d/imt-2020/Documents/S01-1_Requirements%20for%20IMT-2020_Rev.pdf

National Institute of Standards and Technology. (2019). *NVD - search and statistics*. Nist.gov. https://nvd.nist.gov/vuln/search

Ni, M. (2023). A review on machine learning methods for intrusion detection system. *Applied and Computational Engineering*, 27(1), 57–64. DOI: 10.54254/2755-2721/27/20230148

Rakas, B., Timčenko, V., Kabovic, M. M., & Kabovic, A. V. (2022). Intrusion Detection Systems in Smart Grid. *2022 21st International Symposium INFOTEH-JAHORINA (INFOTEH)*. DOI: 10.1109/INFOTEH53737.2022.9751302

Roddy, M., Truong, T., Walsh, P., Al Bado, M., Wu, Y., Healy, M., & Ahearne, S. (2019). 5G network slicing for mission-critical use cases. *2019 IEEE 2nd 5G World Forum (5GWF)*, 409–414. DOI: 10.1109/5GWF.2019.8911651

Shafique, K., Khawaja, B. A., Sabir, F., Qazi, S., & Mustaqim, M. (2020). Internet of Things (IoT) for next- generation smart systems: A review of current challenges, future trends and prospects for emerging 5G-IoT scenarios. *IEEE Access : Practical Innovations, Open Solutions*, 8(8), 23022–23040. DOI: 10.1109/ACCESS.2020.2970118

Siwakoti, Y. R., Bhurtel, M., Rawat, D. B., Oest, A., & Johnson, R. (2023). Advances in IoT security: Vulnerabilities, enabled criminal services, attacks and countermeasures. *IEEE Internet of Things Journal*, 10(13), 1–1. DOI: 10.1109/JIOT.2023.3252594

Sultan, A. (2022, August 8). *5G system overview*. 3GPP. https://www.3gpp.org/technologies/5g-system- overview

Vittal, S., Dixit, U., Sovitkar, S. P., Sowjanya, K., & Antony Franklin, A. (2023). Preventing cross network slice disruptions in a zero-trust and multi-tenant future 5G networks. *2023 IEEE 9th International Conference on Network Softwarization (NetSoft)*, 227–231. DOI: 10.1109/NetSoft57336.2023.10175424

Wang, J., Roy, H., Alam, S., Rao, T., Ahshrup, S., & McCluskey, W. (2021). The Impact of 5G on the European Economy. In *Accenture*. Accenture., https://www.accenture.com/content/dam/accenture/final/a-com- migration/manual/r3/pdf/pdf-144/Accenture-5G-WP-EU-Feb26.pdf

Xue, K., Piñeiro, J., Yu, Y., Hong, J., Yin, X., & Xie, S. (2023). Performance and reliability of 5G communications for USV-UAV critical applications. *2023 17th European Conference on Antennas and Propagation (EuCAP)*. DOI: 10.23919/EuCAP57121.2023.10132977

Yalli, J. S., Hasan, M. H., & Badawi, A. (2024). Internet Of Things (IOT): Origin, Embedded Technologies, Smart Applications and its Growth in the Last Decade. *IEEE Access : Practical Innovations, Open Solutions*, 12, 1–1. DOI: 10.1109/ACCESS.2024.3418995

Zou, Z., Chen, T., Chen, J., Hou, Y., & Yang, R. (2021, March 1). *Research on network security risk and security countermeasures of 5G technology in power system application*. IEEE Xplore. DOI: 10.1109/IAEAC50856.2021.9390826

KEY TERMS AND DEFINITIONS

Cloud Native: An approach in building applications upon cloud computing infrastructure. A rising trend in cybersecurity and AI appliances that benefit greatly from leveraging the scalability, efficiency, and reliability, provided by cloud computing.

Denial-of-Service (DoS): Among the most common cyberattacks, where it aims to disrupt the availability of digital services via flooding them with enough network traffic to use up or overwhelm the supported capacity.

Federated Learning (FL): A machine learning technique that performs model training in a distributed and decentralised manner across multiple devices. These decentralised nodes collaboratively train the model without sharing raw local data, protecting private data.

Man-in-the-Middle (MITM): A type of cyberattack which aims to covertly intercept the communications between two parties, potentially breaching communication confidentiality or even integrity by modifying intercepted messages.

Mobile Edge Computing (MEC): A network architecture of cloud computing that extends computational work to the edge of mobile networks to reduce latency. Often employed by IoT networks that require low-latency but also don't require intense computational power.

Neural Network: A type of machine learning model made up of interconnected nodes, organized into layers. These neurons process information and pass it along to the next layer, similar to how biological neurons transmit signals. Commonly used by IDS due its effectiveness in natural language processing and handling large volumes of data.

Orthogonal Frequency-Division Multiplexing (OFDM): A digital modulation technique that enables high-speed data transfer required by wireless communications such as 5G and WiFi. It achieves this by dividing transmission data across the frequency spectrum orthogonally to avoid interference.

Radio Area Network (RAN): The edge of wireless networks that connects user equipment, such as mobile phones or IoT devices, to the core network via a backhaul link. This is where physical base stations, i.e. cell towers, come into play.

Zero-Day: A cyberattack that exploits unknown vulnerabilities within a system. Amongst the hardest cyberattacks to defend against as they're unpredictable, and evade signature-based defensive systems.

Chapter 9
Machine Learning in Digital Forensic Analysis

Angel Justo Jones
https://orcid.org/0009-0007-9740-6611
University of Virginia, USA

ABSTRACT

Machine learning (ML) is transforming digital forensic analysis by enhancing the speed, accuracy, and depth of evidence examination and interpretation. This chapter explores the integration of ML algorithms into digital forensic workflows, including anomaly detection, pattern recognition, and predictive modeling. It discusses how various machine learning techniques, such as supervised and unsupervised learning, deep learning, and reinforcement learning, are applied to tasks like data classification, incident response, and evidence triage. Challenges such as model interpretability, data privacy, and adversarial attacks are addressed alongside emerging solutions to improve robustness and reliability. Through case studies and practical applications, this chapter underscores the impact of machine learning on evolving forensic capabilities, contributing to more efficient investigations and enhanced decision-making processes.

1. INTRODUCTION

Digital forensics has evolved considerably in recent years as investigators face increasingly complex challenges in analyzing and interpreting digital evidence. The integration of Machine Learning (ML) within digital forensics represents a significant advancement, offering tools that can handle large volumes of data, recognize intricate patterns, and automate traditionally manual tasks (Bhawna & Mahajan, 2024; Dunsin et al., 2024). The application of ML within digital forensics brings speed,

DOI: 10.4018/979-8-3373-0857-9.ch009

efficiency, and scalability to investigations, which is crucial given the exponential increase in digital crime and the widespread use of technology in modern society.

A few key factors drive the need for ML in digital forensics. First, digital devices' sheer volume of data creates substantial obstacles for forensic analysts. Traditional forensic techniques may struggle to handle the volume and complexity of data in cases involving terabytes of information, necessitating a scalable, automated approach (Ganesh, 2017; Jeong, 2020). Additionally, with cybercrimes' diverse and evolving nature, identifying patterns and understanding relationships within data has become increasingly critical. ML techniques like anomaly detection and predictive modeling aid in uncovering hidden patterns, enabling investigators to detect malicious activities with greater accuracy (Hall et al., 2022; Irons & Lallie, 2014).

The use of ML in digital forensics is multifaceted, spanning several applications. For example, ML algorithms assist in data classification, making it easier to identify relevant data among massive datasets. Natural Language Processing (NLP) models help analyze textual evidence, while image and video recognition algorithms process multimedia files, identifying pertinent evidence in formats like photos and recordings (Costantini et al., 2019; Zangana & Omar, 2020). Moreover, ML models, such as neural networks and decision trees, enable digital forensics to detect irregularities and anomalies within network traffic, which is vital for investigating network-based crimes like Distributed Denial of Service (DDoS) attacks and unauthorized access (Rizvi et al., 2022; Omar, 2024).

The growing sophistication of cyber threats has also led to the need for explainable AI (XAI) in digital forensics, where transparency and accountability are essential (Kelly et al., 2020; Sikos, 2021). Explainable AI models make it easier for forensic analysts to interpret and justify findings to legal stakeholders, which is a crucial component in court proceedings. This transparency facilitates better trust in AI-driven forensics, allowing the presentation of forensic findings in an understandable format for non-technical stakeholders (Jarrett & Choo, 2021; Hall et al., 2022).

ML in digital forensics not only enhances traditional forensic methods but also introduces new ways to anticipate and respond to cyber threats. For instance, predictive models are used to detect potential threats and vulnerabilities within networks, allowing for proactive security measures (Tyagi et al., 2024; Wright et al., 2012). By anticipating attacks, forensic investigators can mitigate risks before they lead to severe breaches, thus strengthening overall cybersecurity (Adam & Varol, 2020; Huff et al., 2023).

As ML applications in digital forensics continue to expand, challenges also arise. Data privacy, ethical concerns, and potential biases within ML models are significant issues. Ensuring that ML algorithms provide accurate and unbiased results is essential, as errors can lead to wrongful conclusions in investigations (Iqbal et al., 2020; Gholami & Omar, 2024). Additionally, digital forensics often involves sensitive data, making privacy-preserving ML techniques essential to protect individuals' rights and comply with regulations (Manasa & Kumar, 2022; Hamza & Omar, 2013).

Overall, the integration of ML into digital forensics represents a transformative shift in the field. By automating data processing, enhancing pattern recognition, and providing actionable insights, ML offers substantial advantages for digital investigations. However, as the field evolves, careful consideration of ethical implications and model accuracy will be crucial for sustainable, responsible implementation (Dunsin et al., 2022; Zangana et al., 2024). In this chapter, we explore the multifaceted roles of ML in digital forensics, examining key methodologies, challenges, and future directions in this emerging domain.

2. OVERVIEW OF MACHINE LEARNING TECHNIQUES USED IN FORENSICS

Machine learning (ML) has rapidly transformed the field of digital forensics, enhancing the efficiency, accuracy, and speed of forensic investigations. The integration of ML into forensics enables practitioners to handle vast volumes of digital data, detect intricate patterns, and automate complex analytical processes. This section explores various ML techniques applied in digital forensics, including supervised, unsupervised, and reinforcement learning models, as well as recent advances such as explainable AI and hybrid systems.

To grasp the role of machine learning in digital forensics, it is essential to understand the main techniques applied in forensic investigations. The figure below provides a high-level overview of the primary machine learning approaches, including supervised, unsupervised, and reinforcement learning, as well as emerging methods like explainable AI and hybrid systems.

Figure 1. Machine Learning Techniques in Digital Forensics

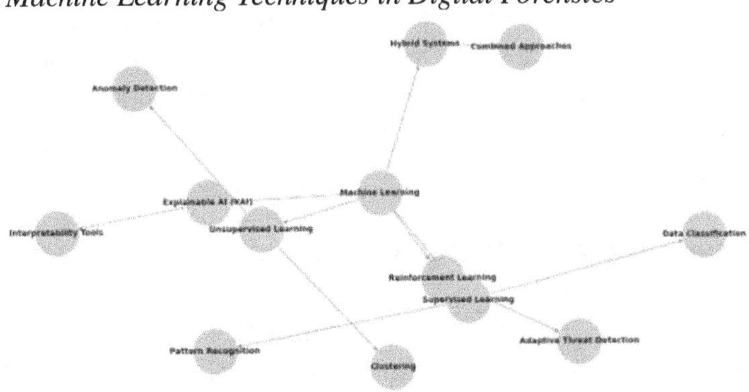

2.1 Supervised Learning in Forensic Investigations

Supervised learning, where algorithms learn from labeled datasets, has been widely used in digital forensics to classify and predict instances of digital evidence. These models are trained on known patterns of cyber threats, which helps them recognize similar threats in new data. For example, classifiers like Support Vector Machines (SVMs) and Random Forests are effective in categorizing malware samples and identifying anomalies in network traffic (Bhawna & Mahajan, 2024). Supervised models are particularly valuable in scenarios requiring pattern recognition, such as distinguishing legitimate from malicious network behavior, or identifying anomalies in file access patterns (Iqbal et al., 2020).

2.2 Unsupervised Learning for Anomaly Detection

Unsupervised learning techniques are also critical in forensic analysis, especially in situations where labeled data is scarce. These models identify patterns or clusters within data without prior labels, making them highly useful for anomaly detection tasks. Techniques like clustering and Principal Component Analysis (PCA) allow forensic experts to flag unusual behaviors that may indicate a security breach or suspicious user activities. For instance, clustering algorithms have been applied in network forensics to detect atypical user behaviors that may indicate malicious intent (Costantini et al., 2019; Dunsin et al., 2022).

2.3 Reinforcement Learning in Adaptive Forensic Systems

Reinforcement learning (RL) has potential applications in digital forensics, particularly for adaptive systems that evolve based on environmental feedback. In cybersecurity contexts, RL algorithms can be designed to learn optimal responses to digital threats over time. For example, RL-based models may adapt detection strategies as they observe attacker behaviors, thereby refining their approach to forensic analysis (Ganesh, 2017). Although RL is less common than supervised and unsupervised techniques in forensics, recent advances suggest it could be instrumental in incident response systems that autonomously adapt to new types of threats (Moustafa, 2022).

2.4 Deep Learning and Neural Networks

Deep learning (DL), particularly Convolutional Neural Networks (CNNs) and Recurrent Neural Networks (RNNs), has had a profound impact on digital forensics. These models are adept at processing large volumes of data and identifying subtle patterns that may elude traditional methods. For example, CNNs are used to analyze image and video evidence, while RNNs help in sequence analysis, making them suitable for processing time-series data like network traffic logs (Hall et al., 2022; Zangana et al., 2024). Advanced DL methods have been employed to enhance text classification accuracy, malware detection, and phishing threat identification (Omar, 2024; Zangana, Mohammed, Sallow, & Sallow, 2024).

2.5 Explainable Artificial Intelligence (XAI)

One of the challenges in applying ML to digital forensics is ensuring model interpretability. Explainable AI (XAI) techniques are essential in forensic investigations, as they provide transparency in decision-making processes, allowing forensic experts to understand and trust the model's output. This is especially important when forensic results are presented as evidence in court, as transparency can affect the outcome of legal proceedings. Techniques such as LIME (Local Interpretable Model-agnostic Explanations) and SHAP (SHapley Additive exPlanations) have been integrated into forensic tools to make ML models more interpretable and accountable (Kelly et al., 2020; Hall et al., 2022).

Explainable AI in digital forensics often involves a trade-off between accuracy and interpretability. Models with high interpretability may be less complex and, therefore, slightly less accurate, while highly accurate models tend to be more complex and challenging interpretability. The graph below illustrates this relationship, helping to clarify why forensic applications often balance these factors.

Figure 2. Accuracy vs. Interpretability in Explainable AI Models

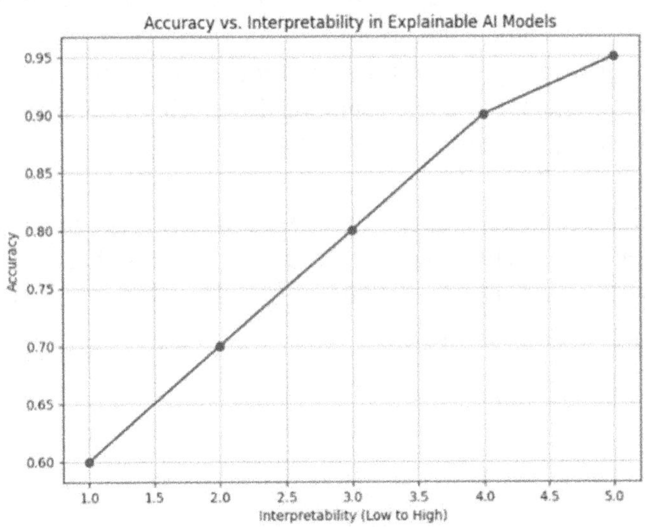

2.6 Hybrid Approaches and Future Directions

Given the diversity of digital evidence and cyber threats' complexity, hybrid approaches combining multiple ML techniques are increasingly favored. For example, integrating supervised and unsupervised learning can enhance the robustness of forensic tools by improving both classification accuracy and anomaly detection capabilities (Jeong, 2020; Jones & Omar, 2024). Additionally, hybrid systems that blend AI with traditional forensic methodologies are being developed to adapt to evolving digital environments, thereby providing comprehensive and adaptable forensic solutions (Irons & Lallie, 2014).

As ML techniques continue to advance, digital forensics is expected to leverage these innovations for more accurate and efficient evidence analysis. Emerging areas such as transfer learning and federated learning show promise in handling distributed forensic data while maintaining privacy. These techniques could address data privacy issues in cross-jurisdictional investigations, enabling forensic experts to collaborate while respecting local data laws (Adam & Varol, 2020; Rizvi et al., 2022). Furthermore, using synthetic data in training forensic models may help mitigate data scarcity issues, enabling the development of more robust detection algorithms (Gholami & Omar, 2023).

3. APPLICATIONS OF MACHINE LEARNING IN DIGITAL FORENSIC ANALYSIS

Machine Learning (ML) has increasingly become a cornerstone in digital forensic analysis, providing enhanced capabilities to handle the complexity and volume of digital evidence. By automating critical tasks and improving detection accuracy, ML algorithms aid forensic professionals in identifying, analyzing, and preserving evidence with greater efficiency and precision. This section explores various applications of ML in digital forensics and highlights how these technologies are reshaping the field.

The applications of AI in digital forensics are diverse, encompassing areas such as anomaly detection, malware analysis, and evidence classification. The network diagram below maps out these applications, illustrating the interconnected roles AI technologies play in forensic analysis.

Figure 3. AI Applications in Forensic Analysis

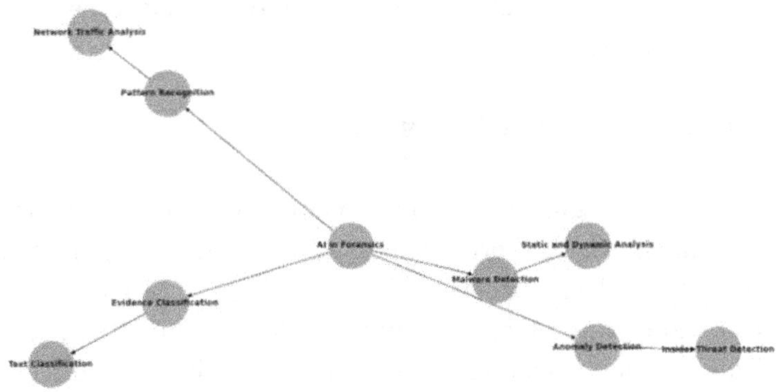

3.1. Pattern Recognition and Anomaly Detection

One of the primary applications of ML in digital forensics is pattern recognition and anomaly detection, enabling forensic analysts to identify irregularities in digital environments. ML algorithms can detect unusual patterns or behaviors indicative of a security breach or malicious activity through supervised and unsupervised learning. Costantini, De Gasperis, and Olivieri (2019) emphasize that AI-driven pattern matching enhances investigators' ability to identify complex attack patterns that might be missed by traditional methods.

Techniques like clustering and classification have been employed to detect anomalies in network traffic, aiding in identifying instances of unauthorized access, data exfiltration, and other cyber threats. Irons and Lallie (2014) noted that intelligent forensics leveraging ML models allow investigators to distinguish between legitimate and potentially malicious activities, thus reducing false positives.

3.2. Malware Detection and Analysis

Malware detection remains a crucial aspect of digital forensics, with ML offering powerful tools for identifying and classifying various types of malware. Deep learning models, such as Convolutional Neural Networks (CNNs), have proven effective in distinguishing between benign and malicious files, enabling forensic teams to respond more quickly to incidents. As Omar (2024) demonstrates, optimized CNN models have shown exceptional promise in revolutionizing malware detection accuracy.

AI and ML also facilitate dynamic and static analysis of malware. According to Rughani (2017), ML algorithms enhance traditional techniques by identifying subtle patterns in malware behavior that may not be evident through static analysis alone. Additionally, as Jarrett and Choo (2021) argue, the automation brought by AI tools can significantly reduce the time required to analyze large volumes of potentially infected files.

3.3. Automated Evidence Classification

The vast quantity of digital data involved in investigations necessitates automated methods for classifying and prioritizing evidence. ML algorithms can assist in categorizing digital artifacts such as images, documents, and network logs, allowing investigators to focus on high-priority items. Rizvi et al. (2022) highlight that ML-driven classification models help streamline the processing of digital evidence, especially in network forensics.

Natural language processing (NLP) models are particularly effective in classifying text data, such as emails or chat logs, which are often critical in cases involving cyber harassment or corporate fraud. Huff et al. (2023) discuss how NLP-based ML models facilitate rapid classification and extraction of relevant information from large datasets, making it easier to build cases based on communication records.

3.4. Behavioral Analysis and Insider Threat Detection

Behavioral analysis is another area where ML contributes significantly to digital forensics. By analyzing user behaviors, ML algorithms can detect deviations from established baselines, which may indicate an insider threat or other suspicious activity. Jeong (2020) proposes that machine learning can proactively identify behavioral anomalies, thus enabling organizations to mitigate risks before they escalate.

AI techniques are also invaluable in distinguishing between intentional and accidental actions, which is crucial for assessing potential insider threats. Hall, Sakzad, and Choo (2022) advocate for explainable AI models that provide transparency in digital forensics, helping forensic professionals understand and trust the decision-making process of ML algorithms when analyzing user behaviors.

3.5. Enhancing Digital Investigations Through Explainable AI (XAI)

Explainable AI (XAI) is gaining traction in digital forensics as it addresses one of the field's critical challenges: interpretability. XAI allows forensic experts to understand the reasoning behind ML-generated insights, which is essential for presenting evidence in legal contexts. Kelly et al. (2020) emphasize that XAI not only provides clarity but also enhances the credibility of AI-driven findings, making it easier for experts to justify decisions in court.

Applications of XAI are particularly relevant in cases involving deep learning models, which are often seen as "black boxes." Hall et al. (2022) argue that integrating XAI can bridge the gap between the advanced capabilities of AI and the need for transparency in legal proceedings, thereby strengthening the role of AI in digital forensics.

3.6. Automation of Routine Forensic Tasks

Automation in digital forensics reduces the workload on forensic analysts by handling repetitive and time-consuming tasks. Adam and Varol (2020) describe the application of AI in automating evidence gathering, data extraction, and preliminary analysis, allowing human investigators to focus on more complex tasks. Automation driven by ML can significantly expedite the investigative process, particularly in cases where large datasets require rapid initial assessment.

As Dunsin, Ghanem, and Quazzane (2022) note, in environments with limited resources, ML-driven automation can compensate for the lack of skilled personnel, ensuring that critical evidence is not overlooked due to resource constraints.

3.7. Network and Cloud Forensics

ML plays a crucial role in analyzing vast amounts of data generated in network and cloud environments. In network forensics, ML techniques are applied to detect intrusion patterns, analyze network flows, and track data exfiltration activities. Bhawna and Mahajan (2024) discuss how ML-based intrusion detection systems are becoming essential in network forensics, enabling real-time detection and response to security incidents.

In cloud forensics, where data is distributed across multiple servers and locations, ML algorithms help gather and correlate data from various sources. Hamza and Omar (2013) emphasize that AI can support cloud forensic investigations by analyzing large-scale data logs and identifying suspicious activities across cloud-based applications.

3.8. Future Directions in AI for Digital Forensics

As ML applications in digital forensics continue to evolve, future research is likely to focus on improving the robustness, accuracy, and interpretability of forensic tools. According to Zangana et al. (2024), advancements in cyber AI and emerging technologies such as blockchain could further enhance digital forensic methodologies by providing more secure and verifiable records of forensic activities.

Future directions may also include the integration of large language models (LLMs) for natural language understanding in forensics, as discussed by Gholami and Omar (2024). These models could assist in analyzing vast volumes of text data, such as chat logs and emails, enhancing the overall efficiency and effectiveness of digital investigations.

In conclusion, ML applications have revolutionized digital forensic analysis by enhancing automation, accuracy, and the ability to process vast datasets. However, ongoing advancements and research in explainability, security, and emerging technologies will be crucial to fully realizing the potential of AI in digital forensics. This transformation, as described by various scholars, marks a significant step forward in how forensic professionals approach evidence gathering, interpretation, and preservation in today's digital age.

4. MACHINE LEARNING PIPELINES FOR FORENSIC INVESTIGATIONS

Machine learning (ML) pipelines are pivotal in automating complex workflows in digital forensic investigations. With advances in artificial intelligence (AI), ML-based forensic pipelines streamline data collection, evidence processing, and pattern recognition, enhancing accuracy and efficiency in forensic tasks (Bhawna & Mahajan, 2024; Costantini et al., 2019). These pipelines typically consist of stages such as data preprocessing, feature extraction, model training, and evaluation, all of which are essential for the rapid and effective identification of digital artifacts relevant to cybercrime investigations.

In digital forensics, the use of machine learning involves several critical stages, from data collection to model deployment. The following flowchart outlines a typical forensic ML pipeline, highlighting stages such as data preprocessing, feature extraction, model training, and evaluation. Each step is essential for preparing and refining models for accurate forensic analysis.

Figure 4. Data Processing Pipeline for Forensic Machine Learning

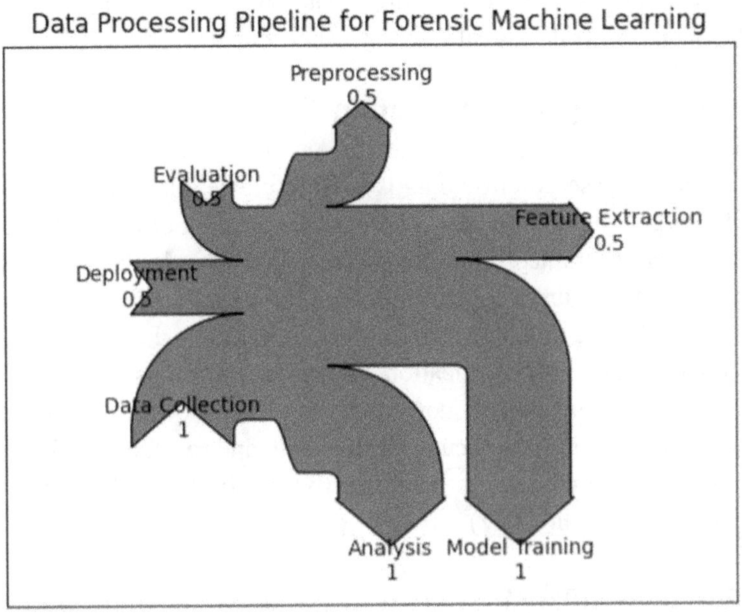

4.1. Data Collection and Preprocessing

Data in forensic investigations often originates from diverse and complex sources, including network logs, mobile devices, and cloud environments (Iqbal et al., 2020; Hamza & Omar, 2013). A comprehensive data collection phase ensures that investigators have access to all potential evidence, while preprocessing is necessary to handle inconsistent data formats, remove noise, and fill in missing information. Using AI for data preprocessing enables systems to recognize patterns within massive datasets, automatically reducing human oversight (Adam & Varol, 2020). Techniques such as natural language processing (NLP) assist in extracting meaningful information from text-based data, which is particularly useful in analyzing social media and communication logs (Gholami & Omar, 2023).

4.2. Feature Extraction and Selection

Feature extraction transforms raw data into useful information that ML models can analyze. In digital forensics, features may include timestamps, IP addresses, and user activity patterns. Feature selection algorithms then identify the most relevant features to improve model performance and reduce computational overhead (Kelly et al., 2020). By using AI-driven feature extraction techniques, forensic practitioners can identify crucial evidence, such as unusual activity patterns, indicating potential security breaches or insider threats (Jeong, 2020; Zangana et al., 2024).

4.3. Model Training and Evaluation

In the training phase, forensic data is used to create machine learning models capable of recognizing patterns and anomalies indicative of cyber threats. These models are generally trained on a large dataset that includes both malicious and benign activities to ensure they can differentiate normal behaviors from threats (Dunsin et al., 2024). Common approaches in digital forensics include supervised learning models, such as classification algorithms, and unsupervised learning, which is often applied in anomaly detection (Jarrett & Choo, 2021; Zangana et al., 2024). Evaluation metrics like accuracy, precision, and recall are critical to assess the reliability of these models, as they directly impact the credibility of forensic conclusions (Dunsin et al., 2022).

4.4. Deployment and Automation

Once trained, ML models are deployed within forensic environments to perform continuous monitoring and analysis. Deployment often involves integrating models with existing digital forensic tools, enabling real-time detection and rapid response to suspicious activities. Automated systems equipped with ML pipelines can significantly reduce the time required to process evidence, allowing investigators to focus on more complex aspects of the investigation (Irons & Lallie, 2014; Ganesh, 2017). Automation also allows these systems to handle vast data streams from network logs, reducing the chances of missing critical evidence (Rizvi et al., 2022).

4.5. Explainable AI and Interpretation of Results

A significant challenge in digital forensics is making AI models interpretable to ensure transparency and reliability in court settings. Explainable AI techniques enable forensic practitioners to understand and trust model outputs, which is essential when evidence is scrutinized in legal proceedings (Hall et al., 2022). Methods such as model-agnostic explanations and feature importance rankings provide insights into the model's decision-making process, helping investigators justify their findings and enhance accountability (Kelly et al., 2020).

4.6. Addressing Challenges and Future Directions

Despite the advantages, there are challenges in implementing ML pipelines in forensic investigations. Issues such as data privacy, model robustness, and computational resource requirements present obstacles in practical forensic applications. Forensic investigations require models that can operate efficiently under constraints, such as limited access to computing power, which calls for optimized algorithms (Mitchell, 2014; Moustafa, 2022). Future research may focus on improving model resilience to adversarial attacks and enhancing compatibility with edge computing devices to support investigations in resource-limited settings (Manasa & Kumar, 2022; Zangana & Omar, 2025).

Overall, machine learning pipelines provide a systematic and efficient framework for digital forensics, improving both the accuracy and speed of investigations. As AI continues to evolve, integrating robust ML models with forensic processes will likely lead to more effective detection and analysis of cyber threats, setting the foundation for next-generation digital forensics (Omar, 2024; Tyagi et al., 2024).

5. CHALLENGES AND LIMITATIONS OF USING ML IN DIGITAL FORENSICS

Machine learning (ML) has become increasingly valuable in digital forensics, especially in automating data processing and enhancing investigative efficiency. However, despite its strengths, several significant challenges and limitations impede its full potential in this field.

1. **Data Complexity and Volume** Digital forensics often involve analyzing vast amounts of data from various sources, including computers, mobile devices, and networks. Handling this volume effectively requires not only computational power but also efficient ML algorithms to process and interpret it. However, standard ML models often struggle to handle the heterogeneous and unstructured nature of forensic data. According to Adam and Varol (2020), the diverse nature of digital artifacts complicates ML-based analysis and interpretation, as traditional algorithms are often not designed for such data complexity.
2. **Quality and Relevance of Data** In digital forensics, the quality and relevance of data used to train ML models are paramount. For instance, many ML applications require labeled data for supervised learning, but forensic datasets are rarely labeled due to privacy concerns and the sensitive nature of the data (Jeong, 2020). This limitation forces forensic practitioners to rely on synthetic or generalized datasets, which may not fully represent real-world conditions

(Gholami & Omar, 2023). Furthermore, without relevant, high-quality data, ML models may produce unreliable results, which is a major concern in legal contexts where accuracy is critical.

3. **Explainability and Transparency** One of the most significant limitations of using ML in digital forensics is the "black-box" nature of many algorithms, especially deep learning models. As Hall, Sakzad, and Choo (2022) discuss, the lack of transparency in ML decisions can create legal and ethical issues, as forensic investigators are often required to explain their findings in court. Explainable AI (XAI) solutions are essential for forensic applications to build trust and facilitate understanding of how conclusions are reached. However, developing interpretable models without sacrificing accuracy remains a challenging goal (Kelly et al., 2020).
4. **Adaptability to Rapidly Evolving Threats** Digital threats evolve rapidly, and ML models need constant updates to remain effective. Traditional ML models, once trained, struggle to adapt to new types of malware, attack vectors, or forensic artifacts without extensive retraining. This limitation is critical in digital forensics, where emerging cyber threats constantly challenge existing defenses (Rizvi et al., 2022). Dunsin et al. (2022) highlight that constrained environments, such as low-resource devices or offline investigations, exacerbate this issue, as these systems may lack the capacity for ongoing model updates.
5. **Bias and Model Integrity** ML models can inadvertently carry biases introduced during the training phase, which could lead to skewed interpretations or incorrect conclusions. In digital forensics, such biases can be particularly damaging, potentially affecting case outcomes (Tyagi et al., 2024). Costantini, De Gasperis, and Olivieri (2019) point out that without careful data curation and bias mitigation strategies, forensic ML models may unintentionally favor specific patterns that do not align with broader investigative needs, leading to incomplete or misleading analyses.
6. **Privacy and Ethical Concerns** The use of ML in digital forensics raises substantial privacy and ethical issues, particularly around the storage, processing, and use of sensitive personal data. For example, models that are not securely managed could inadvertently expose sensitive data, violating privacy rights (Omar, 2022). Additionally, forensic investigators must consider the ethical implications of using AI in highly sensitive cases, as mistakes or misuse of these technologies could have severe consequences (Hamza & Omar, 2013).
7. **Resource Constraints and Computational Limitations** Effective ML applications in digital forensics often demand significant computational resources, which can be a limitation in environments with restricted access to advanced hardware (Dunsin et al., 2022). Resource-constrained environments, such as those in remote locations or smaller organizations, may not have the computa-

tional power required for advanced ML models, limiting their applicability and efficacy in real-time investigations (Omar, 2021).

8. **Integration with Existing Forensic Frameworks** Integrating ML with established forensic frameworks and tools poses challenges in terms of compatibility and standardization. Many digital forensics processes have been designed without ML in mind, making it difficult to incorporate these models effectively. Jones et al. (2023) emphasize the importance of interoperability between ML and existing digital forensics systems, noting that without standardized integration, ML models may fail to enhance investigative workflows as intended.
9. **Cybersecurity Risks** ML models themselves are vulnerable to cyber attacks, including adversarial attacks and model poisoning, which can significantly affect their reliability. In a forensic context, the security of ML models is essential, as compromised models could mislead investigations (Zangana et al., 2024). Cybersecurity measures must be robustly implemented in ML-based forensic systems to prevent attackers from manipulating models and tampering with forensic findings.
10. **Challenges in Forensic Automation** While automation through ML holds promise for improving forensic efficiency, fully automating complex investigative processes remains challenging. Bhawna and Mahajan (2024) note that ML-based automation may struggle with complex cases that require nuanced judgment, as current models lack the contextual understanding necessary to make informed decisions in ambiguous scenarios. As a result, while ML can assist in automating repetitive tasks, complete automation in digital forensics is still out of reach.

In summary, while ML has substantial potential to enhance digital forensic processes, these challenges and limitations must be carefully managed to ensure its reliability, accuracy, and ethical use. Addressing these issues requires ongoing research, technological advancements, and a commitment to transparency and accountability in forensic applications.

6. CASE STUDIES AND REAL-WORLD APPLICATIONS

This section delves into case studies and real-world applications, examining how artificial intelligence (AI) has been integrated into digital forensics and cybersecurity to address evolving threats. Through AI advancements, the field of digital forensics has become more efficient, allowing professionals to respond to increasingly complex cyber incidents.

6.1 AI in Digital Forensics

The integration of AI in digital forensics has allowed for automation and efficiency in identifying, analyzing, and responding to cyber incidents. The study by *Adam and Varol (2020)* demonstrates how digital forensics tools enhanced by intelligent systems streamline the investigation process, enabling faster response times in detecting malicious activities. Additionally, Bhawna and Mahajan (2024) explore how AI-based analytics in digital forensics can improve the detection of anomalies, which is crucial for identifying unauthorized access and breaches.

Furthermore, the research by *Costantini et al. (2019)* highlights the synergy between AI and digital forensics, emphasizing how machine learning algorithms aid in sifting through vast data sets to uncover hidden patterns, especially in criminal investigations. As digital forensic investigations become more complex, AI tools provide robust solutions, offering accurate data analysis and reducing human error. Studies like that of *Rizvi et al. (2022)* affirm this trend, showing how AI techniques like neural networks and deep learning models aid in network forensics and detecting cyber-attacks in real-time.

6.2 AI-Enhanced Incident Response

AI has proven effective in incident response by providing proactive security measures. *Dunsin et al. (2022)* demonstrate that AI-driven incident response tools can operate in constrained environments, which is critical in real-time cybersecurity applications. They show that AI can assist in identifying potential threats before they escalate, thereby minimizing damage. *Jeong (2020)* also provides insights into how AI algorithms are leveraged to categorize security threats, allowing digital forensics teams to prioritize and respond efficiently to the most pressing risks.

In addition, *Irons and Lallie (2014)* discuss how AI-based intelligent forensics can analyze complex data structures and assist in decision-making, proving invaluable in responding to incidents swiftly. The study by *Hall et al. (2022)* explores the potential of explainable AI in digital forensics, making AI algorithms transparent and understandable for investigators, who can then verify and trust the system's findings when responding to threats.

6.3 Applications of AI in Cybersecurity and Threat Detection

In cybersecurity, AI's role has expanded from merely assisting in digital forensic investigations to actively preventing cyber threats. The use of machine learning in cybersecurity, as explored by *Jones et al. (2023)*, has facilitated the advancement of threat detection methods that can identify new attack patterns, such as zero-day vulnerabilities. *Zangana et al. (2024)* delve into the application of AI to assess and improve firewall rules, which significantly enhances an organization's security posture by preemptively blocking suspicious activities.

Similarly, *Mitchell (2014)* discusses AI-based pattern matching in a digital forensic context, which assists in identifying recurring attack patterns and applying preventive measures. These proactive capabilities align with *Tyagi et al. (2024)*, who review AI-based cyber defense mechanisms, stressing the importance of adaptive learning models to protect against dynamic threats in digital infrastructures.

6.4 Case Study: AI and Email Phishing Detection

Email phishing remains a prevalent cyber threat, with AI providing new solutions for its detection and mitigation. *Zangana et al. (2024)* explore cybernetic deception techniques, specifically examining AI's role in analyzing phishing email patterns. Their study outlines how AI models detect phishing attempts by analyzing the language and structure of emails, allowing organizations to filter out malicious messages before they reach employees.

6.5 Blockchain and AI in Digital Forensics

Blockchain technology, when combined with AI, enhances digital forensic processes by ensuring data integrity and security. For example, *Zangana (2024)* reviews blockchain-based timestamping tools, which provide verifiable records that are tamper-resistant, ensuring evidence preservation during forensic investigations. This application supports broader forensic needs, particularly in maintaining the chain of custody for digital evidence.

6.6 AI in Cloud and Network Forensics

With the rise of cloud computing, AI-based digital forensic tools have also expanded to address unique challenges in cloud environments. *Hamza and Omar (2013)* examine cloud computing security, illustrating how AI assists in monitoring cloud networks for abuse and misuse. In a complementary study, *Mohammed et al. (2018)* discuss the use of AI in wireless sensor network security, specifically in detecting wormhole attacks, showcasing the versatility of AI in different networking environments.

Moreover, *Ganesh (2017)* highlights AI's applicability in network forensics, where it can analyze traffic and detect unusual patterns indicative of malicious activity. These methods have made network forensics a more efficient field, as large volumes of network data are now analyzed quickly to detect anomalies, contributing to faster resolution of security incidents.

6.7 The Role of Large Language Models (LLMs) in Digital Forensics

Large Language Models (LLMs) have shown promise in enhancing digital forensics through natural language processing (NLP) capabilities. *Gholami and Omar (2023)* explore the efficiency gains from synthetic data use in training LLMs, while *Gholami and Omar (2024)* assess the application of student-teacher models in large-scale data analysis. These studies illustrate LLMs' role in handling vast datasets, such as communication logs, and identifying suspicious language patterns, which is invaluable for forensic teams during investigations.

Omar and Zangana (2025) further expand on LLM applications, highlighting their utility in software vulnerability detection, which has broader implications for forensic investigations, as software vulnerabilities often precede security breaches.

In conclusion, these case studies and applications showcase the depth of AI's integration into digital forensics and cybersecurity. With AI tools, digital forensics can adapt to the ever-evolving landscape of cyber threats, providing organizations with proactive security solutions and efficient incident response capabilities. The convergence of AI, blockchain, and LLMs highlights an emerging paradigm in digital forensics, promising a future where intelligent systems handle the complexities of cybersecurity threats and incident investigations autonomously.

7. LEGAL AND ETHICAL CONSIDERATIONS

In the rapidly evolving field of digital forensics, integrating artificial intelligence (AI) technologies raises complex legal and ethical issues that must be considered alongside technical advancements. As digital forensics moves towards the inclusion of sophisticated AI-driven tools, professionals must address these issues to ensure compliance with laws, maintain ethical standards, and uphold public trust. The ethical concerns surrounding AI in digital forensics involve privacy, transparency, accountability, bias, and data security. Simultaneously, legal considerations pertain to regulatory compliance, data protection laws, and evidentiary standards.

7.1 Privacy Concerns and Data Protection

AI in digital forensics poses significant privacy concerns, especially when it involves handling sensitive personal data. The ability of AI systems to analyze vast amounts of data can lead to potential overreach, infringing upon individuals' privacy rights. Forensic investigations often access confidential or private information, increasing the risk of unintentional breaches or misuse of data. As noted by Hall, Sakzad, and Choo (2022), the need for "explainable AI" frameworks has emerged as a solution to balance the power of AI with privacy constraints by making AI decisions more transparent and justifiable.

Data protection laws, including GDPR in Europe, mandate strict requirements for data handling and storage, particularly in forensics, where data integrity is paramount (Adam & Varol, 2020). Compliance with these regulations ensures that data subjects' rights are respected while allowing investigators to proceed lawfully. The use of anonymization techniques and other privacy-preserving methods is recommended to mitigate risks (Jeong, 2020).

7.2 Transparency and Accountability

Transparency in AI-driven digital forensics is critical to maintaining accountability. Digital forensic tools often operate as "black boxes," making it difficult for users to understand how conclusions are derived, which can complicate the judicial process. AI models must be designed to ensure that outputs can be easily interpreted, especially in high-stakes legal scenarios where forensic evidence can impact case outcomes (Kelly et al., 2020). The necessity of interpretable and explainable AI models is emphasized by Costantini, De Gasperis, and Olivieri (2019), who highlight that opaque models may hinder trustworthiness and credibility in legal proceedings.

Accountability also remains a core concern, as errors in forensic conclusions could result in wrongful convictions or overlooked criminal activities. For instance, Bhawna and Mahajan (2024) point out that accountability in digital forensics involves clarifying responsibilities for AI-driven decisions, such as identifying which stakeholders (software developers, forensic analysts, or AI designers) are responsible for errors or unintended outcomes in the analysis process.

7.3 Ethical Use of Artificial Intelligence

The ethical use of AI in digital forensics extends beyond legal requirements, necessitating that AI applications in this field uphold values of fairness, integrity, and impartiality. Bias in AI algorithms, often introduced unintentionally through training data, can lead to discriminatory practices. For instance, if an AI model is trained on a biased dataset, it may disproportionately flag certain groups or demographics in forensic investigations (Dunsin, Ghanem, & Quazzane, 2022). The inclusion of diverse and balanced datasets is critical to mitigating such bias, ensuring the fair treatment of all individuals involved.

Further ethical considerations arise in the use of deceptive techniques, such as cybernetic deception in digital forensics, which aim to detect phishing and other malicious activities by simulating adversarial scenarios. While effective, this approach may inadvertently violate ethical standards if it misleads innocent users or circumvents their consent (Zangana, Mohammed, Sallow, & Sallow, 2024). Striking a balance between effectiveness and ethical boundaries remains a priority.

7.4 Regulatory and Compliance Challenges

The legal landscape for AI in digital forensics is still developing, presenting challenges in maintaining consistent regulatory standards across different jurisdictions. Regulatory frameworks, such as those governing cybersecurity and data privacy, are essential to guide ethical AI usage, but they often lag behind the technology's advancements. Omar and Zangana (2024) emphasize that the rapid deployment of AI in security applications has outpaced regulatory progress, leading to ambiguities in acceptable practices and compliance guidelines.

In response, some scholars advocate for the establishment of international standards that would help streamline legal requirements across borders. Such standards could define protocols for data handling, evidence authentication, and AI accountability (Huff et al., 2023). Meanwhile, legal practitioners and forensic experts must stay informed of current regulations to prevent inadvertent violations, especially concerning cross-border data transfer and international investigative collaborations.

7.5 Standards of Evidence and Forensic Integrity

AI-driven digital forensic evidence must meet stringent legal standards to be admissible in court. In digital forensics, the reliability and integrity of AI methods are scrutinized under the rules of evidence, which often require forensic techniques to be widely accepted and validated by the scientific community (Irons & Lallie, 2014). Establishing AI tools as credible sources of forensic evidence requires rigorous validation and peer review, as the accuracy and reproducibility of AI-based forensic tools can significantly impact judicial outcomes (Mitchell, 2014).

Moreover, ethical concerns regarding AI's role in evidence collection, storage, and analysis must be managed with caution. Ganesh (2017) notes that evidence gathered through AI may need to undergo additional scrutiny to verify its reliability, thus requiring forensic analysts to be skilled not only in AI technology but also in the legal standards that underpin admissible evidence. Regular audits and updates to AI systems are suggested to maintain their forensic integrity and ensure they comply with legal standards.

In conclusion, addressing legal and ethical considerations in AI-driven digital forensics is essential to ensuring that technological advancements align with societal expectations and judicial requirements. By incorporating transparent, accountable, and fair AI practices, professionals in the field can uphold both the ethical principles and the legal frameworks critical to the field's credibility and public trust.

8. FUTURE DIRECTIONS AND RESEARCH OPPORTUNITIES

The field of digital forensics is poised for significant advancements through the integration of artificial intelligence (AI) and machine learning (ML) technologies. The potential to improve digital forensic processes, evidence analysis, and overall cybersecurity posture creates a promising trajectory for future research and application. This section explores several key directions and research opportunities for enhancing digital forensics through AI.

8.1 Enhanced AI Integration for Incident Response and Investigation

In the realm of digital forensics, the adoption of AI in incident response and investigative processes offers the potential to improve both speed and accuracy. AI-driven automation can facilitate quicker identification of malicious activities, reduce response times, and mitigate potential damages. Future research should focus on optimizing these capabilities within constrained environments, particularly in low-resource settings or during remote investigations, as highlighted by Dunsin et al. (2022) and Dunsin et al. (2024). Developing robust AI solutions that can function effectively in resource-constrained environments would benefit organizations operating in remote areas or with limited infrastructure.

8.2 Advancing Explainable AI in Digital Forensics

One crucial challenge for AI in digital forensics is the "black box" nature of some AI models, which can limit the transparency of decision-making processes. To address this, researchers like Hall et al. (2022) and Kelly et al. (2020) have explored Explainable AI (XAI) as a means to provide interpretable insights into AI-driven forensic analysis. Future research could focus on enhancing XAI methods to improve trust in AI applications within digital forensics, making it easier for investigators to understand and justify AI-based conclusions in court settings. This approach is critical to ensure that AI-driven evidence can stand up to legal scrutiny and support judicial decisions.

8.3 AI for Proactive Threat Intelligence

As cyber threats become more complex, there is a need for digital forensic systems that not only respond to attacks but also proactively identify and mitigate threats. Research by Jeong (2020) and Ganesh (2017) emphasizes the potential for AI in threat prediction and prevention. Future investigations can focus on integrating predictive analytics to assess potential risks and alert systems to suspicious behavior patterns in real-time, moving digital forensics from a reactive to a proactive stance. Moreover, the work by Wright et al. (2012) on cybersecurity in mobile environments highlights the importance of securing emerging digital landscapes where proactive threat intelligence will be critical.

8.4 AI-Driven Pattern Recognition and Automation in Forensic Analysis

Incorporating AI-based pattern recognition can streamline the forensic process by identifying pertinent data faster and with higher precision. Pattern recognition models, as outlined by Mitchell (2014) and Rughani (2017), can assist in discerning relevant data from vast datasets, a task that often consumes significant time and resources in traditional forensic analysis. Future research could focus on refining these models to handle increasingly sophisticated cyber threats and the growing volume of data from connected devices and networks.

8.5 Leveraging Large Language Models (LLMs) in Digital Forensics

Recent advances in LLMs have opened new pathways for digital forensics, particularly in software vulnerability detection and analyzing vast textual data from cyber incidents. As indicated by Gholami and Omar (2023, 2024) and Zangana and Omar (2025), LLMs can be applied to identify vulnerabilities in real-time, automate the extraction of critical information from text, and streamline forensic reporting. Future research could explore the potential of LLMs to handle multilingual data sources and provide real-time analysis of communication data, enhancing the detection of subtle patterns in text data that might indicate malicious activity.

8.6 AI and Blockchain for Enhanced Data Integrity in Forensic Investigations

Blockchain technology offers a decentralized, immutable ledger that can ensure the integrity and provenance of digital evidence. Zangana (2024) discusses the potential for blockchain-based timestamping tools to verify forensic data's authenticity, while Karthikeyan et al. (2023) highlight the promise of combining AI with blockchain for tamper-proof record-keeping. Future research could focus on designing blockchain-enabled frameworks that integrate AI models for real-time evidence validation, ensuring that digital forensics processes are both transparent and secure.

8.7 Tackling Privacy and Ethical Concerns in AI-Driven Digital Forensics

The implementation of AI in digital forensics raises ethical considerations, particularly regarding privacy and data security. Research by Omar and Zangana (2025) and Irons and Lallie (2014) has underscored the importance of addressing these concerns to maintain public trust in forensic investigations. Future research should focus on developing privacy-preserving AI models that allow forensic analysis without compromising individuals' privacy. This may involve advancements in differential privacy and federated learning, enabling the analysis of encrypted data without exposing sensitive information.

8.8 Summary

The application of AI and ML in digital forensics represents a paradigm shift in how digital evidence is gathered, analyzed, and interpreted. Future research in this domain can benefit from continued exploration into areas like Explainable AI, LLMs, blockchain integration, and privacy-preserving techniques. Collaborative efforts between academia, industry, and government will be essential to advance these technologies, ensuring they are robust, reliable, and legally sound for forensic purposes. Embracing these advancements will not only enhance the effectiveness of digital forensics but also help to stay ahead of increasingly sophisticated cyber threats.

9. CONCLUSION

This chapter has examined the growing influence of artificial intelligence (AI) on digital forensics, emphasizing how AI technologies are reshaping investigative processes. As digital environments expand in complexity and the volume of digital evidence grows exponentially, the need for sophisticated tools capable of processing large datasets and delivering accurate analyses has become critical. AI-driven techniques, including machine learning algorithms and neural networks, are now central to enhancing forensic investigations' speed, efficiency, and accuracy. These tools are increasingly relied upon to analyze massive data sources, detect patterns indicative of cyber threats, and automate repetitive tasks, which frees forensic experts to focus on more intricate aspects of their investigations.

The integration of AI in digital forensics has brought forward both significant opportunities and distinct challenges. On one hand, AI provides powerful mechanisms for automating tasks, identifying complex patterns, and predicting potential security threats with greater precision than traditional methods. However, the dependency on AI also introduces challenges related to algorithmic bias, explainability, and the security risks posed by adversarial attacks on AI models themselves. These challenges underscore the need for a balanced approach incorporating AI while addressing its limitations and vulnerabilities. Furthermore, legal and ethical considerations remain paramount, as forensic evidence derived from AI systems must meet rigorous standards for reliability and interpretability in court.

Future advancements in AI, such as explainable AI and advanced neural architectures, promise to further revolutionize the field of digital forensics. As researchers and practitioners continue to address existing limitations, AI-based digital forensics will likely become even more indispensable in combating cybercrime, ensuring data integrity, and safeguarding digital environments. The continuous evolution of this field presents promising research opportunities that will advance both forensic methodologies and the development of resilient, transparent AI models.

In summary, AI holds immense potential to transform digital forensics, making it more effective and adaptable to emerging threats. By harnessing the strengths of AI and mitigating its risks, digital forensic professionals can create more robust systems capable of addressing the demands of modern cybersecurity. This integration will not only enhance investigative capabilities but also contribute to the development of a more secure and resilient digital landscape.

REFERENCES

Adam, I. Y., & Varol, C. (2020, June). Intelligence in digital forensics process. In *2020 8th International Symposium on Digital Forensics and Security (ISDFS)* (pp. 1-6). IEEE. DOI: 10.1109/ISDFS49300.2020.9116442

Costantini, S., De Gasperis, G., & Olivieri, R. (2019). Digital forensics and investigations meet artificial intelligence. *Annals of Mathematics and Artificial Intelligence*, 86(1), 193–229. DOI: 10.1007/s10472-019-09632-y

Dunsin, D., Ghanem, M. C., Ouazzane, K., & Vassilev, V. (2024). A comprehensive analysis of the role of artificial intelligence and machine learning in modern digital forensics and incident response. *Forensic Science International Digital Investigation*, 48, 301675. DOI: 10.1016/j.fsidi.2023.301675

Dunsin, D., Ghanem, M. C., & Quazzane, K. (2022). The use of artificial intelligence in digital forensics and incident response in a constrained environment. *International Journal of Information and Communication Engineering*, 16(8), 280–285.

Ganesh, V. (2017). Artificial intelligence applied to computer forensics. *International Journal (Toronto, Ont.)*, 5(5).

Gholami, S., & Omar, M. (2023). Does Synthetic Data Make Large Language Models More Efficient? *arXiv preprint arXiv:2310.07830.*

Gholami, S., & Omar, M. (2024). Can a student large language model perform as well as its teacher? In *Innovations, Securities, and Case Studies Across Healthcare, Business, and Technology* (pp. 122-139). IGI Global. DOI: 10.4018/979-8-3693-1906-2.ch007

Hall, S. W., Sakzad, A., & Choo, K. K. R. (2022). Explainable artificial intelligence for digital forensics. *Wiley Interdisciplinary Reviews: Forensic Science*, 4(2), e1434.

Hamza, Y. A., & Omar, M. D. (2013). Cloud computing security: Abuse and nefarious use of cloud computing. *International Journal of Computer Engineering Research*, 3(6), 22–27.

Huff, A. J., Burrell, D. N., Nobles, C., Richardson, K., Wright, J. B., Burton, S. L., Jones, A. J., Springs, D., Omar, M., & Brown-Jackson, K. L. (2023). Management Practices for Mitigating Cybersecurity Threats to Biotechnology Companies, Laboratories, and Healthcare Research Organizations. In *Applied Research Approaches to Technology, Healthcare, and Business* (pp. 1-12). IGI Global.

Iqbal, F., Debbabi, M., Fung, B. C., Iqbal, F., Debbabi, M., & Fung, B. C. (2020). Artificial intelligence and digital forensics. *Machine Learning for Authorship Attribution and Cyber Forensics*, 139-150.

Irons, A., & Lallie, H. S. (2014). Digital forensics to intelligent forensics. *Future Internet*, 6(3), 584–596. DOI: 10.3390/fi6030584

Jarrett, A., & Choo, K. K. R. (2021). The impact of automation and artificial intelligence on digital forensics. *WIREs Forensic Science*, 3(6), e1418. DOI: 10.1002/wfs2.1418

Jeong, D. (2020). Artificial intelligence security threat, crime, and forensics: Taxonomy and open issues. *IEEE Access : Practical Innovations, Open Solutions*, 8, 184560–184574. DOI: 10.1109/ACCESS.2020.3029280

Jones, A., & Omar, M. (2024). Codesentry: Revolutionizing Real-Time Software Vulnerability Detection With Optimized GPT Framework. *Land Forces Academy Review*, 29(1), 98–107. DOI: 10.2478/raft-2024-0010

Jones, R., & Omar, M. (2024). Revolutionizing Cybersecurity: The GPT-2 Enhanced Attack Detection and Defense (GEADD) Method for Zero-Day Threats. *International Journal of Informatics* [INJIISCOM]. *Information System and Computer Engineering*, 5(2), 178–191.

Jones, R., Omar, M., Mohammed, D., Nobles, C., & Dawson, M. (2023). Harnessing the Speed and Accuracy of Machine Learning to Advance Cybersecurity. In *2023 Congress in Computer Science, Computer Engineering, & Applied Computing (CSCE)* (pp. 418-421). IEEE. DOI: 10.1109/CSCE60160.2023.00074

Karthikeyan, P., Pande, H. M., & Sarveshwaran, V. (Eds.). (2023). *Artificial intelligence and blockchain in digital forensics*. CRC Press.

Kelly, L., Sachan, S., Ni, L., Almaghrabi, F., Allmendinger, R., & Chen, Y. (2020). *Explainable artificial intelligence for digital forensics: opportunities, challenges and a drug testing case study*. Digital Forensic Science.

Manasa, S., & Kumar, K. P. (2022). Digital forensics investigation for attacks on artificial intelligence. *ECS Transactions*, 107(1), 19639–19645. DOI: 10.1149/10701.19639ecst

Mitchell, F. R. (2014). An overview of artificial intelligence based pattern matching in a security and digital forensic context. *Cyberpatterns: Unifying Design Patterns with Security and Attack Patterns*, 215-222.

Mohammed, D., Omar, M., & Nguyen, V. (2018). Wireless sensor network security: Approaches to detecting and avoiding wormhole attacks. *Journal of Research in Business. Economics and Management*, 10(2), 1860–1864.

Moustafa, N. (2022). *Digital Forensics in the Era of Artificial Intelligence*. CRC Press. DOI: 10.1201/9781003278962

Nguyen, V., Mohammed, D., Omar, M., & Banisakher, M. (2018). The Effects of the FCC Net Neutrality Repeal on Security and Privacy. [IJHIoT]. *International Journal of Hyperconnectivity and the Internet of Things*, 2(2), 21–29. DOI: 10.4018/IJHIoT.2018070102

Omar, M. (2021). New insights into database security: An effective and integrated approach for applying access control mechanisms and cryptographic concepts in Microsoft Access environments.

Omar, M. (2022). *Machine Learning for Cybersecurity: Innovative Deep Learning Solutions*. Springer Brief. https://link.springer.com/book/978303115

Omar, M. (2024). From Attack to Defense: Strengthening DNN Text Classification Against Adversarial Examples. In *Innovations, Securities, and Case Studies Across Healthcare, Business, and Technology* (pp. 174-195). IGI Global.

Omar, M. (2024). Revolutionizing Malware Detection: A Paradigm Shift Through Optimized Convolutional Neural Networks. In *Innovations, Securities, and Case Studies Across Healthcare, Business, and Technology* (pp. 196-220). IGI Global. DOI: 10.4018/979-8-3693-1906-2.ch011

Omar, M., & Zangana, H. M. (Eds.). (2024). *Redefining Security With Cyber AI*. IGI Global., DOI: 10.4018/979-8-3693-6517-5

Omar, M., & Zangana, H. M. (Eds.). (2025). *Application of Large Language Models (LLMs) for Software Vulnerability Detection*. IGI Global., DOI: 10.4018/979-8-3693-9311-6

Rizvi, S., Scanlon, M., Mcgibney, J., & Sheppard, J. (2022). Application of artificial intelligence to network forensics: Survey, challenges and future directions. *IEEE Access : Practical Innovations, Open Solutions*, 10, 110362–110384. DOI: 10.1109/ACCESS.2022.3214506

Rughani, P. H. (2017). Artificial Intelligence Based Digital Forensics Framework. *International Journal of Advanced Research in Computer Science*, 8(8), 10–14. DOI: 10.26483/ijarcs.v8i8.4571

Sikos, L. F. (2021). AI in digital forensics: Ontology engineering for cybercrime investigations. *WIREs Forensic Science*, 3(3), e1394. DOI: 10.1002/wfs2.1394

Tyagi, A. K., Kumari, S., & Richa. (2024). Artificial Intelligence-Based Cyber Security and Digital Forensics: A Review. *Artificial Intelligence-Enabled Digital Twin for Smart Manufacturing*, 391-419.

Wright, J., Dawson, M. E.Jr, & Omar, M. (2012). Cyber security and mobile threats: The need for antivirus applications for smartphones. *Journal of Information Systems Technology and Planning*, 5(14), 40–60.

Zangana, H. M., Mohammed, A. K., Sallow, A. B., & Sallow, Z. B. (2024). Cybernetic Deception: Unraveling the Layers of Email Phishing Threats. [INJURATECH]. *International Journal of Research and Applied Technology*, 4(1), 35–47.

Zangana, H. M., & Mohammed, D. (2025). Foundations of Large Language Models in Software Vulnerability Detection. In Omar, M., & Zangana, H. (Eds.), *Application of Large Language Models (LLMs) for Software Vulnerability Detection* (pp. 41–74). IGI Global., DOI: 10.4018/979-8-3693-9311-6.ch002

Zangana, H. M., & Omar, M. (2020). Threats, Attacks, and Mitigations of Smartphone Security. *Academic Journal of Nawroz University*, 9(4), 324–332. DOI: 10.25007/ajnu.v9n4a989

Zangana, H. M., & Omar, M. (2025). Harnessing the Power of Large Language Models for Cybersecurity: Applications, Challenges, and Future Directions. In Omar, M., & Zangana, H. (Eds.), *Application of Large Language Models (LLMs) for Software Vulnerability Detection* (pp. 1–40). IGI Global., DOI: 10.4018/979-8-3693-9311-6.ch001

Chapter 10
Behavioral Analysis and User Profiling in Forensic Investigations

Angel Justo Jones
https://orcid.org/0009-0007-9740-6611
University of Virginia, USA

Bianca Montes Jones
Capitol Technology University, USA

ABSTRACT

In the rapidly evolving field of digital forensics, the integration of behavioral analysis and user profiling has emerged as a critical component for enhancing investigation accuracy and efficiency. This chapter explores the role of behavioral analysis in forensic investigations, focusing on how user profiling techniques can be utilized to identify behavior patterns, track digital footprints, and detect anomalous activities. We examine various methods for collecting, analyzing, and interpreting user data from diverse digital sources, including social media, browsing history, and mobile devices. Furthermore, we discuss the challenges forensic experts face in handling large volumes of data, maintaining privacy, and ensuring the integrity of evidence. This chapter aims to provide insights into the growing importance of behavioral analysis and user profiling for modern forensic investigations in the digital age through a combination of AI-driven tools and traditional forensic methodologies.

DOI: 10.4018/979-8-3373-0857-9.ch010

1. INTRODUCTION

Digital forensics has become an essential field in investigating cybercrimes, helping to identify, preserve, and analyze digital evidence in a legally sound manner. As technology advances, the role of artificial intelligence (AI) and machine learning (ML) has gained significant prominence in enhancing digital forensic investigations, making them more efficient, accurate, and scalable. Among the key aspects of digital forensics, behavioral analysis, and user profiling play a crucial role in identifying patterns, reconstructing events, and making sense of complex data.

Behavioral analysis in the context of digital forensics involves the study of user actions, system behaviors, and digital footprints left behind during an investigation. This analysis can reveal insights into how individuals interact with systems, how they access sensitive information, and the types of anomalies that can indicate malicious behavior. By applying AI and machine learning, investigators can automate much of the process of identifying suspicious patterns or deviations in user behavior, reducing the workload and increasing the accuracy of investigations.

User profiling is another critical aspect of digital forensics, wherein investigators develop a profile of a user's typical behavior, preferences, and activities based on digital interactions. This profiling helps forensic investigators differentiate between normal and suspicious behavior by using algorithms that analyze large volumes of data. Through the combination of behavioral analysis and user profiling, forensic experts are better equipped to trace a suspect's actions and intentions, even when those actions are deliberately hidden.

The need for sophisticated tools to analyze digital evidence has never been more pressing as the world becomes increasingly interconnected through the Internet of Things (IoT), cloud computing, and social media. Artificial intelligence has the potential to significantly enhance the capabilities of digital forensic investigators by not only automating routine tasks but also offering advanced techniques for anomaly detection, predictive analysis, and even decision-making in ambiguous situations.

This chapter explores the integration of behavioral analysis and user profiling in the context of digital forensics, with a particular focus on how AI can be leveraged to improve the process. We will highlight recent advancements in AI-based tools' application in analyzing digital evidence, identifying user behavior patterns, and profiling individuals involved in cybercrime. Additionally, the chapter will delve into the challenges and opportunities in this area, exploring how AI can help overcome traditional limitations in digital forensics.

Recent research has provided a solid foundation for the application of AI in digital forensics. For example, Bhawna and Mahajan (2024) discuss how AI perspectives are reshaping the field of digital forensics by enabling more efficient cyber threat detection, while Costantini, De Gasperis, and Olivieri (2019) examine the intersection of AI and digital forensics from both a theoretical and practical standpoint. Furthermore, the use of AI in forensic investigations is explored in several studies, such as Dunsin, Ghanem, and Quazzane (2022), who highlight AI's role in enhancing the accuracy and efficiency of digital investigations, and Zangana et al. (2024), who review various tools for analyzing network security that could aid digital forensics.

The integration of AI technologies into digital forensics not only advances the investigative process but also adds a layer of complexity in managing and interpreting the vast amounts of data generated during such investigations. This chapter, therefore, aims to provide an in-depth understanding of how behavioral analysis and user profiling are essential components of modern digital forensic investigations underpinned by the capabilities of AI.

2. THEORETICAL FOUNDATIONS OF BEHAVIORAL ANALYSIS IN DIGITAL FORENSICS

The integration of behavioral analysis into digital forensics has emerged as a crucial framework for enhancing investigative practices. Behavioral analysis in digital forensics seeks to understand and interpret human actions and patterns of behavior within the context of digital environments. This approach has become particularly important as cybercrimes grow increasingly sophisticated, with perpetrators employing various tactics that often blur traditional boundaries of digital and physical investigations.

Behavioral analysis aims to bridge the gap between technical forensic methods and the human element behind cybercrimes. According to Adam and Varol (2020), intelligence in the digital forensics process is pivotal in distinguishing between routine cyber events and malicious activities. Intelligence is gathered through understanding behavior patterns within digital environments, facilitating more accurate incident detection and response strategies. This approach becomes even more powerful when augmented by Artificial Intelligence (AI), which can analyze vast quantities of data to identify subtle patterns in user behavior that may not be immediately apparent through conventional forensics techniques (Bhawna & Mahajan, 2024).

AI has significantly expanded the role of behavioral analysis in digital forensics. Machine learning algorithms, for instance, can automate identifying unusual behavior patterns across networks and devices. Zangana et al. (2024) highlight how AI can be applied to network traffic analysis to uncover hidden threats, such as advanced persistent threats (APTs), by recognizing deviations from normal user or system behavior. Such insights are essential for proactive security measures and can greatly improve the efficacy of forensic investigations, as they allow for faster identification of potential breaches.

Costantini, De Gasperis, and Olivieri (2019) emphasize that combining AI with behavioral analysis helps forensic investigators not only identify known patterns but also predict potential new forms of attacks. This predictive capability is particularly important in the era of dynamic cyber threats, where traditional forensic methods may struggle to keep up with evolving tactics. Dunsin et al. (2022) further argue that using AI-driven behavioral analysis in constrained environments, such as those with limited resources, can dramatically enhance incident response capabilities, making forensic investigations more agile and scalable.

Additionally, behavioral analysis in digital forensics is indispensable for understanding and combating deception. Zangana, Omar, and colleagues (2024) explore the intricate dynamics of cybernetic deception, including the analysis of fraudulent activities such as phishing, which often rely on manipulating human behavior. AI's role in such analyses is to decode the behavioral cues of both the perpetrator and the victim, enabling forensic experts to detect deceptive strategies more effectively.

One critical challenge in integrating behavioral analysis into digital forensics is ensuring the explainability of AI models. As noted by Hall, Sakzad, and Choo (2022), the lack of transparency in AI-driven decision-making can pose significant obstacles in legal contexts where forensic evidence needs to be understood and accepted by courts. This has led to growing interest in explainable AI (XAI) in digital forensics, which aims to provide clear justifications for AI-driven conclusions. This is especially important when forensic results are used as evidence in criminal proceedings.

The growing significance of AI and behavioral analysis in digital forensics is further reflected in the work of Jeong (2020), who discusses the security threats and crimes posed by AI and the need for forensics systems to address such risks. AI not only plays a role in analyzing and predicting criminal behavior but also represents a new frontier in cybercrime techniques, which digital forensics must continually adapt to address.

In forensic investigations, the importance of context cannot be overstated. Sikos (2021) discusses how ontology engineering can support AI in understanding the contextual elements of cybercrimes, from the intentions of the attacker to the impact of the crime on the victim. This contextual understanding is central to behavioral analysis, as it allows investigators to interpret digital evidence not just from a technical perspective but with a deeper insight into the motivations and strategies behind the behavior. Tyagi et al. (2024) also recognize this by suggesting that AI-based systems need to account for both the technical and psychological aspects of cyber threats, particularly in cases of fraud or social engineering.

Moreover, AI and machine learning can assist in identifying behavioral anomalies in real-time, which is particularly critical in fast-moving environments such as cloud computing. As highlighted by Hamza and Omar (2013), cloud computing environments present new challenges in cybersecurity, where traditional forensics methods often struggle due to the distributed and ephemeral nature of cloud infrastructures. By applying behavioral analysis, digital forensics can offer more effective tracking and investigation of activities across diverse cloud platforms.

In addition to incident detection, behavioral analysis through AI can also be instrumental in assessing the response and mitigation efforts during and after a cyber event. For instance, Jarrett and Choo (2021) discuss the impact of automation in digital forensics, specifically in automating response mechanisms that take into account the behavior of both attackers and defenders. The role of AI in automating these processes can significantly improve the speed and efficiency of forensic investigations, reducing the time required to mitigate damage and prevent further incidents.

To understand how behavioral analysis contributes to digital forensics, it is essential to examine the steps involved in this process. The flowchart below outlines the stages, starting from data collection and proceeding through analysis, anomaly detection, and evidence reporting. Each stage plays a crucial role in gathering insights into user behaviors and patterns, facilitating the detection of suspicious or malicious activities.

Figure 1. Overview of Behavioral Analysis in Digital Forensics

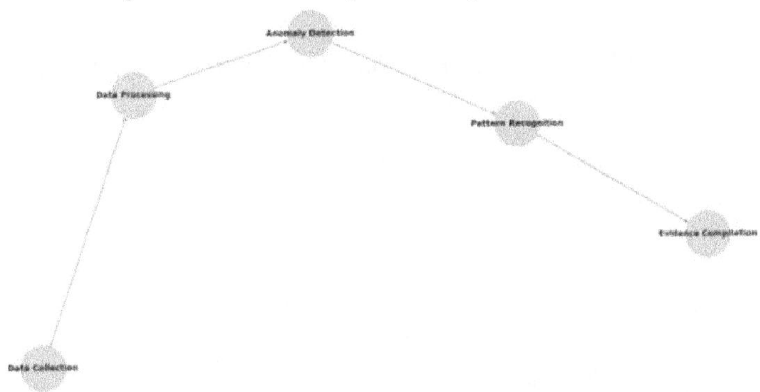

Therefore, the theoretical foundation of behavioral analysis in digital forensics is rooted in the idea that understanding human behavior—through both direct and indirect observations in digital environments—can offer deeper insights into cybercrimes. This multi-faceted approach, blending human psychology, technical forensic analysis, and cutting-edge AI, ensures that forensic investigators are better equipped to handle the complexities of modern cybercrime (Rughani, 2017). By leveraging AI to analyze patterns and behaviors, digital forensics evolves from a reactive process to a proactive one, better capable of anticipating and mitigating cyber threats before they manifest.

3. USER PROFILING TECHNIQUES IN FORENSIC INVESTIGATIONS

User profiling plays a pivotal role in digital forensics investigations, enabling investigators to understand the behaviors, preferences, and patterns associated with a suspect's activities. As digital forensic investigations grow increasingly complex due to the vast volume of data and diverse types of cybercrimes, leveraging user profiling techniques becomes essential. These methods aid in narrowing down potential suspects, analyzing digital footprints, and identifying the nature of cybercrimes. This section delves into the significance of user profiling, the methodologies employed, and how artificial intelligence (AI) and machine learning (ML) are revolutionizing these techniques in digital forensic investigations.

User profiling is essential in digital forensics to understand the behavior, preferences, and patterns of users. This diagram illustrates the main user profiling techniques—data aggregation, pattern recognition, machine learning-based anomaly detection and predictive analytics—and their applications in forensic investigations. Each technique contributes to the accurate identification and differentiation of normal versus suspicious behavior.

Figure 2. Techniques Used in User Profiling for Forensic Investigations

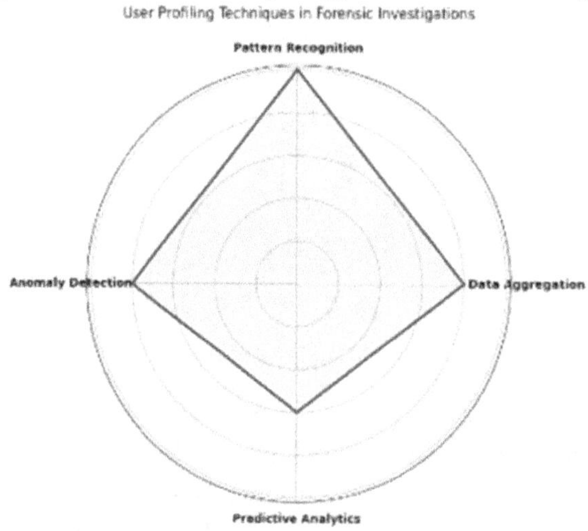

3.1 Traditional User Profiling in Digital Forensics

Historically, user profiling in forensic investigations was focused on analyzing data from devices such as computers, mobile phones, and servers. Forensic investigators typically examined files, logs, internet activity, and other digital traces left by users. These profiles would then be used to match suspicious behaviors with known patterns of criminal activities. Traditional profiling methods primarily relied on manual investigation processes, making it time-consuming and often error-prone (Bhawna & Mahajan, 2024).

Basic user profiling involves identifying patterns in system interactions, such as the websites visited, types of files accessed, communication methods used, and times of activity. By examining system logs, network traffic data, and email communications, investigators could create a preliminary user profile that could be useful in narrowing down suspects. However, this traditional method lacks the efficiency required for modern, large-scale investigations (Bhawna & Mahajan, 2024).

3.2 The Role of Artificial Intelligence and Machine Learning

With the rapid advancements in AI and ML, digital forensics has seen significant improvements in user profiling techniques. AI-based systems can now analyze vast amounts of digital data much faster and with greater accuracy than traditional manual methods. These systems apply algorithms that can detect hidden patterns, unusual activities, or anomalies that might indicate malicious intent (Adam & Varol, 2020).

3.3 Machine Learning for Pattern Recognition:

ML techniques, such as clustering, classification, and anomaly detection, are particularly useful in identifying patterns in digital behavior. These algorithms can analyze large datasets to detect correlations between user actions and predict future activities or behaviors that are characteristic of cybercriminals. For example, in analyzing user login attempts, ML models can identify irregular login behaviors that deviate from the user's typical activities, thus highlighting potential security threats (Zangana, Mohammed, & Omar, 2024).

3.4 Deep Learning and Neural Networks

In more advanced cases, deep learning techniques especially neural networks—have been applied for user profiling in digital forensics. These models can process and analyze data from multiple sources, such as text logs, file access patterns, and even voice or facial recognition data. As these models evolve, they offer better accuracy and can predict user actions with minimal input, making them invaluable tools for investigators (Dunsin, Ghanem, & Quazzane, 2022).

Moreover, AI-powered systems can automate the detection of suspicious behavior across large datasets, reducing the workload of forensic experts and enabling faster identification of potential threats (Zangana & Omar, 2024).

3.5 Behavioral Analysis and Profiling

Behavioral analysis has emerged as a central aspect of digital forensics, aiming to understand the actions and motivations behind a user's digital interactions. This type of profiling goes beyond simple user identification and instead seeks to understand how a user behaves in the digital environment. Theoretical foundations of behavioral analysis include an understanding of psychological and sociological factors that can inform the digital behaviors of individuals (Sikos, 2021). By applying these theories to digital forensics, investigators can build more accurate profiles that help predict future actions, identify covert behaviors, and understand the decision-making processes of suspects.

AI and machine learning play a key role in automating the extraction and analysis of behavioral patterns. For example, AI can identify which files or communications are frequently accessed by a user and flag unusual patterns. Additionally, AI systems can correlate this behavior with broader social engineering tactics used by cybercriminals to manipulate targets, improving the ability of forensic experts to understand criminal psychology (Jeong, 2020).

3.6 Integrating AI with Digital Forensics

Integrating AI into digital forensics has enhanced user profiling techniques and facilitated a more holistic and predictive approach to investigations. AI tools are now capable of integrating data from multiple digital sources, including cloud platforms, social media, and IoT devices. This allows forensic investigators to build comprehensive profiles of suspects based on their activities across different digital platforms (Zangana & Omar, 2025). By combining information from disparate sources, AI offers the potential for uncovering hidden relationships and patterns that would have been difficult to detect using traditional methods.

The integration of AI within digital forensics brings a structured and efficient approach to investigations. This workflow outlines the AI-driven digital forensics process, from data extraction to anomaly detection, analysis, and reporting. AI plays a crucial role in each stage, automating repetitive tasks, enhancing pattern recognition, and enabling predictive insights that support forensic investigators.

Figure 3. AI-Driven Workflow in Digital Forensics Investigations

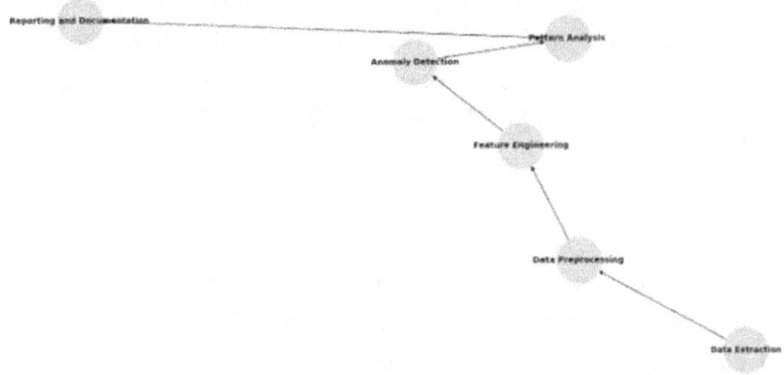

3.7 Case Studies in AI-Driven User Profiling:

In real-world applications, AI systems have been employed in various cybercrime investigations. For instance, AI-powered user profiling tools were successfully used in identifying patterns of insider threats and detecting phishing attempts by analyzing communication patterns across email and social media platforms (Zangana et al., 2024). Such systems can predict fraudulent activity based on previous user behaviors and known attack vectors, offering valuable insights for investigators during the critical stages of an investigation.

3.8 Challenges and Future Directions

While AI and machine learning have greatly enhanced user profiling techniques in digital forensics, challenges still remain. One of the primary issues is the risk of false positives or misidentifications due to incomplete data or inaccurate models. Investigators must therefore ensure that the AI systems used for profiling are properly trained and continually updated with new data to improve their accuracy (Tyagi, Kumari, & Richa, 2024).

Additionally, privacy concerns and ethical considerations must be considered when building AI systems for digital forensics. Profiling individuals based on their digital behavior may lead to privacy violations if not managed correctly. To mitigate these risks, it is essential to implement strict data protection protocols and ensure that AI tools comply with existing legal frameworks for digital evidence (Costantini, De Gasperis, & Olivieri, 2019).

In the future, advancements in AI technologies, such as explainable AI (XAI), will play a crucial role in improving user profiling for digital forensics. By providing transparency in decision-making, XAI models can help forensic experts better understand how AI systems arrive at conclusions and improve their trust in these systems for legal proceedings (Hall, Sakzad, & Choo, 2022).

3.9 Summary

User profiling techniques are indispensable in digital forensics, helping investigators understand criminal behaviors, track suspect activities, and detect anomalies across digital platforms. Integrating AI and ML technologies has revolutionized these techniques, enabling faster, more accurate, and predictive analysis of user actions. As digital forensics continues to evolve, AI-based systems will remain a core component in identifying and preventing cybercrime. However, accuracy, privacy, and ethics challenges must be continuously addressed.

4. AI-ENHANCED BEHAVIORAL ANALYSIS TOOLS AND TECHNIQUES

The application of Artificial Intelligence (AI) in digital forensics has significantly advanced the ability to analyze and interpret digital evidence. One of the core components of modern forensic investigations is behavioral analysis, where AI plays a crucial role in detecting, categorizing, and predicting activities associated with cybercrimes. This section explores AI-enhanced behavioral analysis tools and techniques, emphasizing how AI methodologies transform digital forensic investigations' landscape.

The use of AI in behavioral analysis allows forensic investigators to leverage machine learning, natural language processing, and anomaly detection, providing deeper insights into user behaviors and aiding the identification of potential threats. This bar chart illustrates the application areas and their relative impact on the forensic investigation process, focusing on automation, speed, and predictive accuracy.

Figure 4. AI-Driven Applications in Behavioral Analysis for Forensics

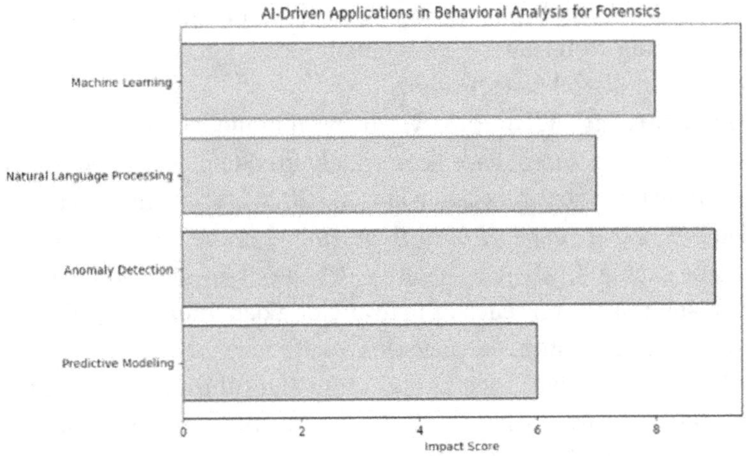

4.1. Behavioral Analysis in Digital Forensics

Behavioral analysis involves examining patterns of behavior exhibited by users, devices, or systems during digital interactions to detect anomalies or illicit activities. In digital forensics, this technique is vital in identifying suspicious behavior such as unauthorized access, fraud, or insider threats (Bhawna & Mahajan, 2024). AI technologies such as machine learning (ML), deep learning, and natural language processing (NLP) have proven effective in augmenting behavioral analysis by automating the identification of complex patterns from vast amounts of data (Zangana et al., 2024).

AI-enhanced behavioral analysis offers several advantages, including the ability to:

- Detect hidden patterns that may go unnoticed by traditional forensic tools.
- Automate time-consuming processes, improving the efficiency of investigations.
- Provide more accurate and reliable results by learning from historical data.

4.2. AI Techniques in Behavioral Analysis

AI-based methods applied to behavioral analysis in digital forensics range from supervised learning to unsupervised anomaly detection, each designed to tackle specific aspects of digital investigations.

Machine Learning (ML): Supervised learning models, such as decision trees and support vector machines, have been widely used to classify and categorize behaviors based on historical data (Dunsin et al., 2024). These models are trained on labeled datasets and are capable of distinguishing between normal and anomalous activities. For example, ML can identify deviations in network traffic patterns, which could suggest the presence of malware or a data breach (Iqbal et al., 2020).

Unsupervised Learning: In scenarios where labeled data is unavailable, unsupervised learning models, such as clustering algorithms and anomaly detection techniques, are employed. These models can identify new, previously unknown threats by detecting outliers in behavioral data (Costantini, De Gasperis, & Olivieri, 2019). For instance, an unsupervised model might detect abnormal system access patterns that suggest an ongoing cyberattack or intrusion (Dunsin et al., 2022).

Natural Language Processing (NLP): NLP is particularly useful in analyzing textual data from email communications, social media posts, or chat logs. AI-powered NLP algorithms can detect phishing attempts, sentiment analysis, and the use of deceptive language (Zangana et al., 2024). Such applications are vital in email forensics, where malicious actors often disguise their intentions through language (Zangana & Omar, 2020).

4.3. AI in Network Forensics

In network forensics, AI-driven tools can analyze large volumes of network traffic to detect malicious activities. Traditional forensic methods often fall short due to the high volume and complexity of modern network data. AI-based behavioral analysis tools excel in processing network traffic patterns and identifying subtle anomalies that indicate security threats (Rizvi et al., 2022).

For instance, machine learning models can be used to analyze network logs for signs of Distributed Denial of Service (DDoS) attacks or identify data exfiltration attempts (Jarrett & Choo, 2021). These models can adapt to evolving attack vectors by continuously learning from new data, making them highly effective in dynamic environments.

4.4. Explainable AI (XAI) in Behavioral Analysis

While AI models offer impressive performance in behavioral analysis, one of the challenges is the "black-box" nature of many algorithms, making it difficult for forensic experts to interpret the decision-making process of AI models. Explainable AI (XAI) aims to address this challenge by providing clear and understandable insights into how a model reaches its conclusions (Hall et al., 2022).

In digital forensics, XAI is crucial for ensuring the transparency and accountability of AI-driven investigations. For example, when an AI model identifies an anomalous user behavior, XAI techniques can provide forensic investigators with a rationale behind the decision, such as pointing to specific network activities or system logs contributing to the anomaly detection (Sikos, 2021). This is vital for ensuring that AI-driven conclusions are admissible in legal contexts, where understanding the reasoning behind findings is essential.

4.5. AI for Predictive Forensics

Predictive forensics is another area where AI techniques are making a significant impact. By leveraging historical data, AI models can predict future cybercrimes based on existing behavioral patterns. These models use various techniques, including time-series analysis and recurrent neural networks (RNNs), to forecast criminal activities before they occur (Ganesh, 2017). Predictive analytics can help forensic teams focus their efforts on high-risk targets and prevent future breaches by identifying vulnerabilities in advance.

4.6. AI in Incident Response and Automation

AI-enhanced behavioral analysis tools also play a key role in incident response. Machine learning algorithms can automatically analyze system logs, network traffic, and user behavior to identify signs of an ongoing cyberattack or system compromise. This rapid identification is crucial in minimizing the damage caused by an attack. Once a threat is identified, AI systems can assist in automating responses, such as isolating affected systems or blocking malicious IP addresses (Dunsin et al., 2024).

Moreover, AI can optimize incident response workflows by prioritizing alerts based on the severity of the detected threat. This allows forensic teams to focus on the most critical incidents first, improving overall response times and efficiency (Tyagi, Kumari, & Richa, 2024).

4.7. Challenges and Future Directions

While AI-enhanced behavioral analysis tools offer significant advancements in digital forensics, several challenges remain to address. One of the main concerns is the quality and quantity of data needed to train AI models effectively. In many forensic investigations, data may be incomplete or inconsistent, which can lead to less accurate results (Jeong, 2020). Additionally, the evolving nature of cyberattacks requires AI models to continuously adapt, which can be resource-intensive.

The future of AI in behavioral analysis will likely involve integrating multiple AI techniques, such as combining supervised and unsupervised learning with NLP and XAI, to create more robust and adaptable forensic tools. Researchers are also exploring the use of synthetic data to improve AI model training and performance (Gholami & Omar, 2024).

4.8 Summary

AI-enhanced behavioral analysis tools are revolutionizing digital forensics by automating complex tasks, improving the accuracy of investigations, and enabling predictive capabilities. As these technologies continue to evolve, their ability to detect and respond to cyber threats in real-time will become increasingly vital. However, data quality, model interpretability, and adaptability challenges remain. Addressing these issues will be crucial for realizing the full potential of AI in digital forensics (Zangana et al., 2024).

5. APPLICATIONS OF BEHAVIORAL ANALYSIS AND PROFILING IN FORENSICS

Behavioral analysis and profiling have become essential components in digital forensics, enabling investigators to interpret and connect digital evidence with criminal activities. This integration has been further enhanced by artificial intelligence (AI) technologies, which allow for more nuanced and sophisticated approaches to investigating cybercrimes. The primary application of behavioral analysis in digital forensics lies in understanding the actions, motives, and patterns of cybercriminals by analyzing their behavior in digital environments. In this context, profiling involves gathering and synthesizing data from digital artifacts to build profiles of suspects or threat actors.

5.1. Behavioral Analysis in Cybercrime Investigations

Behavioral analysis in digital forensics helps investigators piece together the actions and decision-making processes of cybercriminals. Experts can identify a suspect's digital footprint by analyzing logs, communication patterns, and system interactions. For instance, the behavior of a hacker might be assessed through the sequence of their actions, from gaining unauthorized access to the network to the exfiltration of sensitive data. AI can assist in detecting anomalous patterns in digital behavior that align with known tactics used by cybercriminals. Adam and Varol (2020) highlight the role of digital intelligence in the forensic process, emphasizing how behavioral data can inform investigative strategies. Furthermore, Dunsin et al. (2022) discuss how AI can be applied to analyze digital traces of cybercriminals, improving the speed and accuracy of investigations in constrained environments.

5.2. AI and Machine Learning in Behavioral Profiling

Machine learning (ML) and AI have revolutionized behavioral analysis application in forensics. These technologies help build predictive models based on historical data, which can be used to anticipate future criminal activities. By using large data-sets, AI systems can learn to identify patterns in the way cybercriminals operate, potentially identifying unknown threats before they fully materialize. Zangana et al. (2024) emphasize the potential of AI to enhance digital forensics by analyzing network traffic, logs, and other digital evidence to automatically generate behavior profiles of attackers. This predictive profiling can lead to proactive measures to prevent cybercrime. Additionally, the ability of AI systems to handle vast amounts of data quickly has proven invaluable in identifying abnormal behaviors that might go unnoticed by human investigators (Bhawna & Mahajan, 2024).

5.3. Application of Behavioral Analysis in Incident Response

In digital forensics, responding quickly and effectively to an incident is paramount. Behavioral analysis plays a crucial role in incident response by helping teams identify the source and nature of the threat. AI-driven tools can rapidly analyze behavioral data from compromised systems and help responders understand the specific tactics and techniques used by attackers. Dunsin et al. (2024) discuss the integration of AI in incident response, focusing on how it aids in rapidly identifying the behaviors associated with an attack, thus improving the forensic investigation's efficiency. Moreover, profiling attackers based on their digital behavior can help investigators attribute the attack to a specific group or individual, providing a clearer direction for follow-up actions.

5.4. Profile Generation for Threat Actor Identification

Digital forensics often requires creating profiles of cybercriminals to link them to specific crimes or types of attacks. Behavioral profiling is essential in this regard, as it involves constructing a detailed view of a suspect's methods, motivations, and previous actions. AI tools can process large volumes of data, such as email headers, metadata, and server logs, to identify patterns associated with certain threat actors. Zangana et al. (2024) discuss how profiling can be applied to phishing attacks, where behavioral analysis helps identify specific techniques and tools cybercriminals use to deceive victims. By mapping these techniques, investigators can develop a more comprehensive understanding of the criminal's behavior, which may ultimately lead to their identification and capture.

5.5. Explaining the Role of Artificial Intelligence in Behavioral Analysis

Artificial intelligence has enhanced the capabilities of forensic investigations by providing automated solutions for analyzing large datasets and identifying suspicious behaviors. Hall et al. (2022) explore how explainable AI (XAI) techniques are crucial in digital forensics, as they provide transparency in the decision-making process of AI systems. This is especially important when AI models are used to identify and classify behavioral patterns that might be linked to cybercrimes. These explainable models enable forensic experts to trust AI's findings and understand the reasoning behind the identification of certain behaviors as suspicious.

Moreover, the integration of AI in digital forensics also facilitates the automation of repetitive tasks, allowing forensic experts to focus on more complex aspects of the investigation. Jarrett and Choo (2021) note the growing importance of AI in automating data collection, analysis, and reporting in digital forensic investigations, thus accelerating the entire forensic process.

5.6. Challenges and Future Directions

Despite the potential of behavioral analysis and AI in digital forensics, several challenges remain. One major concern is the need for high-quality data to train AI models effectively. Behavioral profiling is only as good as the data fed into the system, and if the data is incomplete or biased, the AI's conclusions may be flawed. Furthermore, as cybercriminals continuously evolve their tactics, the profiles created by AI systems must be updated regularly to reflect the latest trends in criminal behavior (Iqbal et al., 2020).

The future of behavioral analysis in forensics lies in the continuous improvement of AI models and the integration of advanced techniques, such as deep learning, which can enhance the accuracy of threat actor profiling. Additionally, as cybercrimes become more complex, integrating AI-driven behavioral analysis with other technologies, such as blockchain forensics and threat intelligence platforms, will further strengthen digital investigations. Costantini et al. (2019) highlight the synergy between AI and digital forensics in evolving to meet new challenges in cybercrime investigation.

In conclusion, behavioral analysis and profiling in digital forensics have proven to be invaluable in understanding and solving cybercrimes. With the ongoing advancements in AI and machine learning, the future of digital forensics looks promising, providing forensic experts with more sophisticated tools to investigate, prevent, and respond to cyber threats. However, ongoing research and development are necessary to address the challenges of evolving cyber threats and improve the accuracy and reliability of AI-based forensic techniques.

6. CHALLENGES AND LIMITATIONS IN BEHAVIORAL ANALYSIS AND PROFILING

Behavioral analysis and profiling in digital forensics play a crucial role in understanding the actions and motivations behind cybercrimes. By analyzing digital footprints left behind by users, investigators can make inferences about potential suspects and attack methods and predict future cyber activities. However, while the potential for using behavioral analysis in digital forensics is significant, some several challenges and limitations must be addressed to enhance its accuracy, reliability, and effectiveness.

6.1. Data Volume and Complexity

One of the most significant challenges in digital forensics is dealing with data's vast volume and complexity. Modern digital systems generate enormous amounts of data, from emails to logs and network traffic. Behavioral profiling, especially when applied to large datasets, faces the challenge of distinguishing between normal and anomalous behavior. Machine learning algorithms, when applied to these data sets, need to be trained on vast amounts of labeled data, which is often difficult to obtain, especially in cases of novel or advanced persistent threats.

The complexity of analyzing multiple data sources, such as social media, email communication, or cloud storage logs, compounds the difficulty of building reliable behavioral models (Zangana et al., 2024). Additionally, the heterogeneity of data—where different formats, structures, and protocols are involved—adds an extra layer of complexity to the analysis (Rizvi et al., 2022).

6.2. Limited Training Data and Privacy Concerns

Developing accurate behavioral models in digital forensics often requires access to extensive training datasets. However, the nature of digital crime often means that investigators may not have access to adequate or diverse datasets, especially when dealing with new attack methods or high-level cybercriminals (Dunsin et al., 2024). Furthermore, the use of personal data in behavioral analysis raises significant privacy concerns. Ensuring that the data used in profiling is not invasive or violates privacy rights is critical for maintaining the ethical standards of digital forensics (Jeong, 2020; Dunsin et al., 2022).

6.3. Interpretation and Explainability

Artificial intelligence (AI) and machine learning (ML) have been increasingly incorporated into behavioral profiling techniques in digital forensics, but a major limitation lies in the interpretability of these systems. The use of "black-box" algorithms, where the decision-making process is not transparent, makes it difficult to understand why certain behaviors are classified as suspicious or normal. This lack of explainability can hinder the judicial use of AI in digital forensics, as the reliance on complex models can lead to legal and ethical concerns about accountability (Hall et al., 2022; Costantini et al., 2019).

For example, while machine learning can identify patterns of unusual behavior that might suggest malicious intent, the system's inability to explain these patterns in human-readable terms makes it harder to corroborate the findings with traditional investigative methods (Sikos, 2021). This limitation is especially critical in situations where legal proceedings are involved, and the evidence needs to be verifiable and interpretable.

6.4. Behavioral Variability

Human behavior, especially online, is highly variable and influenced by many factors, including psychological states, external environments, and personal goals. Digital forensics often struggles to accommodate this variability, leading to false positives or missed connections. Even within the same individual, online behavior can vary significantly depending on the context. A legitimate user may perform actions that appear suspicious if the system fails to account for contextual factors (Zangana et al., 2024).

Furthermore, cybercriminals frequently adapt their tactics, often changing their behaviors to avoid detection. This adaptability creates a dynamic environment where behavioral patterns may quickly become obsolete, reducing the efficacy of previous profiling models.

6.5. Ethical and Legal Implications

The ethical challenges associated with behavioral profiling are also significant. The use of AI in digital forensics requires careful handling of sensitive personal data, and inappropriate or excessive use could lead to violations of privacy or civil liberties (Adam & Varol, 2020). Moreover, when misapplied, behavioral analysis risks unfairly profiling individuals based on patterns that do not necessarily indicate malicious intent. This is particularly problematic when combined with issues related to racial or social profiling, which could lead to discriminatory practices.

There is also the concern of unintended biases in the training data for machine learning algorithms. If these datasets contain biases, they can affect the analysis outcome, potentially leading to unfair conclusions about individuals or groups (Dunsin et al., 2024). Addressing these biases is critical to ensuring the fairness and accuracy of behavioral profiling systems in digital forensics.

6.6. Evolving Nature of Cybercrime

The rapidly evolving nature of cybercrime adds another layer of complexity to behavioral analysis. New attack techniques, such as phishing, ransomware, and advanced persistent threats, are constantly emerging, and behavioral analysis models must be regularly updated to stay effective. Unfortunately, this constant evolution means that behavioral profiling models can quickly become outdated or ineffective against new types of cybercrimes (Zangana et al., 2024; Jarrett & Choo, 2021).

Furthermore, cybercriminals are becoming increasingly sophisticated in evading detection. They use techniques like obfuscation, anonymization, and encrypted communication to hide their tracks, making it harder for behavioral profiling systems to detect patterns of malicious activity (Zangana et al., 2025). In these cases, traditional data collection and analysis methods may no longer be sufficient to accurately profile behavior.

6.7 Summary

While behavioral analysis and profiling offer promising potential for enhancing digital forensics and cybercrime investigations, the challenges associated with data volume, privacy concerns, explainability, behavioral variability, and the evolving nature of cybercrime must be carefully addressed. By continuing to develop AI-based tools and frameworks that are not only effective but also ethical and transparent, digital forensics can continue to evolve to meet the demands of modern cyber threats (Bhawna & Mahajan, 2024; Mitchell, 2014).

As the field advances, it will be essential to establish robust standards for the use of behavioral profiling in digital forensics, ensuring that these techniques contribute meaningfully to investigations without compromising individual rights or the accuracy of the findings (Costantini et al., 2019; Zangana et al., 2024).

7. CASE STUDIES AND REAL-WORLD APPLICATIONS

In recent years, integrating artificial intelligence (AI) in digital forensics has been an area of significant interest, offering the potential to revolutionize cybercrime investigations. AI enhances the capabilities of digital forensics by automating complex tasks, improving the accuracy of evidence analysis, and providing more efficient responses to cyber threats. This section presents key case studies and real-world applications that highlight the critical role of AI in advancing digital forensics.

7.1 AI in Digital Forensics and Incident Response

Digital forensics has always been a crucial component of incident response, allowing investigators to analyze and recover critical information from digital devices. The growing complexity of cyberattacks, especially in the era of advanced persistent threats (APT), has led to a rise in the adoption of AI technologies. One prominent example is the use of AI to detect and mitigate email phishing attacks. Zangana et al. (2024) explore how AI can be utilized to identify deceptive behaviors in email phishing schemes, significantly improving incident response times by automating the detection process. Their study highlights the power of machine learning algorithms in identifying phishing emails by analyzing patterns and anomalies in email content and metadata.

In another case study, Dunsin et al. (2022) examine how AI has been deployed in constrained environments to enhance digital forensic investigations. They demonstrate that AI can process large amounts of forensic data in real-time, providing investigators with faster insights into cybersecurity incidents. This technology is particularly valuable in scenarios where time is critical, such as during the investigation of ransomware attacks. The authors discuss how machine learning models can be trained to recognize known attack vectors, helping forensic experts pinpoint the root cause of security breaches more efficiently.

7.2 AI-Driven Automated Analysis in Forensic Investigations

The automation of forensic processes has led to an increase in the speed and precision of digital forensic investigations. For example, Costantini et al. (2019) explore the use of AI to automate the analysis of large volumes of digital evidence, such as network traffic logs and file systems. Their study reveals that AI-powered tools can reduce the burden on forensic investigators by autonomously categorizing data, identifying anomalies, and prioritizing potential leads for further investigation. This reduces the workload of forensic teams, allowing them to focus on more complex tasks that require human expertise.

Similarly, Hall et al. (2022) discuss the implementation of explainable AI (XAI) models in digital forensics, which can provide clear reasoning behind decisions made by AI systems. By enhancing transparency, XAI improves the trustworthiness of AI tools in forensic investigations. Their research illustrates how AI can not only assist in detecting cybercrime but also provide explanations that forensic experts can use in court to support their findings. This is particularly important in criminal investigations, where evidence must be presented in a way that is understandable to judges and juries.

7.3 Cybersecurity and AI-Powered Digital Forensics

In cybersecurity, AI has proven to be indispensable in enhancing organizations' overall security posture. Zangana and Omar (2024) provide a comprehensive review of network firewall rule analyzers, which use AI to optimize the configuration of security rules and improve the efficiency of firewalls. By leveraging machine learning algorithms, these analyzers can detect vulnerabilities in firewall configurations that could be exploited by attackers. The study emphasizes the importance of AI in preventing security breaches by identifying potential weaknesses in network defenses before they can be exploited.

AI's role in cybersecurity extends beyond just firewall optimization. Jones et al. (2024) introduce the concept of GPT-2-enhanced attack detection and defense methods, where AI is used to detect zero-day vulnerabilities in cybersecurity systems. Their approach integrates natural language processing (NLP) with traditional security measures, providing organizations with an advanced layer of protection against emerging threats. This hybrid method can quickly adapt to new types of attacks by analyzing patterns in large datasets, such as security logs and threat intelligence feeds.

7.4 AI Applications in Digital Forensics Investigations for Mobile and Cloud Security

The increasing reliance on mobile devices and cloud-based systems has introduced new challenges for digital forensics experts. Mobile devices, in particular, present unique difficulties due to their compact size, varied operating systems, and the encryption used by many applications. Zangana et al. (2020) explore the complexities of smartphone security, discussing how AI can assist in detecting and mitigating threats like malware and unauthorized access. Their study examines AI-based approaches for analyzing mobile data and identifying vulnerabilities that cybercriminals could exploit.

AI has also become crucial in cloud computing environments, where security threats and incidents are often harder to detect due to the distributed nature of the infrastructure. Hamza and Omar (2013) explore the abuse of cloud computing and the challenges it poses for digital forensics. They suggest that AI-based tools can help address these challenges by automating the analysis of cloud logs and detecting suspicious activities that could indicate a breach. The use of AI in cloud security investigations has become essential as more organizations migrate their operations to the cloud, increasing the need for effective and efficient forensic techniques.

7.5 Enhancing Forensic Analysis with AI-Based Pattern Recognition

The application of AI in pattern recognition is another key area of digital forensics. AI algorithms are adept at identifying patterns in data, whether in network traffic, file systems, or user behavior. Mitchell (2014) provides an overview of AI-based pattern matching techniques in digital forensics, focusing on their ability to detect security threats in real time. These pattern recognition techniques can be used to identify suspicious activity such as unauthorized access attempts, data exfiltration, and abnormal network behavior, significantly enhancing the speed and accuracy of forensic investigations.

Furthermore, Rizvi et al. (2022) survey the challenges and future directions of AI in network forensics. Their research outlines how machine learning can be applied to detect advanced persistent threats (APT) in network traffic, enabling forensic investigators to pinpoint suspicious activity patterns more efficiently. AI-driven network forensics tools can automate the detection of threats, allowing security teams to respond to potential attacks faster and with greater precision.

7.6 Future Directions for AI in Digital Forensics

The future of AI in digital forensics holds significant promise. As cyber threats continue to evolve, so too must the tools and techniques used to investigate them. AI's ability to process vast amounts of data, recognize patterns, and make decisions with minimal human intervention positions it as a game-changer in the field. Zangana et al. (2025) and Kelly et al. (2020) suggest that the integration of blockchain and AI could further enhance the integrity and authenticity of digital evidence, particularly in cases involving data tampering or fraudulent digital signatures.

In addition to improving forensic analysis, AI has the potential to reduce human error, standardize investigative processes, and provide consistent, repeatable results. As AI tools become more advanced and accessible, they will likely become an integral part of the digital forensics toolkit, helping investigators solve complex cybercrime cases more efficiently and accurately.

7.7 Summary

AI is undeniably transforming digital forensics landscape, providing powerful tools for automating investigations, detecting threats, and ensuring the integrity of digital evidence. From email phishing detection to advanced network forensics and cloud security, AI applications are proving to be indispensable in addressing the growing complexity of cybercrime. As AI continues to evolve, its integration with digital forensics will only deepen, further enhancing the ability to combat cyber threats and safeguard digital assets across industries.

8. LEGAL AND REGULATORY CONSIDERATIONS

The integration of Artificial Intelligence (AI) in digital forensics brings with it a complex web of legal and regulatory challenges that need to be navigated to ensure the proper handling of evidence and compliance with privacy and security standards. These challenges involve issues related to data privacy, the admissibility of AI-generated evidence in court, and the evolving landscape of laws governing cybersecurity, digital forensics, and AI technologies. As the intersection between AI and digital forensics expands, it is crucial to understand the legal implications accompanying AI deployment in criminal investigations and cybersecurity responses.

8.1 Data Privacy and Protection

One of the foremost legal concerns in digital forensics is ensuring that the collection and analysis of digital evidence through AI tools comply with data privacy regulations such as the General Data Protection Regulation (GDPR) in the European Union, as well as various national privacy laws. AI systems employed in digital forensics often process large volumes of sensitive data, raising the potential for data breaches or the inadvertent exposure of personal information. Legal frameworks such as GDPR impose strict requirements on data handling, including the principles of data minimization and the right to erasure, which must be respected when AI tools are used in forensics (Adam & Varol, 2020).

Moreover, AI's role in extracting and analyzing data from devices such as smartphones, computers, and cloud environments poses risks in terms of unauthorized access to private information. Laws around consent, particularly in the context of obtaining and processing digital evidence, are critical in ensuring compliance with privacy standards (Zangana et al., 2020). Thus, organizations employing AI in forensic investigations must ensure that these systems are designed to minimize the risk of data misuse and to align with legal frameworks that protect individuals' privacy.

8.2 Admissibility of AI-Generated Evidence

As AI technologies become more embedded in the forensic process, questions arise regarding the admissibility of AI-generated evidence in court. Traditional forensic methods, such as human testimony or manual analysis of digital evidence, are well-established in legal proceedings. However, AI-generated evidence, particularly from machine learning models, poses new challenges for courts and regulatory bodies. Issues regarding the transparency, explainability, and reliability of AI-generated results are central to debates about the admissibility of such evidence in legal contexts.

The growing reliance on AI tools such as facial recognition, anomaly detection systems, and predictive analytics in forensics demands that these tools be subject to rigorous validation and certification processes to ensure their accuracy and prevent potential bias or errors. AI-driven forensics tools must meet standards that guarantee they can withstand legal scrutiny, much like traditional forensic methods, and this may involve adopting best practices for validating AI models before they are used in criminal investigations (Dunsin et al., 2022; Hall et al., 2022).

Regulatory bodies, including courts and law enforcement agencies, must establish clear guidelines regarding the admissibility of AI-generated evidence. These guidelines should address the need for transparency in AI model decision-making processes, ensuring that forensic tools are not "black boxes" but instead offer traceable and explainable outcomes (Costantini et al., 2019). As such, explainable AI (XAI) is becoming a crucial area of focus to ensure that AI systems in forensics are interpretable by legal professionals (Hall et al., 2022).

8.3 Ethical Implications and Bias in AI Forensics

Another significant legal and regulatory issue in digital forensics is the potential for bias in AI systems. Many AI models are trained on large datasets that may reflect societal biases or gaps in data, leading to the possibility of unfair or discriminatory outcomes. In the context of digital forensics, biased AI tools could result in wrongful accusations or unfair treatment of individuals based on flawed evidence. For example, AI tools used in facial recognition or behavioral analysis could misidentify suspects or flag individuals unfairly based on demographic factors (Zangana et al., 2024; Gholami & Omar, 2023).

To mitigate such risks, AI systems used in digital forensics must be regularly audited to detect and address biases. Ethical frameworks emphasizing fairness, accountability, and transparency must be integrated into designing and deploying AI forensics tools. Legal regulations may evolve to require such audits to ensure that AI systems do not inadvertently reinforce existing prejudices or violate individuals' rights (Jeong, 2020).

8.4 International and Cross-Border Legal Issues

In the realm of digital forensics, the global nature of the internet and cybercrimes creates challenges for law enforcement and forensic investigators. AI tools used for cross-border investigations must comply with international laws and treaties related to data sovereignty, cybersecurity, and digital evidence collection. The transfer of data across borders often involves complex legal considerations, particularly when the data is subject to different legal regimes that may not align on issues such as data privacy or the handling of sensitive information (Sikos, 2021).

International cooperation among law enforcement agencies and between governmental and non-governmental organizations is essential to navigate these cross-border challenges. Regulations that govern data-sharing and international collaboration must evolve to address the emerging role of AI in digital forensics, especially as AI tools become crucial in detecting and investigating crimes that transcend national boundaries (Moustafa, 2022).

8.5 Regulatory Compliance for AI Tools

As AI systems become central to digital forensics, it is essential for the tools used in investigations to adhere to industry standards and regulatory compliance frameworks. Regulatory bodies such as the National Institute of Standards and Technology (NIST) in the United States and the European Union Agency for Cybersecurity (ENISA) have been instrumental in providing guidelines and best practices for the use of AI in cybersecurity and digital forensics. These regulatory frameworks set standards for the development, testing, and deployment of AI tools, ensuring that they are secure, reliable, and aligned with legal requirements (Karthikeyan et al., 2023).

Compliance with such regulations not only helps ensure the legitimacy of AI tools in forensic investigations but also provides confidence to legal professionals, ensuring that AI-generated evidence can be trusted in court. For example, frameworks for cybersecurity incident response that incorporate AI tools must demonstrate compliance with regulations on the handling of electronic evidence, proper chain of custody, and the protection of sensitive data (Zangana & Omar, 2025).

8.6 Summary

As digital forensics continues to evolve with the integration of AI, legal and regulatory considerations must keep pace with technological advancements. Issues related to data privacy, the admissibility of AI-generated evidence, ethical concerns about bias, and the complexities of international regulations present challenges for the use of AI in forensic investigations. To ensure that AI in forensics is both effective and compliant with legal frameworks, it is crucial to establish clear standards for AI tools, enhance transparency and explainability, and develop ethical guidelines that address the potential risks of bias and data misuse. By doing so, the integration of AI in digital forensics can enhance security while respecting privacy and legal rights.

9. FUTURE DIRECTIONS AND RESEARCH OPPORTUNITIES

The integration of Artificial Intelligence (AI) into digital forensics has revolutionized the way investigators approach cybercrime, data breaches, and incident response. As digital environments grow increasingly complex and cybercriminal techniques evolve, AI offers transformative potential in enhancing the capabilities of digital forensics. However, there are still numerous opportunities for research and development in this area, which could lead to more efficient, secure, and automated investigative processes. This section outlines key future directions and research opportunities, drawing from various studies on AI and digital forensics.

9.1. Enhancing Explainability and Transparency in AI Models

One of the prominent challenges in applying AI in digital forensics is the "black-box" nature of many machine learning models, particularly deep learning algorithms. Although these models have proven effective in detecting anomalies, classifying data, and identifying cybercrime activities, their lack of transparency limits their adoption in critical fields like forensics, where evidence presentation in court requires clear and understandable explanations. Research efforts should focus on explainable AI (XAI) to improve model interpretability without sacrificing performance. Studies like **Hall, Sakzad, and Choo (2022)** and **Kelly et al. (2020)** discuss the challenges and opportunities for incorporating XAI into digital forensics, ensuring that AI systems can provide understandable and defensible outputs in judicial settings.

9.2. Advancing AI Algorithms for Incident Response and Automation

The growing volume of data in digital forensics calls for increasingly sophisticated AI systems capable of automating various aspects of investigation. AI-powered tools could automatically categorize and prioritize incidents, helping investigators identify the most critical threats first. **Dunsin et al. (2024)** highlight the potential of AI and machine learning to streamline incident response, especially in constrained environments. Moreover, automated tools can reduce human error, expedite investigations, and improve response times in urgent cybersecurity scenarios. Research should explore developing more robust, real-time AI models that can autonomously manage, detect, and respond to cybersecurity incidents, making the process more efficient and scalable.

9.3. Synthetic Data for Training AI Models

Training AI systems, particularly deep learning models, requires vast amounts of labeled data, which is often unavailable or difficult to collect in the domain of digital forensics. **Gholami and Omar (2023)** discuss the potential of synthetic data in improving the efficiency of AI models. Future research could explore using simulated or synthetic datasets to train forensic AI systems, particularly in scenarios where real-world data is scarce or sensitive. The generation of synthetic data could help overcome privacy and legal constraints while providing a wealth of information for machine learning models, improving their accuracy and reliability.

9.4. Application of AI in Digital Evidence Analysis

Digital forensics relies heavily on analyzing vast amounts of data, ranging from network traffic logs to digital images and files. **Costantini, De Gasperis, and Olivieri (2019)** explore the intersection of AI and digital forensics, noting that AI techniques such as pattern recognition and natural language processing (NLP) can be pivotal in handling diverse digital evidence. AI's ability to process large datasets efficiently and recognize patterns that may be overlooked by humans is critical for identifying malicious activity or traces of cybercrimes. Researchers should focus on AI applications that can automate the extraction, processing, and interpretation of digital evidence, such as identifying steganography in images or detecting hidden information in network traffic.

9.5. AI for Cybercrime Prevention and Detection

AI's potential to enhance cybersecurity extends beyond post-incident forensics; it can play a crucial role in preventing crimes before they occur. AI-based systems can proactively identify vulnerabilities, predict attacks, and implement preventive measures. **Rughani (2017)** argues for the integration of AI in cybersecurity to predict potential cybercrimes, such as phishing or advanced persistent threats (APTs), and take preventive actions. Further research in AI-driven anomaly detection and predictive modeling could lead to more resilient security infrastructures capable of anticipating and mitigating attacks before they fully manifest.

9.6. Security and Privacy Concerns in AI-Based Forensics

As AI increasingly integrates into digital forensics, concerns regarding the security and privacy of both forensic data and AI models become paramount. **Bhawna and Mahajan (2024)** note the dual-edged nature of AI, where the same technology that can enhance forensic capabilities can also introduce new vulnerabilities. Researchers should focus on securing AI models from adversarial attacks, where malicious actors manipulate the model to produce erroneous outputs. Moreover, privacy concerns arise when AI systems analyze sensitive personal data. Future research should aim at developing AI models that are secure, robust, and capable of operating in compliance with privacy regulations.

9.7. Blockchain for Digital Forensics and Evidence Integrity

Blockchain technology offers promising solutions to ensure the integrity of digital evidence, which is a critical aspect of any forensic investigation. **Zangana (2024)** explores how blockchain-based timestamping tools can enhance evidence authenticity and prevent tampering. Blockchain's decentralized and immutable nature makes it an ideal candidate for storing digital evidence, ensuring that the data remains unaltered throughout the investigation process. Future research could focus on integrating blockchain with AI to create automated forensic systems that analyze data and securely store and validate evidence.

9.8. AI-Driven Threat Intelligence and Cyber Deception

Cyber deception techniques, such as honeypots and decoy systems, are becoming increasingly common in cybersecurity. **Zangana, Mohammed, Sallow, and Sallow (2024)** discuss the application of AI in cyber deception, emphasizing how AI can create realistic decoys that mislead attackers. Future research could explore how AI can enhance the effectiveness of cyber deception strategies by dynamically adapting to evolving attack tactics. AI-driven threat intelligence systems could detect and analyze deceptive tactics, improving incident response and helping organizations stay ahead of cybercriminals.

9.9. Interdisciplinary Approaches to Digital Forensics and AI

The integration of AI into digital forensics requires an interdisciplinary approach that combines expertise in computer science, law, and cybersecurity. **Sikos (2021)** advocates for the creation of ontologies and frameworks that can bridge the gap between AI systems and forensic investigators. Future research should focus on developing standards and methodologies that enable seamless collaboration between AI tools and human forensic experts. Interdisciplinary research will be essential to ensuring that AI systems in digital forensics are technically advanced, legally sound, and ethically responsible.

9.10 Summary

AI has the potential to significantly enhance the capabilities of digital forensics, from automating investigations to providing deeper insights into cybercrimes. However, there is still much to explore in terms of enhancing the explainability, efficiency, and security of AI systems used in forensics. By addressing the challenges related to data quality, model transparency, and ethical concerns, researchers can pave the way for more effective and reliable AI-driven forensic investigations. As the field evolves, interdisciplinary research will be key to advancing both AI technology and forensic practices, ensuring that digital forensics remains a critical component of cybersecurity in the future.

10. CONCLUSION

The integration of artificial intelligence (AI) in digital forensics has opened up transformative possibilities, driving innovation and enhancing the capabilities of forensic investigations. As cyber threats evolve in sophistication, traditional digital forensics methods struggle to keep up with the growing volume and complexity of data. AI, particularly through machine learning and pattern recognition techniques, has shown immense promise in automating and augmenting the digital investigation process. By leveraging AI, forensic experts can now more efficiently analyze vast amounts of digital evidence, identify anomalies, and detect security breaches faster than ever before.

However, the incorporation of AI into digital forensics is not without challenges. There are still significant hurdles related to data privacy, explainability of AI models, and the ethical implications of automated decision-making in legal contexts. As AI systems become more autonomous in forensic analysis, ensuring transparency, accountability, and fairness in their applications remains crucial. These issues need to be addressed through the development of ethical frameworks, legal standards, and AI technologies that are not only effective but also responsible and compliant with existing regulations.

Looking forward, the future of digital forensics will be closely tied to AI and machine learning advancements. The increasing use of AI tools will enable investigators to work more quickly and accurately, unlocking new potentials for digital evidence analysis. However, this future will require continuous collaboration between AI researchers, cybersecurity experts, legal professionals, and policymakers to ensure that the adoption of AI in digital forensics progresses in a manner that benefits both security and privacy. By doing so, AI will continue to play a central role in strengthening the effectiveness and reliability of digital forensic investigations in the face of evolving cyber threats.

In conclusion, while AI offers substantial promise for the future of digital forensics, its successful implementation will depend on overcoming several key challenges. With careful development, ethical oversight, and collaborative efforts, AI can reshape the landscape of digital forensics, improving investigative outcomes and contributing to a safer, more secure digital environment.

REFERENCES

Adam, I. Y., & Varol, C. (2020, June). Intelligence in digital forensics process. In *2020 8th International Symposium on Digital Forensics and Security (ISDFS)* (pp. 1-6). IEEE. DOI: 10.1109/ISDFS49300.2020.9116442

Costantini, S., De Gasperis, G., & Olivieri, R. (2019). Digital forensics and investigations meet artificial intelligence. *Annals of Mathematics and Artificial Intelligence*, 86(1), 193–229. DOI: 10.1007/s10472-019-09632-y

Dunsin, D., Ghanem, M. C., Ouazzane, K., & Vassilev, V. (2024). A comprehensive analysis of the role of artificial intelligence and machine learning in modern digital forensics and incident response. *Forensic Science International Digital Investigation*, 48, 301675. DOI: 10.1016/j.fsidi.2023.301675

Dunsin, D., Ghanem, M. C., & Quazzane, K. (2022). The use of artificial intelligence in digital forensics and incident response in a constrained environment. *International Journal of Information and Communication Engineering*, 16(8), 280–285.

Ganesh, V. (2017). Artificial intelligence applied to computer forensics. *International Journal (Toronto, Ont.)*, 5(5).

Gholami, S., & Omar, M. (2023). Does Synthetic Data Make Large Language Models More Efficient? *arXiv preprint arXiv:2310.07830.*

Gholami, S., & Omar, M. (2024). Can a student large language model perform as well as its teacher? In *Innovations, Securities, and Case Studies Across Healthcare, Business, and Technology* (pp. 122-139). IGI Global. DOI: 10.4018/979-8-3693-1906-2.ch007

Hall, S. W., Sakzad, A., & Choo, K. K. R. (2022). Explainable artificial intelligence for digital forensics. *Wiley Interdisciplinary Reviews: Forensic Science*, 4(2), e1434.

Hamza, Y. A., & Omar, M. D. (2013). Cloud computing security: Abuse and nefarious use of cloud computing. *International Journal of Computer Engineering Research*, 3(6), 22–27.

Huff, A. J., Burrell, D. N., Nobles, C., Richardson, K., Wright, J. B., Burton, S. L., Jones, A. J., Springs, D., Omar, M., & Brown-Jackson, K. L. (2023). Management Practices for Mitigating Cybersecurity Threats to Biotechnology Companies, Laboratories, and Healthcare Research Organizations. In *Applied Research Approaches to Technology, Healthcare, and Business* (pp. 1-12). IGI Global.

Iqbal, F., Debbabi, M., Fung, B. C., Iqbal, F., Debbabi, M., & Fung, B. C. (2020). Artificial intelligence and digital forensics. *Machine Learning for Authorship Attribution and Cyber Forensics*, 139-150.

Irons, A., & Lallie, H. S. (2014). Digital forensics to intelligent forensics. *Future Internet*, 6(3), 584–596. DOI: 10.3390/fi6030584

Jarrett, A., & Choo, K. K. R. (2021). The impact of automation and artificial intelligence on digital forensics. *WIREs Forensic Science*, 3(6), e1418. DOI: 10.1002/wfs2.1418

Jeong, D. (2020). Artificial intelligence security threat, crime, and forensics: Taxonomy and open issues. *IEEE Access : Practical Innovations, Open Solutions*, 8, 184560–184574. DOI: 10.1109/ACCESS.2020.3029280

Jones, R., & Omar, M. (2024). Revolutionizing Cybersecurity: The GPT-2 Enhanced Attack Detection and Defense (GEADD) Method for Zero-Day Threats. *International Journal of Informatics* [INJIISCOM]. *Information System and Computer Engineering*, 5(2), 178–191.

Jones, R., Omar, M., Mohammed, D., Nobles, C., & Dawson, M. (2023). Harnessing the Speed and Accuracy of Machine Learning to Advance Cybersecurity. In *2023 Congress in Computer Science, Computer Engineering, & Applied Computing (CSCE)* (pp. 418-421). IEEE. DOI: 10.1109/CSCE60160.2023.00074

Karthikeyan, P., Pande, H. M., & Sarveshwaran, V. (Eds.). (2023). *Artificial intelligence and blockchain in digital forensics*. CRC Press.

Kelly, L., Sachan, S., Ni, L., Almaghrabi, F., Allmendinger, R., & Chen, Y. (2020). *Explainable artificial intelligence for digital forensics: opportunities, challenges and a drug testing case study*. Digital Forensic Science.

Manasa, S., & Kumar, K. P. (2022). Digital forensics investigation for attacks on artificial intelligence. *ECS Transactions*, 107(1), 19639–19645. DOI: 10.1149/10701.19639ecst

Mitchell, F. R. (2014). An overview of artificial intelligence based pattern matching in a security and digital forensic context. *Cyberpatterns: Unifying Design Patterns with Security and Attack Patterns*, 215-222.

Mohammed, D., Omar, M., & Nguyen, V. (2018). Wireless sensor network security: Approaches to detecting and avoiding wormhole attacks. *Journal of Research in Business. Economics and Management*, 10(2), 1860–1864.

Moustafa, N. (2022). *Digital Forensics in the Era of Artificial Intelligence*. CRC Press. DOI: 10.1201/9781003278962

Nguyen, V., Mohammed, D., Omar, M., & Banisakher, M. (2018). The Effects of the FCC Net Neutrality Repeal on Security and Privacy. [IJHIoT]. *International Journal of Hyperconnectivity and the Internet of Things*, 2(2), 21–29. DOI: 10.4018/IJHIoT.2018070102

Omar, M. (2021). New insights into database security: An effective and integrated approach for applying access control mechanisms and cryptographic concepts in Microsoft Access environments.

Omar, M. (2022). *Machine Learning for Cybersecurity: Innovative Deep Learning Solutions*. Springer Brief. https://link.springer.com/book/978303115

Omar, M. (2024). From Attack to Defense: Strengthening DNN Text Classification Against Adversarial Examples. In *Innovations, Securities, and Case Studies Across Healthcare, Business, and Technology* (pp. 174-195). IGI Global.

Omar, M. (2024). Revolutionizing Malware Detection: A Paradigm Shift Through Optimized Convolutional Neural Networks. In *Innovations, Securities, and Case Studies Across Healthcare, Business, and Technology* (pp. 196-220). IGI Global. DOI: 10.4018/979-8-3693-1906-2.ch011

Omar, M., & Zangana, H. M. (Eds.). (2024). *Redefining Security With Cyber AI*. IGI Global., DOI: 10.4018/979-8-3693-6517-5

Omar, M., & Zangana, H. M. (Eds.). (2025). *Application of Large Language Models (LLMs) for Software Vulnerability Detection*. IGI Global., DOI: 10.4018/979-8-3693-9311-6

Rizvi, S., Scanlon, M., Mcgibney, J., & Sheppard, J. (2022). Application of artificial intelligence to network forensics: Survey, challenges and future directions. *IEEE Access : Practical Innovations, Open Solutions*, 10, 110362–110384. DOI: 10.1109/ACCESS.2022.3214506

Rughani, P. H. (2017). Artificial Intelligence Based Digital Forensics Framework. *International Journal of Advanced Research in Computer Science*, 8(8), 10–14. DOI: 10.26483/ijarcs.v8i8.4571

Sikos, L. F. (2021). AI in digital forensics: Ontology engineering for cybercrime investigations. *WIREs Forensic Science*, 3(3), e1394. DOI: 10.1002/wfs2.1394

Tyagi, A. K., Kumari, S., & Richa. (2024). Artificial Intelligence-Based Cyber Security and Digital Forensics: A Review. *Artificial Intelligence-Enabled Digital Twin for Smart Manufacturing*, 391-419.

Wright, J., Dawson, M. E.Jr, & Omar, M. (2012). Cyber security and mobile threats: The need for antivirus applications for smartphones. *Journal of Information Systems Technology and Planning*, 5(14), 40–60.

Zangana, H. M., Mohammed, A. K., Sallow, A. B., & Sallow, Z. B. (2024). Cybernetic Deception: Unraveling the Layers of Email Phishing Threats. [INJURATECH]. *International Journal of Research and Applied Technology*, 4(1), 35–47.

Zangana, H. M., & Mohammed, D. (2025). Foundations of Large Language Models in Software Vulnerability Detection. In Omar, M., & Zangana, H. (Eds.), *Application of Large Language Models (LLMs) for Software Vulnerability Detection* (pp. 41–74). IGI Global., DOI: 10.4018/979-8-3693-9311-6.ch002

Zangana, H. M., & Omar, M. (2020). Threats, Attacks, and Mitigations of Smartphone Security. *Academic Journal of Nawroz University*, 9(4), 324–332. DOI: 10.25007/ajnu.v9n4a989

Zangana, H. M., & Omar, M. (2025). Harnessing the Power of Large Language Models for Cybersecurity: Applications, Challenges, and Future Directions. In Omar, M., & Zangana, H. (Eds.), *Application of Large Language Models (LLMs) for Software Vulnerability Detection* (pp. 1–40). IGI Global., DOI: 10.4018/979-8-3693-9311-6.ch001

Chapter 11
Advancements in Image Integrity Verification Techniques and Challenges in AI-Driven Forensics

Mona Moussa
https://orcid.org/0000-0002-3647-1993
Electronics Research Institute, Egypt

Rasha Shoitan
https://orcid.org/0000-0003-0372-4293
Electronics Research Institute, Egypt

ABSTRACT

In the internet era, images and videos face significant danger from criminals seeking to manipulate and conceal evidence of their crimes. The authenticity of image and video evidence cannot be guaranteed, making it challenging to consider them strong proof in a law court. The ongoing competition between researchers developing forgery detection tools and forgers creating more sophisticated manipulation techniques adds complexity to creating a universal tool for efficiently detecting various types of forgeries. Numerous approaches have been proposed to assess the authenticity of images; this chapter conducts a comprehensive literature review and comparative analysis of recent effective techniques designed to discover image forgeries. The emphasis is on addressing copy-move and splicing attacks frequently encountered in such scenarios. The chapter also identifies commonly used datasets and evaluation metrics in this field. The chapter also highlights existing challenges

DOI: 10.4018/979-8-3373-0857-9.ch011

and provides valuable insights into potential future directions for research in image forgery detection.

INTRODUCTION

With the rapid progress of consumer technologies like image editing tools and artificial intelligence, altering and fabricating digital images has become more accessible and cost-effective. While some image modifications are benign, such as improving visual appeal, others serve harmful objectives, like distorting facts to propagate misinformation about people, groups, or incidents, or even constructing false evidence for criminal defense. The proliferation of such deceptive images presents serious risks to legal systems, global markets, economic stability, and national security. Therefore, in recent years, the field of digital forensics, and specifically image forensics, has naturally shifted its focus to identifying deliberate modifications in digital images. Methods for identifying these alterations are broadly classified into active and passive techniques, as illustrated in figure 1. Active techniques involve embedding a watermark or signature into the original image immediately upon capture. The key challenge lies in designing an insertion method that is robust enough to withstand minor, unintended alterations such as noise or compression during transmission, while remaining sensitive to subtle, intentional manipulations introduced by human intervention. A significant drawback of active techniques is that they need prior knowledge of an image, which means that it is not applicable when dealing with images from unknown sources (V. Sharma et al., 2016). Additionally, given the vast number of images being captured daily, it becomes impractical to embed a watermark or signature in every single image. Consequently, there is a growing demand for methods capable of detecting image forgery in images from unknown sources. To address this need, passive detection methods have been developed as an alternative. Unlike active techniques, passive approaches do not rely on any prior information about the image. Instead, they work solely by analyzing the image's data, without requiring any external input. Passive forgery attacks can generally be categorized into image retouching, image splicing, and copy-move techniques. Specifically, the process of image retouching involves subtle modifications that enhance or reduce certain features of an image. This technique is widely used in fields such as magazines and film photography, where images are enhanced to improve their appearance. For instance, specific elements, like the removal of wrinkles, are adjusted to achieve the desired aesthetic outcome. While these modifications are typically intended for enhancement rather than deception, they still qualify as forgery because they compromise the authenticity of the original image (P. Sharma et al., 2023). In addition to retouching, image splicing is another prevalent passive tampering technique. It is based on creating a new image using image fragments from distinct sources without post-processing, thus it is challenging to discern fabrications since the source images are absent (Fakhrulddin Abdulqader et al., 2023). Usually, there exists a donor image that is used to take a portion of it to be inserted in a host image as shown in figure 2. Although the changes in the image are not noticed by the naked eye, it disturbs some features of the image such as high order Fourier statistics as well as causing defects at the edges. These perceptions can consequently be utilized to identify fake content.

Figure 1. Image forgery types

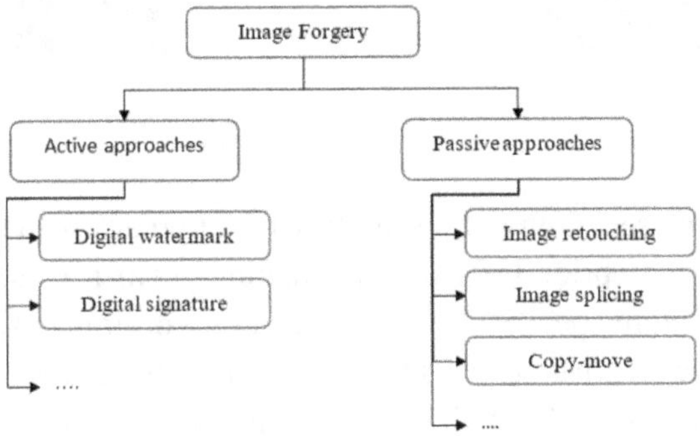

Figure 2. Procedure of image splicing forgery

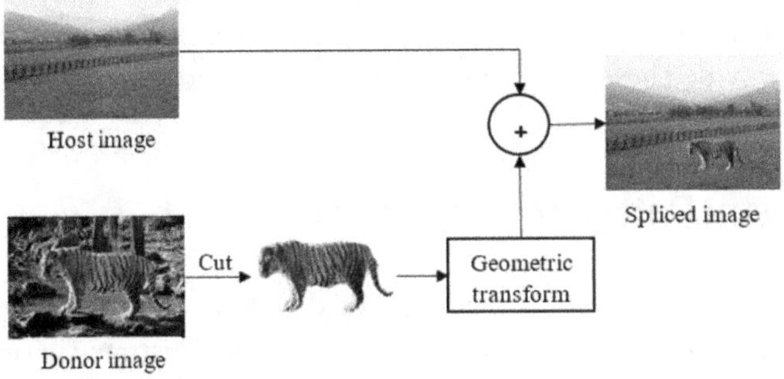

Copy-move forgery is another prevalent passive tampering technique, where a portion of an image is duplicated, as illustrated in figure 3. This technique can be detected using two main methods: block-matching and point-based approaches. Block-matching involves dividing the image into overlapping blocks, afterwards, features are extracted from these blocks and compared to identify similarities. On the other hand, point-based techniques extract relevant key points from the image and match them to find similar areas (Ardizzone et al., 2015a).

Figure 3. Procedure of copy-move forgery

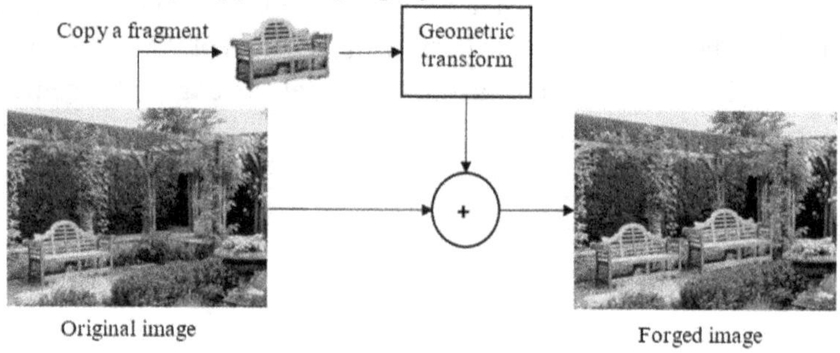

This chapter focuses on investigating passive approaches to forgery detection, which do not rely on prior information, making them a challenging yet more generalized goal. More specifically, we concentrate on image splicing and copy-move attacks as they are true attacks not just enhancing approaches such as image retouching. By addressing the evolving threats posed by increasingly sophisticated manipulation techniques, this work aims to contribute to developing more robust and reliable tools. These advancements are crucial for ensuring the integrity of digital evidence, ultimately strengthening its role in legal, investigative, and forensic contexts. In this chapter, the sections are laid out as follows: section 3 details several image manipulation detection techniques. Section 4 includes the benchmark datasets as well as the evaluation metrics. A summary of the covered research and a discussion is provided in section 5. Finally, challenges and future research directions are found in section 6.

Image Forgery Detection Techniques

The section outlines various methods for detecting image forgery, which are classified based on their core conceptual approaches, as illustrated in figure 4. These approaches include Error Level Analysis (ELA)-based methods, which examine compression artifacts; image partitioning-based methods, which analyze image segments for inconsistencies; and dominant features-based methods, which focus on characteristic patterns. Additionally, segmentation-based and JPEG header-based methods target anomalies in image regions or metadata, while object detection-based approaches focus on identifying manipulated objects within the image. Deep learning-based methods leverage neural networks to learn and identify forgery patterns, offering advanced capabilities in automated detection. In the subsequent subsections, these methods are detailed to provide a comprehensive understanding of their principles and applications.

Figure 4. Image forgery detection approaches taxonomy

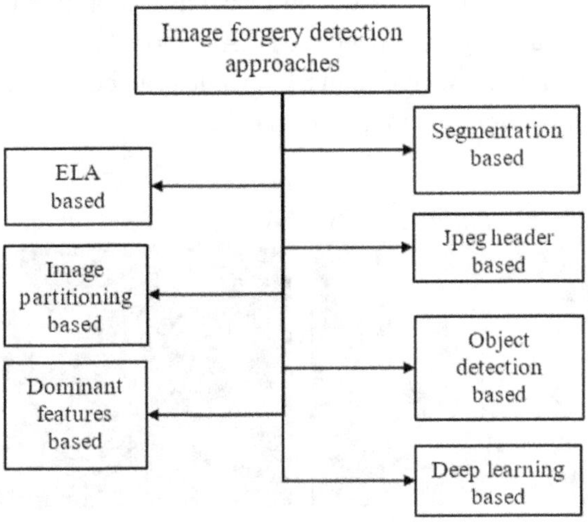

Error Level Analysis (ELA) based approaches

ELA (Warif et al., 2015) is a powerful tool for spot manipulation that occurs in lossy compressed image formats such as JPEG images. It works by analyzing the distribution of error that is introduced when the image is resaved at a particular compression rate, so it highlights areas in the image having different compression levels. JPEG utilizes a lossy compression algorithm, meaning that with each resaving process, the image loses quality. JPEG operates on an 8x8 pixel grid, compressing each square separately. If the image remains untouched, the 8x8 squares display the same level of error potential. However, when a JPEG image undergoes further resaving, all 8x8 squares tend to stabilize to similar error levels. In contrast, edits made to specific areas of an image cause those regions to display error levels distinct from the rest, making such manipulations detectable through ELA. The process of ELA involves generating a difference map of an image through intentionally resaving an image at a predetermined high error rate (i.e. 95%), then the difference between the initial image and the resaved version is then calculated and analyzed. The result highlights the varying degrees of compressions, making it easier to detect any edits that occurred, where modified portions of the image exhibit distinct compression rates as bright spots on the difference map.

Figure 5 illustrates how ELA reveals manipulations in an image. In figure 5(a), an original image is shown alongside its corresponding ELA after resaving it at a quality of 95%. In contrast, figure 5(b) presents an edited version of the image, in addition to the corresponding ELA due to resaving it at a quality of 95%. As observed, in the case of an original image the ELA is more homogenous. However, in the edited version, a distinct variation in ELA values can be seen in the manipulated region, clearly highlighting the area that was altered.

Figure 5. (a) An original image and its ELA. (b) A forged image and its ELA

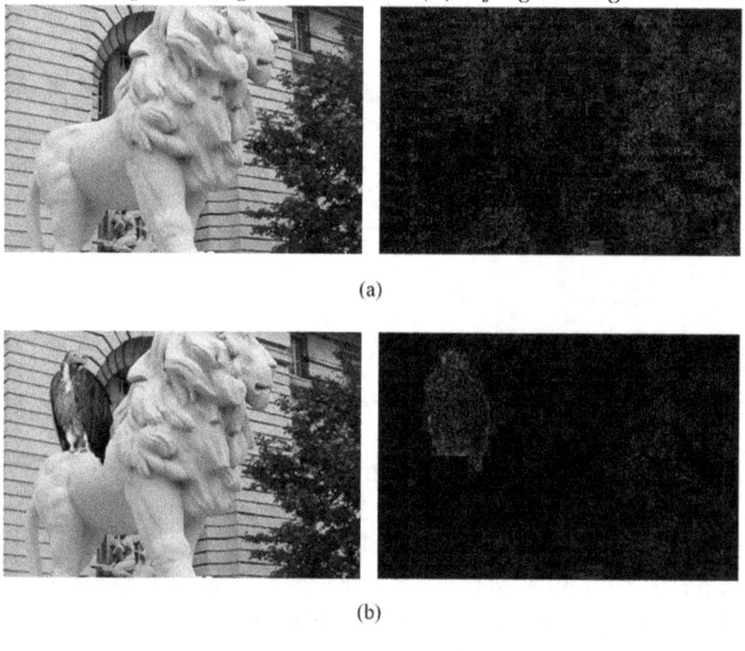

(a)

(b)

Numerous research studies utilize ELA as input to deep learning networks, training the models to classify images as either manipulated or authentic based on the ELA data and corresponding ground truth labels. Chakraborty et al. (Chakraborty et al., 2022a) propose employing a dual-branch convolutional neural network (CNN) combined with two preprocessing methods: ELA and Spatial Rich Model (SRM). SRM is derived from 30 high-pass filters and is used for steganalysis by discovering inconsistencies to reflect the residual images containing noise. These two inputs are fed into the two separate branches of the network to detect forgery images. While, Chakraborty et al. (Chakraborty et al., 2022b), target detecting forgeries in social media content. The first step is generating an ELA image to highlight inconsistencies in compression levels, then the ELA is preprocessed, resized, and normalized before being fed into the CNN. The proposed CNN is a lightweight architecture that requires few resources and parameters resulting in faster training.

Sri et al. (Sri et al., 2021) and Nagm et al. (Nagm et al., 2024) combine ELA with CNN to categorize fake images. Nagm et al. construct a CNN model that is formed from two successive convolution layers, these layers are then followed by a max pooling layer and two dense layers. Moreover, to improve model generalization, two dropout layers are inserted between different layers. Similarly, Sudiatmika et al. (Sudiatmika et al., 2019) combine ELA and deep learning to distinguish real images from forged ones by analyzing differences in compression levels. Specifically, ELA is applied to detect variations in compression ratios between original and tampered images, which is then fed as input into a VGG-16 model to classify images as either authentic or forged. On the other hand, Ali et al. (Ali et al., 2022) demonstrate the effect of the compression factor variation of the ELA on the results quality. Their proposed system depends on a lightweight CNN-based architecture to detect image forgeries based on the differences between original and recompressed images. The architecture consists of three convolutional layers, each with 32 filters and ReLU activation, followed by a dense layer with 256 neurons and a final output layer with two sigmoid neurons. As a result, the method effectively detects both splicing and copy-move forgeries. Walia (Walia et al., 2022) et al. start the process of forgery detection by computing the ELA value and then passing it to a Local Binary Pattern (LBP) (Alhindi et al., 2018) to generate a new feature map. LBP is a highly effective technique for describing the texture of images. It works by thresholding the neighboring pixels concerning the current pixel's value and then encoding the resulting local texture information. Consequently, this makes LBP a useful tool for vast computer vision tasks like classification, detection, and recognition. Moreover, explainable artificial intelligence (XAI) (Adadi & Berrada, 2018) is used as a feature selection approach to identify the precise features that cause irregular behavior in the dataset of manipulated images. Finally, the generated feature maps are then passed to a deep residual network (ResNet-50) to train them for classification.

Image partitioning-based approaches

Partitioning-based techniques rely on segmenting an image into smaller regions, whether in its original state or after transformation into another domain. This segmentation is commonly achieved using super-pixels, square patches (overlapping or non-overlapping), or in a triangular shape. These smaller regions are then analyzed to detect inconsistencies or repetitions. Generally, these methods are more effective for tackling copy-move forgery, which involves duplicating a section of the image and repositioning it within the same image. The segmentation facilitates an effective comparison of analogous regions to pinpoint duplicated patterns. In contrast, they are less effective for splicing forgery, which involves combining parts from different images, as this type of forgery does not usually result in repeated patterns within the same image. For instance, Islam et al. (Islam et al., 2018) identify image tampering by dividing the chroma components of an image into non-overlapping blocks of fixed size. Following this, a 2D Discrete Cosine Transformation (DCT) block is applied to define changes due to forgery in local frequency distribution. Moreover, LBP is utilized as a texture descriptor for the 2D-DCT to enhance the artifacts. The relevant inter-cell values of the LBP blocks are summed up to be used as feature values to be fed to a support vector machine (SVM) to classify images as authentic or fake.

Similarly, Reddy et al. (Reddy et al., 2021) propose a system for copy-move forgery detection as shown in figure 6. Initially, the image is divided into super-pixels using Simple Linear Iterative Clustering (SLIC) super-pixel segmentation algorithm. Afterward, three feature extraction techniques namely; Residual Neural Network (ResNet), Scale Invariant Feature Transform (SIFT), and Speeded Up Robust Features (SURF) are applied to each super-pixel. Finally, the features of each super-pixel are combined and matched with other super-pixels to identify regions exposed to copy-move forgery. In contrast, Ardizzone et al. (Ardizzone et al., 2015b) introduce an approach for recognizing and detecting copy-moved regions in images. This technique can identify the existence of these copied regions and reveal certain portions of them. Their method lies somewhere between block-based and point-based methods, it focuses on analyzing the structure of objects within the image, represented as a network of triangles. Initially, they extract points of interest from the image using three commonly used detectors, namely SIFT, SURF, and Harris. Subsequently, a Delaunay triangulation is constructed based on these extracted points, effectively dividing the image into triangles encompassing pixels with highly similar characteristics. However, a notable limitation of such keypoint-based techniques is their inability to detect regions within homogeneous areas of the scene, as such areas often lack sufficient interest points for detection.

Figure 6. Copy-move forgery detection based on super-pixel matching.

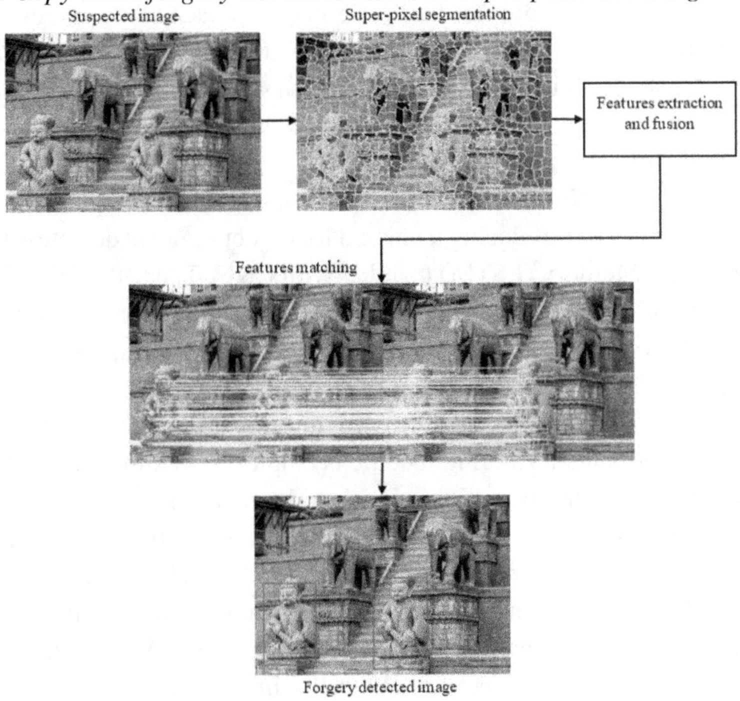

Huang (Huang & Ciou, 2019) propose a keypoint-based image forensic method designed to detect copy-move forgery using a combination of the Helmert transformation and SLIC superpixel segmentation. The system starts by extracting the key points and their descriptors from the image using the SIFT algorithm and then these points are matched in pairs based on their similarity. Afterward, the Helmert transformation uses spatial distance and geometric constraints to group the matching pairs to get the coarse forgery regions (compact clusters). At this point, Helmert transformation improves robustness against scaling, rotation, and compression. These regions are then refined to remove isolated regions and errors. Lastly, forgery regions are localized more precisely using the SLIC algorithm. Although this technique is robust against JPEG compression and geometric transformations (scaling, rotation), it is not powerful against recurring, symmetric, as well as smooth forms for tampering areas. Khudhair et al. (Khudhair et al., 2023) propose a copy-move forgery detection that initiates with the preprocessing of input images, converting them from RGB to grayscale. Following this, the image undergoes segmentation into overlapping blocks of dimensions 11 × 11. Singular Value Decomposition (SVD) is then applied to extract features from each block, capturing both geometric and arithmetic aspects of the image. SVD, known for its reliability and robustness as an orthogonal matrix decomposition method, ensures invariance to scaling and rotation. Subsequently, the norm value is calculated for each block, representing the diagonal matrix derived from the SVD transformation. Blocks with similar norms are identified, and the weight is computed for each subgroup of such similar norms. This systematic approach aids in determining whether a block has undergone copy-move manipulation.

Lu and Niu (Lu & Niu, 2020) address the challenges of exemplar-based image inpainting forensics by introducing a method for object removal detection based on Long Short Term Memory (LSTM) together with CNN. The task of the CNN is to explore anomalous similar patches based on patch matching for nearest neighbors leveraging CNN's strong learning capabilities to improve search speed and accuracy. Whereas, the LSTM network works on refining the results by reducing the false detection rate by distinguishing the normal texture consistent areas from suspicious ones. On the other hand, a filtering module is employed to eliminate disturbances caused by post-processing operations aiming to improve the robustness. Verma et al. (Verma et al., 2018) propose a system, demonstrated in figure 7, which begins by dividing an image into non-overlapping patches of size 128 × 128 pixels. Then, raw DCT coefficients are generated from each patch. Each one of these patches is processed and classified separately using a CNN network. Afterward, a majority vote is held to make a final decision about the image. This method focuses on identifying compression artifacts like quantization, rounding, and truncation noise rather than image content, making the system independent of scene context. The experimental results prove the system's scalability for detecting up to five compression cycles. (Tan et al., 2023) introduces a unified pipeline for Constrained Image Splicing Detection and Localization (CISDL). The aim is to integrate feature extraction with correlation matching using a target-aware attention mechanism. Here correlation matching is performed between the probe and donor images by revealing the relationship between related image patches. A multi-scale projection method is integrated into the attention mechanism so that it can perform matching among patches of images having different scales which increases the robustness of the proposed system against scale transformations.

Figure 7. Forgery detection depending on non-overlapping patches

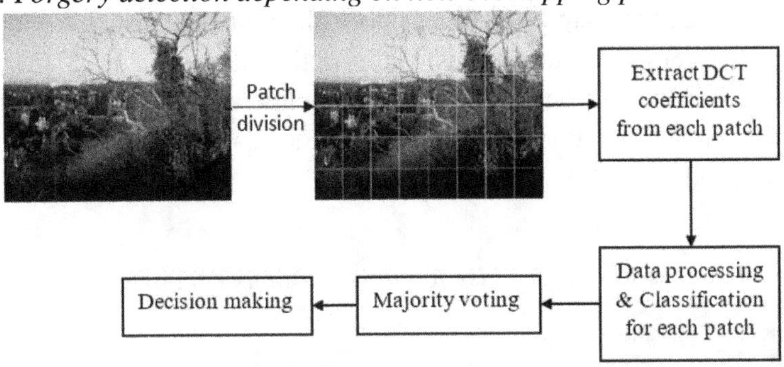

Dominant features-based approaches

This category of approaches depends on the premise that a tampered region exhibit disparities from the surrounding authentic area, particularly in terms of inconsistencies such as noise, texture, and intensities. To illustrate, Xiang and Acuna (Z. Xiang & Acuna, 2020) classify image manipulation depending on discovering noise inconsistencies in an image. The system generates a group of residual images for the suspected image to discard the image content and highlight existing noise in an image, aiming to increase the detection robustness by using various residuals. Finally, a one-class SVM is adapted to classify the images. Furthermore, Zhou et al. (Zhou et al., 2018) propose a Faster R-CNN network that consists of two streams as shown in figure 8. The network is specifically designed to detect tampered regions in manipulated images. The RGB stream extracts features from the RGB image input, focusing on detecting tampering artifacts such as strong contrast differences and unnatural boundaries. In parallel, the noise stream extracts noise features using a steganalysis model filter layer to identify inconsistencies in noise between tampered and authentic regions. To further improve the network performance, a bilinear pooling layer is applied to fuse the features from the two streams. This enables the incorporation of the spatial occurrence of the two modalities. The whole network is trained end-to-end for optimal performance and the result is in the form of a bounding box that surrounds the tampered region.

In contrast, Das and Naskar (Das & Naskar, 2024) construct an image-splicing detection method that relies on Haralick features and textural features that are extracted from the Gray Level Co-occurrence Matrix (GLCM) of the image, and the system localizes the spliced regions as well. The method begins by transforming the suspected image into a grayscale and extracts Haralick and textural features from it. The next phase includes feature correlation and the removal of the correlated feature using Sequential Forward Selection (SFS) to choose the most significant features to decrease the feature set dimension. Following this, Principle Component Analysis (PCA) is employed for dimensionality optimization. Finally, SVM classifier is utilized to classify whether the image is authentic and spliced. Additionally, a 10-fold cross-validation is conducted to validate the model's performance, ensuring its robustness and reliability.

Figure 8. Combining RGB and noise features for tampering detection

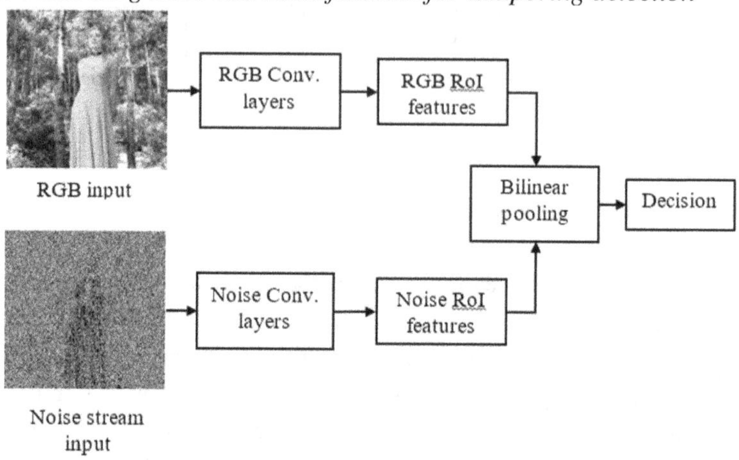

Al-Shamasneh and Ibrahim (Al-Shamasneh & Ibrahim, 2024) propose an image splicing model that combines deep features automatically generated using a CNN from the color image with the Sonine functions-based feature extraction model. This model utilizes some pieces of evidence about the likelihood of the given image pixels to discover spliced texture details. After the feature extraction stage, the classification phase starts by deploying SVM to differentiate between spliced and authentic images. Similarly, Ding et al. (Ding et al., 2023) introduce a dual-channel U-Net model to detect image splicing forgery, the model can localize the forged region at the pixel level. The model accepts two inputs; the first is the RGB features of the suspected image. The second input is the residual image features extracted from the suspected image using high-pass filters, where residual image features hold the tampered area's edge information. The model consists of three main parts: an encoder for feature extraction, a dual-feature fusion mechanism, and a decoder. Specifically, a VGG-16 model is adapted for encoding the RGB channel to extract deep features. The dual-feature fusion mechanism integrates features at different scales, enabling a richer semantic understanding of the context. Meanwhile, the decoder reconstructs the high-resolution tampered region by mapping the extracted features to the original image size.

In a related vein, A. Xiang et al. (A. Xiang et al., 2024) introduce an image splicing attack detection combining Discrete Wavelet Transform (DWT), DCT, and SVM classifier. The system recognizes spliced edges using this integration between statistical characteristics of natural images and machine learning techniques. The feature extraction process utilizes DWT and DCT transformations, focusing on DC and AC components, which typically follow Gaussian and Generalized Gaussian Distributions (GGD), respectively. Splicing operations disrupt these patterns, and the system models these changes using block-based DCT transformations. Subsequently, the extracted features are fed into an SVM classifier to determine the authenticity of the image. Although the system achieves high results, it has a challenging point facing complex textures such as Texture-to-Smooth and Texture-to-Texture categories. To address this limitation, deeper feature extraction methods could be explored. Furthermore, Liang et al. (Liang et al., 2024) introduce a Multi-Scale Feature Attention Fusion Network (MFAF-Net) that depends on an encoder-decoder architecture to detect spliced images. The network integrates two modules; the Multi-Scale Atrous Feature Attention (MAFA) and the Multi-Branch Attention Mechanism (MBAM) modules. MAFA is employed to extract rich contextual features across different scales of high-level feature fusion. Two attention mechanisms are used in the MAFA module, the first is channel attention which exploits inter-channel relationships between features by employing max pooling and average pooling across spatial dimensions. The second is spatial attention which uses the spatial relationships between features. Average pooling and max pooling are used successively to aggregate channel information from the channel dimension. Then, convolutional layers process the aggregated statistical features. In parallel, two MBAM branches, having Res2Net50 as their backbone, aim to refine low-level features by learning pixel relationships through context and local detail branches, improving pixel-level attention. The proposed system (MFAF-Net) overcomes the imbalance between positive and negative samples by employing dice loss and weighted binary cross entropy loss.

Segmentation-based approaches

In forgery detection, some research approaches treat the task as segmentation, aiming to identify the exact boundaries of tampered regions in an image by labeling each pixel as either authentic or forged. Gao et al. (Gao et al., 2022) develop a network that localizes copy-move and splicing forgeries through an end-to-end process utilizing ResNet101 as a backbone. The proposed system combines the RGB stream, frequency stream, and boundary artifact localization within a single framework.

First, the Adaptive Frequency Selection (AFS) module identifies tampering clues by selecting relevant frequency data. Next, the Adaptive Cross-Attention Fusion (ACF) module combines RGB and frequency features to enhance feature representation. Finally, the Boundary Artifact Location (BAL) network improves detection by identifying subtle boundary traces of manipulation. These three components are optimized together, ensuring their complementary strengths are leveraged for accurate forgery localization. Further, Wu et al. introduce the ManTra-Net network (Wu et al., 2019) to detect forged images. The architecture begins with a local detection algorithm using a Z-score feature that indicates how each local feature is far from a reference one. This is achieved by recognizing dominant features in the image and then identifying regions of features with adequate differences from the mean value to be defined as anomalous. To address the challenge of regions exposed to various manipulations, a multi-resolution analysis is employed, collecting a sequence of Z-score features using different window sizes. Subsequently, a convolutional LSTM network (Chao et al., 2018) analyzes these Z-score feature deviations. Finally, the VGG architecture is utilized for the classification step. Further, Niloy et al. (Niloy et al., 2023) aim to differentiate the unaltered and modified regions of an image enabling a clear separation of the feature distributions between both regions by adapting a Contrastive Learning Module as shown in figure 9. The technique depends on the assumption that there are differences in the feature's statistics as intensity, color, and noise. ResNet is used as a backbone to construct a two-stream encoder network, the first stream is an RGB encoder and the other is a Steganalysis Rich Model (SRM) filter (Fridrich & Kodovský, 2012) encoder. SRM filters are designed to function as high-pass filters that work by boosting the high-frequency information of the input image. As a result, these filters are capable of highlighting the edge information more effectively. The output of these two streams is merged and supplied to the Atrous Spatial Pyramid Pooling (ASPP) (Chen et al., 2017) module, which effectively extracts multi-scale features by expanding the field of view. The ASPP block's output features are passed through two heads; a segmentation head and a projection head. The segmentation head generates the ultimate prediction mask, while the projection head produces features utilized in the contrastive learning module. The projection head is active only during the training phase of the contrastive loss to learn the mapping in the feature space to effectively distinguish between genuine and altered regions.

Bappy et al. (Bappy et al., 2019) resent the detection of manipulated regions in an image as a semantic segmentation task, employing a deep learning architecture that combines a hybrid CNN and LSTM model. The encoder, built using a CNN, extracts spatial feature maps. Since certain manipulations, such as downsampling, upsampling, and compression, are more effectively identified in the frequency domain, the LSTM processes frequency domain features to learn correlations between patches. Subsequently, a decoder network reconstructs a binary mask that defines the manipulated regions by mapping the low-resolution feature maps to a pixel-level representation. Guillaro et al. (Guillaro et al., 2023) address the forgery localization task as a supervised binary segmentation problem. The approach involves a fusion architecture that relies on transformers. This architecture integrates the RGB image with Noiseprint++, a learned noise-sensitive fingerprint. Noiseprint++ is specifically trained on real data in a self-supervised manner, allowing it to effectively capture and incorporate artifacts related to both the internal and external processing of the camera. Through the parallel branches of the system, features from both the input image and Noiseprint++ are extracted using a shared encoder architecture derived from a semantic segmentation method. Furthermore, Zhao and Tian (Zhao & Tian, 2022) propose a multiscale fusion lightweight segmentation network for detecting image splicing. Their methodology enhances MobileNet version 2 by removing the classification layers, modifying structural blocks, and integrating dilated convolutions to preserve spatial information. They also skip some connections from the original network to enhance feature extraction from earlier network layers and decrease the parameters and the operations. Max pooling is employed for the down sampling process to reduce information loss, while a pyramid pooling module is used to capture multi-scale global information that enables pixel-level classification which is essential for forgery localization.

Aminu et al. (Ahmad Aminu et al., 2021) use the training images dataset and the corresponding ground truth to train a classification network based on a UNET architecture as a backbone. The proposed deep residual UNET model enhances image tampering detection and localization by utilizing the strengths of the UNET architecture, residual learning, and dilated convolutions. The traditional UNET is modified to join residual units in both the encoder and decoder paths to simplify efficient information propagation as well as to speed up the training step. Furthermore, dilated convolutions are employed to expand the receptive field to enable the network to capture global tampering artifacts while keeping a reduced computational load.

Figure 9. Adapting RGB and SRM encoders for forgery detection

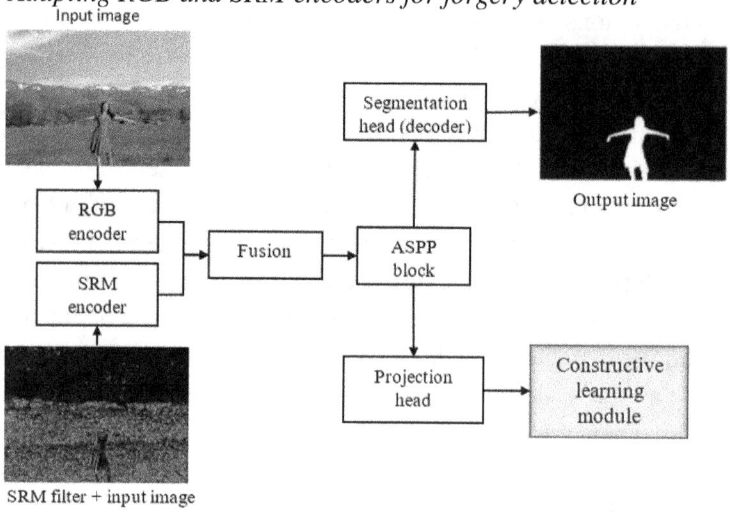

Sun et al. (Sun et al., 2022) propose an Edge-enhanced Transformer (ET) to localize tampered regions at both pixel and edge levels. The model aims to reduce false alarms by incorporating edge information into a transformer-based framework. A two-branch edge-aware transformer is used to comprise splicing edge clues. This model utilizes both deep and shallow layers to capture features related to both global tampering traces and subtle splicing edge artifacts, aiding in the localization of tampered regions task. To generate more effective features, a self-attention-based feature enhancement module is employed to highlight edge-area artifacts, suppress noise, and strengthen vital signals. Finally, the decoder produces the detailed forgery and edge maps.

Mazumdar et al. (Mazumdar & Bora, 2022) present a two-stream encoder-decoder network that depends on both low-level and high-level image features for the detection of fake regions. The first stream is the image-stream encoder-decoder (ISED), which captures high-level artifacts such as artificial edges, unnatural contrasts, and inconsistent blur from the input RGB image. While the second stream is the noise-stream encoder-decoder (NSED), it identifies low-level inconsistencies, such as variations in noise residuals, by applying a set of high-pass filters at the encoder's input. Each stream produces coarse feature maps which are then up sampled to generate dense feature maps using the corresponding decoder of each stream. Finally, the concatenated dense maps are then passed to a convolutional layer with a sigmoidal activation to produce a pixel-wise probability map that classifies each pixel in an image as forged or authentic. This technique can effectively detect and localize splicing, copy-move, and content removal forgeries.

JPEG-header based approaches

The quantization table, presented in the JPEG image file's header, reflects the amount of information lost during compression. This table can be used to estimate both single and double JPEG compression in a suspected image. In the case of double compression, only the secondary quantization table is preserved in the file, as shown in figure 10. This difference allows for distinguishing between the two types of compression by analyzing the presence of the secondary quantization table. To address this challenge, Park et al. (Park et al., 2018) develop a deep convolutional network to detect whether an image has undergone single or double JPEG compression. The network accepts both quantization tables and histogram features as inputs. For the histogram features input, DCT coefficient statistical characteristics are more appropriate to rely on than the RGB image since JPEG compression primarily modifies the statistical properties of individual blocks rather than altering the overall semantic content of an image.

Figure 10. (a) Original image having the same JPEG quantization table. (b) The image after manipulation. (c) Original and altered regions have different JPEG characteristics

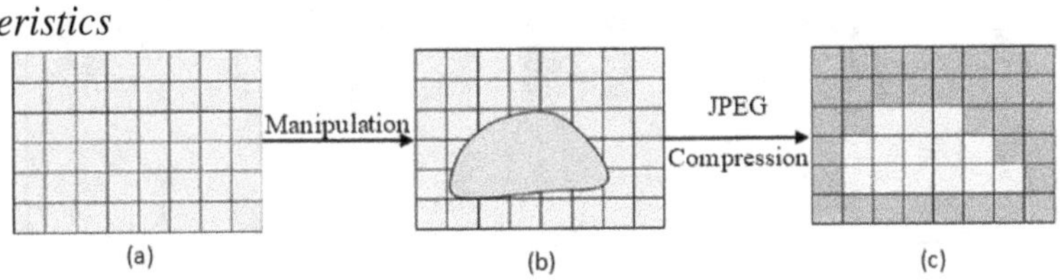

Object-based approaches

Paying significant attention to specific image content leads to recognizing and verifying whether it has been intentionally manipulated or is genuine. Ensuring the authenticity of human faces is particularly crucial in this context. In this regard, Ganguly et al. (Ganguly et al., 2022) create a deep learning model that incorporates a visual attention technique to distinguish between manipulated media (videos or images), generated through deep fake methods, and authentic ones. A lightweight attention mechanism technique is employed to prioritize relevant features for effective decision-making. The process begins with extracting the human face region from video frames, which are then processed through a pretrained Xception model to obtain feature maps. Subsequently, a visual attention mechanism is applied to highlight the residual artifacts of deep fake video manipulations. Figure 11 illustrates the process:

(A) represents the cropped face generator responsible for extracting and detecting frames and cropping faces. (B) demonstrates the generation of feature maps using the Xception model from the cropped face images. (C) portrays the functioning of the soft attention network applied to the feature maps. Finally, (D) showcases the classification network, comprising two dense layers and a softmax layer.

Moreover, B et al. (B & Bhaskar Reddy, 2023) present an object-based copy-move identification approach leveraging deep learning, as shown in figure 12. The proposed technique employs a Deep CNN that is enhanced through transfer learning from GoogLeNet's pre-trained parameters. The process begins with utilizing the You Only Look Once (YOLO) technique to identify objects within the image. Subsequently, appropriate features within each object are extracted through the VGG network. A Fractional Leader Harris Hawks Optimization (FLHHO) algorithm is developed to optimize the Deep CNN's performance by improving the exploitation phase of the Leader Harris Hawks Optimization using the fractional concept.

Figure 11. Detecting faces manipulation using visual attentions (Ganguly et al., 2022)

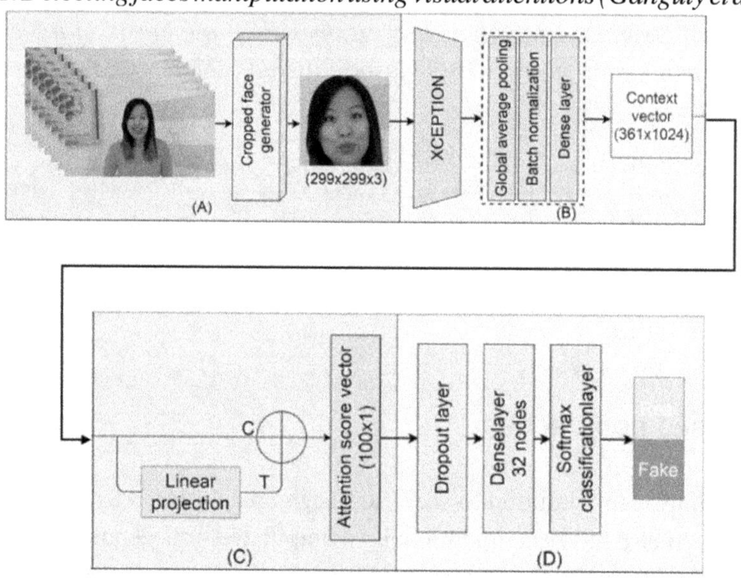

Figure 12. An object-based copy-move identification

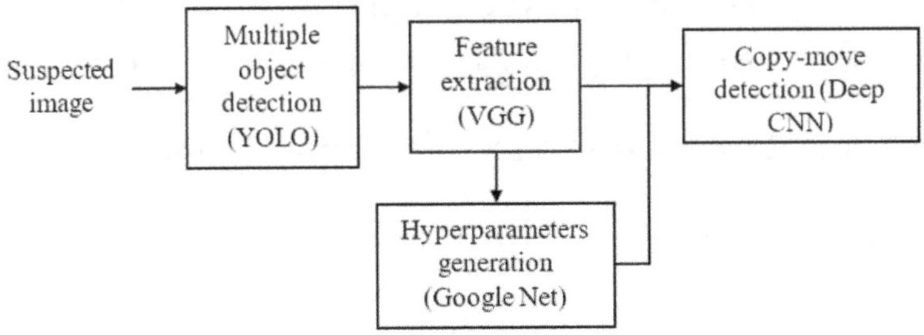

Deep learning-based approaches

Some systems are designed to feed images directly into a deep learning network without undergoing any preprocessing or feature extraction. In this setup, features are automatically acquired through the network without the need for human intervention. For instance, Diallo et al. (Diallo et al., 2019) propose a system that trains a CNN model to extract distinctive camera model features from image patches to be classified into original or forged patches. The framework addresses the challenges that occur in transformations such as compression, noising, resizing, and filtering, ensuring a tampered image detection algorithm that maintains robustness against these manipulations. Similary, Hosny et al. (Hosny et al., 2023) adapt a lightweight CNN model for detecting image splicing. The model consists of four convolutional layers, four max-pooling layers, one global average pooling layer, and one fully connected layer. In contrast, MiniNet (Tyagi & Yadav, 2023), a CNN model used by Tyagi and Yadav (2023) for image-level fake image detection, features a concise architecture with only eight layers. MiniNet consists of four convolutional layers, each followed by a max-pooling layer, and no residual or skip connections are needed to so that to speed up the training process. Furthermore, Qazi et al. (Qazi et al., 2022) employ transfer learning by leveraging YOLO CNN weights to adapt an architecture built on the ResNet50 deep network. This adaptation aims to identify instances of image splicing forgeries. In a similar vein, Nguyen & Huynh (Nguyen & Huynh, 2023) develop an image splicing detection model that designed to work efficiently on limited memory machines. The model offers an improvement for VGG 16, where residual networks are used to avoid the vanishing gradient. Lastly, Ramirez-Rodriguez et al. (Ramirez-Rodriguez et al., 2024) introduce a deep learning approach that depends on a Siamese neural network to identify image splicing manipulation. The Siamese network architecture consists of two identical branches that share weights and image features for effective feature extraction. The goal is to compare the image blocks and identify tampered areas, so a K-means algorithm is utilized to recognize similar centroids formed from the features extracted by the Siamese neural network, helping to locate the duplicated regions in the image.

Benchmark Datasets and Used Evaluation Metrics

Benchmark datasets

Numerous datasets are employed in the training of image manipulation detection systems. In this section, we provide descriptions of the most commonly utilized datasets.

- **CASIA 1** (Dong et al., 2013) comprises a total of 1721 images, with 800 being original and 921 classified as forgeries, in addition to the ground truth masks. The images have a resolution of either 384 × 256 or 256 × 384 and are stored in JPG format. The dataset involves manipulated samples through splicing and copy-move forgery. Additionally, post-processing techniques such as filtering and blurring are applied to enhance the images. Figure 13 displays some images from the CASIA 1 dataset.

Figure 13. Sample from CASIA 1 dataset. (a) Original images and (b) Tampered images

(a) Original images

(b) Tampered images

- **CASIA 2** (Dong et al., 2013) consists of 12,616 images, comprising 7,492 originals and 5,124 forgeries. The images have a fixed resolution of 900 × 600 and are available in BMP, TIFF, or JPG formats. The dataset contains ground truth masks. Manipulations in the dataset involve splicing and copy-move forgery, while post-processing includes image enhancement techniques like filtering and blurring applied to the samples. Some images of the CASIA 2 dataset can be seen in Fig. 14.

Figure 14. Sample from CASIA 2 dataset. (a) Original images and (b) Tampered images

(a) Original images

(b) Tampered images

- **Columbia** (Columbia Uncompressed Image Splicing Detection Evaluation CUISDE) (Hsu & Chang, 2006) dataset is composed of 363 images, featuring 183 originals and 180 forgeries, as shown in Fig. 15. The images vary in resolution, ranging from 568 × 757 to 768 × 1152. The dataset uses BMP and TIFF formats for its image files.

Figure 15. Sample from Columbia dataset. (a) Original images and (b) Tampered images

(a) Original images

(b) Tampered images

- **NIST 16** (*Nist Nimble 2016Datasets.*Https://Www.Nist.Gov/Itl/Iad/Mig/Nimble-Challenge-2017-Evaluation/., n.d.) comprises 584 image samples accompanied by ground-truth masks. The samples undergo manipulations involving splicing, copy-move, and removal, followed by post-processing to conceal any visible traces, as shown in Fig. 16.

Figure 16. Sample from NIST 16 dataset. (a) Original images and (b) Tampered images

(a) Original images

(b) Tampered images

- **COVERAGE** (Wen et al., 2016) is a relatively compact collection of 100 images along with their ground-truth masks, averaging a size of 400×486. This dataset specifically targets copy-move forgery, aiming to camouflage tampering artifacts by incorporating similar objects into the pasted regions. Some images of the dataset can be seen in Fig. 17.

Figure 17. Sample from COVERAGE dataset. (a) Original images and (b) Tampered images

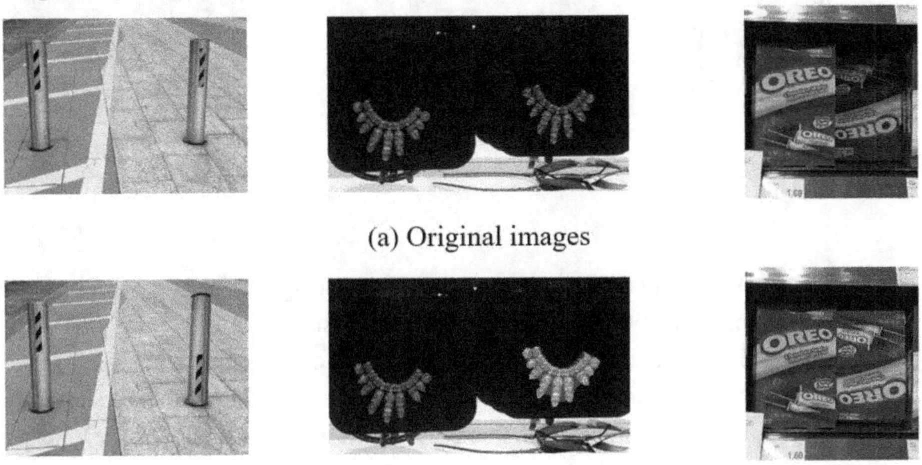

(a) Original images

(b) Tampered images

- The Multiple Image Splicing dataset (**MISD**) (Kadam et al., 2021) is categorized as a splicing dataset. It consists of 918 high-quality images that are annotated and deemed realistic, as shown in Fig. 18. These images are classified as either spliced or original, with the dataset containing 300 images created through multiple splicing and 618 original images. The images are stored in JPG format, each with dimensions of 384 × 256. Additionally, ground truth masks are provided for all the images in the dataset.

Figure 18. Sample from MISD dataset. (a) Original images and (b) Tampered images

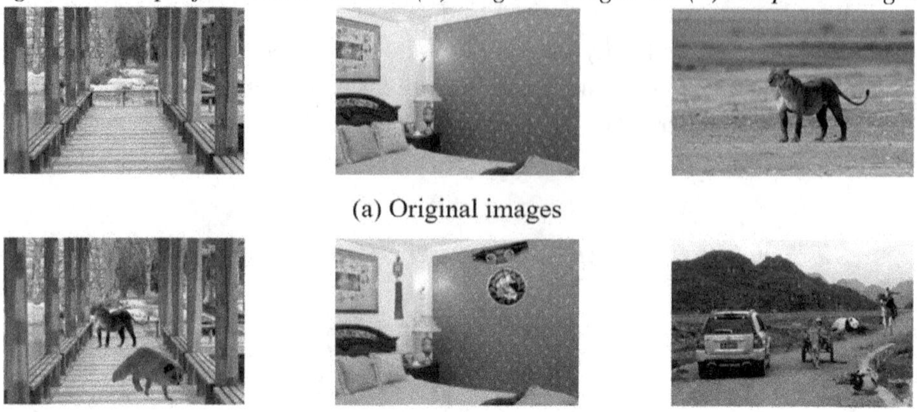

(a) Original images

(b) Tampered images

- The **CoMoFoD** dataset (Dijana et al., 2013) is designed for copy-move forgery and comprises 260 images ranging in dimensions from 512 × 512 to 3000 × 2000. This dataset includes both original and forged images, where forgery is applied through techniques such as translation, rotation, scale adjustments, distortion, or a combination of these manipulations. Samples of the dataset are shown in Fig. 19.

Figure 19. Sample from CoMoFoD dataset. (a) Original images and (b) Tampered images

(a) Original images

(b) Tampered images

Evaluation metrics

The performance metrics used in forgery detection applications are the same as those used for binary classification problems. In these applications, there are two classes: authentic and forged. These classes can be attributed to the entire image or pixel level. The evaluation of these systems relies on four key measures:

- **TP (True Positive):** Refers to the situation where forged pixels/images are correctly detected as forged pixels/images.
- **FP (False Positive):** Refers to the situation where authentic pixels/images are mistakenly detected as forged pixels/images.
- **FN (False Negative):** Refers to the situation where forged pixels/images are erroneously missed and considered as authentic pixels/images.
- **TN (True Negative):** Refers to the situation where authentic pixels/images are correctly detected as authentic pixels/images.

Based on these measures, these evaluation metrics are defined as follows:

1. **Precision:** It is a metric used to determine the accuracy of a machine learning model's predictions for the positive class. It can be calculated by dividing the number of accurate positive predictions (true positives) by the total number of instances that the model predicted as positive (including both true positives and false positives) as shown in Fig. 20. Simply, precision provides an answer to the question: how many retrieved items are relevant?

$$Percision = \frac{TP}{TP + FP}$$

2. **Recall:** It assesses the accuracy of a system in correctly identifying positive instances from the total number of positive samples in the dataset. To calculate recall, we can divide the number of true positives by the total number of positive instances, as shown in Fig. 20. It is important to note that the latter consists of both true positives (successfully identified cases) and false negatives (missed cases). In simpler terms, recall addresses the question of whether or not a system is capable of identifying all instances belonging to the positive class. How many relevant items are retrieved?

$$Recall = \frac{TP}{TP + FN}$$

Figure 20. Precision and recall metrics calculations

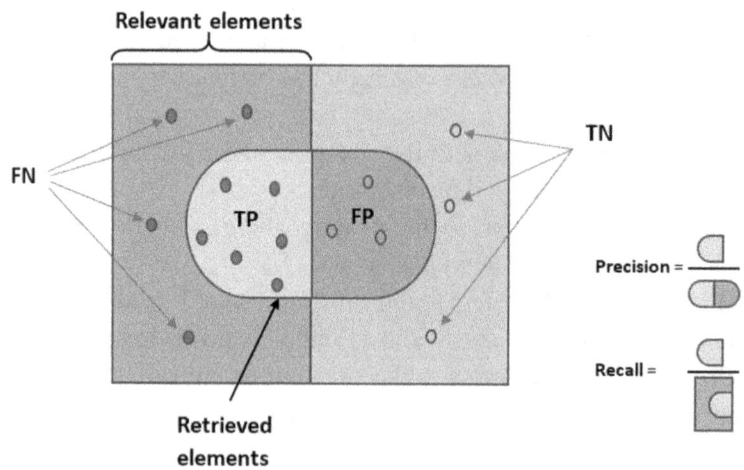

3. **Accuracy:** Is a quantitative measure that determines the frequency of correct predictions a system makes. This metric can be calculated by dividing the number of accurate predictions by the total number of predictions made. In simpler terms, accuracy provides an answer to the question: How often is the system correct?

$$Accuracy = \frac{TP + TN}{TP + TN + FP + FN}$$

4. **F1 score:** Is a valuable metric to consider when aiming for a balance between Precision and Recall. It becomes precious in scenarios where there is an uneven distribution of classes. By incorporating both precision and recall into a single metric, the F1 Score provides a symmetrical representation. An F1 score of 1.0 signifies perfect precision and recall, while a value of 0 indicates that either precision or recall is zero.

$$F1\ score = 2 \times \frac{Percision \times Recall}{Percision + Recall}$$

5. **The AUC (Area Under the ROC Curve):** it is a metric that quantifies the two-dimensional area under the entire Receiver Operating Characteristic (ROC) curve. The ROC curve is a graphical representation that illustrates the performance of a classification model across various classification thresholds. This curve compares two key parameters, the True Positive Rate, and the False Positive Rate, as they vary with different classification thresholds. By adjusting the classification threshold, more items can be classified as positive, resulting in an increase in both False Positives and True Positives.
6. **Confusion matrix:** it is used to visualize four outcomes (TP, TN, FP, FN) in one table, as shown in Fig. 21.

Figure 21. Confusion matrix of 2-class classification

		Predicted	
		Forgery	Authentic
Actual	Forgery	TP	FN
	Authentic	FP	TN

7. **Intersection over Union (IoU):** it is a widely used evaluation metric for assessing the accuracy of object detection algorithms. It can be applied to any algorithm that produces predicted bounding boxes. By comparing the ground-truth bounding box with the predicted bounding box, IoU quantifies the degree of overlap between the two boxes. A higher IoU value indicates a larger region of overlap.

$$IoU = \frac{Area\ of\ intersection\ of\ two\ boxes}{Area\ of\ union\ of\ two\ boxes}$$

Discussion

This section summarizes the surveyed approaches and conducts a comparative analysis, as outlined in Table 1, considering the datasets employed and the corresponding outcomes. The findings suggest that methods relying on features directly influenced by image forgeries generally yield higher accuracy compared to those dependent on conventional image features. Conversely, deep learning approaches outperform classical classification methods. These results indicate the potential benefits of combining handcrafted features with deep learning classification, encouraging a hybrid approach for enhanced performance.

Table 1. A comparison of various approaches for detecting image forgery.

Authors	Year	Forgery detection	Approach	Dataset	Evaluation metric	Result
ELA based approaches						
Chakraborty et al., 2022a	2022	Splicing Copy-move	ELA, image residual + dual-branch CNN.	CASIA v2	Accuracy F1 score	0.986 0.99
Chakraborty et al., 2022b	2022	Splicing Copy-move	ELA+CNN	CASIA v2	**Validation** Accuracy F1 score	0.962 0.976
Nagm et al., 2024	2024	Splicing Copy-move	ELA+CNN	CASIA v2	**Testing** Accuracy	0.94
Sudiatmika et al., 2019	2019	Splicing Copy-move	ELA+VGG16	CASIA v2	**Training** Accuracy	0.922
Ali et al., 2022	2022	Splicing Copy-move	ELA+ a lightweight CNN	CASIA v2	**Validation** Accuracy	0.922

continued on following page

Table 1. Continued

Authors	Year	Forgery detection	Approach	Dataset	Evaluation metric	Result
ELA based approaches						
Walia et al., 2022	2022	Splicing Copy-move	ELA+ LBP+ XAI+ ResNet	CASIA v1	Accuracy	0.931
				CASIA v2		0.995
				IMD 2020		0.981
				DVMM		0.991
Image partitioning-based approaches						
Islam et al., 2018	2018	Splicing Copy-move	LBP + 2D-DCT+SVM	Columbia	AUC	0.975
				CASIA v1		0.977
				CASIA v2		0.998
Reddy et al., 2021	2021	Copy-move	Extract ResNet, SIFT & SURF from Image superpixel and match them.	Private dataset	-	-
Ardizzone et al., 2015b	2015	Copy-move	Divide the image into triangles according to the SIFT, SURF& Harris extracted features and matches them.	Private dataset	-	-
Huang & Ciou, 2019	2019	Copy-move	Apply SIFT to image super-pixels and match pairs.	CMH1	F1 score	0.971
				CMH2		0.979
				CMH3		0.915
				CMH4		0.918
				D0		0.887
				D1		0.947
				D2		0.828
Khudhair et al., 2023	2023	Copy-move	Extracts SVD from image's non-overlapping blocks to capture geometric aspects of the image.	CASIA & CoMoFoD	F1-score	99.1
Lu & Niu, 2020	2020	Copy-move	CNN find similar patches based on patch matching	Private dataset	Accuracy	0.948
Verma et al., 2018	2018	Splicing Copy-move	DCT of non-overlapping patches+ CNN classifies each patch+ a majority voting for final decision	UCID	Accuracy	97.45
Authors	**Year**	**Forgery detection**	**Approach**	**Dataset**	**Evaluation metric**	**Result**
Tan et al., 2023	2023	Splicing	Integrates feature extraction and correlation using attention mechanism for patch matching.	CASIA	F1 score	0.952
Dominant features-based approaches						

continued on following page

Table 1. Continued

Authors	Year	Forgery detection	Approach	Dataset	Evaluation metric	Result
ELA based approaches						
Z. Xiang & Acuna, 2020	2020	Splicing Copy-move	One class SVM classify images depending on discovering noise inconsistencies.	Private dataset	AUC F1 score	0.92 0.77
Zhou et al., 2018	2018	Splicing Copy-move	A two-branch Faster R-CNN network.	NIST 16	F1 score AUC	0.937
				CASIA		0.795
				Columbia		0.858
				Coverage		0.817
Ding et al., 2023	2023	Splicing	Dual-channel U-Net model	CASIA v2	Accuracy	0.979
				Colombia		0.9727
Das & Naskar, 2024	2024	Splicing	Haralick and textural features extracted from the gray level co-occurrence matrix is used to localize spliced regions.	Columbia	Accuracy	0.83
				DSO-1		0.95
Al-Shamasneh & Ibrahim, 2024	2024	Splicing	deep features + Sonine functions-based feature extraction model+ SVM	CASIA v2	Accuracy	0.989
A. Xiang et al., 2024	2024	Splicing	DWT+ DCT + SVM	Columbia	Accuracy	0.96
Segmentation-based approaches						
Gao et al., 2022	2022	Splicing Copy-move	Localize forgery depending on RGB, frequency and boundary artifacts	CASIA v1	F1 score	0.597
				Coverage		0.518
				NIST 16		0.357
Wu et al., 2019	2019	Splicing Copy-move	Z-score feature+ LSTM + VGG	Dresden Image Database and KCMI	AUC	0.7
Niloy et al., 2023	2023	Splicing Copy-move	Two-stream encoder network. 1) RGB encoder and 2) SRM filter encoder	NIST 16	AUC	0.997
				CASIA		0.863
				IMD-20		0.899
Bappy et al., 2019	2019	Splicing Copy-move	A hybrid CNN and LSTM model.	NIST 16	AUC	0.794
				IEEE Forensics		0.758
				Coverage		0.712

continued on following page

Table 1. Continued

Authors	Year	Forgery detection	Approach	Dataset	Evaluation metric	Result
ELA based approaches						
Guillaro et al., 2023	2023	Splicing Copy-move	Combine RGB features and noise-sensitive fingerprint features to adapt a supervised binary segmentation system based on transformers.	CASIA	F1 score AUC	0.822 0.916
				Coverage		0.735 0.77
				Columbia		0.914 0.996
				NIST 16		0.47 0.760
Authors	**Year**	**Forgery detection**	**Approach**	**Dataset**	**Evaluation metric**	**Result**
Zhao & Tian, 2022	2022	Splicing	MobileNet segmentation algorithm	CASIA	F1 score	83.2
				Columbia		88.1
Ahmad Aminu et al., 2021	2021	Splicing Copy-move	Deep residual UNET model	CASIA v2	F1 score AUC	0.703 0.889
				Columbia		0.754 0.922
				NIST 16		0.75 0.92
				MICC		0.824 0.93
Sun et al., 2022	2022	Splicing	A two-branch transformer relying on forgery and edges features	CASIA v1	F1 score	0.633
				CASIA v2		0.681
				NC 2016		0.944
Mazumdar & Bora, 2022	2022	Splicing Copy-move	A two-stream encoder-decoder network	NIST 16	F1 score AUC	0.62 0.95
				CASIA v1		0.41 0.81
				Columbia		0.86 0.88
JPEG-header based approaches						
Park et al., 2018	2018	Splicing Copy-move	A CNN is used depending on JPEG image file's header and DCT histogram features	Private dataset	Accuracy	92.76
Object-based approaches						
Ganguly et al., 2022	2022	Deepfake for human faces	Pretrained Xception model + visual attention mechanism	Face Forensics++	Accuracy	0.993
				Celeb-DF (V2)	AUC	96.04

continued on following page

Table 1. Continued

Authors	Year	Forgery detection	Approach	Dataset	Evaluation metric	Result
ELA based approaches						
B & Bhaskar Reddy, 2023	2023	Copy-move	YOLO+ VGG & GoogLeNet or feature extraction + CNN classifier	MISD	Accuracy	0.93
Deep learning-based approaches						
Ramirez-Rodriguez et al., 2024	2024	Splicing	Siamese neural network + K-means	CASIA v2	Accuracy	0.986
Hosny et al., 2023	2023	Splicing	A lightweight CNN model	CASIA v1	Accuracy	0.991
				CASIA v2		0.993
				Columbia		1
Tyagi & Yadav, 2023	2023	Copy-Move	CNN	CASIA	F1 score	0.91
				Coverage		0.882
Qazi et al., 2022	2022	Splicing	ResNet50 built on YOLO CNN weights	CASIA v1	Accuracy	0.81
				CASIA v2		0.993
Nguyen&Huynh, 2023	2023	Splicing	ResNet-50 is used to enhance VGG-16 to avoid vanishing gradient	CASIA v2	Accuracy	0.925

Challenges and future research directions

Detecting image forgery presents challenges, particularly in enhancing the precision of localizing tampered regions within manipulated images. Another critical consideration is the need to minimize computational complexity in future research. Additionally, upcoming work should address emerging challenges, such as the detection of deep fake content, to ensure comprehensive and effective approaches in the field of image forensics. To support this, it is crucial to create realistic datasets that cover a range of attacks and diverse image extensions. These images should resemble those commonly shared on social media, depicting malicious attacks from a semantic standpoint. The dataset must include associated ground-truth masks, which are essential for both the training phase and system evaluation.

Relying on a complete end-to-end deep learning system is a worthy objective, but it encounters several challenges. The primary challenge is constructing a system of reasonable size that can be trained efficiently and deliver prompt decisions. Therefore, a robust lightweight network capable of detecting various forms of tampering is needed. The second challenging aspect involves improving the feature extraction stage, a fundamental step crucial to the functioning of any system. The comparative analysis in this chapter establishes that segmentation-based methods typically rely on pixel-based evaluation, which may lead to lower accuracy performance than approaches that depend on image-based evaluation. On the other hand, object-based methods face limitations in widespread applicability as they depend solely on specific objects. While partitioning-based methods are commonly employed to identify copy-move more than splicing, they may suffer from rough boundaries in the resulting output. Methods that incorporate a pre-processing step with a deep learning network have demonstrated superior accuracies. Consequently, these approaches emerge as the most promising avenue for further research, emphasizing the need to develop systems that integrate deep learning approaches with traditional techniques that emphasize the effect of tampering on the extracted features.

Competing interests: The authors declare that they have no competing interests or financial conflicts to disclose.

REFERENCES

Adadi, A., & Berrada, M. (2018). Peeking Inside the Black-Box: A Survey on Explainable Artificial Intelligence (XAI). *IEEE Access : Practical Innovations, Open Solutions*, 6, 52138–52160. DOI: 10.1109/ACCESS.2018.2870052

Ahmad Aminu, A., Nnanna Agwu, N., & Steve, A. (2021). Detection and Localization of Image Tampering using Deep Residual UNET with Stacked Dilated Convolution. In *IJCSNS International Journal of Computer Science and Network Security* (Vol. 21, Issue 9). DOI: 10.22937/IJCSNS.2021.21.9.28

Al-Shamasneh, A. R., & Ibrahim, R. W. (2024). Image Splicing Forgery Detection Using Feature-Based of Sonine Functions and Deep Features. *Computers, Materials & Continua*, 78(1), 795–810. DOI: 10.32604/cmc.2023.042755

Alhindi, T. J., Kalra, S., Ng, K. H., Afrin, A., & Tizhoosh, H. R. (2018). *Comparing LBP, HOG and Deep Features for Classification of Histopathology Images*. http://arxiv.org/abs/1805.05837 DOI: 10.1109/IJCNN.2018.8489329

Ali, S. S., Ganapathi, I. I., Vu, N.-S., Ali, S. D., Saxena, N., & Werghi, N. (2022). Image Forgery Detection Using Deep Learning by Recompressing Images. *Electronics (Basel)*, 11(3), 403. DOI: 10.3390/electronics11030403

Ardizzone, E., Bruno, A., & Mazzola, G. (2015a). Copy–Move Forgery Detection by Matching Triangles of Keypoints. *IEEE Transactions on Information Forensics and Security*, 10(10), 2084–2094. DOI: 10.1109/TIFS.2015.2445742

Ardizzone, E., Bruno, A., & Mazzola, G. (2015b). Copy–Move Forgery Detection by Matching Triangles of Keypoints. *IEEE Transactions on Information Forensics and Security*, 10(10), 2084–2094. DOI: 10.1109/TIFS.2015.2445742

Bappy, J. H., Simons, C., Nataraj, L., Manjunath, B. S., & Roy-Chowdhury, A. K. (2019). Hybrid LSTM and Encoder–Decoder Architecture for Detection of Image Forgeries. *IEEE Transactions on Image Processing*, 28(7), 3286–3300. DOI: 10.1109/TIP.2019.2895466 PMID: 30703026

Chakraborty, S., Chatterjee, K., & Dey, P. (2022a). *Detection of Image Tampering Using Deep Learning, Error Levels & Noise Residuals*. 1–17. DOI: 10.21203/rs.3.rs-2174562/v1

Chakraborty, S., Chatterjee, K., & Dey, P. (2022b). Discovering Tampered Image in Social Media Using ELA and Deep Learning. *SN Computer Science*, 3(5), 392. DOI: 10.1007/s42979-022-01311-w

Chao, Z., Pu, F., Yin, Y., Han, B., & Chen, X. (2018). Research on real-time local rainfall prediction based on MEMS sensors. In *Journal of Sensors* (Vol. 2018). DOI: 10.1155/2018/6184713

Chen, L.-C., Papandreou, G., Schroff, F., & Adam, H. (2017). *Rethinking Atrous Convolution for Semantic Image Segmentation.* http://arxiv.org/abs/1706.05587

Das, D., & Naskar, R. (2024). Image splicing detection using low-dimensional feature vector of texture features and Haralick features based on Gray Level Co-occurrence Matrix. *Signal Processing Image Communication*, 125, 117134. Advance online publication. DOI: 10.1016/j.image.2024.117134

Diallo, B., Urruty, T., Bourdon, P., & Fernandez-Maloigne, C. (2019). Improving Robustness of Image Tampering Detection for Compression. In *Lecture Notes in Computer Science (including subseries Lecture Notes in Artificial Intelligence and Lecture Notes in Bioinformatics): Vol. 11295 LNCS* (pp. 387–398). DOI: 10.1007/978-3-030-05710-7_32

Dijana, T., Zupancic, I., Grgic, S., & Grgic, M. (2013). CoMoFoD—New database for copy-move forgery detection (pp. 49–54). In *Proceedings ELMAR-2013.*

Ding, H., Chen, L., Tao, Q., Fu, Z., Dong, L., & Cui, X. (2023). DCU-Net: A dual-channel U-shaped network for image splicing forgery detection. *Neural Computing & Applications*, 35(7), 5015–5031. DOI: 10.1007/s00521-021-06329-4 PMID: 34404963

Dong, J., Wang, W., & Tan, T. (2013). CASIA Image Tampering Detection Evaluation Database. *2013 IEEE China Summit and International Conference on Signal and Information Processing*, 422–426. DOI: 10.1109/ChinaSIP.2013.6625374

Fakhrulddin Abdulqader, M., Dawod, A. Y., & Zeki Ablahd, A. (2023). Detection of tamper forgery image in security digital mage. *Measurement. Sensors*, 27, 100746. DOI: 10.1016/j.measen.2023.100746

Fridrich, J., & Kodovský, J. (2012). *Rich Models for Steganalysis of Digital Images.*

Ganguly, S., Mohiuddin, S., Malakar, S., Cuevas, E., & Sarkar, R. (2022). Visual attention-based deepfake video forgery detection. *Pattern Analysis & Applications*, 25(4), 981–992. DOI: 10.1007/s10044-022-01083-2

Gao, Z., Sun, C., Cheng, Z., Guan, W., Liu, A., & Wang, M. (2022). TBNet: A Two-Stream Boundary-Aware Network for Generic Image Manipulation Localization. *IEEE Transactions on Knowledge and Data Engineering*, •••, 1–16. DOI: 10.1109/TKDE.2022.3187091

Guillaro, F., Cozzolino, D., Sud, A., Dufour, N., & Verdoliva, L. (2023). *TruFor: Leveraging All-Round Clues for Trustworthy Image Forgery Detection and Localization*. 20606–20615. DOI: 10.1109/CVPR52729.2023.01974

Hosny, K. M., Mortda, A. M., Lashin, N. A., & Fouda, M. M. (2023). A New Method to Detect Splicing Image Forgery Using Convolutional Neural Network. *Applied Sciences (Basel, Switzerland)*, 13(3), 1272. Advance online publication. DOI: 10.3390/app13031272

Hsu, Y., & Chang, S. (2006). Detecting Image Splicing using Geometry Invariants and Camera Characteristics Consistency. *2006 IEEE International Conference on Multimedia and Expo*, 549–552. DOI: 10.1109/ICME.2006.262447

Huang, H.-Y., & Ciou, A.-J. (2019). Copy-move forgery detection for image forensics using the superpixel segmentation and the Helmert transformation. *EURASIP Journal on Image and Video Processing*, 2019(1), 68. DOI: 10.1186/s13640-019-0469-9

Islam, M. M., Karmakar, G., Kamruzzaman, J., Murshed, M., Kahandawa, G., & Parvin, N. (2018). Detecting Splicing and Copy-Move Attacks in Color Images. *2018 Digital Image Computing: Techniques and Applications (DICTA)*, 1–7. DOI: 10.1109/DICTA.2018.8615874

Kadam, K. D., Ahirrao, S., & Kotecha, K. (2021). Multiple image splicing dataset (Misd): A dataset for multiple splicing. In *Data* (Vol. 6, Issue 10). DOI: 10.3390/data6100102

Khudhair, Z. N., Mohamed, F., Rehman, A., Saba, T., & Bahaj, S. A. (2023). Detection of Copy-Move Forgery in Digital Images Using Singular Value Decomposition. *Computers, Materials & Continua*, 74(2), 4135–4147. DOI: 10.32604/cmc.2023.032315

Liang, E., Zhang, K., Hua, Z., & Jia, X. (2024). Multi-Scale Feature Attention Fusion for Image Splicing Forgery Detection. *ACM Transactions on Multimedia Computing Communications and Applications*, 3698770. Advance online publication. DOI: 10.1145/3698770

Lu, M., & Niu, S. (2020). A detection approach using lstm-cnn for object removal caused by exemplar-based image inpainting. In *Electronics (Switzerland)* (Vol. 9, Issue 5). DOI: 10.3390/electronics9050858

Mazumdar, A., & Bora, P. K. (2022). Two-stream encoder–decoder network for localizing image forgeries. *Journal of Visual Communication and Image Representation*, 82, 1–11. DOI: 10.1016/j.jvcir.2021.103417

Nagm, A. M., Moussa, M. M., Shoitan, R., Ali, A., Mashhour, M., Salama, A. S., & Hamada, I. (2024). *Detecting image manipulation with ELA- CNN integration : a powerful framework for authenticity verifi cation.* 1–18. DOI: 10.7717/peerj-cs.2205

Nguyen, H. L., & Huynh, K. T. (2023). *A Deep Learning Model for Splicing Image Detection.* REV Journal on Electronics and Communications., DOI: 10.21553/rev-jec.335

Niloy, F. F., Kumar Bhaumik, K., & Woo, S. S. (2023). CFL-Net: Image Forgery Localization Using Contrastive Learning. In *Proceedings - 2023 IEEE Winter Conference on Applications of Computer Vision, WACV 2023* (pp. 4631–4640). DOI: 10.1109/WACV56688.2023.00462

Park, J., Cho, D., Ahn, W., & Lee, H. K. (2018). Double JPEG Detection in Mixed JPEG Quality Factors Using Deep Convolutional Neural Network. In *Lecture Notes in Computer Science (including subseries Lecture Notes in Artificial Intelligence and Lecture Notes in Bioinformatics): Vol. 11209 LNCS* (pp. 656–672). DOI: 10.1007/978-3-030-01228-1_39

Qazi, E. U. H., Zia, T., & Almorjan, A. (2022). Deep Learning-Based Digital Image Forgery Detection System. *Applied Sciences (Basel, Switzerland)*, 12(6), 2851. Advance online publication. DOI: 10.3390/app12062851

Ramirez-Rodriguez, A. E., Arevalo-Ancona, R. E., Perez-Meana, H., Cedillo-Hernandez, M., & Nakano-Miyatake, M. (2024). AISMSNet: Advanced Image Splicing Manipulation Identification Based on Siamese Networks. *Applied Sciences (Basel, Switzerland)*, 14(13), 5545. Advance online publication. DOI: 10.3390/app14135545

Reddy, V., Vaghdevi, K., & Kolli, D. K. (2021). Digital image forgery detection using SUPER pixel segmentation and HYBRID feature point mapping. *European Journal of Molecular and Clinical Medicine*, 8(2), 1485–1500.

Sharma, P., Kumar, M., & Sharma, H. (2023). Comprehensive analyses of image forgery detection methods from traditional to deep learning approaches: an evaluation. In *Multimedia Tools and Applications* (Vol. 82, Issue 12, pp. 18117–18150). DOI: 10.1007/s11042-022-13808-w

Sharma, V., Jha, S., & Kumar Bharti, R. (2016). Image Forgery and it's Detection Technique: A Review. In *International Research Journal of Engineering and Technology.*

Sri, C. G., Bano, S., Deepika, T., Kola, N., & Pranathi, Y. L. (2021). Deep Neural Networks Based Error Level Analysis for Lossless Image Compression Based Forgery Detection. *2021 International Conference on Intelligent Technologies (CONIT)*, 1–8. DOI: 10.1109/CONIT51480.2021.9498357

Sudiatmika, I. B. K., Rahman, F., Trisno, T., & Suyoto, S. (2019). Image forgery detection using error level analysis and deep learning. [Telecommunication Computing Electronics and Control]. *TELKOMNIKA*, 17(2), 653. DOI: 10.12928/telkomnika.v17i2.8976

Sun, Y., Ni, R., & Zhao, Y. (2022). ET. *Edge-Enhanced Transformer for Image.*, 29, 1232–1236.

Tan, Y., Li, Y., Zeng, L., Ye, J., Wang, W., & Li, X. (2023). Multi-scale Target-Aware Framework for Constrained Splicing Detection and Localization. *MM 2023 - Proceedings of the 31st ACM International Conference on Multimedia*, 8790–8798. DOI: 10.1145/3581783.3613763

Tyagi, S., & Yadav, D. (2023). MiniNet: A concise CNN for image forgery detection. *Evolving Systems*, 14(3), 545–556. DOI: 10.1007/s12530-022-09446-0

Verma, V., Agarwal, N., & Khanna, N. (2018). DCT-domain deep convolutional neural networks for multiple JPEG compression classification. *Signal Processing Image Communication*, 67, 22–33. DOI: 10.1016/j.image.2018.04.014

Walia, S., Kumar, K., Agarwal, S., & Kim, H. (2022). Using XAI for Deep Learning-Based Image Manipulation Detection with Shapley Additive Explanation. In *Symmetry* (Vol. 14, Issue 8). DOI: 10.3390/sym14081611

Wen, B., Zhu, Y., Subramanian, R., Ng, T.-T., Shen, X., & Winkler, S. (2016). COVERAGE — A novel database for copy-move forgery detection. *2016 IEEE International Conference on Image Processing (ICIP)*, 161–165. DOI: 10.1109/ICIP.2016.7532339

Wu, Y., AbdAlmageed, W., & Natarajan, P. (2019). ManTra-Net: Manipulation Tracing Network for Detection and Localization of Image Forgeries With Anomalous Features. *2019 IEEE/CVF Conference on Computer Vision and Pattern Recognition (CVPR)*, 9535–9544. DOI: 10.1109/CVPR.2019.00977

Xiang, A., Zhang, J., Yang, Q., Wang, L., & Cheng, Y. (2024). *Research on Splicing Image Detection Algorithms Based on Natural Image Statistical Characteristics*. http://arxiv.org/abs/2404.16296

Xiang, Z., & Acuna, D. E. (2020). *Scientific Image Tampering Detection Based On Noise Inconsistencies: A Method And Datasets*. arXiv preprint arXiv:2001.07799. DOI: 10.21203/rs.2.22943/v1

Zhao, D., & Tian, X. (2022). A Multiscale Fusion Lightweight Image-Splicing Tamper-Detection Model. In *Electronics (Switzerland)* (Vol. 11, Issue 16). DOI: 10.3390/electronics11162621

Zhou, P., Han, X., Morariu, V. I., & Davis, L. S. (2018). Learning Rich Features for Image Manipulation Detection. *2018 IEEE/CVF Conference on Computer Vision and Pattern Recognition*, 1053–1061. DOI: 10.1109/CVPR.2018.00116

KEY TERMS AND DEFINITIONS

Attention Model: Is a mechanism that improves the neural network performance by focusing on the most relevant parts of the input data while processing it. In image processing, it concentrates on specific image regions that are most important for a given task.

Discrete Cosine Transform (DCT): Is a mathematical tool used in image processing to convert an image from a pixel value representation into frequency-domain data. This representation form can be used to separate low-frequency components (like smooth variations) from less significant high-frequency ones (like edges or noise). Tasks such as image and video compression, noise reduction, and feature extraction can relay on DCT.

Long Short-Term Memory (LSTM): Is a type of recurrent neural network (RNN) designed to capture long-term dependencies in sequential data. LSTM uses specialized gating mechanisms to regulate the flow of information, allowing them to learn patterns over extended sequences.

Recurrent Neural Network (RNN): Is a type of neural network designed to process sequential data by maintaining a hidden state that captures information about previous inputs.

Scale Invariant Feature Transform (SIFT): Is a computer vision algorithm that is used to detect and describe local features in images. It identifies key points and extracts distinctive descriptors for them. SIFT descriptors are invariant to scale, rotation, and moderate illumination and view angle changes.

Speeded Up Robust Features (SURF): Is a computer vision algorithm similar to SIFT but optimized for speed making it more suitable for real-time applications.

Support Vector Machine (SVM): Is a supervised machine learning algorithm that is used for classification and regression tasks. It works on finding the optimal decision boundary between different classes by maximizing the margin between data points closest to the boundary. It is used in the image processing field in tasks such as object recognition, image classification, face detection, and handwriting recognition.

Visual Geometry Group (VGG): Is a deep convolutional neural network architecture. VGG-16 is composed of 16 layers (13 convolutional layers and 3 fully connected layers). It uses a 3x3 convolutional kernel to extract features and utilizes max-pooling layers to reduce the spatial dimensions.

Chapter 12
Navigating Emerging AI Technologies and Future Trends in Cybersecurity and Forensics

Pranjal Khare
https://orcid.org/0000-0002-9937-9588
O.P. Jindal Global University, India

Vishambhar Raghuwanshi
https://orcid.org/0009-0009-1365-1850
Manipal University, India

ABSTRACT

Artificial Intelligence (AI) has transformed digital forensics and cybersecurity, enhancing efficiency and accuracy in combating cybercrime and analyzing evidence. This chapter will explore AI's capabilities in handling vast data, identifying patterns, reconstructing crime scenes, and detecting anomalies that have revolutionized investigations.. However, these technologies also pose challenges, including ethical concerns, algorithmic bias, privacy issues, and potential misuse. In cybersecurity, AI facilitates real-time threat detection, fraud prevention, and cross-border cooperation against cyberattacks. Despite these advancements, addressing challenges like international legal inconsistencies, transparency, and ethical implications is critical. As AI evolves, its integration into forensic science and cybersecurity holds immense potential to uphold justice and security, demanding balanced governance to ensure ethical and lawful applications.

DOI: 10.4018/979-8-3373-0857-9.ch012

INTRODUCTION

A specialized branch of forensic science known as digital forensics is a subspecialty that involves analysis of digital media in gathering, acquiring, examining, and through documented and authenticated methods, putting into evidence such digital information. Originally developed in the late 20th century to handle cybercrimes using very basic technology, digital forensics is proven to be a necessary course for managing the expansive field that contains technologies, methods and processes that are involved in crime investigation. In its simplest terms, digital forensics seeks to provide methods that make the evidence collected more residual and credible, and that's why it plays a central role in both justice and defense systems.

The roots of computer forensics date back to the early 1980s when personal computers started to become popular thereby accompanying new forms of computer related crime. During the early years of computing and computer crime investigation, the concepts of digital evidence and scientific investigation of the digital environment were in their infancy, and the two main branches of digital forensic tools, computer forensics and network forensics, consisted of little more than rudimentary techniques and methods for data recovery from hard drives and more basic structures like email systems and rudimentary networks. Nevertheless, the constant increase of digital storage space, mobility of technology devices, and the appearance of cloud-based technology have made digital forensics become broader and much more intricate. Today, it includes subdomains like computer forensics, network forensics, digital communications forensics, or mobile device forensics and multimedia forensics. This evolution is due to the emergence of novelties in the digital environment not only in technology but also in the ability of methodologies to incorporate developments of criminal practice (Gaona, 2024).

The distributed computing environment provided by the use of the internet and shift from separate systems that are difficult to connect make up a new age in digital forensic practice. Fraud including identity theft, hacking and espionage were on the rise and detectives had to design equipment for data mining. At the same time, the use of encryption technologies and anonymization tools around the world was a new problem, which forced forensic specialists to develop constantly. Digital forensics functions in an extremely diverse community, which requires investigators to detect secured communication, work with numerous terabytes of data, and consider the differences in the legal treatment of digital evidence among states.

Artificial Intelligence (AI) has become a revolution in cybersecurity and forensic science because it solves many problems related to the scale, complexity, and constant changes in the digital environment. For instance, in cybersecurity, machine learning and deep learning are employed to provide predictions of attacks in real time and thereby reduce risks significantly from the norms applied in legacy systems.

The applied use of Artificial intelligence in the field of forensic science implies automation, increased efficiency and standardization of operations, and helps the investigatory department find patterns that the human eye might not be able to spot.

Another benefit of the use of AI by firms is that AI computes very large data at a very high speed. As the type of traffic that networks generate today grows bigger it becomes almost impossible for human analysts to sit and detect the anomalies by themselves. The progressive use of AI in such systems offers enhanced algorithms for analyzing these forms of datasets in real time to identify threats. For example, IDS based on machine learning can analyze several previous and current packets and discover that the current one deviates from the norm – and mark the attempt at a network breach. Likewise, AI-based endpoint protection solutions can determine the future actions of malware, due to previous actions, thus are more efficient in providing protection against new threats (Begg, 2024).

In forensic science AI supports different kinds of text and media content as well as text and audio message and video, still images and logs of network activity. One of AI's subfields, Natural Language Processing (NLP), has been particularly useful in mining records of communication for signs suggestive of a criminal act. For instance, NLP can be employed in identifying key words or strings related to fraud or terrorism in emails and chat transcripts. Deep learning technologies are used to perform the examination of image material, for example, to recognize people's faces in surveillance videos or to identify peculiarities of digital images that may have the nature of manipulation. This is useful to find hidden or latent relationships or patterns based on a large dataset of social media data where relationships and interaction can be mapped including potential criminal groups (Yadav, 2024).

There are many reasons for using AI and not only in the analysis of forensics but also in the evidence collection and their proving as well. Application of the block chain, which can interoperate with AI systems, formalizes and proves the incorporation of digital evidence, to eliminate issues associated with data alteration. Also, through learning the missing data or contaminated one, the algorithms may even restore the files, making the evidence aspects of digital artifacts precious. For example, they can retrieve torn apart files from the edges of the failed hard drives or reconstruct missing frames in surveillance videos.

AI technology has great potential when incorporated in the areas of cybersecurity and forensic science. There are some limitations though. Adversarial AI, where an attacker employs AI techniques to bypass detection systems or to mask herself from forensic algorithms, is a real threat. Additionally, the susceptibility of the findings to external validation in legal processes increases the doubts about the application of AI for political purposes due to the concerns of interpretability and reproducibility of the analyses. However, again, looking at the advantages of applying artificial intelligence in these fields, far exceeds the weaknesses hence making it an essential tool when it comes to cybersecurity and forensic.

Since the current world is so dependent on technology, and cyber criminals are increasingly becoming more and more innovative, the examination of Artificial Intelligence based security and forensic solutions has become critical. The digitization of the world economy compounded by developing Internet of Things (IoT), 5G networks and cloud services has provided a favorable ecological niche for cybercriminals. Malware, specifically ransomware, breaches, and cyber spying have become more rampant and complex threatening the existence of individuals, companies, and government bodies. Under such a context, knowing the function of AI in embracing these risks is not just a theoretical endeavor but a necessity in society (Saini, 2023).

Machine learning and artificial intelligence can be used to implement security on computers and other critical structures rather than wait for attacks to happen when they are already successful. The conventional security measures that conceptually enchant an organization's computer system, for instance firewalls and antivirus software, are of little utility against modern threat actors. Due to the use of machine learning algorithms AI systems can even learn more about threats and adapt to them, thus providing great opportunities for the organizations to counteract attackers. For instance, threat intelligence solutions collect and process data of different types to identify potential threats, and to act accordingly. This capability is especially relevant in today's terms for defending critical industries including healthcare, finance, and security of nations (Roush, 2024).

AI can also be considered essential for forensic technologies mainly because of the possibilities to boost the efficacy of criminal investigations. A digital crime has some form of residue that is usually hard to decipher by conventional methods of investigation. AI tools are of great help in this regard as they are able to assist with the time-consuming repetitive jobs, for instance going through logs or defining what kind of data within heaps of data is relevant. Besides, it speeds up the probes, which would otherwise be time-consuming, and minimizes the chances of the interference of human error. In addition, AI can identify complex relationships and trends that are easily overlooked by detectives and other criminal analysts hence making differentials in understanding the behavior and likelihood of criminals.

The third and equally important underlying question to consider when it comes to artificial intelligence-based forensic technologies is how the AI technologies address legal and ethical concerns of digital forensic evidence. That is because as the amount of digital evidence increases, it becomes very difficult to handle and maintain its genuineness and authenticity when it is presented in court. Overall, technologies that are able to check and identify digital artifacts meet another important function, that is the documentation of the chain of custody. Of course, there are ethical implications of using AI; for example, algorithmic decision making might be prejudiced in some way, and the increase in surveillance. These problems are complex and require a better appreciation of the opportunity and risk to positively deploy AI technology.

Furthermore, the integration of AI in the field of forensic practices has consequences for cooperation on the international level regarding combating transnational incidents of cybercrime. Many cybercrime incidents are international in nature and hence the crime fighting effort is best done internationally across borders. AI-related technologies support this integration of processes by establishing best practice norms for these investigations while also allowing for instantaneous data exchange. For example, it can help to decode encrypted messages or to identify the global connections between cybercriminals, which should lead to a more joined-up approach to combat existing threats (Pattnaik, 2024).

All in all, the synergy of AI, cybersecurity, and forensic science is at the heart of radical notations in societies' combating of digital threats and criminal investigations. With the ever-increasing advances in the functional web and digital environment, the dependence on AI technologies is only going to strengthen in future, therefore, there remains a great necessity to undertake continued research and development in the given domain. Thus, only when the strengths, weaknesses and the ethical issues pertaining to AI are known, stakeholders can use it to transform virtual environments into safer sources. The academic study of these technologies, therefore, lays a useful groundwork for growth, for policymaking, as well as for the construction of a robust new information age.

Understanding Emerging AI Technologies

Machine learning, especially Artificial intelligence has turned out to be an essential aspect of cybersecurity and digital forensics due to its distinctive advantage in data analysis and pattern recognition as well as in threat identification. As we can see these days, cyber operations are highly technological and the amount of data available and under attack has grown to levels that require more than human intelligence. AI in its machine learning and deep learning frameworks offers real time and adaptive solutions for writing optimized programs to scan for susceptibility, forecast threats, and avoid risks.

Intending threat detection, AI works with the help of structuralized and unstructured patterns, and with the help of them, systems are able to detect unusual activities, which indicate threats. Signatures by nature of the fundamental approach face a severe problem of ineffectiveness since they operate based on sets of rules that are organized in advance. Instead, AI uses theoretical and actual data to develop improved algorithms allowing the discovery of new forms of attack. To illustrate, in the case of machine learning models, it is possible to implement net flow analysis mechanisms to detect any anomalies that may emanate from normal behavior of a network, and alert relevant authorities of higher-level threats before they occur. Machine learning threat detection systems also use big data analysis to gauge the prospects of future attack, which provides organizations with an option to strengthen their security in advance (Schneider & Breitinger, 2023).

Pattern recognition is yet another fundamental component of the AI procedure that is most valuable for the recognition of trends or inconsistencies in large data sets. Some of the most advanced algorithms are deep learning models that attempt to model the brain's neural network and are phenomenal in identifying precise features across disparate forms of data, whether texts, images, or numbers. This capability is highly recommended in forensic investigations since there could be several indicators hidden by large amounts of digital evidence. Meanwhile, AI can review other transactions to grasp what sequences are abnormal with the objective of identifying and preventing fraud (Jurva, 2024). With these analyses automated, not only does AI assist in expediting the investigating process effectively, but also, the resulting data is more accurate, significantly reducing the chance of false positives or negatives.

Another transformation feature is the capacity of AI to process large amounts of data in real time, especially in the big data setting. Computer Forensics and Cybersecurity usually concern examination of considerable terabytes of information containing system logs, communication records, or other types of digital evidence. Sophisticated algorithms used by AI-based tools filter through this data and pull-out things which are useful for investigation and which information should be given priority. Further, the NLP subbranch of AI helps to deal with textual information, for instance, emails, chat history, social networks' interactions. NLP enables the extract of the hidden intention and relation by searching the embedded key-terms, positive/negative bias or any linguistic anomaly (Suryal et al., 2024).

Possibly the most effective use of AI in cybersecurity and forensics can be applied to the study of patterns of communication used in the commission of frauds and cybercrimes. Today's communications protocols including; email, chatting, and social media networks are often the tools of choice for criminals involved in fraud and cybercrimes such as phishing and identity theft. The high number and variety of these communications pose a complex problem that is hard to solve by the customary investigative methods. AI, however, eradicates these problems since it autonomously identifies dangerous activities and reveals kinship.

Apart from this, AI applied systems exploit NLP and machine learning algorithms to evaluate communication content and context. For instance, phishing emails will always display other linguistic behaviors like grammatical mistakes, sense of urgency and links that seem again abnormal. The characteristics of phishing attempts can be learned by various AI algorithms that would allow providing their automated detection and categorization. In a similar way, AI can examine the timelines of an interaction and the responses given, to determine when and if the subject is being dishonest in cases such as computer fraud crimes.

Apart from single messages, AI outperforms in recognizing the topological correspondence between relations and detecting a large number of crimes. Machine learning is applied in graph analytics that helps to build and analyze the relationship map of the communication pattern applied in constructing the communication graph to map the number of important nodes and how they are interconnected. Organized cybercrimes, for example, fraud rings, ransomware operations, are challenging to counter with separate teams; more people work in coordination in such crime groups. When these networks are depicted, key players, direction of the information, and halting of criminal activities can be easily identified.

It also helps to have AI filtering through multilingual, cross-platform conversations in addition to the sources of information it analyzes. Hackers, especially criminals, are known to use different methods, languages or codes or work on different platforms. Translating and sentiment analysis that can be added to NLP models allow deciphering these communications and eliminate language barriers in comprehensively describing criminal scenarios. Further, the combination of AI in analyzing social media entails the identification of fake news dissemination, cyber bullying or planning of criminal activities hence can prompt an early intervention.

AI's contributions to solving crimes are not limited to being used in processing large volumes of data but involve creative uses of AI in matters like creation of crime scenes and certification of digital evidence. However, the emergence of AI has brought new problems such as the widespread use of fake data, which violates the work of forensic activities. Of all the uses, those for recreating crime scenes are one of the most fascinating areas where AI shows a great deal of promise. The awareness of London attacks and the subsequent investigations have shown that modern technologies such as VR and AR complemented by AI algorithms let investigators recreate events using digital evidence only. For example, video or still images, GPS, or IOT records taken at or near the scene of the crime or can be incorporated in a virtual environment allowing an accurate depiction of the crime scene. This approach is also helpful in setting up scenarios for the event sequences and when explaining to juries and other related parties during trials. AI's capability of handling spatial data with such precision means that it is easier for these reconstructions to be both accurate and credible and thus make for credible evidence (Singh, 2023).

Another area where AI equips the processes is in the identification and validation of the authenticity of digital evidence, potential issues regarding tampering or forging of which are relevant to any process. This technique is used in conjunction with blockchain/Artificial Intelligence technology, where creating involute blocks for protected digital artifacts, consequently guaranteeing their credibility during the investigation process. Furthermore, AI also is capable of identifying obvious tampering indications in compressed formats such as, articles or documents in photo, or jpegs, noisy signals, beep sounds in recordings, discrepancies in metadata or alignment. These capabilities are particularly valuable where the evidential provenance is an issue, as they utilize standard protocols which can be applied to pseudo-validation.

Nevertheless, there exists a new problem regarding forensic science, called deepfake technologies. Deepfakes are considered as an example when AI reduces the trustworthiness of digital forensics – the more realistic fake images, videos, or audio are generated. For instance, an actual crime suspect can be portrayed in what looks like a confession through a deepfake video or clean evidence can be discredited with a primary video showing fake evidence through the Deepfake video. In normally not possible for the human eye to distinguishing one between the deepfake and a real video most of the times, this is the reason why deepfake detection machinery calls for sophisticated AI solutions that can recognize small discrepancies that cannot be imitated, for instance, neurological twitches, inconsistent light or tone variations in the sound. Although current ongoing research also has shown the possibility of implementation, the highly dynamic pace of development of deepfake technology requires constant creation of breakthroughs.

Another problem connected with the application of AI in forensics is adversarial AI and when the attackers use the AI system's weaknesses to avoid being caught or change the result. For instance, adversarial attacks take a form where slight noise is added to input data to confuse the AI into either completely misidentifying it or simply not noticing important evidence. Mitigating these threats, therefore, calls for strongly encrypted models of AI and multi-disciplinary cooperative endeavors to set best practices in AI security.

AI has largely revolutionized how threats are handled in cybersecurity and how forensic scientists approach investigations and analyze evidence. Using such capabilities as threat identification, pattern matching, and communication analysis, AI gives unbelievable opportunities for fighting cybercriminals and detecting fraud. At the same time, novel uses such as crime scene enhancements, and evidence verification increase the effectiveness of criminal investigations. Nevertheless, the threats proposed by newest phenomena such as deepfakes and adversarial AI prove existing necessity in further research, ethical regulation, and cooperation. Having quantified the impact of AI on the future of digital forensics, its future status both as an enabler and a disruptor should be monitored, and the adoption process should be even more careful.

Legal Frameworks Governing AI Applications in Cybersecurity and Forensics

Legal frameworks governing the application of AI in cybersecurity and forensics are complex and orchestrated by a combination of laws due to the various ways that nations approach the fast-growing innovative technology. Globally, the European Union has been looking forward to the passage of its Artificial Intelligence Act, an advanced legal instrument intended to provide a general framework for the proper ethical and safe use of AI. This regulation categorizes AI systems based on risk including unacceptable risk, high risk, limited risk, and minimal risk. And it also places significant restrictions on high-risk systems such as systems used in control or law enforcement. In this respect, EU strategies put on transparency, accountability and human supervision, to reduce the risks while encouraging innovations.

Currently, there is no comprehensive AI legislation in the United States and various AI rules and regulations are contained in different pieces of legislation governing activities in different sectors of the economy. Regarding ethical practices of AI in cybersecurity the FTC holds the role of an ethicist while its primary objectives are consumer protection and privacy. For instance, some countries like California have put in place thick laws including the CCPA to protect the data that AI systems process. However, one disadvantage of such an oriented system is the absence of the federal law that has led to the appearance of the discussion regarding the thin regulation for emerging AI issues.

On the other hand, China has fully endorsed an aggressive regulatory strategy that uses AI in achieving state objectives such as security and order. The Cybersecurity Law of China and related regulations on AI ethics state control and maintain that AI systems must be in the state's interest. Despite the solidity and versatility of offered solutions, this approach questions privacy and surveillance in the sphere of forensic and cybersecurity.

On the contrary, during the current year, and its early stages, India has been found quite inexperienced in terms of AI regulation. The proposed Digital Personal Data Protection Act, 2023, and on-going debate on the robust, an emergent AI policy are some steps that are not aggressive but constructive. The goal is to retain an association on innovation while formulating the right strategies regarding data and ethical sensitivity including cybersecurity and digital forensics.

The United Nations and the Organization for Economic Co-operation and Development have, for instance, supported the idea of similar AI regulation. For example, the OECD has developed the OECD princess on AI which is not even legally binding with focus on human rights, transparency and accountability. They guide the nature and actions of national policies up to international cooperation in managing AI.

Regarding the international variation of the legal frameworks presented, we find the conflict between innovation and regulation raging, jurisdictions seeking to advance technologies and provide adequate social protection simultaneously. With the growing integration of AI in ever more domains of cybersecurity and forensics, an internationally coherent framework, based on agreed-upon ethical principles, will prove crucial in facing the increasingly global character of threats and of investigations in cyberspace.

Challenges and Limitations of AI in Cybersecurity and Forensics

Incorporation of artificial intelligence (AI) has fast advanced the research and application in the practices of cybersecurity and forensic work. But it has also brought up novel problems of privacy, privacy invasion, and the possibilities for abuse of these technologies. To brief, these challenges provoke ethical, legal and practical issues that should be met to have a fair advanced intelligent system.

The use of surveillance systems, especially those driven by Artificial intelligence (AI) is on the rise due to the increasing adoption by governments and organizations for surveillance, and as a way of preventing crime. Biometrics, including face and behavior recognition, combined with the analysis of network traffic, increases its capacity to track the movements of targeted persons in real time. These capabilities increase the security of the public as well as investigation effectiveness but come with unique dangers to privacy (Noonan, 2024). The application of AI for monitoring citizens en masse without any respect to their right to privacy as has been practiced in some jurisdictions, there is discussion on whether citizens' liberties have been suppressed with a possibility of formation of surveillance society.

Other important considerations include data protection in the context of AI application in forensics. A lot of the time investigations involve personal data that is deemed to be sensitive; fingerprints, bank records or call logs. This information is processed by the AI systems to compile information and there are implications towards security of data as well as the misuse of the same. As an example, cyberattacks on the inadequately protected forensic databases may endanger not only the result of investigations and cases under investigation but also the private lives of persons involved in criminal proceedings. Furthermore, many organizations have no well-defined rules on data anonymization/retention hence the risk of misuse increases since the data collected may be used or sold without the knowledge of the data providers.

The susceptibility of AI in cyberspace and forensic applications cover both the intentional and accidental applications. On one side, the AI systems can be easily exploited by cybercriminals to launch complex cyber-attacks, avoid being detected or tampering with the digital artifacts. For instance, adversarial AI approaches involve the development of inputs that manipulate AI signal processing, for example, by placing changes beyond human perception such as the slight distortion of the appearance of an image or modifying an audio track in a way that it is discernible by AI software but not by humans. However, reckless utilization can stem from greatly developed or insufficiently tested creditable AI applications which causes wrong estimations of the threats or flaws in comprehending evidence. This is made worse by the fact that many AI algorithms are not very transparent; it is hard to tell where one went wrong or there was even bias (Li, 2024).

AI systems applied in a forensic environment are based on the capability of the data set used in calibrated AI algorithms with high reliability and accuracy. The results derived from the biased or unrepresentative dataset can largely reduce the performance of AI and produce wrong outcomes which have massive legal and ethical implications.

It has become common practice to find prejudice in AI training data sets originating from previous imbalances in society, bigotry or inadequate tools and techniques of data collection. For example, facial recognition algorithms delivered worse accuracy to people of color because of insignificant samples of their races in training data sets. It can lead to either false positives or false negatives, and certain populations are more likely to be put into either category than others. In the use of these technologies in forensic investigations these mistakes can result in charges being made, brought or dismissed, or evidence rejected, consequently, the public trust in the justice system is undermined.

The legal concern of having unbiased AI systems in forensic is complex in the following ways. First, they contradict the principle of equal treatment and AI decision-makers might discriminate against some people based on AI's methodological errors. Second, they create concern as to the status of the AI-derived evidence as proof or evidence in the court. Justice around the globe is struggling to address goals of admissibility and neutrality of AI evidence, especially when biases are found in the algorithms. Sometimes, specific AI-based evidence was rejected under the principle that it is not scientifically admissible. Third, biased AI systems put an organization or a government at legal risk for any harm that results from the use of AI. Legal cases of discrimination/negligence or violation of the Data protection laws show the importance of social scrutiny, responsible stewardship in the operating deployment of AI in societies.

Reducing biases in forensic AI systems requires a more elaborate strategy. This includes end-to-end sample differentiation, effective testing procedures as well as more code transparency in procedures. Multidisciplinary work is necessary to promote fairness and accuracy of AI systems as well as to make them adhere to justice.

Moreover, regulations address the issue with AI bias and put specific requirements into addressing the use of AI in legal contexts.

AI is growing fast and therefore the legal provisions governing its use in forensics are lagging because barriers to their development and enforcement have not been closed. These gaps are due to the coalition's inability to develop unified global standards, problems of defining many terms in legal practices, and delays in response to new issues. To this end, one of the problems that may be observed when managing AI regulation in forensics is influenced by the lack of international conventions. AI technologies are used in different jurisdictions that possess different legal frameworks, cultural practices and technological sophistication. This situation causes inconsistencies in how AI is managed or regulated, especially in international investigations. For instance, some nations have set down restrictive data regulatory policies that limit the application of AI in surveillance or forensic systems while some nations do not have articulated comprehensive legislation, thereby allowing uncontrolled app of AI. The foregoing brings about a fragmentation that hampers the collaborative effort towards fighting cybercrimes and other cross-border offenses because there are legal and procedural hurdles in sharing of evidential materials generated by the AI technology.

Another major void is the lack of sufficient legal definitions and legal models of regulation of AI solutions with the help of artificial intelligence. This is because legal tools based on the accountability of actions, based on known motives, do not fit into the concept of creating an autonomous or even semi-autonomous AI system. For example, the question of who is most directly responsible for wrongful prediction or other forms of bias when using forensic AI systems is still very much open and can that place the liability on the software developers and those who use this software or is it with the algorithms themselves. Just like with regular AI algorithms, there is no clear understanding of such issues as algorithm transparency, reproducibility, and explainability that makes it difficult to decide whether the AI-generated evidence can be admitted in court.

New phenomena, deepfakes, adversarial AI, and the legal regulation of applying algorithms to make decisions also reveal that the modern legal framework is insufficient here. Recently introduced deepfake technologies, which involve creation of pseudo real images or videos and even pseudo real audio, are quite problematic when it comes to forensic and judicial applications. The differing handling of digital evidence thus challenges the reliability of AI-derived insights and calls for changes to legal rules on evidence admissibility. Moreover, concerns have been raised on issues of discrimination, misuse and most importantly the ethical use of AI in surveillance and forensics. Ten of these recommendations entail: development of the legal frameworks to cover for these concerns with appropriate ethical standards (Malik, 2024).

The integration of AI with cybersecurity and forensics has raised some ethical concerns thus requiring the establishment of a good governance structure on the use of intelligence. Major issues that one can identify include Inaccurate or biased algorithms that perpetrate bias and discriminations, privacy issues, and abuse of the artificial intelligence technologies. For example, machine learning and big data in cybersecurity are very useful, can work with imbalanced or skewed datasets and output profiling and surveillance where there is none. Likewise, the use of AI in forensic context presupposes cooperation with large amounts of personal data that undoubtedly raises numerous privacies issues and jeopardizes the data protection from unauthorized access most of the time. Such challenges require compliance with the numerous and clear ethical standards that exist like the GDPR and ethical guidelines by bodies such as the IEEE. These frameworks capture concepts like; equity, responsibility, confidentiality, and the AI systems must work without touching on basic human rights. Moreover, as the role of AI deepens in these areas, giving more importance to ethical, technological, and legal symbiosis, with ethicists, technologists, and legal scholars is vital for addressing these moral questions raised by these domains. Introducing ethical values as integrating factors in the AI's development and deployment process, the stakeholders can find a suspect balance between the freedom to innovate and the freedom of the individuals.

Closing these gaps calls for engagement from the governments, the international organizations and civil society actors. First, unsettlement of the guidelines for the creating, launching, and regulating of forensic AI systems on the international level is a considerable issue. These standards should include privacy and data handling and transparency of artificial intelligence techniques as well as use of the evidence produced by the artificial intelligence in the courtroom. Second, there is the need to bring legal changes in relation to corresponding shifts in the capabilities and problems of AI systems. It also involves coming up with brand new legal constructs like algorithmic liability and transparency, and procedures for assessing AI affairs on a regular basis. Third, another crucial factor that should prevail is interdisciplinary contact in order to integrate technological, ethical and societal perspectives into regulation.

With AI now being integrated into cybersecurity and forensic sciences it has revolutionized the approach to digital investigations by providing capability to augmented threat detection, data analysis and creation of evidence. These have brought in certain new problems which are based on surveillance problems, data security problems and misuse of AI technologies. This misrepresentation of training data sets brings inaccuracies in forensic results, and possible legal consequences; therefore, there is a need for bias-free and reliable AI systems. Furthermore, the existing and emerging issue with resource allocation and licensing, gaps in legal norms in AI usage in forensic examinations prove that there is an urgent need for drafting harmonized standards for AI and updated definitions of AI in the legal system as well as mechanisms for solving emerging issues. Because of these developments, the application of AI in forensics will depend on the actions and inputs of technologists, legal systems, and policymakers in effecting AI in ways that respect justice, accountability, and, more importantly, human rights.

Future Trends in Cybersecurity and Forensics

Evidently, innovations that include drones and other auto pilot instruments with features of artificial intelligence have greatly improved the collection and analysis of evidence in today's forensic cases. These technologies provide far more than what is achievable with traditional approaches and help law enforcement plus forensic professionals do their jobs more effectively, accurately and safely within many real-life situations. Still, they are important members of forensic science to which they also bring some ethical, legal and technical issues that need to be thought thoroughly.

Today, drones or UAVs are among the essential means of acquiring evidence in crime scenes or disaster areas and other areas not easily accessible. The use of intelligent drones can avoid obstacles, capture images and even create complex 3D maps of crime scenes and share the area view in general with investigators, thus giving them an accurate picture. For instance, drones are more and more used in crime scenes to search for the victims, estimate the degree of building destruction and assess the possible threats to the environment when people are not involved. In the same way, in mass shootings or cases of arson, drones with thermal imaging cameras and AI object detection systems can easily identify additional objects such as weapons, fuel sources or bodies, which may otherwise go unnoticed (Agrawal, 2024).

Robotic systems, as independent tools, have also broadened the spectrum of forensic inquiries. Artificial intelligence integrated into robots is used to inspect dangerous objects like chemical or biological substances at a crime scene or a war theatre. These systems can recognize chemical compounds, sample them, and sometimes even analyze them on-site, which lessens the dangers of having to intervene manually. Also, AI based robotic systems are being designed for forensic pathology, where robotics aid in the postmortem examination with extraordinary precision and dexterity. For instance, robotic arms with integrated software processes can capture intricate studies on wounds and cause of death explorations and in a minimally invasive approach (Yanthan, 2024).

Nevertheless, the application of drones and other autonomous instruments in the collection of physical evidence presents a number of ethical and legal issues. The use of drones for surveillance and gathering evidence, especially in city states, has raised concerns which pivot on issues of privacy and misuse. In addition, concerns over the admissibility of evidence in cases where an autonomous system has been utilized because the nature of the algorithm specifically or the process by which it was developed generally is not clear or transparent, nor can it be regarded as free from bias. Meeting these challenges needs setting of clear standard rules, which govern the use of these technologies since they may lead to complimenting ethical and or legal norms.

Due to the advancement of the IT infrastructure across the world, the population of cross-border cyber-crimes is also growing in equal measures which call for international cooperation to address. Machine learning technologies are the key components of the international measures of countering, preventing, and investigating cybersecurity threats, along with promoting cooperation between law enforcement agencies, governments and non-governmental organizations. Such collaborations do not only exploit the strengths of Artificial Intelligence but also encompass other issues such as the territorial issue, data exchange, and law standardization.

Probably the most effective example of using AI in international cooperation is the identification of threats in cyberspace. Artificial Intelligence and machine learning are capable of processing big data from other regions and looking for patterns that are considered to be associated with cyber threats like phishing scams or ransomware, or APTs. Such information is spread globally among partners to prevent consequences of cybercrimes before the situation aggravates. For example, Europol is home to the European Cybercrime Centre (EC3), an agency that works together with global Law Enforcement Agency players and private sector partners in the development of artificial intelligence-based threat intelligence applications, all aimed at improving the overall cybersecurity posture of society (Khaitan, 2023).

AI equally is indispensable when it comes to evidence collection and evaluation during cross-border investigations of cybercrimes. Applying AI to cybercrime investigation can map the history of the attack, decipher encrypted messages, and replicate actions throughout the world. It is these capabilities that are especially important in situations related to the functioning of the dark web, where anonymity and encryption are major problems for conventional investigation. In that context, translation based on artificial intelligence helps to ensure translation of correspondence and data and simplify interaction between multicultural teams.

However, cross-border collaboratives that may apply the use of AI are faced with some of the following challenges. Thus, it inhibits the sharing of information because the legal standards, both in data protection as well as in AI implementation are not consistent around the globe putting the participating entities in a position where they must battle with different laws. Also, sovereignty of data and misuse of shared intelligence becomes a question that forms the base of mistrust and noncooperation. To resolve such problems international treaties and directives for example the Budapest Convention on Cybercrime need to be signed to set base for international cooperation which will not infringe on individual privacy, security and legal systems of the collaborating countries.

Quantum AI or Quantum computing AI is the biggest revolutionary change in the cybersecurity and the forensic investigation field. Quantum AI is not completely developed now but it has the capabilities to transform encryption methods, big data analytics and threat identification in cyberspace. But it also brings in great risk, especially in the realm of cryptography and computer science investigations. Encryption, one of the fundamental pillars of cybersecurity, is based upon utilization of numerous algorithms to assert confidentiality. Today's encrypting schemes like the RSA and AES are defined to be resistant to attacks by classical computing systems. However, the rise of quantum computing means that those methods are rather dangerous as quantum algorithms, like Shor's Means for example, can defeat many of the present-day encryption systems even more efficiently compared to classical computers. Incorporating this display, already with the possibility to process and analyze many data simultaneously, Quantum AI could improve this ability, making most of the existing encryption algorithms pointless.

In a forensic context, quantum AI creates suggestions for data analysis and evidence processing which are impossible to crack from a traditional perspective. Thus, optimization problems are well solved by quantum computers, and the amounts of data of genetic code matches, or other evidence such as multiple records of computers' activity, can be analyzed significantly faster when using quantum methods. For instance, quantum AI might be applied for the identification of DNA samples or finding correlations in financing transactions that sign certain fraudulent activities. Moreover, the unstructured data input, and processing capabilities of quantum AI such as in audio recordings or video materials, social media, etc., may revolutionize the recreation of the events or the verification of the electronic evidence (Alghamdi, 2021).

Because of quantum AI for encryption as well as for forensic purposes, it also contains some negative aspects. One of the chief threats presented by quantum computers relates to their capacity to render encryption systems ineffective; this threatens information security especially because data of a sensitive nature can be stored in digital forensic databases. Besides, the daily use of quantum-safe cryptosystems is a necessity, which however is not an easy or implementable task. The use of quantum AI combined with the traditional ones is also ethical and legal issues like the permissibility of quantum derived evidence in the court trial and the chances of the malicious actors producing quantum technologies.

For these challenges to be overcome, academies, governments and private organizations should fund the development of quantum-safe encryption algorithms and draft legislation on the usage of Quantum AI in forensics. Another important factor is multiregional cooperation; it is necessary because the development of quantum technologies occurs on an international level. The use of drones in crime scenes, cognitive autonomous tools, and quantum artificial intelligence in cyber security and forensic science is the new future of evidence gathering, analysis and cross border cooperation. These technologies bring with them incredible possibilities but incomprehensible difficulties that have to be solved through legal, ethical and technical means. Thus, as forensic science progresses in the future, it depends on the stakeholders in ensuring that the AI tools are used to support justice, security and respect for human rights (Zaid & Garai, 2024).

Case Studies and Real-world Applications

Cybersecurity has become the new buzzword in the world, and with the help of Artificial Intelligence (AI), the world of cybersecurity has evolved drastically. Real time analysis, predictive model and adaptive learning has made AI a powerful tool that strengthens the organizations' cyber security against complex cyber threats. Similarly, its use in forensic cases has also been equally helpful in the revelation of absolute key evidence in changing the techniques of investigations. Although AI has been implemented in cybersecurity and forensics, its implementation has not been without challenges, as we observed in cases where it was failed or hacked.

AI has proved itself invaluable in preventing major cyberattacks and is now rightfully considered an essential part of contemporary cybersecurity measures. Among the most successful applications of AI is its application in combating ransomware attacks, which are rapidly becoming a global problem for businesses and governments. Last year, AI solutions such as Darktrace used machine learning to spot suspicious patterns in network traffic which is indicative of early ransomware operations (Sharma et al., 2019). The system was thus able to identify small anomalies of user behavior or facility in a network, allowing organizations to control the threat before encryption processes started; thus, saving millions of dollars.

Another huge success area that has exploited the use of AI is the financial industry, especially in its fight against fraud. Some major financial institutions use IBM's Truster and SAS Fraud Management to analyze transactional data in real-time while locating any fraudulent transactions with ease and accuracy. For example, AI techniques can identify provocative characteristics of extension, for which transactions might be potentially fraudulent and which might not attract the attention of human enthusiasts. It has helped to reduce the cases of fraud which has as your result shown a direct impact to the customer loyalty (Kim et al. 2023).

AI has also played a significant factor in threat intelligence and prediction, its capabilities being key in the analysis of great threats in the community. Microsoft Azure Sentinel is an example of AI used when considering huge amounts of data from various sources, as well as the identification of new threats and recommendations for their consideration in cybersecurity departments. An example is when Azure Sentinel identified a synchronized phishing attack on a healthcare organization during the COVID-19 crisis (Dunsin et al., 2023). Through the metadata analysis of emails and the association of this data with recognized threat types, it was possible to provide timely countermeasures in order to protect potential individual patient data.

AI has also caused a revolution in forensic science, making the advancements that were earlier unthinkable if traditional techniques were to be used. In recent years, the case of the Golden State Killer in the United States turned out to be an eye opener for the world to use Artificial Intelligence in the forensic process. Law enforcement officers were able to use specially designed AI methods of genetic genealogy to compare the collected biological materials at the scene of the crime with the public database of genealogy. In the case of pinpointing of familial relations, and, therefore, construction of a suspect family tree AI was successful in helping the police to identify the perpetrator of a crime that had remained unsolved due to traditional investigation methods for more than three decades (Tariq et al., 2023).

The use of AI in digital forensics has been most significant where there is huge data collection. For instance, in a big insider trading scandal AI algorithms were employed to sort through terabytes of emails and chat messages to find messages implicating the criminals. The system using NLP procedures could mark the conversations that include some prohibited keywords and examples of unlawful actions for further analysis, significantly minimizing the time needed for the control of the messages.

Also, cases of using an AI-powered facial recognition system when it is necessary to indicate villains during an investigation. Chinese authorities were able to employ an AI surveillance application to track down a fleeing suspect watching a concert with 60 thousand people in 2019 (Saini et al., 2024). The general efficiency shown by this technology meant that the matching algorithms that read and map faces in real time were ideal for public security and police work.

Nonetheless, there are negative aspects in the use of AI, and these have brought out the end weaknesses as well as the misuse of the matters. There is, for instance, the dangerous vulnerability of AI systems to adversarial perturbation, whereby the inputs are designed to deceive AI in some way. For instance, the authors have shown that small changes to an image that cannot be noticed by a human eye lead AI facial recognition system to incorrect people identification (Parkinson & Khan, 2024). When AI programs or models have such weaknesses, the dependability of such systems in matters of high-risk nature like in crime investigations and security at borders, is questionable.

One common failure was the controversial implementation of artificial intelligence in policing services, particularly in predictive policing services. Research about the algorithm utilized in United States law enforcement agencies conducted in 2020 established that the tech was racially biased resulting in targeted minorities. These biases were said to have originated from datasets of historical crime statistics, which captured systematic unfairness in the application of the police force. The consequent errors contributed not only to the loss of the public's confidence but also to the subject of ethical questions about the enforcement of fair AI policing tools.

AI's adversaries have also had their fair share as far as challenges are concerned as expected. Traditional hackers have incorporated artificial intelligence into their operations from increasing the automation of phishing emails to even developing new forms of malware. For instance, in 2019, security specialists found out that deepfake AI was used to forge the CEO's voice to scam $243,000. This incident supported the thesis that AI can be used for both sides of conflict, defense and attack.

In another incident, in September 2017, Equifax lost personal details of over 147 million customers due to data breach, an incident that has underlined the importance of artificial intelligence breach detection systems. In the aftermath of this event, Equifax began to rely on machine learning algorithms that would handle real-time monitoring of irregularities. These algorithms utilized large datasets to determine and prevent other possible risks and showed how AI can improve vulnerability management and breaches.

Similarly, The WannaCry attack that happened in the year 2017 targeted more than 200000 systems across 150 different countries. Consequently, cybersecurity companies such as Symantec or Kaspersky Lab adapted AI-based tools to define the ransomware activity. These AI models could replicate the malware's algorithm and provide countermeasures faster and hence one could state that such usage results in minimizing the respective organizations' losses from downtime and data breach. AI has enhanced facial identification methods in forensic investigations. In the case of Golden State Killer other law enforcement agencies employed AI powered facial reconstruction software algorithm to map DNA phenotyping to old sketches of suspects. It is this technology that helped to fast forward the probe and culminated in an arrest several years after the crime.

In addition, the use of computer algorithms has from time to time produced ambiguous findings when applied on forensic investigations. In one instance an AI algorithm which was designed to forecast recidivism rates in the US criminal justice system has been deemed to be less precise compared to a mere guess in some instances. Some of the concerns raised on the reliability of the system and the ethical issues of using it to deliver justice in courts, can be put to the system's lack of explainability (Thurzo et al., 2021).

Balancing with the benefits to adopting the use of AI in cybersecurity and forensics, there is a need to ensure that safeguard measures are put in place to address the following vices; There is the need to ensure that development and deployment of AI incorporates the following considerations; The blind and bias issues can be easily detected and mitigated through good test and validation methods applicable to AI programs. Thirdly, all stakeholders, government, academia, and private companies need to work together on setting up international norms and standards for AI implementation.

Furthermore, the reinforcement of adversarial resilience can improve the security of AI systems, adversarial training and robust algorithm designs, for instance. Further investment in XAI can also enhance AI decision-making amongst forensic and cybersecurity domains to bolster the accountability inherent in the technology. AI adoption has widely seeped into the field of cybersecurity and forensic science and has produced incredible results, as witnessed from stamping out cyberattacks or solving previously unsolvable criminal cases and improving investigative actions. It has certain drawbacks and weaknesses which should be taken into consideration when considering its application and utilization in considerable detail. The book shows how the concerns of bias, adversarial attacks, and ethical issues can be resolved to make the best out of artificial intelligence adoption for its rights use. The subject areas of which these lessons were derived shall continue to define the future of AI driven innovations in cybersecurity as well as in forensic services.

CONCLUSION AND WAY FORWARD

Cybersecurity and forensic science have become major areas where artificial Intelligence (AI) has been adopted as a solution to the problems of an advanced society. For threat identification, crime solving as well as digital investigation and protection, not only has capability of advanced analytics, pattern recognition and predictive modelling transformed the process but also the underlying paradigms. This relevance is because artificial intelligence can cope with big data, provide near real-time response to new threats, and support sophisticated decision-making by automating and/or making processes intelligent. Nonetheless, such change should be made with compliance with the principles of the right ethical standards and proper framework to see to it that the resultant positive impact is received by all.

The use of artificial intelligence in cybersecurity has become highly vital to tackle all the challenges of modern day's cyber threats. Hackers, using complex strategies and tools, have very dangerous impacts on people, businesses, and states. Traditional security solutions have failed in the provision of protection against the relatively new cybersecurity threats and risks, and solutions that rely on Artificial Intelligence provide an extended level of first-line defense. It means that through the help of machine learning algorithms AI can analyze the anomalous pattern of the traffic on the network and predict the type of threat that is suitable for the attack and prevent them before occurring. These capabilities have not only improved the organization's ability to perform its cybersecurity functions effectively but has also diminished the cost and brand image loss ensuing from cyber threats (Kosta et al., 2024).

Specifically, in forensic science, AI has changed investigative paradigms as a means of processing large data sets and delivering new means of searching for and interpreting evidence. AI solutions cover a wide field of needs and requirements starting from face recognition and voice identification, up to genome identification and risk analysis. These tools have been found very useful in solving otherwise unsolvable cases as this illustrated a big impact of AI in delivery of justice.

Thus, the importance of AI in designing safer ecosystems will increase as the existing ecosystem changes in the future. Novel technologies ranging from quantum computing and distributed ledgers to fifth generation wireless communication have redefined and recalibrated the parameters for cybersecurity and forensic science as well as the potential role for artificial intelligence in these fields. In this context, AI is on the cusp of playing a dual role of protecting organizations from potential cyber threats while at the same time helping organizations wield AI to discover latent threats and foster creativity.

In cybersecurity, the future of AI is in making learning systems that can learn on the fly or in real-time and improve themselves. These systems will take advantage of continual learning algorithms in order to find new threat modes, including those not seen before. For example, AI could be applied to manage the new attack surface that rises from the increasingly popular Internet of Things (IoT) devices. When combining AI with the blockchain, cybersecurity frameworks can guarantee the secure pass and store data with little risk as those of traditional breaches.

Consequently, applications of AI are also likely to have great impact on forensic science and analysis for refining and improving measure and accuracy involved in the identification of evidential findings. Tools like drones, automatic analysis of the crime scene and computerized profiling will enhance the capability of investigators. The ability of the AI tools in identifying multimedia content, breaking encrypted codes and identifying real deep fakes shall be essential in tackling the current and future angled crimes. In addition, more cross-border cooperation arrangements determined and supported by the AI systems will set up a combination against transnational crimes, which is a global aspect of the AI's application in society to creating justice and security environments.

Nonetheless, the enhanced use of AI in cybersecurity and forensics leads to having to solve problems associated with its application. Algorithmic risks or bias, data privacy and protection as well as appropriate use of the new technologies are some of the issues that must be most addressed to minimize creation of new social injustices by the new technologies. The ongoing work on the explainable AI that allows us to give clear, easily understandable, and reasonable answers to legal questions will be of great significance in forensic implementations. Moreover, the creation of the framework for AI governance on the global level will be important for increasing credibility and accountability in cases of its application on a transnational level.

The fast-moving AI technology emphasizes the need to design and implement more studies as a means of fully capturing the benefits of this technology while dealing with the associated consequences. Thus, the real progression of the state of the art and science of AI in educational organizations, technology companies and in the policies supporting them would require paradigmatic synergy in which academic sectors technology and policy sectors can synergistically work together. The emphasis in funding of research in AI must be placed on ideas like adversarial robustness, diversity of the data that AI algorithms are trained on, and the principles of the utilization of AI. As such they will help to increase the dependability and efficiency of the systems while at the same time helping to create trust in adoption of the AI systems (El-din, 2022).

Besides, it is crucial to focus on building an organizational culture that would let the company meet the emerging threats connected with cyber technologies and criminality. Cyber criminals and hackers are constantly in a state of continuous improvement when it comes to their criminal activities and therefore so should be the professionals and scientists in the cyber security and cyber forensic fields. Future trends that can enable proactive protective measures should top the list of AI driven innovations to counter potential adversaries. However, forensic researchers need to look for interesting innovative usages of AI for evidence gathering and examination and not forgetting existing and future developments such as quantum computing and neuromorphic engineering.

Issues of ethical concern must always be placed before more advancement and use of artificial intelligence. The current highly developed AI technologies contain a bivalent potential whereby they can also be used for dangerous objectives. This fact indicates the necessity of strict ethical rules and control mechanisms. AI systems should reflect the ACE (Accountability, Explainability, and Ethics) criteria as a set of requirements in shaping efficient AI systems that would integrate attributes of fairness, accountability, and transparency in delivering their services. Also, privacy must be ensured, all individual's data should be protected against unlawful usage in case of AI investigations and surveillance.

Simply we cannot overemphasize the importance of policymakers to regulate and set up ethical standards for the use of AI. National states and the international community must move forward to elaborate complex legal systems that would manage the application of AI in cyber security and cyber forensics. These frameworks should respond to questions like algorithmic accountability, data protection and -use of AI in law enforcement. Thus, the goal of all policy makers should be to harmonize such legislation throughout the world and to encourage international co-operation in the broad perception of such a vision of Artificial Intelligence systems being used to deliver justice and security rather than the opposite.

The case of AI as applied to cybersecurity and forensic science best reveals the possibility of making the digital world safer and more just. Encrypting cyber threats to the advanced solving of various crimes, the use of AI in managing the problems of the world's interconnectedness is obvious. But it also entails a good deal of commitments that need prudent evaluation of possible ethical, legal, and social effects. The work on AI in cybersecurity and forensics are the key areas that consist of research and innovations, and professionals from different fields. Here, the key message is that, if stakeholders get engaged in the adequate and ethical deployment of AI, all its beneficial features will be unleashed while all the potential unfavorable effects will be effectively mitigated. Over time, therefore, the value of using and applying the technology in an appropriate manner will be vital in making sure that its gains will be felt by all. Thus, AI will successfully recreate the very paradigm of cybersecurity and forensic science, as well as stimulate further development of a safer and more equal environment in the digital world.

REFERENCES

Agrawal, V. (2024). 20 Emerging Cybersecurity Trends to Watch Out in 2025. *Simplilearn*. https://www.simplilearn.com/top-cybersecurity-trends-article

Alghamdi, M. I. (2021). Digital Forensics in Cyber Security—Recent Trends, Threats, and Opportunities. *IntechOpen*. https://www.intechopen.com/chapters/76151

Begg, D. (2024). Applications and Challenges of Artificial Intelligence for Digital Forensics. *Westoahu Cybersecurity*. https://westoahu.hawaii.edu/cyber/forensics-weekly-executive-summmaries/applications-and-challenges-of-artificial-intelligence-for-digital-forensics/

Dunsin, D., Ghanem, M. C., Ouazzane, K., & Vassilev, V. T. (2024). A comprehensive analysis of the role of artificial intelligence and machine learning in modern digital forensics and incident response. *ResearchGate*. https://www.researchgate.net/publication/378241312_A_comprehensive_analysis_of_the_role_of_artificial_intelligence_and_machine_learning_in_modern_digital_forensics_and_incident_response

El-din, E. A. A. (2022). Artificial Intelligence in Forensic Science: Invasion or Revolution? *Egyptian Society of Clinical Toxicology Journal, 10*(2), 20-32. https://esctj.journals.ekb.eg/article_272046_4694247be2fec3aa3f89e32768714bae.pdf

Gaona, J. (2024). The Role of AI in Forensics. *Marymount University*. https://marymount.edu/blog/the-role-of-ai-in-forensics/

Jurva, G. (2024). Unlocking Justice: 2 Ways AI Is Impacting Evidence Analysis and Forensics. *Everlaw*. https://www.everlaw.com/blog/ai-and-law/unlocking-justice-ai-evidence-analysis-forensics/

Khaitan, A. (2023). Top 5 Trends For Digital Forensics in 2023. *Cyber Express*. https://thecyberexpress.com/top-5-trends-for-digital-forensics-in-2023/

Kim, K., Alshenaifi, I. M., Ramachandran, S., Kim, J., Zia, T., & Almorjan, A. (2023). Cybersecurity and Cyber Forensics for Smart Cities: A Comprehensive Literature Review and Survey. *Sensors (Basel)*, 23(7), 3681. DOI: 10.3390/s23073681 PMID: 37050740

Kosta, S., Jain, S., & Suwalka, I. (2024). AI Revolutionizing Forensic Analysis: Enhancing Efficiency and Accuracy in Crime Investigation. *International Advanced Research Journal in Science, Engineering and Technology, 11*(2), 226-229. https://iarjset.com/wp-content/uploads/2024/06/IARJSET-ICMART-41.pdf

Li, F. (2024). Application and challenges of artificial intelligence in cybersecurity. *ResearchGate*. https://www.researchgate.net/publication/379012606_Application_and_challenges_of_artificial_intelligence_in_cybersecurity

Malik, K. (2024). AI in Cybersecurity: Benefits and Challenges. *Astra*. https://www.getastra.com/blog/ai-security/ai-in-cybersecurity/

Noonan, L. (2024). Exploring the Benefits and Challenges of AI in Cyber Security. *Meta Compliance*. https://www.metacompliance.com/blog/data-breaches/benefits-and-challenges-of-ai-in-cyber-security

Parkinson, S., & Khan, S. (2024). The role of Artificial Intelligence in digital forensics: Case studies and future directions. *Assessment & Development Matters*, 16(1), 42–47. DOI: 10.53841/bpsadm.2024.16.1.42

Pattnaik, P. (2024). The Impact Of Artificial Intelligence On Forensic Science. *Lawyers Club India*. https://www.lawyersclubindia.com/articles/the-impact-of-artificial-intelligence-on-forensic-science-16676.asp

Roush, Z. (2024). Digital Forensics: The Good, the Bad, and the AI-Generated. *ACEDS*. https://aceds.org/digital-forensics-the-good-the-bad-and-the-ai-generated-aceds-blog/

Saini, K., Sonone, S. S., Sankhla, M. S., & Kumar, N. (2024). Artificial Intelligence in Forensic Science: An Emerging Technology in Criminal Investigation Systems. *ResearchGate*. https://www.researchgate.net/publication/382035324_Artificial_Intelligence_in_Forensic_Science_An_Emerging_Technology_in_Criminal_Investigation_Systems

Saini, S. (2023). Unveiling the Impact of Artificial Intelligence in Forensic Science. *Geeta University*. https://blog.geetauniversity.edu.in/unveiling-the-impact-of-artificial-intelligence-in-forensic-science/

Schneider, A. & Breitinger, F. (2023). Towards AI forensics: Did the artificial intelligence system do it?. *Journal of Information Security and Applications*. https://doi.org/DOI: 10.1016/j.jisa.2023.103517

Sharma, B. K., Joseph, M. A., Jacob, B., & Miranda, L. C. (2019). Emerging trends in Digital Forensic and Cyber security- An Overview. *2019 Sixth HCT Information Technology Trends (ITT)*, 309-313. https://www.semanticscholar.org/paper/Emerging-trends-in-Digital-Forensic-and-Cyber-An-Sharma-Joseph/503186f6126c8c7e3c265b8bdcfc71b61059bab1

Singh, W. U., & Singh, K. P. (2023). The transformative role of artificial intelligence in forensic medicine and toxicology. *Journal of Medical Society*, 37(3), 101–102. https://journals.lww.com/jmso/fulltext/2023/37030/the_transformative_role_of_artificial_intelligence.1.aspx. DOI: 10.4103/jms.jms_54_24

Suryal, A., Vishwakarma, P., & Malik, A. (2024). Impact of Artificial Intelligence in Digital Forensics: a Review Study. *EasyChair*. https://easychair.org/publications/preprint/52Gz

Tariq, U., Ahmed, I., Bashir, A. K., & Shaukat, K. (2023). A Critical Cybersecurity Analysis and Future Research Directions for the Internet of Things: A Comprehensive Review. *Sensors (Basel)*, 23(8), 4117. DOI: 10.3390/s23084117 PMID: 37112457

Thurzo, A., Kosnacova, H. S., Kurilova, V., Kosmel, S., Benus, R., Moravansky, N., Kova, P., Kuracinova, K. M., Palkovic, M., & Varga, I. (2021). Use of Advanced Artificial Intelligence in Forensic Medicine, Forensic Anthropology and Clinical Anatomy. *Health Care*, 9(11), 1545. DOI: 10.3390/healthcare9111545 PMID: 34828590

Yadav, R. T. (2024). AI-Driven Digital Forensics. *International Journal of Scientific Research & Engineering Trends, 10(*4), 1673-1681. https://ijsret.com/wp-content/uploads/2024/07/IJSRET_V10_issue4_353.pdf

Yanthan, N. (2024). Future of Cybersecurity - Trends and Scope. *Sprintzeal*. https://www.sprintzeal.com/blog/future-of-cybersecurity

Zaid, T., & Garai, S. (2024). Emerging Trends in Cybersecurity: A Holistic View on Current Threats, Assessing Solutions, and Pioneering New Frontiers. *Blockchain in Healthcare Today*, 7(1). Advance online publication. DOI: 10.30953/bhty.v7.302 PMID: 38715765

Chapter 13
Future Trends in AI and Digital Forensics

Hewa Majeed Zangana
https://orcid.org/0000-0001-7909-254X
Duhok Polytechnic University, Iraq

Shuai Li
University of Oulu, Finland

ABSTRACT

As artificial intelligence (AI) continues to evolve, it is reshaping the landscape of digital forensics, introducing new tools, methodologies, and challenges. This chapter explores the anticipated future trends in AI that are poised to transform digital forensic practices. Key areas of focus include the integration of machine learning for enhanced evidence analysis, AI-driven automation for streamlining investigative processes, and advances in natural language processing to improve data interpretation. The chapter also addresses emerging challenges such as adversarial AI, ethical considerations, and the complexities of handling AI-generated evidence. By examining these trends, the chapter aims to provide a comprehensive overview of the trajectory of AI in digital forensics and its potential impact on forensic methodologies, legal frameworks, and cybersecurity.

1. INTRODUCTION TO THE EVOLUTION OF AI IN DIGITAL FORENSICS

The integration of artificial intelligence (AI) into digital forensics has dramatically transformed the way forensic investigators handle, analyze, and interpret digital evidence. As technology advances, the scope and complexity of digital evidence

DOI: 10.4018/979-8-3373-0857-9.ch013

have increased, necessitating sophisticated tools to manage and analyze vast datasets more efficiently. AI, particularly through its machine learning (ML) and deep learning (DL) techniques, has become instrumental in facilitating this shift. From enhancing data extraction and classification to detecting anomalies and patterns, AI plays a pivotal role in augmenting the capabilities of digital forensics professionals, ultimately driving more accurate and timely investigations.

Historically, digital forensics relied on traditional methods that were primarily manual and labor-intensive, involving the inspection of data storage devices and the extraction of relevant information using basic pattern-matching techniques (Bhawna & Mahajan, 2024; Ganesh, 2017). These early methodologies often fell short in terms of efficiency and scalability, particularly as digital data grew in volume and complexity. AI's introduction brought about transformative changes, enabling the automation of repetitive tasks, thereby significantly reducing the time required for forensic analysis (Bhawna & Mahajan, 2024; Costantini, De Gasperis, & Olivieri, 2019). Techniques like neural networks and pattern recognition algorithms have allowed forensic analysts to identify correlations and anomalies within large datasets with unprecedented accuracy (Jarrett & Choo, 2021; Rizvi, Scanlon, McGibney, & Sheppard, 2022).

A significant development in AI-based digital forensics has been its application in malware analysis, intrusion detection, and fraud detection. These areas have benefited from machine learning models capable of learning from vast datasets, recognizing patterns, and predicting malicious behavior (Rughani, 2017; Dunsin, Ghanem, & Quazzane, 2022). This evolution also includes advancements in natural language processing (NLP), which enables automated analysis of textual evidence in criminal cases, including emails, social media posts, and chat logs (Gholami & Omar, 2023; Iqbal, Debbabi, & Fung, 2020).

The growing adoption of AI has not only streamlined digital forensics processes but also opened up new avenues for addressing previously challenging areas, such as predictive forensics and behavioral analysis. Predictive forensics leverages AI to anticipate potential cyber threats and cybercrimes, thereby supporting proactive security measures (Tyagi, Kumari, & Richa, 2024). Meanwhile, behavioral analysis, which focuses on understanding the actions and motivations of cybercriminals, has become increasingly sophisticated with the help of AI algorithms that detect behavioral patterns and outliers (Sikos, 2021; Jeong, 2020).

Another area of significant evolution is the development of explainable AI (XAI) within digital forensics. With growing demands for transparency, XAI provides forensic investigators with insights into AI model decisions, making the process of digital evidence analysis more understandable and legally defensible (Hall, Sakzad, & Choo, 2022; Kelly et al., 2020). The need for interpretability in AI-driven forensic analysis is paramount as legal proceedings require that the basis of digital evidence and analysis be clear to non-expert stakeholders, such as judges and jurors (Hall et al., 2022; Kelly et al., 2020).

Moreover, AI applications in digital forensics have expanded into specialized areas, such as cyber deception and adversarial AI, where techniques are developed to deceive malicious actors and detect deception in cyber activities. Cyber deception, for instance, is used to trap cybercriminals by presenting false information or decoys, effectively misleading them (Zangana, Mohammed, Sallow, & Sallow, 2024). Adversarial AI, conversely, is used to identify and counteract attempts to manipulate AI models, thus ensuring the reliability and robustness of AI-driven forensic investigations (Omar, 2024).

To illustrate the transformative journey of AI in digital forensics, from manual methods to the integration of machine learning and deep learning, the following timeline highlights key milestones. This visual representation underscores the rapid progression and its implications for forensic investigations.

Figure 1. Timeline of AI Advancements in Digital Forensics

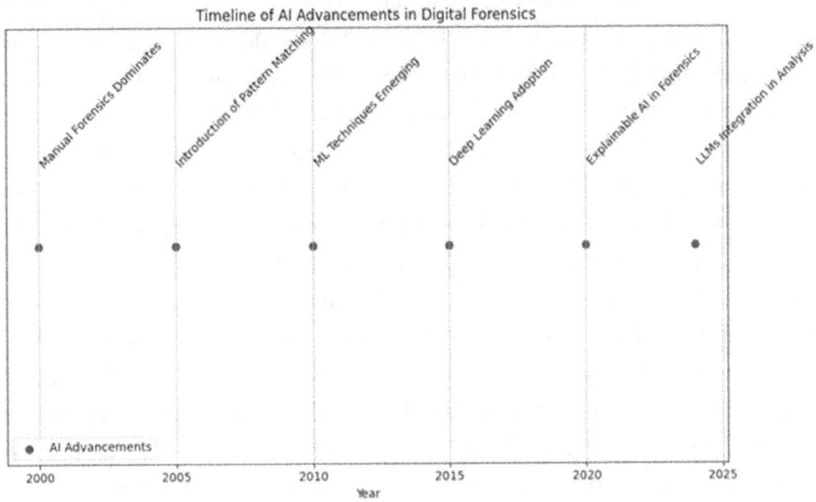

The transition from traditional to AI-based digital forensics represents a substantial leap in how cyber investigations are conducted. This shift not only allows investigators to handle the increasing volume and complexity of digital evidence but also equips them with tools to address the challenges of emerging threats. As AI technologies continue to evolve, their application in digital forensics will likely expand, leading to more sophisticated, efficient, and transparent investigative processes (Zangana, 2024; Dunsin et al., 2024). The future holds the promise of further innovations, including real-time analytics, advanced predictive capabilities, and AI-driven adaptive forensics, which will continue to transform the field.

2. EMERGING AI TECHNOLOGIES AND THEIR IMPACT ON DIGITAL FORENSICS

The rapid advancements in artificial intelligence (AI) have brought transformative changes to the field of digital forensics, offering novel approaches to analyze, detect, and understand cyber incidents. By integrating AI, digital forensics has expanded its capability to handle large volumes of data and intricate patterns in a highly efficient and accurate manner. This section discusses key AI technologies that are reshaping digital forensics, their applications, and the implications they hold for the future.

2.1. Machine Learning in Digital Forensics

Machine learning (ML), a subset of AI, has revolutionized data analysis in digital forensics by enabling systems to learn from past data and identify patterns without explicit programming. ML algorithms can analyze massive datasets, detect anomalies, and even anticipate security breaches. For example, Dunsin et al. (2022) highlight the effectiveness of ML in incident response, especially in resource-constrained environments where rapid analysis is crucial. This capability is particularly useful in cases requiring quick turnaround, as it minimizes the time spent on manual investigation and helps identify potential threats more accurately.

In network forensics, ML models have shown significant promise in identifying patterns indicative of malicious activity, such as unusual traffic behaviors or potential intrusion attempts (Rizvi et al., 2022). These models analyze historical data to predict similar incidents, thus enhancing the speed and accuracy of forensic investigations (Iqbal et al., 2020). Such applications illustrate the value of ML in automating and enhancing traditional forensic processes, allowing analysts to address complex cases with precision.

AI techniques vary in their application and effectiveness within digital forensics. The bar chart below compares key techniques—machine learning, deep learning, and explainable AI—based on accuracy, scalability, and interpretability.

Figure 2. Comparison of AI Techniques in Digital Forensics

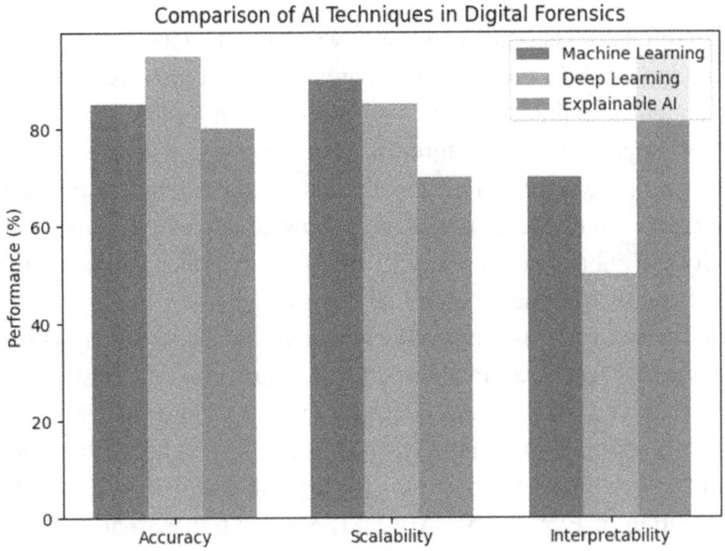

2.2. Deep Learning for Image and Text Analysis

Deep learning, a more advanced form of ML, has proven highly effective for analyzing complex data types, including images and text. In digital forensics, deep learning models are used extensively in image recognition, aiding investigators in tasks such as identifying individuals in surveillance footage or extracting relevant text data from images (Moustafa, 2022). For example, Convolutional Neural Networks (CNNs) are frequently employed for image classification tasks, which can be instrumental in identifying critical evidence during investigations.

Natural language processing (NLP), a facet of deep learning, enables AI to analyze textual data and extract meaning from it. In the context of digital forensics, NLP aids in examining chat logs, emails, and other forms of digital communication to detect signs of criminal intent or activity. NLP applications are crucial for forensic investigations in cases involving potential phishing attacks or online fraud, as discussed by Zangana et al. (2024) in their analysis of cybernetic deception and email phishing threats.

2.3. Explainable AI in Forensic Analysis

As digital forensics becomes increasingly reliant on AI, the need for explainable AI (XAI) has grown. XAI provides transparency into AI models, enabling forensic analysts to understand and trust the conclusions drawn by these systems. Explainability is particularly crucial in forensic investigations, where evidence derived from AI-driven processes must be legally sound and defensible in court. Hall et al. (2022) explore the integration of XAI in forensic processes, demonstrating how explainability can enhance the credibility of digital evidence and help investigators better understand the rationale behind AI decisions.

The importance of XAI is especially evident in cases where analysts must justify their findings to non-technical stakeholders or in courtrooms where evidence from AI systems is scrutinized (Kelly et al., 2020). For instance, in drug testing and similar sensitive investigations, explainable AI models can help validate the processes and outcomes of forensic analyses, bolstering the legal standing of AI-derived evidence.

The integration of Explainable AI (XAI) ensures transparent decision-making in digital forensics. The workflow diagram below captures the sequential stages, from evidence acquisition to explainable AI-enhanced analysis, providing insights into how forensic investigators use AI tools effectively.

Figure 3. Workflow of AI-Driven Digital Forensics

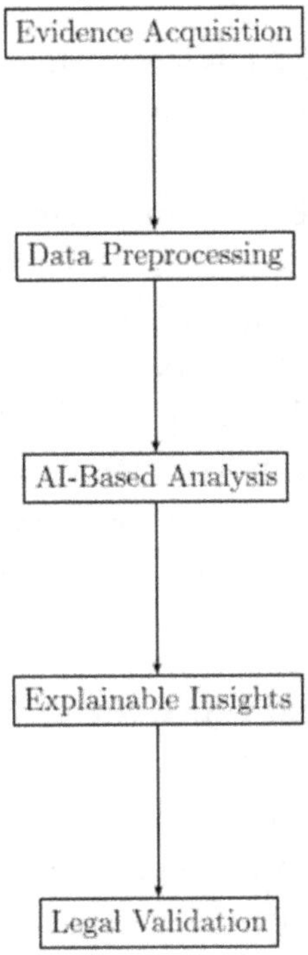

2.4. Large Language Models (LLMs) in Forensic Investigations

Large Language Models (LLMs), such as GPT-based architectures, represent a significant leap in AI capabilities, especially for tasks involving text analysis and information synthesis. In digital forensics, LLMs have the potential to examine large amounts of textual data, assisting investigators in cases involving social media analysis, dark web monitoring, and real-time communication monitoring. By parsing complex text patterns, LLMs can uncover insights that may otherwise go unnoticed, thus enhancing the depth of forensic investigations (Omar & Zangana, 2025).

Forensic applications of LLMs are still emerging, but recent research suggests that LLMs can play a pivotal role in vulnerability detection and threat analysis (Jones & Omar, 2024). By training these models on cybersecurity-related datasets, LLMs can identify potential security vulnerabilities within software systems or network configurations, offering an advanced level of protection and insight for forensic analysts.

2.5. AI-Based Behavioral Analysis

Behavioral analysis, aided by AI, is a powerful approach in digital forensics for identifying malicious or suspicious activity by analyzing patterns of behavior across digital environments. Tools that utilize AI-based behavioral analysis examine user activity, looking for irregular patterns that may signal an insider threat or unauthorized access. Adam and Varol (2020) demonstrate how AI-enhanced behavioral analysis tools can be integrated into forensic workflows to identify unusual patterns, such as unauthorized login attempts or data transfers.

This method is particularly relevant in forensics for identifying persistent threats and understanding the methods used by attackers. Behavioral analysis not only aids in detection but also provides insights into how and why certain security incidents occur, offering valuable context that can inform future security measures (Jeong, 2020).

2.6. Blockchain and Digital Forensics

Blockchain technology, with its immutability and transparency, is becoming an essential tool in digital forensics, particularly for maintaining the integrity of digital evidence. Blockchain can create tamper-proof records of forensic findings, ensuring that evidence is stored securely and can be verified throughout the investigation process. Zangana (2024) explores blockchain-based timestamping tools, which ensure that digital evidence remains unaltered and traceable throughout forensic analysis.

By combining AI with blockchain, forensic tools can offer enhanced security and trustworthiness of evidence, especially in high-stakes cases where evidence integrity is paramount (Omar & Zangana, 2024). This combination can be particularly effective in scenarios where multiple investigators or agencies collaborate, as blockchain provides a decentralized and transparent method for tracking forensic activities and evidence custody.

2.7 Summary

AI technologies are reshaping the field of digital forensics, offering advanced tools that enhance speed, accuracy, and reliability in cyber investigations. From machine learning and deep learning for complex data analysis to explainable AI and LLMs for legal defensibility, these tools are critical for modernizing forensic processes. As the field continues to evolve, the integration of blockchain with AI, along with advances in behavioral analysis, will further strengthen digital forensics, making it more resilient to emerging cyber threats. However, the reliance on AI also introduces new challenges, including issues of transparency, model bias, and the need for ongoing training, as noted by Bhawna and Mahajan (2024). Addressing these challenges will be essential for the sustainable and effective application of AI in digital forensics.

3. INTEGRATION OF AI WITH EMERGING TECHNOLOGIES

The integration of Artificial Intelligence (AI) with emerging technologies has been transformative across many fields, particularly in the realms of cybersecurity and digital forensics. As these fields evolve, AI's synergy with technologies like blockchain, cloud computing, large language models (LLMs), and the Internet of Things (IoT) is facilitating advanced solutions for security challenges and forensic investigation.

3.1 AI and Blockchain

Blockchain technology offers a decentralized and immutable ledger, which is invaluable for digital forensics. The integration of AI with blockchain enhances security and efficiency in forensic data handling. AI algorithms can be employed to analyze blockchain transactions, identify anomalies, and detect patterns of malicious activity. For example, blockchain timestamping tools, as explored by Zangana (2024), can create reliable, tamper-proof logs of forensic evidence, further strengthening forensic integrity. This combination also supports cyber deception and anti-phishing strategies, as AI algorithms identify suspicious patterns, flagging potential phishing attacks before they can cause harm (Zangana et al., 2024).

The synergy between AI and blockchain offers unparalleled capabilities in evidence integrity. The following diagram outlines the integration of AI analysis and blockchain-based timestamping to secure forensic evidence.

Figure 4. AI-Blockchain Synergy in Evidence Integrity

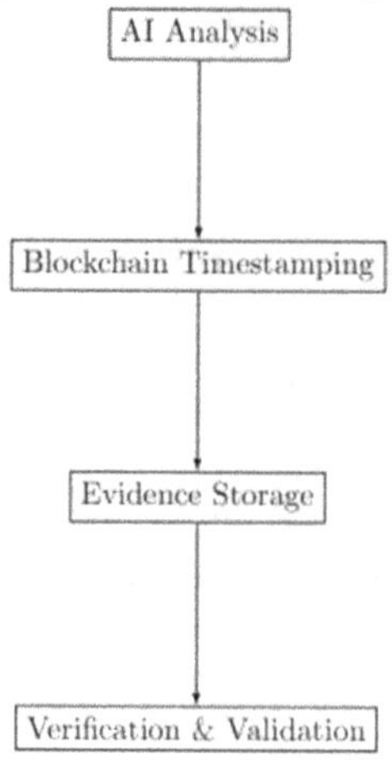

3.2 AI and Cloud Computing

Cloud computing offers scalable and efficient data storage solutions, critical for handling vast amounts of digital forensic data. The combination of AI and cloud infrastructure can address challenges associated with data privacy and security. AI-enhanced cloud systems can efficiently process large volumes of forensic data and automate malware detection and incident response. Studies have emphasized the importance of applying AI to monitor and detect abusive practices within cloud environments (Hamza & Omar, 2013). In high-stakes digital forensics, leveraging cloud AI enables rapid analysis, which is essential for incident response (Dunsin et al., 2022).

3.3 AI and Large Language Models (LLMs)

Large Language Models (LLMs) such as GPT-3 and BERT have shown considerable promise in the domain of cybersecurity and digital forensics. LLMs can analyze vast quantities of text data, extracting critical information relevant to forensic investigations. Their capabilities extend to software vulnerability detection, as they help identify code vulnerabilities or potential exploits within complex systems (Omar & Zangana, 2025). The use of synthetic data has further optimized LLM efficiency, allowing for more comprehensive training and improved model accuracy in recognizing cyber threats (Gholami & Omar, 2023).

3.4 AI and IoT

With the rise of IoT devices, digital forensics faces new challenges related to data privacy and device authentication. AI can process and analyze the massive influx of data from IoT devices, which is essential for identifying patterns of malicious behavior and securing IoT infrastructures. AI-based methods, including machine learning, are used to detect and counteract cyber threats within IoT networks, such as Distributed Denial of Service (DDoS) attacks and device intrusions (Jeong, 2020). Moreover, AI has been applied in network forensics, enabling forensic experts to track IoT communication patterns and identify security breaches (Rizvi et al., 2022).

3.5 Explainable AI (XAI)

In digital forensics, Explainable AI (XAI) has emerged as a critical requirement. XAI aims to make AI decision-making processes more transparent, which is vital for forensic investigations that require clear, accountable evidence. For instance, Hall et al. (2022) discuss the applications of XAI in digital forensics, highlighting how it provides investigators with comprehensible insights into AI's decision-making processes. This transparency aids forensic experts in establishing accountability and reliability in AI-driven findings.

3.6 AI-Enhanced Automation

Automation powered by AI has revolutionized several aspects of digital forensics, from data collection to evidence analysis. Automation allows for quicker processing times, enabling forensic experts to focus on complex investigative tasks. Studies have shown that automation reduces human error and ensures the accuracy and reliability of digital evidence (Jarrett & Choo, 2021). Furthermore, automated AI systems enhance the speed of forensic processes, which is crucial when working within constrained environments or time-sensitive situations (Dunsin et al., 2022).

3.7 Summary

The integration of AI with emerging technologies is revolutionizing the field of digital forensics. The advancements provided by blockchain, cloud computing, LLMs, IoT, and XAI enable more sophisticated and efficient forensic methods. By combining these technologies, forensic investigators can better manage the complexities of modern cyber threats, providing reliable, transparent, and accurate solutions to digital security challenges. As these integrations continue to evolve, they hold significant potential for further strengthening the forensic capabilities necessary in an increasingly digitized and interconnected world.

4. ANTICIPATING FUTURE CHALLENGES IN AI-DRIVEN FORENSICS

As artificial intelligence (AI) continues to revolutionize digital forensics, the field faces a growing number of complex challenges. These challenges arise from the need for more sophisticated methodologies to handle diverse digital artifacts, protect privacy, ensure explainability, and respond to evolving cyber threats. AI-driven forensics promises significant advancements in efficiency and accuracy, yet it also brings forward technical, ethical, and operational concerns that must be addressed to maximize its potential and mitigate risks.

4.1. Complexity of Digital Artifacts and Data Volume

With the exponential growth in digital devices, including IoT, mobile platforms, and cloud-based services, the volume and complexity of digital artifacts have increased dramatically. AI-based tools are essential for parsing, analyzing, and extracting meaningful information from this extensive data. However, the integration of AI into forensic processes introduces new hurdles. As Costantini, De Gasperis, and Olivieri (2019) note, the sheer variety of digital data sources challenges AI algorithms to remain adaptable and accurate across heterogeneous environments. The evolving nature of devices and data structures, from encrypted communications to decentralized systems, necessitates continuous refinement of AI models, which may struggle to keep pace with real-time demands (Adam & Varol, 2020; Rizvi et al., 2022).

4.2. Privacy and Ethical Concerns in AI Forensics

Privacy is a significant consideration in AI-driven forensics, especially with the growing use of personal devices and cloud services. The application of AI in digital forensics raises ethical questions regarding data ownership, user consent, and the potential for misuse of sensitive information (Dunsin, Ghanem, & Quazzane, 2022). Investigators often face difficulties balancing the need for data access with respecting user privacy, as data collection and analysis can sometimes overstep ethical boundaries. As Irons and Lallie (2014) highlight, AI must be employed with stringent data governance policies to mitigate the risk of overreach and ensure that forensic investigations remain ethically sound. Additionally, frameworks like explainable AI (XAI) can enhance transparency and accountability, although implementing XAI in complex forensic systems remains challenging (Kelly et al., 2020; Hall, Sakzad, & Choo, 2022).

4.3. Explainability and Trustworthiness of AI Algorithms

Explainability is critical in digital forensics, especially when AI-based findings are used in legal contexts. The black-box nature of many AI models, particularly deep learning algorithms, presents a challenge in explaining forensic outcomes to non-technical stakeholders, including legal professionals and regulatory bodies (Jeong, 2020; Sikos, 2021). As forensic analysis relies on AI for pattern recognition and anomaly detection, the lack of transparency can hinder the acceptance of evidence derived from these methods. Explainable AI techniques, as explored by Hall et al. (2022), offer a potential pathway to improve trust in AI systems, yet they also present computational challenges and may compromise accuracy. Developing transparent, interpretable models is essential to maintaining the integrity of AI-driven forensics.

4.4. Adaptation to Evolving Cyber Threats

The rapidly changing landscape of cyber threats presents an ongoing challenge for AI-driven forensics. Attackers frequently modify tactics to evade detection, utilizing encryption, anonymization, and AI themselves to obscure malicious activities (Manasa & Kumar, 2022). According to Jones et al. (2023), the adaptability of machine learning models is vital in countering zero-day attacks and other sophisticated threats. However, maintaining AI models that are responsive to new attack vectors without incurring significant computational costs remains a key issue. This calls for advanced AI techniques, such as adversarial machine learning, that can predict and respond to emergent cyber tactics (Jarrett & Choo, 2021; Omar, 2024).

4.5. Infrastructure and Resource Constraints

Another concern in deploying AI-based forensic tools is the need for high-performance computing resources, which may not be available in all forensic environments. In constrained environments, such as remote locations or small-scale forensic labs, the limited availability of resources can impede the effective application of advanced AI techniques (Dunsin, Ghanem, Ouazzane, & Vassilev, 2024). Cloud-based AI solutions, as discussed by Hamza and Omar (2013), offer a potential workaround, though they introduce additional concerns around data sovereignty, latency, and security risks.

4.6. Addressing Bias and Model Robustness

Bias in AI algorithms is an ongoing concern, particularly in forensic applications where impartiality is crucial. Bias can emerge from the training data or the model design itself, potentially leading to incorrect conclusions that could impact judicial outcomes (Bhawna & Mahajan, 2024). The incorporation of diverse, representative datasets is essential to mitigate these risks, yet achieving robust, unbiased models remains an industry-wide challenge. Moreover, ensuring that AI models are resilient against adversarial inputs is critical to maintaining reliable forensic outcomes, as discussed by Huff et al. (2023) and Mohammed et al. (2018).

4.7. Integration with Blockchain for Data Integrity

Blockchain technology offers promising opportunities for enhancing the integrity and traceability of digital evidence in AI-driven forensics. Blockchain's immutable ledger can help prevent tampering, ensuring that digital evidence remains authentic and reliable throughout forensic investigations (Zangana, 2024). This integration, however, introduces operational challenges in terms of data storage, retrieval, and computational load. As Ganesh (2017) suggests, combining blockchain with AI in forensics could provide an innovative way to preserve data integrity, yet further research is required to determine the scalability and efficiency of such approaches.

4.8. Future Directions for AI in Digital Forensics

Looking ahead, the future of AI in digital forensics will depend on advancing technologies and interdisciplinary collaboration. Continuous development in AI methodologies, such as reinforcement learning and natural language processing, may enable more sophisticated forensic analysis and broader application contexts (Omar & Zangana, 2025). Moreover, fostering partnerships between forensic experts, legal authorities, and AI researchers will be essential to developing robust frameworks that address both technical and ethical challenges. Ultimately, addressing these future challenges will ensure that AI-driven forensics remains a vital, trusted tool in the fight against cybercrime.

This section, by incorporating the perspectives from a wide range of researchers and practitioners, underscores the multifaceted nature of AI-driven forensics. With advancements in AI, blockchain, and cybersecurity measures, the field can evolve in ways that balance efficacy with ethical responsibility, offering a future that leverages the power of technology for enhanced forensic capabilities.

5. REGULATORY AND LEGAL CONSIDERATIONS FOR AI IN FORENSICS

The integration of artificial intelligence (AI) in digital forensics offers considerable potential, enhancing the accuracy and speed of forensic investigations. However, as forensic AI applications evolve, so does the need for robust regulatory and legal frameworks to guide their use and ensure adherence to ethical standards. Legal considerations surrounding AI in digital forensics largely focus on issues such as evidence admissibility, data privacy, accountability, and algorithmic transparency.

5.1. Evidence Admissibility

AI systems in forensics often generate outputs or insights used in court proceedings, raising questions about the admissibility of AI-derived evidence. Courts may scrutinize the reliability of AI-driven evidence due to the "black-box" nature of many AI models, which can obscure how conclusions are reached (Hall et al., 2022). This is a key concern in high-stakes environments such as criminal trials, where the defense may challenge AI-driven evidence if they lack understanding of its decision-making processes (Jeong, 2020). Legal frameworks must clarify the standards required for AI to meet admissibility criteria, often requiring explainability and reproducibility.

5.2. Privacy and Data Protection

The use of AI in digital forensics often involves analyzing massive datasets that include sensitive information. Privacy regulations, such as the GDPR in Europe, impose strict requirements on the collection, processing, and storage of personal data (Bhawna & Mahajan, 2024). Forensic AI applications must comply with these regulations by implementing data protection measures like anonymization and ensuring that data collection is lawful and proportional to investigative needs (Zangana & Omar, 2025). Moreover, AI-powered forensic tools may inadvertently increase the risk of privacy infringement by uncovering data beyond the scope of investigation, necessitating regulatory safeguards to prevent misuse (Dunsin et al., 2024).

5.3. Accountability and Liability

Accountability in AI forensics is complex, as AI systems often involve collaboration among multiple stakeholders, including developers, law enforcement, and forensic analysts. Determining liability when AI malfunctions or produces erroneous outputs is critical, especially when such errors lead to false accusations or wrongful convictions (Ganesh, 2017). Regulatory frameworks must define clear accountability structures, stipulating who is responsible when an AI system fails and how accountability is distributed across various stakeholders involved in the forensic process (Irons & Lallie, 2014). This may include requirements for regular audits of AI algorithms to ensure compliance with legal standards and best practices (Adam & Varol, 2020).

5.4. Transparency and Explainability

The opaque nature of many AI algorithms, particularly those based on deep learning, poses significant challenges for transparency in forensic contexts. Transparency is essential in establishing trust in AI-assisted forensic methods and ensuring that they can be scrutinized for fairness and accuracy. Hall et al. (2022) highlight the growing demand for "explainable AI" (XAI) in forensics to help stakeholders understand the rationale behind AI decisions, which is vital for upholding the rights of defendants. Tools such as interpretable models and traceable algorithms are increasingly seen as prerequisites in forensic AI applications to provide accountability and facilitate legal assessments (Costantini et al., 2019; Kelly et al., 2020).

5.5. Ethical and Bias Concerns

Bias in AI-driven forensics can lead to discriminatory outcomes, particularly if algorithms are trained on unrepresentative datasets or contain inherent biases in their design (Rizvi et al., 2022). Legal frameworks must address these issues by enforcing standards that minimize bias and ensure equitable treatment across different demographic groups (Gholami & Omar, 2023). Bias mitigation strategies, such as employing diverse training data and regularly assessing algorithms for discriminatory patterns, are essential for ethically sound forensic AI systems (Tyagi et al., 2024).

5.6. Cross-Jurisdictional Challenges

Digital forensics often involves investigations that span multiple jurisdictions, especially in cybercrime cases. Jurisdictional variations in data privacy laws, evidence admissibility standards, and law enforcement procedures present significant challenges for AI applications in digital forensics (Zangana et al., 2024). Harmonizing these disparate legal standards is essential for enabling effective cross-border investigations, which may require international agreements that standardize forensic AI practices (Omar, 2022; Moustafa, 2022).

5.7. Compliance and Best Practices

To promote consistency and compliance, regulatory bodies may establish standards and guidelines for forensic AI applications. These guidelines would offer best practices for the development, deployment, and auditing of AI systems used in forensics. Omar & Zangana (2025) emphasize that adherence to industry standards, such as those set by the ISO/IEC for information security management, could help organizations ensure that AI applications are reliable, secure, and aligned with legal requirements. Compliance with these standards helps build public trust in forensic AI, reinforcing its credibility in legal contexts (Jones et al., 2023; Mitchell, 2014).

5.8 Summary

Legal and regulatory frameworks for AI in digital forensics must evolve to keep pace with technological advancements. A robust legal infrastructure will safeguard individual rights, enhance trust in forensic processes, and ensure that AI's role in digital forensics aligns with societal expectations of fairness and accountability. Future developments in forensic AI regulation will likely focus on balancing the potential of AI technologies to aid justice with the need to protect privacy, prevent bias, and maintain transparency and accountability in forensic investigations (Zangana et al., 2024).

Ensuring that AI applications meet high standards of explainability, data protection, and compliance with legal frameworks will be crucial as forensic AI continues to shape the future of criminal justice.

6. FUTURE SKILLS AND WORKFORCE DEVELOPMENT IN FORENSICS

The rapid advancement of technology in digital forensics necessitates a workforce equipped with specialized skills and knowledge. As digital forensics increasingly integrates artificial intelligence (AI) and machine learning (ML), future forensics professionals will need to develop competencies that align with these transformative technologies. Traditional forensic skills, though foundational, are no longer sufficient on their own; practitioners must also possess expertise in data science, cybersecurity, AI, and ethical considerations related to technology use in criminal investigations.

6.1. AI and Machine Learning Proficiency

The integration of AI in forensics allows for automated and enhanced data analysis, pattern recognition, and predictive modeling. Future forensic professionals must understand the basics of machine learning algorithms and be able to interpret AI-driven insights. For example, deep learning models are being applied to detect anomalies and potential threats in real-time, which is vital in quickly evolving cyberattack scenarios (Ganesh, 2017; Bhawna & Mahajan, 2024). Moreover, to effectively handle AI-driven forensic tools, professionals will need knowledge in selecting and training machine learning models, as well as skills in evaluating the accuracy and reliability of these models (Costantini et al., 2019).

6.2. Knowledge of Cloud and Network Security

As cloud computing and IoT become increasingly common, understanding cloud environments and network security is critical. For instance, forensic experts need to know how to track and interpret digital traces across different platforms and networks (Hamza & Omar, 2013; Jeong, 2020). This shift emphasizes the need for professionals who can apply forensic methods to cloud-based data and manage challenges related to multi-tenant cloud infrastructures. Skills in network analysis, cloud forensics, and understanding potential vulnerabilities in these infrastructures are essential to investigate cybercrimes comprehensively (Mohammed et al., 2018).

6.3. Blockchain and Encryption Skills

Blockchain technology, widely regarded for its security and transparency, has implications for digital forensics, especially in data verification and chain-of-custody issues (Zangana, 2024). Professionals must understand blockchain-based timestamping tools and how encryption protocols can both protect and obscure data. Familiarity with cryptographic concepts will enable forensic investigators to retrieve and interpret encrypted data securely, which is crucial in cases where data privacy and integrity are at stake (Omar, 2024).

6.4. Explainable AI and Interpretability Skills

The adoption of AI in forensic investigations introduces the need for explainable AI (XAI) to ensure that outcomes are interpretable and can withstand legal scrutiny. Forensic analysts must be able to explain how AI algorithms reach specific conclusions, which requires knowledge of interpretability techniques in machine learning (Hall et al., 2022; Kelly et al., 2020). The ability to critically assess AI's decision-making processes will be essential to establish trust in AI-driven forensic findings and to use them as admissible evidence in court (Jarrett & Choo, 2021).

6.5. Ethical and Legal Proficiency

Forensic work often intersects with sensitive legal and ethical issues, especially when it involves the use of invasive technologies. The growing capabilities of AI in tracking, analyzing, and predicting behaviors raise important ethical considerations. Forensic experts must be aware of ethical frameworks that guide responsible use of AI in criminal investigations, ensuring privacy rights and data integrity are respected (Dunsin et al., 2024). This knowledge is critical for handling cases involving personal data and requires an understanding of legal standards and regulations related to digital evidence (Iqbal et al., 2020).

6.6. Cybersecurity Skills

A deep understanding of cybersecurity principles is necessary for forensic experts to detect, prevent, and investigate cyberattacks. Forensics professionals must keep pace with the latest developments in cybersecurity and digital forensics frameworks (Wright et al., 2012). This includes skills in threat detection, incident response, and an awareness of the most recent cyberattack methods. Enhanced understanding of cybersecurity protocols will also enable forensic analysts to collaborate more effectively with cybersecurity teams, thereby strengthening the overall defense against digital threats (Rizvi et al., 2022).

6.7. Large Language Model (LLM) Applications in Forensics

The rise of large language models (LLMs) offers new potential in forensics, especially in analyzing textual data and automating parts of the investigative process. Forensic experts of the future may need to understand how to leverage LLMs for tasks like identifying patterns in communication data or synthesizing large volumes of unstructured information (Omar & Zangana, 2025; Gholami & Omar, 2023). Familiarity with these models, and the ability to understand their limitations, will be invaluable in enhancing the analytical capabilities of forensic investigations.

6.8 Summary

The field of digital forensics is evolving rapidly, driven by advancements in AI, cybersecurity, cloud computing, and blockchain technology. Developing skills in these areas will be essential for future forensic professionals to remain effective in an increasingly complex digital landscape. This interdisciplinary approach to skill development in digital forensics will not only equip practitioners with technical competencies but also prepare them to address ethical, legal, and interpretative challenges, fostering a workforce capable of advancing forensic science in meaningful ways.

7. GLOBAL TRENDS AND COLLABORATIONS

The field of digital forensics is rapidly transforming, propelled by advancements in artificial intelligence (AI) and machine learning (ML) technologies, and the increased connectivity of global systems. As digital forensic techniques continue to evolve, they are increasingly being influenced by global trends such as AI integration, blockchain adoption, and interdisciplinary collaborations. These advancements have paved the way for enhanced investigation methodologies, more effective data analysis, and collaborative approaches to combating cybercrime.

7.1 AI Integration in Digital Forensics

Artificial intelligence plays a critical role in modernizing digital forensic processes, offering significant benefits in areas such as automation, data analysis, and pattern recognition. AI's capabilities enable digital forensics experts to analyze vast amounts of data quickly and accurately, which is essential for identifying cyber threats and criminal activities. For instance, AI models can efficiently categorize and interpret data collected from various digital sources, reducing the time required to investigate incidents (Bhawna & Mahajan, 2024; Costantini et al., 2019). Moreover, AI-based digital forensics tools offer robust methods for data reconstruction, allowing experts to recover and analyze digital evidence that might otherwise be inaccessible (Irons & Lallie, 2014).

The integration of AI in digital forensics has also led to the development of predictive models that assist in identifying potential future threats. AI-driven predictive analytics enables forensic investigators to anticipate cyberattacks and implement preventive measures, bolstering security across systems (Jeong, 2020; Jarrett & Choo, 2021). Furthermore, advancements in explainable AI (XAI) offer transparency in digital investigations, making it easier for investigators to understand and trust AI-generated insights (Hall et al., 2022; Kelly et al., 2020).

7.2 Blockchain Technology in Digital Forensics

Blockchain technology is emerging as another transformative tool in digital forensics, particularly in the area of data integrity and verification. Blockchain's decentralized and immutable nature ensures that digital evidence remains tamper-proof, which is critical for preserving the authenticity of data throughout the investigative process. Blockchain-based timestamping tools are being explored as a means to secure digital evidence, providing a reliable method for verifying the origin and modification history of data (Zangana, 2024). This is especially useful in legal contexts, where the integrity of evidence can be a determining factor in the outcome of a case (Zangana & Omar, 2025).

7.3 Global Collaborative Efforts in Digital Forensics

Collaboration across national and organizational boundaries is essential to address the increasing complexity of cyber threats. Cybercrime is often transnational, and thus, a coordinated global approach to digital forensics is necessary. International bodies and coalitions are working together to establish standards and protocols for data exchange, evidence handling, and the application of AI in forensics. For example, digital forensic experts from various countries collaborate to enhance incident response techniques, ensuring timely and effective actions in the event of cyber-attacks (Moustafa, 2022). These global partnerships facilitate knowledge sharing, standardization of procedures, and advancements in digital forensics methodologies (Adam & Varol, 2020; Hamza & Omar, 2013).

Furthermore, interdisciplinary collaboration is becoming increasingly important. The integration of expertise from fields such as AI, cybersecurity, data science, and law enables digital forensic teams to develop comprehensive approaches to cybercrime investigation. This interdisciplinary approach enhances the ability of forensic teams to adapt to the evolving landscape of cyber threats and to implement innovative solutions (Ganesh, 2017; Huff et al., 2023).

7.4 Addressing Privacy and Ethical Challenges

As digital forensics becomes more reliant on AI and international collaboration, privacy and ethical concerns also become increasingly prominent. Ensuring compliance with international data privacy regulations, such as the General Data Protection Regulation (GDPR), is essential when handling digital evidence across borders. This necessitates the development of protocols that safeguard personal data while allowing investigators to access the information they need (Tyagi et al., 2024; Omar, 2022).

Ethical AI in digital forensics also involves addressing issues such as bias in AI models and ensuring accountability in AI-driven forensic processes. Transparency in AI models is essential for upholding ethical standards in digital investigations, as it helps to mitigate the risk of biased outcomes and ensures that forensic evidence is legally admissible (Sikos, 2021). Additionally, collaboration between regulatory bodies and AI developers is crucial to establishing guidelines that promote fairness and accountability in AI-based forensic applications (Rizvi et al., 2022).

7.5 Future Directions and Emerging Trends

The future of digital forensics lies in the continued integration of AI, the expansion of blockchain applications, and the strengthening of global collaborations. Emerging technologies, such as quantum computing, are expected to play a role in enhancing cryptographic techniques and data analysis capabilities in digital forensics. Additionally, there is a growing interest in utilizing large language models (LLMs) to improve forensic analysis by automating complex data interpretation tasks (Gholami & Omar, 2023; Zangana & Omar, 2025).

Digital forensics is poised to become a more dynamic and collaborative field, with experts from around the world contributing to innovative solutions and standardized practices. Through ongoing research, technological advancements, and international cooperation, digital forensics will continue to evolve, ensuring that it remains an effective tool for combating cybercrime and protecting digital assets (Mitchell, 2014; Wright et al., 2012).

8. CASE STUDIES AND SPECULATIVE SCENARIOS

The intersection of artificial intelligence (AI) and digital forensics has become a dynamic area of study, especially as cyber threats grow in sophistication and variety. This section will examine real-world case studies and provide speculative scenarios to explore the potential applications of AI in digital forensics. Using AI for threat detection and digital investigation has transformed traditional practices and introduced new possibilities and challenges.

8.1 Case Studies in AI-Driven Digital Forensics

1. Enhancing Forensic Investigation with AI and Machine Learning

Adam and Varol (2020) conducted a detailed study on the role of intelligence in digital forensic processes, focusing on how machine learning algorithms enhance forensic capabilities. The case study shows how AI can automate evidence gathering, pattern recognition, and anomaly detection, which allows investigators to process vast datasets quickly. Additionally, this approach enhances the speed and efficiency of forensic investigations by reducing human error, making it suitable for high-stakes environments like corporate security and national defense.

2. Applying AI in Phishing Detection and Network Defense

Zangana, Omar, Al-Karaki, and Mohammed (2024) provide insights into using AI-based systems for network firewall rule analysis to improve security posture and efficiency. The case emphasizes the effectiveness of AI in identifying and responding to network anomalies, including potential phishing attempts. By automating the detection of phishing attacks, AI helps mitigate threats more proactively. These findings align with previous research by Jeong (2020), which categorizes various security threats and emphasizes the importance of AI-driven forensics in mitigating such vulnerabilities.

3. AI and Digital Forensics in Constrained Environments

Dunsin, Ghanem, and Quazzane (2022) highlight the use of AI in digital forensics within constrained environments, such as mobile devices and IoT networks. Their research addresses the challenges of limited computational resources, demonstrating that lightweight AI models can operate effectively under such constraints. This case illustrates the adaptability of AI in forensic investigations, allowing for efficient threat detection even with limited processing power. This study aligns with the work of Wright, Dawson, and Omar (2012), who identified the need for effective mobile security measures.

4. Explainable AI in Digital Forensics

The application of explainable AI (XAI) is gaining traction, especially for enhancing transparency in forensic investigations. Hall, Sakzad, and Choo (2022) present a case study where XAI tools were used to interpret and validate forensic findings, especially in sensitive cases such as drug testing. By providing clear explanations of

AI-driven decisions, XAI facilitates legal scrutiny and helps stakeholders understand forensic evidence more easily. This transparency is critical in building trust in AI technologies within the legal domain, echoing the call for explainable AI in Kelly et al. (2020) and Costantini, De Gasperis, and Olivieri (2019).

5. AI-Powered Detection of Emerging Cyber Threats

Jones, Omar, and colleagues (2023) emphasize the role of machine learning in improving cybersecurity defenses through the rapid identification of zero-day vulnerabilities. Their study highlights AI's capability to detect subtle signs of emerging threats in real-time, which is invaluable in modern forensics where speed is crucial. Similarly, the research by Sikos (2021) demonstrates how ontology engineering with AI can help organize forensic data and create detailed profiles of cybercriminal behavior.

8.2 Speculative Scenarios in AI-Driven Digital Forensics

1. Autonomous Forensic Systems in Future Smart Cities

With the growth of smart cities, autonomous AI-driven forensic systems could monitor public and private networks for potential threats. These systems might leverage machine learning algorithms to detect unusual patterns, enabling real-time response to cyber incidents. For instance, autonomous AI could predict criminal activities by identifying behavioral anomalies across connected infrastructure, inspired by the frameworks proposed by Manasa and Kumar (2022) and Moustafa (2022).

2. AI-Driven Predictive Forensics

Predictive forensics is an emerging concept that uses AI to forecast potential cyber incidents based on historical data, user behavior, and network patterns. As highlighted by Mitchell (2014), pattern recognition plays a crucial role in identifying potential threats before they materialize. By analyzing these patterns, AI could help prevent cybercrimes, moving digital forensics from a reactive to a proactive approach. This anticipatory capability could prove transformative in both corporate and public-sector environments.

3. AI-Augmented Behavioral Analysis for Insider Threats

Insider threats represent a significant challenge in cybersecurity, and AI could offer sophisticated behavioral analysis tools to identify risky behaviors among employees or users within an organization. Inspired by Rizvi et al. (2022), who explore AI's role in network forensics, this speculative scenario posits that AI could track user interactions with sensitive data, flagging deviations from typical behavior patterns that might suggest insider threats. This approach can add a layer of intelligence to traditional monitoring methods, helping organizations protect against internal security breaches.

4. Virtual AI Investigators for Law Enforcement

In the future, AI could serve as virtual investigators within law enforcement agencies, handling basic digital forensics tasks such as analyzing data, sifting through digital evidence, and categorizing potential threats. This would allow human investigators to focus on more complex and nuanced cases, as noted in the studies by Irons and Lallie (2014) and Bhawna and Mahajan (2024). These virtual investigators could even assist in court proceedings by producing evidence reports and supporting explanations that can withstand legal scrutiny.

5. Cybernetic Deception and AI-Driven Forensic Analysis

As cybercriminals adopt more sophisticated tactics, the use of AI for cyber deception analysis has become necessary. For example, Zangana, Mohammed, Sallow, and Sallow (2024) explore the concept of cybernetic deception in phishing attacks, which could be extended to AI systems designed to counteract these tactics. By identifying and responding to deceptive strategies, AI-driven forensic tools can reduce the effectiveness of such attacks, enabling forensic analysts to stay one step ahead of cybercriminals.

6. AI and Blockchain-Enhanced Forensic Evidence Management

Combining AI with blockchain technology could revolutionize evidence management in digital forensics, providing an immutable ledger that enhances transparency and security. Zangana (2024) suggests blockchain-based timestamping as a means of ensuring data integrity, an approach that could prevent tampering and enhance trust in forensic evidence. This speculative scenario envisions AI managing the ledger, cross-referencing timestamps with evidence to verify its authenticity automatically, as also discussed by Omar and Zangana (2024).

9. RECOMMENDATIONS FOR POLICYMAKERS AND PRACTITIONERS

In light of the evolving landscape of digital forensics, artificial intelligence (AI), and cybersecurity, there are critical steps that policymakers and practitioners should consider to enhance digital investigation efforts, mitigate cyber threats, and align with regulatory standards. These recommendations draw on contemporary research and aim to address the complexities faced in the digital forensics domain.

1. **Develop Standardized AI-Integrated Forensic Frameworks**

To cope with the increasing integration of AI in digital forensics, policymakers should prioritize establishing standardized frameworks for AI-enhanced forensic investigations. Given that AI technologies can significantly enhance accuracy and speed in identifying digital threats (Dunsin et al., 2024), these frameworks should outline the legal boundaries, ethical considerations, and procedural guidelines for using AI in digital forensics. This is especially crucial as the boundaries between human and machine-led investigation processes blur (Irons & Lallie, 2014; Jeong, 2020).

2. **Invest in Explainable AI for Transparent Forensic Processes**

Explainable AI (XAI) can assist forensic practitioners and legal authorities in understanding AI-driven findings, fostering trust in AI-based forensic outcomes (Hall et al., 2022; Kelly et al., 2020). Policymakers should encourage investment in XAI research and promote its use across forensic investigations to enhance the interpretability of AI methods. This would help practitioners justify and present evidence in court, where AI decisions may face scrutiny for their lack of transparency (Costantini et al., 2019).

3. **Emphasize Training Programs on AI and Cybersecurity for Forensic Professionals**

With AI's growing role in digital forensics, there is a need for continuous professional development and training in AI, cybersecurity, and digital forensics (Ganesh, 2017). Policymakers should collaborate with educational institutions to integrate specialized training programs that equip forensic practitioners with skills in AI-based tools, methods, and ethics (Moustafa, 2022). Additionally, courses on handling cyber deception, including email phishing detection, should be prioritized to address emerging cyber threats (Zangana et al., 2024).

4. **Enhance Cross-Jurisdictional Collaboration and Data Sharing**

Cyber threats are global, and digital forensics investigations often require collaboration across borders. Policymakers should create frameworks to facilitate secure data sharing between law enforcement and cybersecurity entities across jurisdictions (Bhawna & Mahajan, 2024; Rizvi et al., 2022). Establishing cross-jurisdictional agreements for data exchange and shared resources can improve response times and aid in tracking cyber criminals effectively.

5. **Regulate and Monitor AI Usage in Digital Forensics to Avoid Bias**

AI models can be prone to biases that may impact the accuracy and fairness of forensic results (Jarrett & Choo, 2021). Policymakers must enforce regulations that require forensic AI systems to undergo rigorous testing for biases and ensure these tools are regularly updated. AI should be used cautiously, particularly in cases where legal decisions are impacted by AI-derived evidence, to protect against potential miscarriages of justice (Iqbal et al., 2020).

6. **Implement Cybersecurity Guidelines for AI in Digital Forensics**

As digital forensics increasingly relies on AI, it becomes vital to secure AI systems themselves against attacks (Mohammed et al., 2018). Practitioners should adhere to best practices and frameworks for cybersecurity, which protect AI forensic systems from cyberattacks. The cybersecurity policies should address AI model vulnerabilities and include measures to guard against adversarial attacks that could compromise forensic data integrity (Omar, 2024; Jones et al., 2023).

7. **Adopt Blockchain for Digital Evidence Integrity**

Blockchain technology provides a promising solution for maintaining the integrity of digital evidence by enabling secure, tamper-proof timestamps and verifiable records (Zangana, 2024). Policymakers should consider adopting blockchain-based systems for digital forensics, as this can significantly improve the reliability and chain of custody of evidence, ensuring data authenticity (Hamza & Omar, 2013). Blockchain systems are especially useful in scenarios involving cross-jurisdictional evidence sharing, as they enable tamper-evident trails (Zangana & Omar, 2025).

8. **Invest in Research on the Ethical Implications of AI in Forensics**

Policymakers should support ongoing research into the ethical implications of AI use in digital forensics. Issues such as privacy, accountability, and potential biases necessitate a clear ethical framework (Adam & Varol, 2020). By fostering a proactive approach, policymakers can help forensic practitioners navigate ethical dilemmas related to data privacy and ensure that AI-enhanced forensics remains transparent, fair, and unbiased (Sikos, 2021).

9. **Encourage Collaborative Research Between Academia and Industry**

Bridging the gap between academic research and industry practices in AI and digital forensics can accelerate the development of innovative solutions (Tyagi et al., 2024). Policymakers should promote partnerships and funding for collaborative research efforts, enabling academic institutions and technology companies to advance cutting-edge forensic methods and apply AI to real-world cybersecurity challenges (Zangana & Mohammed, 2025; Omar, 2022).

10. **Expand Awareness Campaigns on AI and Digital Forensics for the Public**

Raising awareness about the role of AI in digital forensics and cybersecurity can foster a better understanding of how personal data may be used in investigations (Wright et al., 2012). Practitioners, with policymakers' support, should conduct campaigns to educate the public on AI's benefits and limitations in digital investigations, promoting transparency and trust in AI-driven forensic processes (Rughani, 2017; Mitchell, 2014).

By implementing these recommendations, policymakers and practitioners can leverage the benefits of AI in digital forensics while addressing potential risks and ethical concerns, ensuring that AI serves as a trustworthy and transparent tool in the fight against cybercrime.

10. CONCLUSION

The integration of artificial intelligence (AI) into digital forensics has significantly transformed how investigations are conducted, offering numerous advantages in terms of efficiency, accuracy, and scalability. AI tools, particularly those powered by machine learning and deep learning, have enhanced the ability to analyze vast datasets, detect patterns, and identify anomalies that would be difficult or even impossible for human investigators to spot. These advancements allow for faster and more reliable detection of cybercrimes, such as data breaches, fraud, and digital evidence manipulation.

Despite the clear benefits, the application of AI in digital forensics also raises several challenges that must be addressed. One of the main concerns is the interpretability of AI models, especially when used in critical investigations where human decision-making is still paramount. Ensuring that AI algorithms are explainable and transparent is essential to maintaining trust and accountability in forensic processes. Furthermore, the complexity and potential biases in AI systems could lead to ethical and legal concerns, especially when these systems are used to make decisions with significant consequences for individuals or organizations.

Looking forward, the role of AI in digital forensics is likely to grow, with emerging technologies such as explainable AI and reinforcement learning offering promising new tools for improving the field. However, the continued development of these technologies must be accompanied by rigorous testing, ethical frameworks, and regulatory oversight to mitigate the risks associated with their use. Collaboration between forensic experts, AI researchers, and policymakers will be essential to ensure that AI tools are used responsibly and effectively in digital investigations.

In conclusion, while AI has the potential to revolutionize digital forensics by improving the speed, accuracy, and scalability of investigations, its integration must be approached carefully and thoughtfully. By addressing the technical, ethical, and legal challenges, stakeholders can unlock the full potential of AI to enhance digital forensics practices and better address the evolving landscape of cyber threats.

REFERENCES

Adam, I. Y., & Varol, C. (2020, June). Intelligence in digital forensics process. In *2020 8th International Symposium on Digital Forensics and Security (ISDFS)* (pp. 1-6). IEEE. DOI: 10.1109/ISDFS49300.2020.9116442

Costantini, S., De Gasperis, G., & Olivieri, R. (2019). Digital forensics and investigations meet artificial intelligence. *Annals of Mathematics and Artificial Intelligence*, 86(1), 193–229. DOI: 10.1007/s10472-019-09632-y

Dunsin, D., Ghanem, M. C., Ouazzane, K., & Vassilev, V. (2024). A comprehensive analysis of the role of artificial intelligence and machine learning in modern digital forensics and incident response. *Forensic Science International Digital Investigation*, 48, 301675. DOI: 10.1016/j.fsidi.2023.301675

Dunsin, D., Ghanem, M. C., & Quazzane, K. (2022). The use of artificial intelligence in digital forensics and incident response in a constrained environment. *International Journal of Information and Communication Engineering*, 16(8), 280–285.

Ganesh, V. (2017). Artificial intelligence applied to computer forensics. *International Journal (Toronto, Ont.)*, 5(5).

Gholami, S., & Omar, M. (2023). Does Synthetic Data Make Large Language Models More Efficient? *arXiv preprint arXiv:2310.07830.*

Gholami, S., & Omar, M. (2024). Can a student large language model perform as well as its teacher? In *Innovations, Securities, and Case Studies Across Healthcare, Business, and Technology* (pp. 122-139). IGI Global. DOI: 10.4018/979-8-3693-1906-2.ch007

Hall, S. W., Sakzad, A., & Choo, K. K. R. (2022). Explainable artificial intelligence for digital forensics. *Wiley Interdisciplinary Reviews: Forensic Science*, 4(2), e1434.

Hamza, Y. A., & Omar, M. D. (2013). Cloud computing security: Abuse and nefarious use of cloud computing. *International Journal of Computer Engineering Research*, 3(6), 22–27.

Huff, A. J., Burrell, D. N., Nobles, C., Richardson, K., Wright, J. B., Burton, S. L., Jones, A. J., Springs, D., Omar, M., & Brown-Jackson, K. L. (2023). Management Practices for Mitigating Cybersecurity Threats to Biotechnology Companies, Laboratories, and Healthcare Research Organizations. In *Applied Research Approaches to Technology, Healthcare, and Business* (pp. 1-12). IGI Global.

Iqbal, F., Debbabi, M., Fung, B. C., Iqbal, F., Debbabi, M., & Fung, B. C. (2020). Artificial intelligence and digital forensics. *Machine Learning for Authorship Attribution and Cyber Forensics*, 139-150.

Irons, A., & Lallie, H. S. (2014). Digital forensics to intelligent forensics. *Future Internet*, 6(3), 584–596. DOI: 10.3390/fi6030584

Jarrett, A., & Choo, K. K. R. (2021). The impact of automation and artificial intelligence on digital forensics. *WIREs Forensic Science*, 3(6), e1418. DOI: 10.1002/wfs2.1418

Jeong, D. (2020). Artificial intelligence security threat, crime, and forensics: Taxonomy and open issues. *IEEE Access : Practical Innovations, Open Solutions*, 8, 184560–184574. DOI: 10.1109/ACCESS.2020.3029280

Jones, R., & Omar, M. (2024). Revolutionizing Cybersecurity: The GPT-2 Enhanced Attack Detection and Defense (GEADD) Method for Zero-Day Threats. *International Journal of Informatics* [INJIISCOM]. *Information System and Computer Engineering*, 5(2), 178–191.

Jones, R., Omar, M., Mohammed, D., Nobles, C., & Dawson, M. (2023). Harnessing the Speed and Accuracy of Machine Learning to Advance Cybersecurity. In *2023 Congress in Computer Science, Computer Engineering, & Applied Computing (CSCE)* (pp. 418-421). IEEE. DOI: 10.1109/CSCE60160.2023.00074

Karthikeyan, P., Pande, H. M., & Sarveshwaran, V. (Eds.). (2023). *Artificial intelligence and blockchain in digital forensics*. CRC Press.

Kelly, L., Sachan, S., Ni, L., Almaghrabi, F., Allmendinger, R., & Chen, Y. (2020). *Explainable artificial intelligence for digital forensics: opportunities, challenges and a drug testing case study*. Digital Forensic Science.

Manasa, S., & Kumar, K. P. (2022). Digital forensics investigation for attacks on artificial intelligence. *ECS Transactions*, 107(1), 19639–19645. DOI: 10.1149/10701.19639ecst

Mitchell, F. R. (2014). An overview of artificial intelligence based pattern matching in a security and digital forensic context. *Cyberpatterns: Unifying Design Patterns with Security and Attack Patterns*, 215-222.

Mohammed, D., Omar, M., & Nguyen, V. (2018). Wireless sensor network security: Approaches to detecting and avoiding wormhole attacks. *Journal of Research in Business. Economics and Management*, 10(2), 1860–1864.

Moustafa, N. (2022). *Digital Forensics in the Era of Artificial Intelligence*. CRC Press. DOI: 10.1201/9781003278962

Nguyen, V., Mohammed, D., Omar, M., & Banisakher, M. (2018). The Effects of the FCC Net Neutrality Repeal on Security and Privacy. [IJHIoT]. *International Journal of Hyperconnectivity and the Internet of Things*, 2(2), 21–29. DOI: 10.4018/IJHIoT.2018070102

Omar, M. (2021). New insights into database security: An effective and integrated approach for applying access control mechanisms and cryptographic concepts in Microsoft Access environments.

Omar, M. (2022). *Machine Learning for Cybersecurity: Innovative Deep Learning Solutions*. Springer Brief. https://link.springer.com/book/978303115

Omar, M. (2024). From Attack to Defense: Strengthening DNN Text Classification Against Adversarial Examples. In *Innovations, Securities, and Case Studies Across Healthcare, Business, and Technology* (pp. 174-195). IGI Global.

Omar, M. (2024). Revolutionizing Malware Detection: A Paradigm Shift Through Optimized Convolutional Neural Networks. In *Innovations, Securities, and Case Studies Across Healthcare, Business, and Technology* (pp. 196-220). IGI Global. DOI: 10.4018/979-8-3693-1906-2.ch011

Omar, M., & Zangana, H. M. (Eds.). (2024). *Redefining Security With Cyber AI*. IGI Global., DOI: 10.4018/979-8-3693-6517-5

Omar, M., & Zangana, H. M. (Eds.). (2025). *Application of Large Language Models (LLMs) for Software Vulnerability Detection*. IGI Global., DOI: 10.4018/979-8-3693-9311-6

Rizvi, S., Scanlon, M., Mcgibney, J., & Sheppard, J. (2022). Application of artificial intelligence to network forensics: Survey, challenges and future directions. *IEEE Access : Practical Innovations, Open Solutions*, 10, 110362–110384. DOI: 10.1109/ACCESS.2022.3214506

Rughani, P. H. (2017). Artificial Intelligence Based Digital Forensics Framework. *International Journal of Advanced Research in Computer Science*, 8(8), 10–14. DOI: 10.26483/ijarcs.v8i8.4571

Sikos, L. F. (2021). AI in digital forensics: Ontology engineering for cybercrime investigations. *WIREs Forensic Science*, 3(3), e1394. DOI: 10.1002/wfs2.1394

Tyagi, A. K., Kumari, S., & Richa. (2024). Artificial Intelligence-Based Cyber Security and Digital Forensics: A Review. *Artificial Intelligence-Enabled Digital Twin for Smart Manufacturing*, 391-419.

Wright, J., Dawson, M. E.Jr, & Omar, M. (2012). Cyber security and mobile threats: The need for antivirus applications for smartphones. *Journal of Information Systems Technology and Planning*, 5(14), 40–60.

Zangana, H. M., Mohammed, A. K., Sallow, A. B., & Sallow, Z. B. (2024). Cybernetic Deception: Unraveling the Layers of Email Phishing Threats. [INJURATECH]. *International Journal of Research and Applied Technology*, 4(1), 35–47.

Zangana, H. M., & Mohammed, D. (2025). Foundations of Large Language Models in Software Vulnerability Detection. In Omar, M., & Zangana, H. (Eds.), *Application of Large Language Models (LLMs) for Software Vulnerability Detection* (pp. 41–74). IGI Global., DOI: 10.4018/979-8-3693-9311-6.ch002

Zangana, H. M., & Omar, M. (2020). Threats, Attacks, and Mitigations of Smartphone Security. *Academic Journal of Nawroz University*, 9(4), 324–332. DOI: 10.25007/ajnu.v9n4a989

Zangana, H. M., & Omar, M. (2025). Harnessing the Power of Large Language Models for Cybersecurity: Applications, Challenges, and Future Directions. In Omar, M., & Zangana, H. (Eds.), *Application of Large Language Models (LLMs) for Software Vulnerability Detection* (pp. 1–40). IGI Global., DOI: 10.4018/979-8-3693-9311-6.ch001

Compilation of References

Aaron, W. C., Irekponor, O., Aleke, N. T., Yeboah, L., & Joseph, J. E. (2024). *Machine learning techniques for enhancing security in financial technology systems.*

Abrahamsen, F. E., Ai, Y., & Cheffena, M. (2021). Communication technologies for Smart Grid: A comprehensive survey. *Sensors (Basel)*, 21(23), 8087. DOI: 10.3390/s21238087 PMID: 34884092

Adadi, A., & Berrada, M. (2018). Peeking Inside the Black-Box: A Survey on Explainable Artificial Intelligence (XAI). *IEEE Access : Practical Innovations, Open Solutions*, 6, 52138–52160. DOI: 10.1109/ACCESS.2018.2870052

Adam, I. Y., & Varol, C. (2020, June). Intelligence in digital forensics process. In *2020 8th International Symposium on Digital Forensics and Security (ISDFS)* (pp. 1-6). IEEE. DOI: 10.1109/ISDFS49300.2020.9116442

Agrawal, V. (2024). 20 Emerging Cybersecurity Trends to Watch Out in 2025. *Simplilearn.* https://www.simplilearn.com/top-cybersecurity-trends-article

Ahmad Aminu, A., Nnanna Agwu, N., & Steve, A. (2021). Detection and Localization of Image Tampering using Deep Residual UNET with Stacked Dilated Convolution. In *IJCSNS International Journal of Computer Science and Network Security* (Vol. 21, Issue 9). DOI: 10.22937/IJCSNS.2021.21.9.28

Al-Awami, S. H., Al-Aty, M. M., & Al-Najar, M. F. (2023). Comparison of IoT architectures based on the seven essential characteristics. *2023 IEEE 3rd International Maghreb Meeting of the Conference on Sciences and Techniques of Automatic Control and Computer Engineering (MI-STA).* DOI: 10.1109/MI-STA57575.2023.10169289

Alazab, M., Venkatraman, S., & Watters, P. (2009). Effective digital forensic analysis of the NTFS disk image. *Ubiquitous Computing and Communication Journal*, 4(1), 551–558.

Aleke, N. (2024). *Combatting deep fakes: Ethical frameworks and technological solutions for preserving integrity in digital media*. Retrieved from https://doi.org/.DOI: 10.4018/979-8-3693-93116.ch010

Alghamdi, M. I. (2021). Digital Forensics in Cyber Security—Recent Trends, Threats, and Opportunities. *IntechOpen*. https://www.intechopen.com/chapters/76151

Alhindi, T. J., Kalra, S., Ng, K. H., Afrin, A., & Tizhoosh, H. R. (2018). *Comparing LBP, HOG and Deep Features for Classification of Histopathology Images*. http://arxiv.org/abs/1805.05837 DOI: 10.1109/IJCNN.2018.8489329

Ali, S. S., Ganapathi, I. I., Vu, N.-S., Ali, S. D., Saxena, N., & Werghi, N. (2022). Image Forgery Detection Using Deep Learning by Recompressing Images. *Electronics (Basel)*, 11(3), 403. DOI: 10.3390/electronics11030403

Al-Shamasneh, A. R., & Ibrahim, R. W. (2024). Image Splicing Forgery Detection Using Feature-Based of Sonine Functions and Deep Features. *Computers, Materials & Continua*, 78(1), 795–810. DOI: 10.32604/cmc.2023.042755

Altaleb, H., & Zoltán, R. (2023, November 1). Addressing cybersecurity challenges in 5G-enabled IoT and critical infrastructures: A comprehensive overview. *2023 IEEE 27th International Conference on Intelligent Engineering Systems (INES)*. DOI: 10.1109/INES59282.2023.10297774

Antwi-Boasiako, A., & Venter, H. (2017). *A model for digital evidence admissibility assessment*. Advances in Digital Forensics XIII. DOI: 10.1007/978-3-319-67208-3_2

Ardizzone, E., Bruno, A., & Mazzola, G. (2015a). Copy–Move Forgery Detection by Matching Triangles of Keypoints. *IEEE Transactions on Information Forensics and Security*, 10(10), 2084–2094. DOI: 10.1109/TIFS.2015.2445742

Balogun, A. M., & Zuva, T. (2017). *Open ethical issues in digital forensic systems*. International Journal of eBusiness and eGovernment Studies, 9(1), 55–71.

Bappy, J. H., Simons, C., Nataraj, L., Manjunath, B. S., & Roy-Chowdhury, A. K. (2019). Hybrid LSTM and Encoder–Decoder Architecture for Detection of Image Forgeries. *IEEE Transactions on Image Processing*, 28(7), 3286–3300. DOI: 10.1109/TIP.2019.2895466 PMID: 30703026

Begg, D. (2024). Applications and Challenges of Artificial Intelligence for Digital Forensics. *Westoahu Cybersecurity*. https://westoahu.hawaii.edu/cyber/forensics-weekly-executive-summmaries/applications-and-challenges-of-artificial-intelligence-for-digital-forensics/

Bhat, W. A., & Quadri, S. M. K. (2010). Review of FAT data structure of FAT32 file system. *Oriental Journal of Computer Science & Technology*, 3(1), 161–164.

Bhawna, & Mahajan, S. (2024). Artificial Intelligence Perspective on Digital Forensics. *Applying Artificial Intelligence in Cybersecurity Analytics and Cyber Threat Detection*, 33-44.

Bradbury, D. (2011). Point to own: The problem with hacking tools. *Computer Fraud & Security*, 2011(11), 12–14. DOI: 10.1016/S1361-3723(11)70114-2

Buyya, R., Vecchiola, C., & Selvi, S. T. (2013). *Mastering cloud computing: foundations and applications programming*. Newnes.

Casino, F., Dasaklis, T. K., Spathoulas, G. P., Anagnostopoulos, M., Ghosal, A., Borocz, I., Solanas, A., Conti, M., & Patsakis, C. (2022). Research trends, challenges, and emerging topics in digital forensics: A review of reviews. *IEEE Access : Practical Innovations, Open Solutions*, 10, 25464–25493. DOI: 10.1109/ACCESS.2022.3154059

Chakraborty, S., Chatterjee, K., & Dey, P. (2022a). *Detection of Image Tampering Using Deep Learning, Error Levels & Noise Residuals*. 1–17. DOI: 10.21203/rs.3.rs-2174562/v1

Chakraborty, S., Chatterjee, K., & Dey, P. (2022b). Discovering Tampered Image in Social Media Using ELA and Deep Learning. *SN Computer Science*, 3(5), 392. DOI: 10.1007/s42979-022-01311-w

Chao, Z., Pu, F., Yin, Y., Han, B., & Chen, X. (2018). Research on real-time local rainfall prediction based on MEMS sensors. In *Journal of Sensors* (Vol. 2018). DOI: 10.1155/2018/6184713

Chatzimiltis, S., Shojafar, M., Mashhadi, M., & Tafazolli, R. (2024). A collaborative Software Defined Network-Based Smart Grid Intrusion Detection System. *IEEE Open Journal of the Communications Society*, 5, 700–711. DOI: 10.1109/OJCOMS.2024.3351088

Chen, L.-C., Papandreou, G., Schroff, F., & Adam, H. (2017). *Rethinking Atrous Convolution for Semantic Image Segmentation*. http://arxiv.org/abs/1706.05587

Cho, G.-S. (2015). Development of an anti-forensic tool for hiding message in a directory index of NTFS. *2015 World Congress on Internet Security (WorldCIS)*, 144–145. https://doi.org/DOI: 10.1109/WorldCIS.2015.7359431

Chow, K. P., Law, F. Y., Kwan, M. Y., & Lai, P. K. (2007, April). The rules of time on NTFS file system. In *Proceedings of the Second International Workshop on Systematic Approaches to Digital Forensic Engineering (SADFE)* (pp. 71–85). IEEE. DOI: 10.1109/SADFE.2007.22

Cohen, F. B. (2010). *Digital forensic evidence examination*. Asp Press.

Colak, A., Guler, N., & Ahmed, K. (2021). Intelligent communication techniques for Smart Grid systems: A survey. *2021 9th International Conference on Smart Grid (IcSmartGrid)*. DOI: 10.1109/icSmartGrid52357.2021.9551027

Costantini, S., De Gasperis, G., & Olivieri, R. (2019). Digital forensics and investigations meet artificial intelligence. *Annals of Mathematics and Artificial Intelligence*, 86(1), 193–229. DOI: 10.1007/s10472-019-09632-y

Craiger, P., & Burke, P. K. (2005). Mac forensics: Mac OS X and the HFS+ file system. *Department of Engineering Technology, University of Central Florida*. Retrieved from https://stars.library.ucf.edu/etd/2167/

Cyber Writers Team. (2023) *What is Digital Forensics? Tools, Types, Phases & History* Cybersecuritynews. Retrieved from https://cybersecuritynews.com/what-is-digital-forensics/

Cybersecurity and Infrastructure Security Agency. (2021). *Potential Threat Vectors To 5G Infrastructure*. Cybersecurity and Infrastructure Security Agency. https://www.cisa.gov/sites/default/files/publications/potential-threat-vectors-5G- infrastructure_508_v2_0%2520%25281%2529.pdf

Cybersecurity in 2024: USB devices continue to pose major threat. Honeywell. (2024). https://www.honeywell.com/us/en/news/2024/04/cybersecurity-in-2024-usb-devices-continue-to-pose-major-threat

D'Orazio, C., Ariffin, A., & Choo, K.-K. R. (2014). iOS Anti-forensics: How can we securely conceal, delete, and insert data? *2014 47th Hawaii International Conference on System Sciences*, 460, 4838–4847. https://doi.org/DOI: 10.1109/HICSS.2014.594

Das, D., & Naskar, R. (2024). Image splicing detection using low-dimensional feature vector of texture features and Haralick features based on Gray Level Co-occurrence Matrix. *Signal Processing Image Communication*, 125, 117134. Advance online publication. DOI: 10.1016/j.image.2024.117134

Deloitte. (2020, March 10). *Global cyber executive briefing*. Deloitte; Deloitte Global. https://www.deloitte.com/global/en/services/risk-advisory/research/Telecommunications.html

Diallo, B., Urruty, T., Bourdon, P., & Fernandez-Maloigne, C. (2019). Improving Robustness of Image Tampering Detection for Compression. In *Lecture Notes in Computer Science (including subseries Lecture Notes in Artificial Intelligence and Lecture Notes in Bioinformatics): Vol. 11295 LNCS* (pp. 387–398). DOI: 10.1007/978-3-030-05710-7_32

Digital Forensics Research Workshop. (n.d.). An analysis of Ext4 for digital forensics. Retrieved from https://dfrws.org/archives/papers/ext4-forensics.pdf

Dijana, T., Zupancic, I., Grgic, S., & Grgic, M. (2013). CoMoFoD—New database for copy-move forgery detection (pp. 49–54). In *Proceedings ELMAR-2013.*

Ding, H., Chen, L., Tao, Q., Fu, Z., Dong, L., & Cui, X. (2023). DCU-Net: A dual-channel U-shaped network for image splicing forgery detection. *Neural Computing & Applications*, 35(7), 5015–5031. DOI: 10.1007/s00521-021-06329-4 PMID: 34404963

Ding, J., Nemati, M., Ranaweera, C., & Choi, J. (2020). IoT connectivity technologies and applications: A survey. *IEEE Access : Practical Innovations, Open Solutions*, 8, 67646–67673. DOI: 10.1109/ACCESS.2020.2985932

Dixit, U., Vittal, S., & A, A. F. (2024). A systematic study for understanding the security risks in 5G Core network. *2024 16th International Conference on COMmunication Systems & NETworkS (COMSNETS)*, 43–48. DOI: 10.1109/COMSNETS59351.2024.10427440

Dong, J., Wang, W., & Tan, T. (2013). CASIA Image Tampering Detection Evaluation Database. *2013 IEEE China Summit and International Conference on Signal and Information Processing*, 422–426. DOI: 10.1109/ChinaSIP.2013.6625374

Dunsin, D., Ghanem, M. C., Ouazzane, K., & Vassilev, V. T. (2024). A comprehensive analysis of the role of artificial intelligence and machine learning in modern digital forensics and incident response. *ResearchGate*. https://www.researchgate.net/publication/378241312_A_comprehensive_analysis_of_the_role_of_artificial_intelligence_and_machine_learning_in_modern_digital_forensics_and_incident_response

Dunsin, D., Ghanem, M. C., Ouazzane, K., & Vassilev, V. (2024). A comprehensive analysis of the role of artificial intelligence and machine learning in modern digital forensics and incident response. *Forensic Science International Digital Investigation*, 48, 301675. DOI: 10.1016/j.fsidi.2023.301675

Dunsin, D., Ghanem, M. C., & Quazzane, K. (2022). The use of artificial intelligence in digital forensics and incident response in a constrained environment. *International Journal of Information and Communication Engineering*, 16(8), 280–285.

EaseUS. (n.d.). File system comparison: NTFS, FAT32, exFAT, and EXT. Retrieved from https://www.easeus.com/diskmanager/file-system.html

Easttom, C. (2022). *Digital forensics, investigation, and response* (4th ed.). Jones & Bartlett Learning.

El-din, E. A. A. (2022). Artificial Intelligence in Forensic Science: Invasion or Revolution? *Egyptian Society of Clinical Toxicology Journal, 10*(2), 20-32. https://esctj.journals.ekb.eg/article_272046_4694247be2fec3aa3f89e32768714bae.pdf

Ericsson. (2022). *5G Core (5GC) network: Get to the core of 5G*. Ericsson.com. https://www.ericsson.com/en/core-network/5g-core

Ericsson. (2024). *Study of 5G as enabler of new power grid architectures*. Ericsson.com. https://www.ericsson.com/en/reports-and-papers/industrylab/reports/bringing-5g-to-power

Esenogho, E., Djouani, K., & Kurien, A. (2022). Integrating Artificial Intelligence Internet of Things and 5G for Next-Generation Smartgrid: A survey of trends challenges and prospect. *IEEE Access : Practical Innovations, Open Solutions*, 10, 1–1. DOI: 10.1109/ACCESS.2022.3140595

Experts question opaque Cybercheck AI crime fighting tool. (2024). AIAAIC. Retrieved from Ghonge, M. M., Pramanik, S., Mangrulkar, R., & Le, D. N. (2022). *Cyber security and digital forensics: Challenges and future trends*. John Wiley & Sons. Github. John The Ripper. Retrieved from https://github.com/magnumripper/

Fakhrulddin Abdulqader, M., Dawod, A. Y., & Zeki Ablahd, A. (2023). Detection of tamper forgery image in security digital mage. *Measurement. Sensors*, 27, 100746. DOI: 10.1016/j.measen.2023.100746

Fan, Y., Li, Y., Zhan, M., Cui, H., & Zhang, Y. (2020). IoTDefender: A Federated Transfer Learning Intrusion Detection framework for 5G IoT. *2020 IEEE 14th International Conference on Big Data Science and Engineering (BigDataSE)*. DOI: 10.1109/BigDataSE50710.2020.00020

Faquir, D., Chouliaras, N., Sofia, V., Olga, K., & Maglaras, L. (2021). Cybersecurity in smart grids, challenges and solutions. *AIMS Electronics and Electrical Engineering*, 5(1), 24–37. DOI: 10.3934/electreng.2021002

Flinders, M., & Smalley, I. (2024, February 20). *What is 5G?* IBM. https://www.ibm.com/topics/5g

Forensics Community. (n.d.). DiffFork. Retrieved from https://github.com/forensics/difffork

Forensics, O. History of Digital Forensics. Retrieved from https://www.oxygenforensics.com

Fortinet. (2023). *Top IoT device vulnerabilities: How to secure IoT devices*. Fortinet. https://www.fortinet.com/resources/cyberglossary/iot-device-vulnerabilities

Franco, D., Fuschini, D., & Rodrigues, T. (2016). How to detect anti-forensic techniques. *eForensics*, 45-69.

Fridrich, J., & Kodovský, J. (2012). *Rich Models for Steganalysis of Digital Images*.

Ganesh, V. (2017). Artificial intelligence applied to computer forensics. *International Journal (Toronto, Ont.)*, 5(5).

Ganguly, S., Mohiuddin, S., Malakar, S., Cuevas, E., & Sarkar, R. (2022). Visual attention-based deepfake video forgery detection. *Pattern Analysis & Applications*, 25(4), 981–992. DOI: 10.1007/s10044-022-01083-2

Gaona, J. (2024). The Role of AI in Forensics. *Marymount University*. https://marymount.edu/blog/the-role-of-ai-in-forensics/

Gao, Z., Sun, C., Cheng, Z., Guan, W., Liu, A., & Wang, M. (2022). TBNet: A Two-Stream Boundary-Aware Network for Generic Image Manipulation Localization. *IEEE Transactions on Knowledge and Data Engineering*, •••, 1–16. DOI: 10.1109/TKDE.2022.3187091

Ghannam, H., & Darwazeh, I. (2019, June 27). A proposal for scalable 5G new radio frames with enhanced throughput. *2019 IEEE 89th Vehicular Technology Conference (VTC2019-Spring)*. DOI: 10.1109/VTCSpring.2019.8746532

Gholami, S., & Omar, M. (2023). Does Synthetic Data Make Large Language Models More Efficient? *arXiv preprint arXiv:2310.07830.*

Gholami, S., & Omar, M. (2024). Can a student large language model perform as well as its teacher? In *Innovations, Securities, and Case Studies Across Healthcare, Business, and Technology* (pp. 122-139). IGI Global. DOI: 10.4018/979-8-3693-1906-2.ch007

Goldman, D. (2015). Navy pays Microsoft $9 million a year for Windows XP. CNN Business. https://money.cnn.com/2015/06/26/technology/microsoft-windows-xp-navy-contract/index.html

Graphica. (2020). *An introduction to 5G architecture*. Graphica. https://just.graphica.com.au/an- introduction-to-5g-architecture/

Greengard, S. (2023, April 28). *Internet ofThings | electronic network*. Encyclopedia Britannica. https://www.britannica.com/science/Internet-of-Things

Grugq. (2005). The art of defiling: Defeating forensic analysis. *Blackhat Briefings*.

Gubanov, Y. (2022). *Preserving chain of custody in digital forensics*. Belkasoft, LinkedIn. Retrieved from https://www.linkedin.com/pulse/preserving-chain-custody-digital-forensics-belkasoft/

Guillaro, F., Cozzolino, D., Sud, A., Dufour, N., & Verdoliva, L. (2023). *TruFor: Leveraging All-Round Clues for Trustworthy Image Forgery Detection and Localization*. 20606–20615. DOI: 10.1109/CVPR52729.2023.01974

Gul, M., & Kugu, E. (2017). A survey on anti-forensics techniques. *2017 International Artificial Intelligence and Data Processing Symposium (IDAP)*, 10 2, 1–6. https://doi.org/DOI: 10.1109/IDAP.2017.8090341

Hall, S. W., Sakzad, A., & Choo, K. K. R. (2022). Explainable artificial intelligence for digital forensics. *Wiley Interdisciplinary Reviews: Forensic Science*, 4(2), e1434.

Hamza, Y. A., & Omar, M. D. (2013). Cloud computing security: Abuse and nefarious use of cloud computing. *International Journal of Computer Engineering Research*, 3(6), 22–27.

Hawaii International Conference on System Sciences, Kauai, HI, USA, January 4–7, 2011, 1–6. Retrieved from .DOI: 10.1109/HICSS.2011.282

Hermon, R., Singh, U., & Singh, B. (2022). Anti-forensic technique using alternate data streams for data hiding in NTFS. *2022 International Conference on Futuristic Technologies (INCOFT)*, 1, 1–5. https://doi.org/DOI: 10.1109/INCOFT55651.2022.10094445

Hong, R.-F., Horng, S.-C., & Lin, S.-S. (2021, November 1). *Machine learning in cyber security analytics using NSL-KDD dataset*. IEEE Xplore. DOI: 10.1109/TAAI54685.2021.00057

Hosny, K. M., Mortda, A. M., Lashin, N. A., & Fouda, M. M. (2023). A New Method to Detect Splicing Image Forgery Using Convolutional Neural Network. *Applied Sciences (Basel, Switzerland)*, 13(3), 1272. Advance online publication. DOI: 10.3390/app13031272

Hsu, Y., & Chang, S. (2006). Detecting Image Splicing using Geometry Invariants and Camera Characteristics Consistency. *2006 IEEE International Conference on Multimedia and Expo*, 549–552. DOI: 10.1109/ICME.2006.262447

Huang, H.-Y., & Ciou, A.-J. (2019). Copy-move forgery detection for image forensics using the superpixel segmentation and the Helmert transformation. *EURASIP Journal on Image and Video Processing*, 2019(1), 68. DOI: 10.1186/s13640-019-0469-9

Huff, A. J., Burrell, D. N., Nobles, C., Richardson, K., Wright, J. B., Burton, S. L., Jones, A. J., Springs, D., Omar, M., & Brown-Jackson, K. L. (2023). Management Practices for Mitigating Cybersecurity Threats to Biotechnology Companies, Laboratories, and Healthcare Research Organizations. In *Applied Research Approaches to Technology, Healthcare, and Business* (pp. 1-12). IGI Global.

IHS Markit, & Omdia. (2020). *The 5G economy in a post-COVID-19 era*. IHS Markit. https://www.qualcomm.com/content/%20dam/qcomm-martech/dm- assets/documents/qualcomm_5g_economy_in_%20a_post-pandemic_era_report_2020.pdf

InfoSec Institute. (n.d.). Computer forensics: Media & file system forensics. Retrieved from https://www.infosecinstitute.com/resources/digital-forensics/computer-forensics-media-file-system-forensics/

International Energy Agency. (2023, July 11). *Smart Grids*. IEA. https://www.iea.org/energy- system/electricity/smart-grids

International Research Journal of Engineering and Technology. (2021). Comparative study on various file system implementations. *International Research Journal of Engineering and Technology, 8*(11), 123–130. Retrieved from https://www.irjet.net/archives/V8/i11/IRJET-V8I11190.pdf

IP with Ease. (n.d.). NTFS file system guide. Retrieved from https://ipwithease.com/ntfs-file-system/

Iqbal, F., Debbabi, M., Fung, B. C., Iqbal, F., Debbabi, M., & Fung, B. C. (2020). Artificial intelligence and digital forensics. *Machine Learning for Authorship Attribution and Cyber Forensics*, 139-150.

Iqbal, W., Abbas, H., Daneshmand, M., Rauf, B., & Abbas, Y. (2020). An in-depth analysis of IoT security requirements, challenges and their countermeasures via software defined security. *IEEE Internet of Things Journal*, 7(10), 1–1. DOI: 10.1109/JIOT.2020.2997651

Irons, A., & Lallie, H. S. (2014). Digital forensics to intelligent forensics. *Future Internet*, 6(3), 584–596. DOI: 10.3390/fi6030584

Islam, M. M., Karmakar, G., Kamruzzaman, J., Murshed, M., Kahandawa, G., & Parvin, N. (2018). Detecting Splicing and Copy-Move Attacks in Color Images. *2018 Digital Image Computing: Techniques and Applications (DICTA)*, 1–7. DOI: 10.1109/DICTA.2018.8615874

Jarrett, A., & Choo, K. K. R. (2021). The impact of automation and artificial intelligence on digital forensics. *WIREs Forensic Science*, 3(6), e1418. DOI: 10.1002/wfs2.1418

Jeong, D. (2020). Artificial intelligence security threat, crime, and forensics: Taxonomy and open issues. *IEEE Access : Practical Innovations, Open Solutions*, 8, 184560–184574. DOI: 10.1109/ACCESS.2020.3029280

Jobin, A., Ienca, M., & Vayena, E. (2019). The global landscape of AI ethics guidelines. *Nature Machine Intelligence*, 1(9), 389–399. https://www.nature.com/articles/s42256019-0088-2. DOI: 10.1038/s42256-019-0088-2

Jones, R., Omar, M., Mohammed, D., Nobles, C., & Dawson, M. (2023). Harnessing the Speed and Accuracy of Machine Learning to Advance Cybersecurity. In *2023 Congress in Computer Science, Computer Engineering, & Applied Computing (CSCE)* (pp. 418-421). IEEE. DOI: 10.1109/CSCE60160.2023.00074

Jones, A., & Omar, M. (2024). Codesentry: Revolutionizing Real-Time Software Vulnerability Detection With Optimized GPT Framework. *Land Forces Academy Review*, 29(1), 98–107. DOI: 10.2478/raft-2024-0010

Jones, R., & Omar, M. (2024). Revolutionizing Cybersecurity: The GPT-2 Enhanced Attack Detection and Defense (GEADD) Method for Zero-Day Threats. *International Journal of Informatics* [INJIISCOM]. *Information System and Computer Engineering*, 5(2), 178–191.

Jones, R., Omar, M., Mohammed, D., Nobles, C., & Dawson, M. (2023). *Harnessing the Speed and Accuracy of Machine Learning to Advance Cybersecurity. In 2023 Congress in Computer Science, Computer Engineering, & Applied Computing (CSCE)*. IEEE.

Jurva, G. (2024). Unlocking Justice: 2 Ways AI Is Impacting Evidence Analysis and Forensics. *Everlaw*. https://www.everlaw.com/blog/ai-and-law/unlocking-justice-ai-evidence-analysis-forensics/

Kadam, K. D., Ahirrao, S., & Kotecha, K. (2021). Multiple image splicing dataset (Misd): A dataset for multiple splicing. In *Data* (Vol. 6, Issue 10). DOI: 10.3390/data6100102

Kai, Z., En, C., & Qinquan, G. (2010). Analysis and implementation of NTFS file system based on computer forensics. *2010 Second International Workshop on Education Technology and Computer Science*, 27, 325–328. https://doi.org/DOI: 10.1109/ETCS.2010.434

Kalafatidis, S., Agrafiotis, G., Giapantzis, K., Lalas, A., & Votis, K. (2024). Experiments with digital security processes over SDN-based cloud-native 5G Core networks. *2024 27th Conference on Innovation in Clouds, Internet and Networks (ICIN)*. DOI: 10.1109/ICIN60470.2024.10494481

Karthikeyan, P., Pande, H. M., & Sarveshwaran, V. (Eds.). (2023). *Artificial intelligence and blockchain in digital forensics*. CRC Press.

Kazim, E., & Koshiyama, A. S. (2021). A high-level overview of AI ethics. *Patterns (New York, N.Y.)*, 2(10), 100333. https://www.cell.com/patterns/fulltext/S2666-3899(21)00157-4 PMID: 34553166

Kelly, L., Sachan, S., Ni, L., Almaghrabi, F., Allmendinger, R., & Chen, Y. (2020). *Explainable artificial intelligence for digital forensics: opportunities, challenges and a drug testing case study*. Digital Forensic Science.

Kerr, O. (2010). The Fourth Amendment and Digital Evidence. *The Journal of Legal Studies*.

Khaitan, A. (2023). Top 5 Trends For Digital Forensics in 2023. *Cyber Express*. https://thecyberexpress.com/top-5-trends-for-digital-forensics-in-2023/

Khan, A. A., Shaikh, A. A., Laghari, A. A., Dootio, M. A., Rind, M. M., & Awan, S. A. (2022). Digital forensics and cyber forensics investigation: Security challenges, limitations, and future directions. *International Journal of Electronic Security and Digital Forensics*, 14(2), 124–150. DOI: 10.1504/IJESDF.2022.121174

Khandelwal, S. (2017). *Here's the NSA employee who kept top secret documents at home*. The Hacker News. Retrieved from https://thehackernews.com/2017/12/nghia-hoang-pho-nsa.html/

Khudhair, Z. N., Mohamed, F., Rehman, A., Saba, T., & Bahaj, S. A. (2023). Detection of Copy-Move Forgery in Digital Images Using Singular Value Decomposition. *Computers, Materials & Continua*, 74(2), 4135–4147. DOI: 10.32604/cmc.2023.032315

Kim, K., Alshenaifi, I. M., Ramachandran, S., Kim, J., Zia, T., & Almorjan, A. (2023). Cybersecurity and Cyber Forensics for Smart Cities: A Comprehensive Literature Review and Survey. *Sensors (Basel)*, 23(7), 3681. DOI: 10.3390/s23073681 PMID: 37050740

Kosta, S., Jain, S., & Suwalka, I. (2024). AI Revolutionizing Forensic Analysis: Enhancing Efficiency and Accuracy in Crime Investigation. *International Advanced Research Journal in Science, Engineering and Technology, 11*(2), 226-229. https://iarjset.com/wp-content/uploads/2024/06/IARJSET-ICMART-41.pdf

Kumar, K., Sofat, S., Jain, S. K., & Aggarwal, N. (2012). *Significance of hash value generation in digital forensics: A case study.* CiteSeerX.

Le, L., Salem, B., Ahad, E., Aitsaadi, N., & Du, X. (2023). 5G-IoT-IDS: Intrusion Detection System for CIoT as Network Function in 5G Core network. *GLOBECOM 2023 - 2023 IEEE Global Communications Conference*. DOI: 10.1109/GLOBECOM54140.2023.10437158

Lee, S., Jo, W., Eo, S., & Shon, T. (2020). ExtSFR: Scalable file recovery framework based on an Ext file system. *Multimedia Tools and Applications*, 79(23), 16093–16111. DOI: 10.1007/s11042-019-7199-y

Li, F. (2024). Application and challenges of artificial intelligence in cybersecurity. *ResearchGate*. https://www.researchgate.net/publication/379012606_Application_and_challenges_of_artificial_intelligence_in_cybersecurity

Liang, E., Zhang, K., Hua, Z., & Jia, X. (2024). Multi-Scale Feature Attention Fusion for Image Splicing Forgery Detection. *ACM Transactions on Multimedia Computing Communications and Applications*, 3698770. Advance online publication. DOI: 10.1145/3698770

Linux Careers Blog. (2022, May). Linux file systems: ext3 vs. ext4. Retrieved from https://linuxcareers.com/blog/2022/05/linux-file-systems-ext3-vs-ext4

Linux Magazine. (2022). The filer. *Linux Magazine, 255.* Retrieved from https://linux-magazine.com/Issues/2022/255/The-Filer

Li, Q., Zhang, Q., Tan, Y. A., Li, Y., & Zheng, J. (2016, January). Research on allocator strategy of FAT32 file system based on Linux & Windows. In *Proceedings of the 2016 International Conference on Intelligent Control and Computer Application (ICCA)* (pp. 248–252). Atlantis Press. DOI: 10.2991/icca-16.2016.58

Liu, F., Liu, K.-S., Chang, C., & Wang, Y. (2016). Research on the technology of iOS jailbreak. *2016 Sixth International Conference on Instrumentation & Measurement, Computer, Communication and Control (IMCCC)*, 644–647. https://doi.org/ DOI: 10.1109/IMCCC.2016.178

Long Path Tool. (n.d.). Long Path Tool. Retrieved from https://longpathtool.com/

Lu, C., Tao, Z., & Yuanyuan, M. (2023). A 5G slice traffic anomaly detection method based on convolution neural network. *2022 7th International Conference on Signal and Image Processing (ICSIP), 34*, 963–967. DOI: 10.1109/ICSIP57908.2023.10270927

Lu, M., & Niu, S. (2020). A detection approach using lstm-cnn for object removal caused by exemplar-based image inpainting. In *Electronics (Switzerland)* (Vol. 9, Issue 5). DOI: 10.3390/electronics9050858

Lu, L., Arpaci-Dusseau, A. C., Arpaci-Dusseau, R. H., & Lu, S. (2013). A study of Linux file system evolution. In *Proceedings of the 11th USENIX Conference on File and Storage Technologies (FAST 13)* (pp. 31–44). USENIX Association.

Lutkevich, B. (2021, April 21). What is NTFS and how does it work? TechTarget. https://www.techtarget.com/searchwindowsserver/definition/NTFS

Magnet Forensics. (n.d.). File system forensics: No longer the gold standard? Part 1. Retrieved from https://www.magnetforensics.com/blog/file-system-forensics-no-longer-the-gold-standard-part-1/

Malik, K. (2024). AI in Cybersecurity: Benefits and Challenges. *Astra*. https://www.getastra.com/blog/ai-security/ai-in-cybersecurity/

Malik, P., Dawar, H., Patel, P., Ahuja, D., & Jain, A. (2024). *Enhancing forensic analysis of digital evidence using machine learning: Techniques, applications, and challenges*. International Journal of Innovative Research in Multidisciplinary Perspectives and Studies (IJIRMPS), Sep-Oct 2024, 1–8. Retrieved from www.ijirmps.org

Manasa, S., & Kumar, K. P. (2022). Digital forensics investigation for attacks on artificial intelligence. *ECS Transactions*, 107(1), 19639–19645. DOI: 10.1149/10701.19639ecst

Maratsi, M. I., Popov, O., Alexopoulos, C., & Charalabidis, Y. (2022). Ethical and legal aspects of digital forensics algorithms: The case of digital evidence acquisition. In *Proceedings of the 15th International Conference on Theory and Practice of Electronic Governance (ICEGOV '22)* (pp. 32–40). Association for Computing Machinery. DOI: 10.1145/3560107.3560114

Mason, S. (Ed.). (2012). *Electronic evidence* (3rd ed.). LexisNexis Butterworths.

Mazumdar, A., & Bora, P. K. (2022). Two-stream encoder–decoder network for localizing image forgeries. *Journal of Visual Communication and Image Representation*, 82, 1–11. DOI: 10.1016/j.jvcir.2021.103417

McFarland, M. (2012). *Why we care about privacy.* Markkula Center for Applied Ethics at Santa Clara University. Retrieved from https://www.scu.edu/ethics/focus-areas/internet-ethics/resources/whywe-care-about-privacy/

Microsoft. (n.d.). Original DOS file system. Princeton University. Retrieved from https://mirror.math.princeton.edu/pub/oldlinux/Linux.old/distributions/cnix/FAT.pdf

Microtek Learning. (n.d.). Understanding hard disks and file systems. Retrieved from https://www.microteklearning.com/pdf/CHFIv10%20Course%20Outline.pdf

Mirzaee, P., Shojafar, M., Pooranian, Z., Asefy, P., Cruickshank, H., & Tafazolli, R. (2021). FIDS: A Federated Intrusion Detection System for 5G Smart Metering network. *2021 17th International Conference on Mobility, Sensing and Networking (MSN)*. DOI: 10.1109/MSN53354.2021.00044

Mitchell, F. R. (2014). An overview of artificial intelligence based pattern matching in a security and digital forensic context. *Cyberpatterns: Unifying Design Patterns with Security and Attack Patterns*, 215-222.

Mohammed, D., Omar, M., & Nguyen, V. (2018). Wireless sensor network security: Approaches to detecting and avoiding wormhole attacks. *Journal of Research in Business. Economics and Management*, 10(2), 1860–1864.

Mohyeldin, E. (2016). *Minimum technical performance requirements for IMT-2020 radio interface(s).* International Telecommunication Union. https://www.itu.int/en/ITU-R/study- groups/rsg5/rwp5d/imt-2020/Documents/S01-1_Requirements%20for%20IMT-2020_Rev.pdf

Moustafa, N. (2022). *Digital Forensics in the Era of Artificial Intelligence.* CRC Press. DOI: 10.1201/9781003278962

Nagm, A. M., Moussa, M. M., Shoitan, R., Ali, A., Mashhour, M., Salama, A. S., & Hamada, I. (2024). *Detecting image manipulation with ELA- CNN integration : a powerful framework for authenticity verifi cation*. 1–18. DOI: 10.7717/peerj-cs.2205

Nance, K., & Ryan, D. J. (2011). Legal aspects of digital forensics: A research agenda. 2011 44th

National Institute of Standards and Technology. (2019). *NVD - search and statistics*. Nist.gov. https://nvd.nist.gov/vuln/search

Nesbo, E. (2021, June 11). 5 ways Apple is securing your device right now. MUO. https://www.makeuseof.com/apple-more-secure-than-android/

Nguyen, H. L., & Huynh, K. T. (2023). *A Deep Learning Model for Splicing Image Detection*. REV Journal on Electronics and Communications., DOI: 10.21553/rev-jec.335

Nguyen, V., Mohammed, D., Omar, M., & Banisakher, M. (2018). The Effects of the FCC Net Neutrality Repeal on Security and Privacy. [IJHIoT]. *International Journal of Hyperconnectivity and the Internet of Things*, 2(2), 21–29. DOI: 10.4018/IJHIoT.2018070102

Niloy, F. F., Kumar Bhaumik, K., & Woo, S. S. (2023). CFL-Net: Image Forgery Localization Using Contrastive Learning. In *Proceedings - 2023 IEEE Winter Conference on Applications of Computer Vision, WACV 2023* (pp. 4631–4640). DOI: 10.1109/WACV56688.2023.00462

Ni, M. (2023). A review on machine learning methods for intrusion detection system. *Applied and Computational Engineering*, 27(1), 57–64. DOI: 10.54254/2755-2721/27/20230148

NIST 800-86. Guide to Integrating Forensic Techniques into Incident Response. Retrieved from https://www.researchgate.net/figure/NISTs-4-phases-forensic-model fig2 263619846/

Noonan, L. (2024). Exploring the Benefits and Challenges of AI in Cyber Security. *Meta Compliance*. https://www.metacompliance.com/blog/data-breaches/benefits-and-challenges-of-ai-in-cyber-security

Omar, M. (2021). New insights into database security: An effective and integrated approach for applying access control mechanisms and cryptographic concepts in Microsoft Access environments.

Omar, M. (2022). *Machine Learning for Cybersecurity: Innovative Deep Learning Solutions*. Springer Brief. https://link.springer.com/book/978303115

Omar, M. (2024). From Attack to Defense: Strengthening DNN Text Classification Against Adversarial Examples. In *Innovations, Securities, and Case Studies Across Healthcare, Business, and Technology* (pp. 174-195). IGI Global.

Omar, M. (2024). Revolutionizing Malware Detection: A Paradigm Shift Through Optimized Convolutional Neural Networks. In *Innovations, Securities, and Case Studies Across Healthcare, Business, and Technology* (pp. 196-220). IGI Global. DOI: 10.4018/979-8-3693-1906-2.ch011

Omar, M., & Zangana, H. M. (Eds.). (2024). *Redefining Security With Cyber AI.* IGI Global., DOI: 10.4018/979-8-3693-6517-5

Omar, M., & Zangana, H. M. (Eds.). (2025). *Application of Large Language Models (LLMs) for Software Vulnerability Detection.* IGI Global., DOI: 10.4018/979-8-3693-9311-6

Operating system market share worldwide. StatCounter Global Stats. (2024, September). https://gs.statcounter.com/os-market-share

Oracle. (n.d.). Understanding Ext4 disk layout, part 1. Retrieved from https://blogs.oracle.com/linux/post/understanding-ext4-disk-layout-part-1

Oracle. (n.d.). Understanding Ext4 disk layout, part 2. Retrieved from https://blogs.oracle.com/linux/post/understanding-ext4-disk-layout-part-2

Park, J., Cho, D., Ahn, W., & Lee, H. K. (2018). Double JPEG Detection in Mixed JPEG Quality Factors Using Deep Convolutional Neural Network. In *Lecture Notes in Computer Science (including subseries Lecture Notes in Artificial Intelligence and Lecture Notes in Bioinformatics): Vol. 11209 LNCS* (pp. 656–672). DOI: 10.1007/978-3-030-01228-1_39

Parkinson, S., & Khan, S. (2024). The role of Artificial Intelligence in digital forensics: Case studies and future directions. *Assessment & Development Matters*, 16(1), 42–47. DOI: 10.53841/bpsadm.2024.16.1.42

Pattnaik, P. (2024). The Impact Of Artificial Intelligence On Forensic Science. *Lawyers Club India.* https://www.lawyersclubindia.com/articles/the-impact-of-artificial-intelligence-on-forensic-science-16676.asp

Perklin, M. (2012). *Def Con.* In Anti-forensics and anti-anti-forensics. Las Vegas, Nevada; Def Con.

Prayudi, Y., & Sn, A. (2015). Digital Chain of Custody: State of the Art. *International Journal of Computer Applications*, 114(5), 1–9. DOI: 10.5120/19971-1856

Qazi, E. U. H., Zia, T., & Almorjan, A. (2022). Deep Learning-Based Digital Image Forgery Detection System. *Applied Sciences (Basel, Switzerland)*, 12(6), 2851. Advance online publication. DOI: 10.3390/app12062851

Rakas, B., Timčenko, V., Kabovic, M. M., & Kabovic, A. V. (2022). Intrusion Detection Systems in Smart Grid. *2022 21st International Symposium INFOTEH-JAHORINA (INFOTEH)*. DOI: 10.1109/INFOTEH53737.2022.9751302

Ramirez-Rodriguez, A. E., Arevalo-Ancona, R. E., Perez-Meana, H., Cedillo-Hernandez, M., & Nakano-Miyatake, M. (2024). AISMSNet: Advanced Image Splicing Manipulation Identification Based on Siamese Networks. *Applied Sciences (Basel, Switzerland)*, 14(13), 5545. Advance online publication. DOI: 10.3390/app14135545

Reddy, V., Vaghdevi, K., & Kolli, D. K. (2021). Digital image forgery detection using SUPER pixel segmentation and HYBRID feature point mapping. *European Journal of Molecular and Clinical Medicine*, 8(2), 1485–1500.

Rizvi, S., Scanlon, M., Mcgibney, J., & Sheppard, J. (2022). Application of artificial intelligence to network forensics: Survey, challenges and future directions. *IEEE Access : Practical Innovations, Open Solutions*, 10, 110362–110384. DOI: 10.1109/ACCESS.2022.3214506

Roddy, M., Truong, T., Walsh, P., Al Bado, M., Wu, Y., Healy, M., & Ahearne, S. (2019). 5G network slicing for mission-critical use cases. *2019 IEEE 2nd 5G World Forum (5GWF)*, 409–414. DOI: 10.1109/5GWF.2019.8911651

Roush, Z. (2024). Digital Forensics: The Good, the Bad, and the AI-Generated. *ACEDS*. https://aceds.org/digital-forensics-the-good-the-bad-and-the-ai-generated-aceds-blog/

Roux, B., & Falgoust, M. (2012). Ethical issues raised by data acquisition methods in digital forensics research. *Journal of Information Ethics*, 21(1), 40–60. DOI: 10.3172/JIE.21.1.40

Rughani, P. H. (2017). Artificial Intelligence Based Digital Forensics Framework. *International Journal of Advanced Research in Computer Science*, 8(8), 10–14. DOI: 10.26483/ijarcs.v8i8.4571

Saini, K., Sonone, S. S., Sankhla, M. S., & Kumar, N. (2024). Artificial Intelligence in Forensic Science: An Emerging Technology in Criminal Investigation Systems. *ResearchGate*. https://www.researchgate.net/publication/382035324_Artificial_Intelligence_in_Forensic_Science_An_Emerging_Technology_in_Criminal_Investigation_Systems

Saini, S. (2023). Unveiling the Impact of Artificial Intelligence in Forensic Science. *Geeta University*. https://blog.geetauniversity.edu.in/unveiling-the-impact-of-artificial-intelligence-in-forensic-science/

Sammons, J. (2014). *The Basics of Digital Forensics: The Primer for Getting Started in Digital Forensics*. Syngress.

Schneider, A. & Breitinger, F. (2023). Towards AI forensics: Did the artificial intelligence system do it?. *Journal of Information Security and Applications*. https://doi.org/DOI: 10.1016/j.jisa.2023.103517

Shafique, K., Khawaja, B. A., Sabir, F., Qazi, S., & Mustaqim, M. (2020). Internet of Things (IoT) for next- generation smart systems: A review of current challenges, future trends and prospects for emerging 5G-IoT scenarios. *IEEE Access : Practical Innovations, Open Solutions*, 8(8), 23022–23040. DOI: 10.1109/ACCESS.2020.2970118

Shamblin, Q. (2024, October 4). Alternate data streams overview. *SANS Digital Forensics and Incident Response Blog*. https://www.sans.org/blog/alternate-data-streams-overview/

Sharma, B. K., Joseph, M. A., Jacob, B., & Miranda, L. C. (2019). Emerging trends in Digital Forensic and Cyber security- An Overview. *2019 Sixth HCT Information Technology Trends (ITT)*, 309-313. https://www.semanticscholar.org/paper/Emerging-trends-in-Digital-Forensic-and-Cyber-An-Sharma-Joseph/503186f6126c8c7e3c265b8bdcfc71b61059bab1

Sharma, P., Kumar, M., & Sharma, H. (2023). Comprehensive analyses of image forgery detection methods from traditional to deep learning approaches: an evaluation. In *Multimedia Tools and Applications* (Vol. 82, Issue 12, pp. 18117–18150). DOI: 10.1007/s11042-022-13808-w

Sharma, V., Jha, S., & Kumar Bharti, R. (2016). Image Forgery and it's Detection Technique: A Review. In *International Research Journal of Engineering and Technology*.

Sikos, L. F. (2021). AI in digital forensics: Ontology engineering for cybercrime investigations. *WIREs Forensic Science*, 3(3), e1394. DOI: 10.1002/wfs2.1394

Singh, W. U., & Singh, K. P. (2023). The transformative role of artificial intelligence in forensic medicine and toxicology. *Journal of Medical Society*, 37(3), 101–102. https://journals.lww.com/jmso/fulltext/2023/37030/the_transformative_role_of_artificial_intelligence.1.aspx. DOI: 10.4103/jms.jms_54_24

Siwakoti, Y. R., Bhurtel, M., Rawat, D. B., Oest, A., & Johnson, R. (2023). Advances in IoT security: Vulnerabilities, enabled criminal services, attacks and countermeasures. *IEEE Internet of Things Journal*, 10(13), 1–1. DOI: 10.1109/JIOT.2023.3252594

Slonopas, A. (2024, March 15). What is digital forensics? A closer examination of the field. American Public University. https://www.apu.apus.edu/area-of-study/information-technology/resources/what-is-digital-forensics/

Solutions, A. D. F. Inc. (2023, July 28). Digital forensics: The military's secret to combating cyber threats. ADF. https://www.adfsolutions.com/adf-blog/digital-forensics-the-militarys-secret-weapon-to-combat-cyber-threats?srsltid=AfmBOooUar16dGj-mMR09kYxzt8zKU_4Ar0d1AnyLcQ9f-q6KmK40jeH

SourceForge. (n.d.). FileXray: Advanced file system analysis tool. Retrieved from https://filexray.sourceforge.net/

Sri, C. G., Bano, S., Deepika, T., Kola, N., & Pranathi, Y. L. (2021). Deep Neural Networks Based Error Level Analysis for Lossless Image Compression Based Forgery Detection. *2021 International Conference on Intelligent Technologies (CONIT)*, 1–8. DOI: 10.1109/CONIT51480.2021.9498357

Stelloh, T. (2024). *An AI tool used in thousands of criminal cases is facing legal challenges*. NBCNews. Retrieved from https://www.nbcnews.com/news/crime-courts/ai-tool-used-thousandscriminal-cases-facing-legal-challenges-rcna149607

Sterniczuk, B. (2022). Comparison of EXT4 and NTFS filesystem performance: Porównanie wydajności systemu plików EXT4 i NTFS. *Journal of Computer Sciences Institute*, 25, 297–300. DOI: 10.35784/jcsi.3004

Sudiatmika, I. B. K., Rahman, F., Trisno, T., & Suyoto, S. (2019). Image forgery detection using error level analysis and deep learning. [Telecommunication Computing Electronics and Control]. *TELKOMNIKA*, 17(2), 653. DOI: 10.12928/telkomnika.v17i2.8976

Sultan, A. (2022, August 8). *5G system overview*. 3GPP. https://www.3gpp.org/technologies/5g-system- overview

Sun, Y., Ni, R., & Zhao, Y. (2022). ET. *Edge-Enhanced Transformer for Image.*, 29, 1232–1236.

Suryal, A., Vishwakarma, P., & Malik, A. (2024). Impact of Artificial Intelligence in Digital Forensics: a Review Study. *EasyChair*. https://easychair.org/publications/preprint/52Gz

Tai, J. (n.d.). Hard disks and file systems. Retrieved from https://john.tai.dev/posts/chfi-notes/module-03/

Tan, Y., Li, Y., Zeng, L., Ye, J., Wang, W., & Li, X. (2023). Multi-scale Target-Aware Framework for Constrained Splicing Detection and Localization. *MM 2023 - Proceedings of the 31st ACM International Conference on Multimedia*, 8790–8798. DOI: 10.1145/3581783.3613763

Tariq, U., Ahmed, I., Bashir, A. K., & Shaukat, K. (2023). A Critical Cybersecurity Analysis and Future Research Directions for the Internet of Things: A Comprehensive Review. *Sensors (Basel)*, 23(8), 4117. DOI: 10.3390/s23084117 PMID: 37112457

The Sleuth Kit. (n.d.). Autopsy digital forensics. Retrieved from https://www.sleuthkit.org/autopsy/

The Sleuth Kit. (n.d.). The Sleuth Kit. Retrieved from https://www.sleuthkit.org/

The SSL Store. What Is a Hash Function in Cryptography? A Beginner's Guide. Retrieved from https://www.thesslstore.com/blog/what-is-a-hash-function-in-cryptography-a-beginners-guide/

Thomas, P., & Morris, A. (2008). An investigation into the development of an anti-forensic tool to obscure USB flash drive device information on a Windows XP platform. *2008 Third International Annual Workshop on Digital Forensics and Incident Analysis*, 60–66. https://doi.org/DOI: 10.1109/WDFIA.2008.13

Thurzo, A., Kosnacova, H. S., Kurilova, V., Kosmel, S., Benus, R., Moravansky, N., Kova, P., Kuracinova, K. M., Palkovic, M., & Varga, I. (2021). Use of Advanced Artificial Intelligence in Forensic Medicine, Forensic Anthropology and Clinical Anatomy. *Health Care*, 9(11), 1545. DOI: 10.3390/healthcare9111545 PMID: 34828590

Ts'o, T. Y. (n.d.). Journaling the Linux ext2fs filesystem. *Massachusetts Institute of Technology*. Retrieved from https://web.mit.edu/tytso/www/linux/ext2intro.html

Tyagi, A. K., Kumari, S., & Richa. (2024). Artificial Intelligence-Based Cyber Security and Digital Forensics: A Review. *Artificial Intelligence-Enabled Digital Twin for Smart Manufacturing*, 391-419.

Tyagi, S., & Yadav, D. (2023). MiniNet: A concise CNN for image forgery detection. *Evolving Systems*, 14(3), 545–556. DOI: 10.1007/s12530-022-09446-0

U.S. Supreme Court, Daubert v. Merrell Dow Pharmaceuticals Inc., United States Reports, vol. 509, pp. 579–601, 1993.

Verma, V., Agarwal, N., & Khanna, N. (2018). DCT-domain deep convolutional neural networks for multiple JPEG compression classification. *Signal Processing Image Communication*, 67, 22–33. DOI: 10.1016/j.image.2018.04.014

Vittal, S., Dixit, U., Sovitkar, S. P., Sowjanya, K., & Antony Franklin, A. (2023). Preventing cross network slice disruptions in a zero-trust and multi-tenant future 5G networks. *2023 IEEE 9th International Conference on Network Softwarization (NetSoft)*, 227–231. DOI: 10.1109/NetSoft57336.2023.10175424

Walia, S., Kumar, K., Agarwal, S., & Kim, H. (2022). Using XAI for Deep Learning-Based Image Manipulation Detection with Shapley Additive Explanation. In *Symmetry* (Vol. 14, Issue 8). DOI: 10.3390/sym14081611

Wang, J., Roy, H., Alam, S., Rao, T., Ahshrup, S., & McCluskey, W. (2021). The Impact of 5G on the European Economy. In *Accenture*. Accenture., https://www.accenture.com/content/dam/accenture/final/a-com- migration/manual/r3/pdf/pdf-144/Accenture-5G-WP-EU-Feb26.pdf

Wen, B., Zhu, Y., Subramanian, R., Ng, T.-T., Shen, X., & Winkler, S. (2016). COVERAGE — A novel database for copy-move forgery detection. *2016 IEEE International Conference on Image Processing (ICIP)*, 161–165. DOI: 10.1109/ICIP.2016.7532339

Wikimedia Foundation. (2024, July 28). RAID. Wikipedia. https://en.wikipedia.org/wiki/RAID

Wong, H. (2020). *Siri, Alexa and unconscious bias: The case for designing fairer AI assistants*. Design Week. Retrieved from https://www.designweek.co.uk/issues/13-19-january-2020/unconsciousbias-ai-voice-assistants/

Wright, J., Dawson, M. E.Jr, & Omar, M. (2012). Cyber security and mobile threats: The need for antivirus applications for smartphones. *Journal of Information Systems Technology and Planning*, 5(14), 40–60.

Wu, Y., AbdAlmageed, W., & Natarajan, P. (2019). ManTra-Net: Manipulation Tracing Network for Detection and Localization of Image Forgeries With Anomalous Features. *2019 IEEE/CVF Conference on Computer Vision and Pattern Recognition (CVPR)*, 9535–9544. DOI: 10.1109/CVPR.2019.00977

Xiang, Z., & Acuna, D. E. (2020). *Scientific Image Tampering Detection Based On Noise Inconsistencies: A Method And Datasets*. arXiv preprint arXiv:2001.07799. DOI: 10.21203/rs.2.22943/v1

Xiang, A., Zhang, J., Yang, Q., Wang, L., & Cheng, Y. (2024). *Research on Splicing Image Detection Algorithms Based on Natural Image Statistical Characteristics*. http://arxiv.org/abs/2404.16296

Xue, K., Piñeiro, J., Yu, Y., Hong, J., Yin, X., & Xie, S. (2023). Performance and reliability of 5G communications for USV-UAV critical applications. *2023 17th European Conference on Antennas and Propagation (EuCAP)*. DOI: 10.23919/EuCAP57121.2023.10132977

X-Ways Software Technology AG. (n.d.). WinHex: Hexadecimal editor and disk forensics tool. Retrieved from https://www.winhex.com/

Yadav, R. T. (2024). AI-Driven Digital Forensics. *International Journal of Scientific Research & Engineering Trends, 10(*4), 1673-1681. https://ijsret.com/wp-content/uploads/2024/07/IJSRET_V10_issue4_353.pdf

Yalli, J. S., Hasan, M. H., & Badawi, A. (2024). Internet Of Things (IOT): Origin, Embedded Technologies, Smart Applications and its Growth in the Last Decade. *IEEE Access : Practical Innovations, Open Solutions*, 12, 1–1. DOI: 10.1109/ACCESS.2024.3418995

Yanthan, N. (2024). Future of Cybersecurity - Trends and Scope. *Sprintzeal*. https://www.sprintzeal.com/blog/future-of-cybersecurity

Zaid, T., & Garai, S. (2024). Emerging Trends in Cybersecurity: A Holistic View on Current Threats, Assessing Solutions, and Pioneering New Frontiers. *Blockchain in Healthcare Today*, 7(1). Advance online publication. DOI: 10.30953/bhty.v7.302 PMID: 38715765

Zangana, H. M. (2024). Exploring Blockchain-Based Timestamping Tools: A Comprehensive Review. Redefining Security With Cyber AI, 92-110.

Zangana, H. M. (2024). Exploring the Landscape of Website Vulnerability Scanners: A Comprehensive Review and Comparative Analysis. Redefining Security With Cyber AI, 111-129.

Zangana, H. M., Omar, M., Al-Karaki, J. N., & Mohammed, D. (2024). Comprehensive Review and Analysis of Network Firewall Rule Analyzers: Enhancing Security Posture and Efficiency. Redefining Security With Cyber AI, 15-36.

Zangana, H. M., Mohammed, A. K., Sallow, A. B., & Sallow, Z. B. (2024). Cybernetic Deception: Unraveling the Layers of Email Phishing Threats. [INJURATECH]. *International Journal of Research and Applied Technology*, 4(1), 35–47.

Zangana, H. M., & Omar, M. (2020). Threats, Attacks, and Mitigations of Smartphone Security. *Academic Journal of Nawroz University*, 9(4), 324–332. DOI: 10.25007/ajnu.v9n4a989

Zatyko, K. (2007). *Commentary: Defining Digital Forensics*. Forensics Magazine.

Zdziarski, J. (2012). *Hacking and securing iOS applications*. O'Reilly Media.

Zhang, N., Jiang, Y., & Wang, J. (2020, January). The research of data recovery on Windows file systems. In *Proceedings of the 2020 International Conference on Intelligent Transportation, Big Data & Smart City (ICITBS)* (pp. 644–647). IEEE. DOI: 10.1109/ICITBS49701.2020.00141

Zhao, D., & Tian, X. (2022). A Multiscale Fusion Lightweight Image-Splicing Tamper-Detection Model. In *Electronics (Switzerland)* (Vol. 11, Issue 16). DOI: 10.3390/electronics11162621

Zhou, P., Han, X., Morariu, V. I., & Davis, L. S. (2018). Learning Rich Features for Image Manipulation Detection. *2018 IEEE/CVF Conference on Computer Vision and Pattern Recognition*, 1053–1061. DOI: 10.1109/CVPR.2018.00116

Zou, Z., Chen, T., Chen, J., Hou, Y., & Yang, R. (2021, March 1). *Research on network security risk and security countermeasures of 5G technology in power system application*. IEEE Xplore. DOI: 10.1109/IAEAC50856.2021.9390826

About the Contributors

Marwan Omar is an accomplished cybersecurity expert and academic, specializing in the intersection of artificial intelligence (AI) and cybersecurity. He currently serves as an Associate Professor of Cybersecurity and AI at the Illinois Institute of Technology, where he leads cutting-edge research on AI security, focusing on the detection and mitigation of advanced cyber threats. Dr. Omar holds multiple advanced degrees, including a PhD in Cybersecurity and a PhD in AI, and has earned numerous industry certifications such as Certified Ethical Hacker (CEH) and SANS Certified Smartphone Forensics Analyst (GASF). His extensive publication record includes books, peer-reviewed journal articles, and conference papers that explore the integration of AI in cybersecurity, with a particular focus on large language models (LLMs) and generalized AI (Gen AI). In addition to his academic pursuits, Dr. Omar is actively involved in industry collaborations and has contributed to numerous high-profile projects aimed at securing AI-driven technologies. His expertise has positioned him as a sought-after advisor and thought leader in the cybersecurity community. As a first-generation American from the Yazidi community in Iraq, Dr. Omar is committed to serving as a beacon of hope and inspiration for underrepresented minorities in STEM fields. His dedication to advancing both the scientific and social aspects of cybersecurity makes him a unique and influential figure in the ongoing dialogue about the future of AI security.

Hewa Majeed Zangana is an Assistant Professor currently affiliated with Duhok Polytechnic University (DPU) in Iraq. He holds a Doctorate in Philosophy (PhD) degree in ITM, which he is currently pursuing at DPU. Prior to his current role, Hewa Majeed Zangana has held various academic and managerial positions. He previously served as an Assistant Professor at Ararat Private Technical Institute and a Lecturer at DPU's Amedi Technical Institute, and Nawroz University. He has also held administrative positions such as Curriculum Division Director - Presidency of DPU, Information Unit Manager of The Research Center at Duhok Polytechnic University,

Head of the Computer Science Department at Nawroz University, and Acting Dean of the College of Computer and IT at Nawroz University. Hewa Majeed Zangana's research interests span a wide range of topics in computer science, including network systems, information security, mobile communication, data communication, and intelligent systems. He has published extensively in peer-reviewed journals such as IEEE, EAI, IGI-Global, Inform, Indonesian Journal of Education and Social Science, TIJAB, INJIISCOM, and AJNU. In addition to his research contributions, Hewa Majeed Zangana has been actively involved in editorial roles such as Editorial Board Member at Applied and Computational Engineering (ewapublishing.org), serving as a Reviewer for the Scientific Journals of Nawroz University. He has also been a member of various scientific committees and administrative bodies at Nawroz University, including the Scientific Curriculum Development Committee, the Student Follow-up Program Committee, and the Committee for the Preparation of the Rules of Procedure for Consultative Offices.

***

Ngozi Tracy Aleke is a Graduate Student at IIT, she has carved a niche for her self by exploring the intercession between law, criminal justice and cybersecurity. Ngozi's goal is to advocate for the responsible and ethical use of technology.

Angel Jones is an Adjunct Professor At the University of Virginia School of Continuing and Professional Studies. Dr. Jones began his 20-year cybersecurity career as a special agent with the U.S. Coast Guard, investigating cybercrime. His expertise has made him the go-to subject matter expert for complex cybersecurity and cyber breach investigation matters. Dr. Jones' experience includes serving as the Chief Information Security Officer for several global firms, proactively protecting organizations from dynamic cyber threats. Further, Dr. Jones holds several industry certifications, including the Certified Information Systems Security Professional (CISSP), Certified Information Security Manager (CISM), Certified Information Systems Auditor (CISA), Certified Chief Information Security Officer (CCISO), Certified in Risk and Information Systems Control (CRISC), Certified Ethical Hacker (CEH), EnCase Certified Examiner (EnCE), Digital Forensics Certified Practitioner (DFCP), AWS Certified Solutions Architect – Professional and AWS Certified Security - Specialty and Project Management Professional (PMP).

Pranjal Khare is a distinguished corporate lawyer and is currently working as a law faculty at O.P. Jindal Global University, India. He specializes in Property Law, Corporate laws, Intellectual Property Rights, and International law. Mr. Pranjal is a highly regarded scholar and has published on numerous issues related to international affairs, economy, politics, data & privacy, artificial intelligence and IP disputes. He is also a frequent speaker at legal conferences and has served as a consultant to numerous law firms and corporations.

Mohamed Trigui is a graduate student at Illinois Institute of Technology, specializing in the intersection of computer science and cybersecurity. His expertise centers on developing innovative security software solutions to address critical challenges in the industry. Mohamed is driven by a passion for problem-solving and advancing the field through innovation.

Index

A

B

C

D

E

F

I

L

M

N

P

Q

S

T

U

W

www.ingramcontent.com/pod-product-compliance
Lightning Source LLC
LaVergne TN
LVHW080608300926
849162LV00005B/1084